APPLIED FINANCE AND ECONOMIC ANALYSIS FOR SCIENTISTS AND ENGINEERS

JAMES R. COUPER
Department of Chemical Engineering
University of Arkansas
Fayetteville, Arkansas

WILLIAM H. RADER
Department of Industrial Engineering
University of Arkansas
Fayetteville, Arkansas

Van Nostrand Reinhold Series in
Managerial Skills in Engineering and Science

VNR VAN NOSTRAND REINHOLD COMPANY
New York

Library of Congress Catalog Card Number: 85–6168
ISBN: 0–442–21856–7

Manufactured in the United States of America

Published by Van Nostrand Reinhold Company Inc.
135 West 50th Street
New York, New York 10020

Van Nostrand Reinhold Company Limited
Molly Millars Lane
Wokingham, Berkshire RG11 2PY, England

Van Nostrand Reinhold
480 Latrobe Street
Melbourne, Victoria 3000, Australia

Macmillan of Canada
Division of Gage Publishing Limited
164 Commander Boulevard
Agincourt, Ontario M1S 3C7, Canada

15 14 13 12 11 10 9 8 7 6 5 4 3 2 1

Library of Congress Cataloging in Publication Data

Couper, James R.
  Applied finance and economic analysis for scientists and engineers.

  (Van Nostrand Reinhold series in managerial skills in engineering and science)
  Includes bibliographies and index.
  1. Corporations—Finance. 2. Capital investments—Evaluation. 3. Business mathematics. I. Rader, William H. II. Title. III. Series: Van Nostrand Reinhold series in managerial skill development in engineering and science.
HG4026.C65 1986   658.1'5'0245   85–6168
ISBN 0–442–21856–7

*To all scientists and engineers who need a broader understanding
of finance and economics to become promotable*

Van Nostrand Reinhold Series in Managerial Skills in Engineering and Science

M. K. Badawy, Series Editor
Virginia Polytechnic Institute and State University

Developing Managerial Skills in Engineers and Scientists: Succeeding as a Technical Manager, by M. K. Badawy

Modern Management Techniques in Engineering and R&D, by J. Balderston, P. Birnbaum, R. Goodman, and M. Stahl

Improving Office Operations: A Primer for Professionals, by Jack Balderston

Managing the Engineering Design Function, by Raymond J. Bronikowski

Applied Finance and Economic Analysis for Scientists and Engineers, by James R. Couper and William H. Rader

Series Introduction

Applied Finance and Economic Analysis for Scientists and Engineers is the fifth volume in the Van Nostrand Reinhold Series in Managerial Skills and Engineering and Science. The series will embody concise and practical treatments of specific topics within the broad area of engineering and R&D management. The primary aim of the series is to provide a set of principles, concepts, tools, and practical techniques for those wishing to enhance their managerial skills and potential.

The series will provide both practitioners and students with the information they must know and the skills they must acquire in order to sharpen their managerial performance and advance their careers. Authors contributing to the series are carefully selected for their experience and expertise. While series books will vary in subject matter as well as approach, one major feature will be common to all volumes: a blend of practical applications and hands-on techniques supported by sound research and relevant theory.

The target audience for the series includes engineers and scientists making the transition to management, technical managers and supervisors, upper-level executives and directors of engineering and R&D, corporate technical development managers and executives, continuing management education specialists, and students in technical management programs and related fields.

We hope that this dynamic series will help readers to become better managers and to lead most rewarding professional careers.

M. K. BADAWAY
Series Editor

PREFACE

With a wealth of experience in industry, we have found that most scientists and engineers, after being promoted to managerial ranks, find themselves confronting financial terminology that is foreign to them. Frequently, technical people find that their background lacks the subject matter in this text. Some technical people attempt to muddle through, not understanding much of what is essential to the managerial concerns of the organization. Others pursue night courses, correspondence courses, or self-studies in accounting, finance, economics, corporate tax, and cost estimation to improve their qualifications for promotion.

This book is written to provide in one text a fundamental understanding of these economic areas. It is designed to provide the scientist or engineer with an introduction to each field with selected references for further study. It has been developed through many years of undergraduate teaching experience to provide technical students with a broader knowledge of elements essential to their ultimate success in managerial roles.

As such, it is suitable for an undergraduate course for technical students, as well as a text for seminars for the practicing scientist or engineer or for easy self-study.

As may be seen from the Contents, the book moves logically from accounting to finance to cost estimating, both capital and operating, and to economics analysis through the time value of money, cash flow, and depreciation and taxation, with the latest rules on depreciation as of the time of writing. Uncertainty analysis based on errors in forecasting is treated from a practical standpoint based on widely-used industrial practice. Managerial attitudes are used in the approach to feasibility analysis and approval of capital appropriations.

Though written to fill a void in the background of technical personnel, it requires no technical background and is of value to all plant managerial personnel whether in maintenance, production, or general management.

We would like to express our appreciation to our wives, Mary and Tonnie, for their patience and for the many hours in which we were taken away from family activities while writing the book. We would also wish to thank Mrs. Vicki Havens for her typing and helpful advice in the composition of the book.

J. R. COUPER
W. H. RADER

CONTENTS

1 PRINCIPLES OF ACCOUNTING

INTRODUCTION

Accounting is the means by which scientists and engineers, managers and owners, creditors and governments, and others are able to assess the health, progress, and financial success of business units and ventures. By the examination of accounting data it is possible to:

1. develop historical trends of costs, sales, machine utilizations, and a host of other data pertinent to economic studies
2. guide investment, expansion, or replacement decisions
3. evaluate management performance
4. analyze product lines
5. compare a company or division with similar industries
6. measure the progress of new products, new manufacturing facilities, new departments

and a host of other areas pertinent to daily life of a business.

It is not necessary for a scientist or engineer to know the details of the art of accounting. But it will greatly enhance his broader understanding of the company for which he works and vastly improve his potential for advancement if he develops enough of an understanding of the principles of accounting to be able to communicate with accountants, financial people, and managers.

THE ACCOUNTING EQUATION

For centuries accounting has been based on what is known as *double entry bookkeeping*. The roots of double entry bookkeeping are found in the accounting equation. Stated in its simplest terms:

$$\text{Assets} = \text{Equities}$$

Assets are things of value. The assets may be tangible assets, such as machinery, furniture, equipment, buildings, or property. Or the assets may be intangible assets, such as copyrights, patents, franchises, trademarks, or goodwill. The only restriction is that they must have value.

Equities are claims against the assets. Anything of value is claimed or owned by someone. The value of that claim or equity cannot exceed the value of the asset. The total claims or ownership against assets must equal the value of the asset.

Equities are broken down into two categories: claims of the owners (insiders) or owners' equity, and claims of the creditors (outsiders) or liabilities. If a person buys an automobile and finances part of the cost, at the time of the purchase, the value of the asset (its cost) is equal to the amount of the loan (equity of the bank) plus the amount of the down payment (equity of the owner). As time passes the value of the asset changes, and so does the equity of the owner and the creditor. Thus to enlarge on the accounting equation:

$$\text{Assets} = \text{Liabilities} + \text{Owners' Equity}$$

This is the more common form of the equation. Any transaction that takes place causes changes in the accounting equation. For example, an increase in assets must be followed by one of the following:

1. An increase in liabilities (e.g., money was borrowed to buy a piece of equipment),
2. An increase in owners' equity (e.g., an owner provided the money to buy a piece of equipment),
3. A decrease in assets (money was taken out of cash to buy a piece of equipment. In this case, total assets do not change, but there is a change in distribution of assets).

A change in one part of the equation as a result of an economic event or transaction must be accompanied by an equal change in another place or places—thus the expression *double entry bookkeeping,* or *double entry accounting.* Assets can be increased or decreased, as can liabilities and owners' equity.

DEBITS AND CREDITS

Economic events that change the accounting equation are recorded in account books. The left side of the account book page has been arbitrarily designated the *debit* side and the right side the *credit* side. This is true regardless of the type of account. Actually as the terms are used in accounting, they mean nothing more than left side or right side.

Because the accounting equation must always remain in balance, the signs in the accounts are always arranged to maintain the balance, if we have debits equaling credits. In an asset account the debit (left side) of the account is always an increase:

$$\underline{Asset} = Liability + Owners' \ Equity$$
$$+ \mid -$$

On the right-hand side of the equation we change the signs, making a debit in liability and owners' equity at a decrease and a credit an increase. This is just the opposite of an asset account because the liability and owners' equity are on the opposite side of the accounting equation:

$$\underline{Asset} \ = \ \underline{Liability} \ + \ \underline{\overset{Owners'}{Equity}}$$
$$+ \mid - \qquad - \mid + \qquad - \mid +$$

Thus any transaction that is an increase in assets must either involve a debit, which would be recorded as an increase to an asset account, a decrease to a liability account, or a decrease in an owners' equity account, and, along with one of the above changes, a balancing or offsetting credit, which would be recorded as a decrease to an asset account, an increase in a liability account, or an increase in an owners' equity account.

A better understanding can be achieved if we use an illustration. I. M. Precise, who had received his doctorate in analytical chemistry and had worked in a laboratory for 10 years, received $99,512 from Uncle Todd's estate. He decided he would invest the entire amount in an analytical laboratory, Precision Plus, and go into business for himself. He placed the inheritance in the bank, and immediately his accounting equation looked as follows:[1]

Assets	=	Liabilities	+	Owners' Equity
Cash				Precision Plus Capital
(1) 99,512				(1) 99,512

Dr. Precise bought a small lot with a metal building on it that had been a cleaning establishment before it went broke. He paid $20,000 cash and took a mortgage for 10 years for $30,000 to meet the agreed purchase price of $50,000. This transaction changed his books as follows:

Assets	=	Liabilities	+	Owners' Equity

Cash		Mortgage Payable	Precision Plus Capital
① 99,512	② 20,000	② 30,000	① 99,512

Building	
② 50,000	

The building needed some revamping to convert it into a laboratory at a cost of $8500:

Assets	=	Liabilities	+	Owners' Equity

Cash		Mortgage Payable	Precision Plus Capital
① 99,512	② 20,000	② 30,000	① 99,512
	③ 8,500		

Building	
② 50,000	
③ 8,500	

Analytical equipment was purchased at a cost of $56,629, with a down payment of $16,000 and a balance of $40,629, which he financed over 5 years, agreeing to pay $2,600 every 3 months:

Assets	=	Liabilities	+	Owners' Equity

Cash		Mortgage Payable	Precision Plus Capital
① 99,512	② 20,000	② 30,000	① 99,512
	③ 8,500	④ 40,629	
	④ 16,000		

Building	
② 50,000	
③ 8,500	

Equipment	
④ 56,629	

Irv needed $1,200 to pay for a new stereo system he had put in his home, so he withdrew the money from his new business:

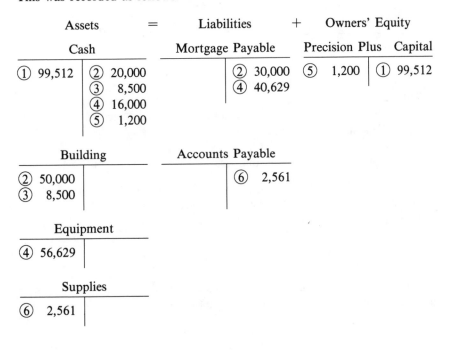

Laboratory chemicals were needed, and a 30-day charge account was established with the chemicals distributor. The purchase amounted to $2,561. This was recorded as follows:

Assets	=	Liabilities	+	Owners' Equity

Cash		Mortgage Payable		Precision Plus	Capital
① 99,512	② 20,000		② 30,000	⑤ 1,200	① 99,512
	③ 8,500		④ 40,629		
	④ 16,000				
	⑤ 1,200				

Building		Accounts Payable	
② 50,000		⑥ 2,561	
③ 8,500			

Equipment	
④ 56,629	

Supplies	
⑥ 2,561	

After 3 months he paid one installment of $2,600 on the analytical equipment, had paid for his initial supply of chemicals, and had just purchased $212 more, leaving the accounts as follows:

Assets	=	Liabilities	+	Owners' Equity

Cash		Mortgage Payable	Precision Plus Capital
① 99,512	② 20,000	② 30,000 ⑤ 1,200 ① 99,512
	③ 8,500 ⑦ 2,600	④ 40,629
	④ 16,000	
	⑤ 1,200	Accounts Payable
	⑦ 2,600	
	⑦ 2,561 ⑦ 2,561	⑥ 2,561
		⑦ 212

Building
② 50,000
③ 8,500

Equipment
④ 56,629

Supplies
⑥ 2,561
⑦ 212

Without going into entries as a result of income from operations, the accounting equation and double entry journals are illustrated. The equation can now be summarized as follows:

Assets	=	Liabilities	+	Owners' Equity
Cash	48,651	Accts. Payable	212	Precision Plus Cap.	98,312
Supplies	2,773	Mortg's. Pay.	68,029		
Equipment	56,629		68,251		98,312
Building	58,500				
	166,553		166,553		

When stated as a balance sheet, the most convertible assets would be listed first, as has been done in the summary above, and assets would be divided into current assets, which in the above summary would include cash and supplies, and long-term assets, which would include equipment and buildings. Short-term liabilities are listed first and are those payments due in 1 year. Long-term liabilities are payments due after 1 year. Payments on long-term loans or mortgages that are due in 1 year are listed as current liabilities.

Long-term assets are usually depreciated over a predetermined schedule. The amount of depreciation and net book value of plant and equipment are listed. Current liabilities include all items and accounts payable within 1 year, including an estimation of income for federal and state taxes due.

Long-term liabilities, in addition to the mortgage listed in the summary above, may also include debentures and bonds.

DATA RECORDING

Though most accounting today is done by entering data into a computer memory in an established company, the process programmed into the computer is based on the older methods of recording, accumulating, and classifying data. The accounting equation, debits and credits, account books, journals, and ledger are all parts of the modern accounting system. The concepts are all fundamental to accounting practice, and the engineer or scientist should be aware of them.

The Journal

The journal is the first book into which any business activity, and thus accounting transaction, is recorded. Journal entries result from such documents as invoices, sales slips, cash register tapes, etc., bearing the date, the transaction, notation of where the debit and credits are to be recorded, and the amount. For example, the activities of I. M. Precise in starting his analytical business would look as shown in Table 1.1. This is referred to as the *2-column* or *general journal.* Special journals may be set up to record particular types of transactions, such as a sales journal. Where special journals are used, the entries are not recorded in the general journal.

The Ledger

A ledger is a group of accounts arranged systematically. Transactions are first recorded in the journal and later transcribed into the individual accounts, which are the ledgers. The column labeled F in Table 1.1 is used to indicate the ledger *folio* or *reference,* thus indicating both that it has been transferred and to where it has been transferred. Transferring the entry from the journal to a ledger is known as *posting.* The ledgers to which our journal entries

Table 1.1   The General Journal

DATE		EXPLANATION	F	DEBIT AMOUNT	CREDIT AMOUNT
1982					
Apr	1	Cash	1	$99512 __	
		I. M. Precise, Capital	2		$99512 __
	4	Property and Building	4	5000 __	
		Cash	1		20000 __
		Mortgage 10 yr	3		30000 __
May	2	Remodeling Building	4	8500 __	
		Cash	1		8500 __
	9	Equipment	5	56629 __	
		Cash	1		16000 __
		Note payable	3		40629 __
Jun	11	To I. M. Precise	2	1200 __	
		Cash	1		1200 __

of Table 1.1 were posted might look like Table 1.2. Thus the journal is the chronological device that records all transactions, while the ledger keeps special accounts. In computer-recorded transactions, journal voucher numbers are chronologically assigned by the computer, and then the date is recorded, and the transaction is assigned to a specific ledger.

Trial Balance

Because debits and credits must always be in balance, a trial balance at the end of a specified accounting period shows the sum of credits and debits for all ledgers to be equal. If we add up our five account ledgers from Table 1.2, we will find that the total of each side is $215,841.00. And thus we have satisfied our trial balance. No income or balance sheet can be prepared until our trial balance proves successful. The trial balance tests mathematically the accuracy of totaling columns in the journals, called *footing,* and balancing ledger accounts.

FINANCIAL REPORTS

The annual report of a corporation usually contains four separate tables:

1. balance sheet
2. income statement
3. statement of retained earnings
4. source and use of funds

Table 1.2 Precision Plus Ledger Accounts

CASH							ACCOUNT NUMBER 1	
1982 Apr 1	Capital	J-1	$99512	--	Apr 4	Property	J-1	$20000 --
					May 2	Remodeling	J-1	8500 --
					9	Equipment	J-1	16000 --
					Jun 11	I. M. Precise	J-1	1200 --

CAPITAL							ACCOUNT NUMBER 2	
Jun 11	Cash to IMP	J-1	$ 1200	--	1982 Apr 1	Capital	J-1	$99512 --

ACCOUNTS PAYABLE							ACCOUNT NUMBER 3	
					Apr 4	Mortgage 10 yr payable qtly	J-1	$30000 --
					May 9	Note payable	J-1	40629 --

PROPERTY AND BUILDING							ACCOUNT NUMBER 4	
Apr 4		J-1	$50000	--				
May 2		J-1	8500	--				

EQUIPMENT							ACCOUNT NUMBER 5	
May 9		J-1	$56629	--				

The balance sheet is usually the first table presented in an annual report. The balance sheet is a record at an instant in time of the financial position of a company on that date. It may be compared to the same statement made one, two, or any number of periods earlier to determine the progress the company has made. The change from year to year in the balance sheet is governed largely by the income statement for the year involved, so we will treat the income statement first.

Income Statement

After a period of operations Irving M. Precise's business may have resulted in a profit. If so, he may have decided to expand, enlarging the building, buying more analytical equipment, hiring some chemists, and exploiting the reputation that he had developed. To do this he needed more money than he could or cared to provide, so he sold common stock in the business.

Table 1.3 Precision Plus, Inc.
Income Statement
Year Ended December 31, 1982.

Net Receipts			$375,000
Less cost of goods manufactured:			
Raw materials (analytical chemicals)			
Inventory, January 1, 1982	6,000		
Plus purchases	56,000		
	62,000		
Less inventory, Dec. 31, 1982	8,000		
Net Raw Materials		54,000	
Direct labor		151,000	
Maintenance and repair		22,000	
Indirect labor		13,000	
Utilities		9,000	
Small tools and equipment		6,000	
			255,000
Gross Profit			120,000
Less operating expenses:			
Advertising		5,000	
Administrative and general and			
selling		42,000	
Lease on autos and trucks		3,000	
			50,000
Gross Operating Income			70,000
Less depreciation			15,000
Net Operating Income			55,000
Interest on mortgages			7,400
Net Income before Income Tax			47,600
Federal and State Tax			10,100
Net Income after Tax			$ 37,500
Earnings per Share			25¢

In a short time the income statement of what is now a corporation might be described in Table 1.3.

Figure 1.1 presents a picture of the cost structure for manufacturing. Included in the figure are common accounting terms used in industry. Unfortunately, the usage of specific cost terms varies from industry to industry and sometimes from company to company within an industry. The terms presented are felt to be those generally used and are included in a larger list (see Table 1.4) of defined types of costs that will be used in this text.

The income statement of Table 1.3 represents our hypothetical company, which is in the chemical analysis business, but the statement could be representative of a small manufacturing concern as well.

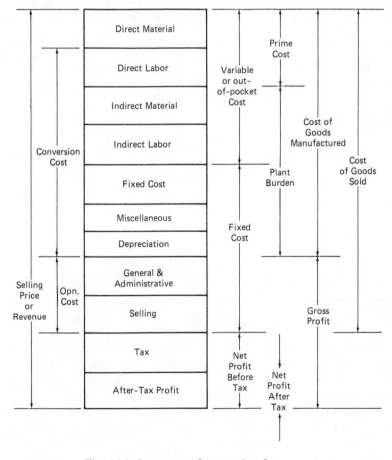

Figure 1.1 Components of costs and profits.

Table 1.4 Definitions of Costs.

TYPE OF COST	DESCRIPTION
Administrative Cost	Includes administrative and office salaries, rent, auditing, legal, engineering, etc.
Capital Cost	The cost of capital, expressed as an interest rate
Conversion Cost	The cost of goods manufactured less the direct material costs, or the cost of converting the direct material into finished product
Depreciation Cost	A noncash expense deductible from income for tax purposes to permit recovery of investment
Direct Cost	The costs identifiable to a unit of output or portion of a business operation, such as direct material or direct labor; also called *prime cost*
Direct Labor Cost	The cost of labor involved in the actual production or service
Direct Material Cost	The cost of materials consumed in or incorporated into a product or service
Distribution Cost	Includes advertising, samples, travel and entertainment, rent, telephone, stationery, postage, freight out, warehousing, etc.
Fixed and Miscellaneous Costs	Includes such items as rent, insurance, depreciation, maintenance, utilities, small tools, and ad valorem and inventory taxes
Fixed Cost	A cost that is independent of the rate of output
Goods Manufactured, Cost of	Also referred to as *total plant costs,* this is the total of prime or direct costs and plant overhead costs
Goods Sold, Cost of	The total of all costs except income taxes that may be deducted from revenue to obtain profit
Gross Profit	Total revenue less cost of goods manufactured
Operating Cost	The general and administrative costs and selling costs
Selling Costs	Salaries and commissions of sales personnel

Balance Sheet

The net profit or loss is posted to the balance sheet to update the financial report. As described earlier in the financial equation, the balance sheet is divided into three main groups: assets, liabilities, and equity. Within the assets and liabilities, subgroups also exist, such as current and fixed assets or liabilities. Fixed assets are properties and equipment owned by the company. Liabilities are debts and mortgages owed by the company. The difference between assets and liabilities is the net worth of the business, which reflects the investment of the owners plus any profits left to accumulate in the business.

Current assets are the properties readily convertible into cash, their ease of convertibility determining their order, with the easiest listed first. Current liabilities are those debts that are payable within 1 year of the date of the financial statement. Fixed assets are those held for long-term use, and fixed or long-term liabilities are those debts payable after 1 year from the date of the financial statement.

The balance sheet of our hypothetical company, Precision Plus, is shown in Table 1.5. It will be noticed that the equation is balanced. That is,

$$\text{Assets} = \text{Liabilities} + \text{Net Worth}$$
$$\text{OR} \quad \$257,484 = \$82,673 + \$174,811$$

In examining the balance sheet, a few observations are appropriate. Though Chapter 6 will discuss depreciation more thoroughly, but notice that land is not depreciated or depreciable. Buildings and equipment are depreciated with the accumulated depreciation reserve shown. This is the total depreciation taken including the last year. The remaining undepreciated value of the asset is its *book value* and is considered to be an estimate of the salvage value of the asset if it were sold at the time of the financial statement.

The net worth of a company consists mainly of capital stock, retained earnings, and paid-in capital. Capital stock is voting common stock. Retained earnings are the earnings over a period of years that have not been paid as dividends to the stockholders, but have instead been plowed back into the business. Retained earnings are usually the subject of a separate statement. As such, they are described in the next section. Paid-in capital is the result of showing capital stock at par value and any amount of money paid in above that par value as paid-in capital.

Retained Earnings

A sample of a retained earnings statement for our hypothetical company is shown in Table 1.6, where the retained earnings for the beginning of the period are added to the net income after tax for the period. From that, the common stock dividend for the period is subtracted to give the retained earnings at the end of the period. This table is also called the *statement of shareholders equity,* for usually any change in number of shares outstanding is noted, and if shares are sold, the revenue from the sale is reported.

Source and Use of Funds

An important portion of a financial statement is a source and use of funds statement. It is generated from comparing the current and previous balance sheets and adding information from the income statement. As an example, let us use our hypothetical example again. Table 1.7 shows a comparison of two consecutive balance sheets. From these balance sheets, if an asset

Table 1.5 Precision Plus Balance Sheet December 31, 1982.

Assets			
Current assets			
Cash		$11,928	
Receivables		41,691	
Inventories			
Reagent chemicals		8,000	
Other supplies		5,254	
Small tools and equipment		13,362	
Total Current Assets			$80,235
Fixed assets			
Land		10,300	
Building	$105,000		
Less accumulated depreciation reserve	28,160		
Net Buildings		76,840	
Equipment	150,236		
Less accumulated depreciation reserve	60,127		
Net Equipment		90,109	
Total Fixed Assets			177,247
Total Assets			$257,484

Liabilities and Net Worth			
Current liabilities			
Accounts payable		12,218	
Taxes payable		8,106	
Current portion of long-term financing		12,700	
Total Current Liabilities			33,024
Fixed liabilities			
Mortgage payable		19,526	
Equipment loan payable		30,123	
Total Fixed Liabilities			49,649
Total Liabilities			82,673
Net worth			
Common stock			150,000
Retained earnings			9,811
Retained surplus (current year)			15,000
Total equity (net worth)			174,811
Total liabilities and equity			$257,484

Table 1.6 Precision Plus Statement of Retained Earnings December 31, 1982.

Retained earnings at beginning of period	$ 9,811
Net income for the period	37,500
	$47,311
Common stock dividend 15¢/share, with 150,000 shares	22,500
Retained earnings at end of period	$24,811

Table 1.7 Comparative Balance Sheets and Source and Use of Funds Precision Plus Co.

	12/31/81	12/31/82	SOURCE	USE
Cash	$ 13,652	$ 11,928	$ 1,724	
Receivables	38,124	41,691		$ 3,567
Inventories	23,813	26,616		2,803
Gross fixed assets	238,627	265,536		26,909
Less: Accumulated depreciation	(73,287)	(88,287)	15,000	
Net fixed assets	165,340	177,249		
Total Assets	240,929	257,484		
Accounts payable	10,106	12,218	2,112	
Taxes payable	5,731	8,106	2,375	
Current portion of long-term debt	12,700	12,700		
Long-term debt	52,581	49,649		2,932
Common stock	150,000	150,000		
Retained earnings	9,811	24,811	15,000	
	$ 240,929	$ 257,484	$36,211	$ 36,211

increases over the year, a use of funds was the result; if it decreases, a source of funds results. The opposite is true of liabilities.

Table 1.8 is a summary of the source and use of funds, which is the normal manner in which it is presented. Table 1.7 is an example of a worksheet required to develop Table 1.8. It will be noted that the major sources of funds were net income and depreciation.

Depreciation as a factor in cash flow will be discussed further in Chapter 6. The major uses of funds were in gross assets expansion and dividends to stockholders.

Table 1.8   Source and Use of Funds Precision Plus Co. 1982.

	AMOUNT		PERCENT
Sources			
Net Income		$37,500	63.9
Depreciation		15,000	25.5
			89.4
Decreases in working capital			
Reduction in cash	$1,724		2.9
Increase in accounts payable	2,112		3.6
Increase in taxes payable	2,375		4.1
Total decrease in working capital		6,211	10.6
Total source of funds		$58,711	100.0
Uses			
Increases in working capital			
Increased receivables	$3,567		6.1
Increased inventories	2,803		4.8
Total increase in working capital		$ 6,370	10.9
Gross fixed assets expansion		26,909	45.8
Decrease in long-term debt		2,932	5.0
Dividend to stockholders		22,500	38.3
Total use of funds		$58,711	100.0

HOW TO READ AN ANNUAL REPORT

Analysts have different purposes in examining an annual report. Equity investors are interested in long-term profitability, efficiency, and dividends, or growth. Unprofitable operations, they know, will erode asset values, and a strong current position may be eroded long-term by inefficient operations. Long-term creditors place emphasis on earning power and operating efficiency. Bankers will look at the firm's short-term liquidity. Management is interested in all aspects of financial analysis, because it must be able to pay long-term and short-term creditors, as well as obtain earnings that will provide growth for and pay dividends to stockholders. Fortunately, the trend in U.S. management is swinging to emphasis on long-term growth, rather than short-term performance at the expense of the long-term picture.

Operating profitability being the first concern of most analysts, we will examine the operating statement first. Having worked with the development and interrelation of the four types of financial reports, we are better able to read financial reports. Most public corporations generally present 2 years in their balance sheet statements and 2 years in their statements of operations. Later in the annual report, an extended report is many times presented covering a summary of financial and operating results for 10 years to permit an analysis of trends of the company in sales, earnings, dividends, and growth in retained earnings.

The Income Statement

Carrying various titles, the income statement, statement of operations, or statement of profit and loss describes how well the company did during the year and may be an indication of how well the company may do in the future. The income statement matches the revenue received from selling goods or services against the cost of manufacturing or of providing the services.

The first item on the statement is the revenue. In manufacturing it is referred to as *net sales*. In services and utilities, this item would be called *operating revenues*. In any case, it represents the primary source of money received by the company from its customers for goods and/or services provided. It is referred to as net sales because returned goods or allowances are deducted. We would expect growth to at least exceed the effects of inflation or no real growth occurs.

The next item presented is entitled cost of goods sold or sometimes cost of sales, which covers the cost of the manufactured goods or costs incurred in the factory, including raw materials, labor (both direct and indirect), and such overhead items as supervision, rent, power, supplies, maintenance and expendable tools, and supplies. Depreciation may be included without detailing it in cost of goods sold, but is usually stated as a part of cost of goods sold. If not stated, it may be found in the source and use of funds statement.

Gross Margin.   The ratio of the cost of goods sold to revenue, expressed as a percentage, should be analyzed particularly as a company trend compared to previous years. Many times the difference between the net sales and cost of goods manufactured, the gross profit, as a percentage of net sales, referred to as *gross margin,* is used for comparisons. If the gross margin percentage is equal to or better than the gross margin for the previous year, then costs have been maintained or improved.

An improvement in gross margin could mean:

1. An increase in sales due to an expanding market or an increased share of the market or a change in product distribution. The latter can be particularly true of a diversified corporation or a conglomerate.
2. Fuller use of idle capacity with constant fixed costs.

3. Less expensive raw materials were used.
4. More efficient methods of production were developed, possibly with new machinery.
5. Higher sales volume reduced inventory, particularly older, lower cost inventory.

Operating Margin. The next item usually appearing is entitled general and administrative costs, selling and administrative costs, or operating costs. These expenses are generally grouped separately from costs of sales to permit examination of selling costs and administrative costs. Selling costs include salesmen's salaries and commissions, advertising and promotions, travel, and entertainment as significant items. Administrative costs include executive salaries, office payroll, office expenses (including computer costs), and similar items.

Subtracting the operating costs from the gross profit gives the operating margin or profit. The operating profit as a percentage of revenue is also a ratio worth examining and comparing to that of previous years. It may also be compared to the *operating margin* of companies in the same type of business. A good source of comparative industries is the *Value Line,* available in most libraries. The *Value Line* presents several ratios for the past 10 years, as well as other interesting data.

Profit Margin on Sales. Though the gross margin and operating margin are of value in analysis, the "bottom line" measures how effectively the firm is being managed. It is computed by directly dividing net income after taxes by sales. It gives, therefore, the profit per dollar of sales. If lower than that of industries in similar businesses, it indicates that the firm's net selling price is low or that its costs, either in manufacturing or in administration or selling, are too high.

Times Interest Earned. Interest expense is also usually stated separately on the income statement. It represents the interest paid to bondholders for the use of their money and is a fixed charge, as it must be paid year after year whether the company makes a profit or loses money. It is another cost of doing business and is subtracted from revenue before calculating income taxes. The ratio of the operating profit before deducting interest expense and income tax to the interest expense is called *times interest earned* and measures the extent to which earnings can decline without resultant financial embarrassment to the firm because of inability to meet annual interest costs. Such an inability to meet obligations could lead to legal action by creditors, possibly leading to bankruptcy. A high ratio will make additional loans easier to obtain.

Fixed Charge Coverage. Recognizing that many firms lease assets and incur long-term obligations under lease contracts, we consider these leases fixed costs and a cost of doing business. As such, a *fixed charge coverage,* expressed as the ratio of the operating profit before deducting interest expense, lease costs, and income tax to lease costs and interest expense, makes this ratio generally preferable to the times interest earned ratio for most financial analyses.

Inventory Turnover. The *inventory turnover* is defined as the sales revenue divided by the value of the inventories, which are usually taken at the lower of cost or market. Excess stocks are unproductive and representative of a low or zero rate of return. A low ratio compared with a similar industry average would cause concern for holding damaged or obsolete materials not worth their stated value.

Average Collection Period. The *average collection period* is an expression of the accounts receivable turnover. It is obtained by dividing the sales by 360 to obtain the daily sales and then dividing the daily sales into the accounts receivable to find the number of days of sales tied up in receivables.

Earnings per Share. One of the more critical ratios of interest to owners of common stock and potential purchasers of equity is earnings per share. Buyers of common stock or suppliers of equity capital are often more concerned with earnings per share than they are with dividends. Earnings per share without dividends means earnings are retained, resulting in an increase in stockholders' equity and usually an increase in stock price. Because of the retained earnings there is less need for floating long-term bonds, thus increasing the margin of safety.

The Balance Sheet

As stated earlier, the balance sheet is a picture of the financial position at a point in time. The difference between two consecutive balance sheet statements reflects the effect of the operating performance or income statement for the intervening year. The ability of the firm to meet its maturing obligations is a major concern of the analyst, and thus we will examine the liquidity ratios.

Current Ratio. The current ratio is calculated by dividing current assets by current liabilities. The current assets include cash, marketable securities, accounts receivable, and inventories. The current liabilities include accounts payable, short-term notes payable, the current portion of long-term liabilities, accrued income taxes, and other accrued expenses, which are largely labor costs and wages. If this ratio is far from the similar industry average, the analyst would probably want to check further.

Quick Assets Ratio, Liquidity Ratio, or "Acid Test." The quick ratio is computed by deducting inventories from current assets, as they are probably not easily converted to cash, and dividing the balance by current liabilities. This ratio defines the firm's ability to pay off short-term obligations without having to rely on liquidation of inventories, which would usually have to be done at discount prices.

Leverage Ratio. The leverage ratio is a measure of the funds supplied by owners compared to the financing supplied by the company's creditors. The leverage ratio implies a number of things:

1. Creditors look to the owners' equity, as stated earlier, as a margin of safety. If owners have supplied a large proportion of the financing, the bonds will have a better rating, and interest rates will be lower.
2. By raising funds through debt, the owners have the benefit of retaining control of the firm with limited investment.
3. If the company earns more on borrowed money than it pays in interest, the return to equity owners is magnified. If assets earn 12% and interest on debt is 10%, there is a 2% differential accruing to the stockholders. If earnings go up to 14%, the differential accruing to the stockholders doubles with only a 17% increase in return on assets. But if earnings drop 25% to 9%, then the differential between the 9% return and the 10% debt must be made up from the stockholders' share of total profits.

Thus high leverage may be dangerous, but low leverage may unduly reduce growth of the firm. Again it may be appropriate to compare the company being studied with companies in similar industries. Firms with low leverage ratios have lower expected returns on equity when the economy is booming, but have less risk of loss when the economy is in a downturn. On the contrary, firms with high leverage ratios run the risks of high losses, but also have the chance of gaining high profits.

Price-Earnings Ratio. Both the price and the return on common stock vary with a multitude of factors. Investors in the stock of a company may inflate the price of a stock because of anticipated earnings due to real or imagined factors. Earnings may vary with economic times. But earnings are quoted with stock prices listed in most newspapers and thus must be considered as a ratio of the greatest interest to investors. If the stock is selling at $24 per share and its earnings are $3 per share, then the price earnings ratio is 8. Inversely, the earnings-to-price ratio indicates the earnings achieved on stock at that price, in this case, 12½%. If annual dividends are $1.44 per share, then the annual return on the stock is 6%. But the stock is also purchased for growth or increase in value as a result of increased earnings and increased dividends.

Fixed Assets Turnover.   The ratio of sales to fixed assets is a measure of the turnover of plant and equipment. It is the sales revenue in dollars divided by the net value of the fixed assets after depreciation. Comparison with other firms in the same industry may indicate whether the assets are effectively used or whether the assets may be outdated and technically obsolete.

Return on Total Assets.   The ratio of net profits after tax to total assets measures the return on total investment, or the ROI, as it is commonly called. This is another measure, in addition to the fixed asset turnover ratio, of the effective use of assets.

Return on Net Worth.   The ratio of net profit after taxes to net worth measures the rate of return on the stockholders' investment. Like earnings per share, the return on net worth measures the effectiveness of the use of the stockholders' equity.

SUMMARY OF RATIOS

The ratios that have been examined can be classified into four basic types: (1) liquidity, (2) leverage, (3) activity, and (4) profitability. Data from the I. M. Precise Co. can be used to calculate each type of ratio, illustrating a financial analysis in practice. Although an almost unlimited number of ratios may be computed, usually a limited number is sufficient. These are reviewed and calculated in Table 1.9.

TREND ANALYSIS

Although the ratio analyses will give a reasonably good picture of a firm's operation, they ignore the dimension of time. A firm may have done things to improve profitability in the short run at the expense of future operations. It may have postponed maintenance of fixed assets to decrease current costs and improve profitability, but this will cause increased costs later. Delaying purchase of modern equipment decreases outlays now and depreciation costs in the short run, but long-term may affect a firm's competitive position.

Table 1.9   Summary of Financial Ratios.

RATIO	FORMULA FOR CALCULATION	CALCULATION	INDUSTRY AVERAGE
Liquidity			
Current	$\dfrac{\text{current assets}}{\text{current liabilities}}$	$\dfrac{88,235}{33,024} = 2.67$ times	2.5 times
Quick or "Acid Test"	$\dfrac{\text{current assets—inventory}}{\text{current liabilities}}$	$\dfrac{53,619}{33,024} = 1.62$ times	1.0 times
Leverage			
Debt-to-total assets	$\dfrac{\text{total debt}}{\text{total assets}}$	$\dfrac{82,673}{257,484} = 32\%$	33%
Times interest earned	$\dfrac{\text{profit before tax plus interest charges}}{\text{interest charges}}$	$\dfrac{47,600}{7,400} = 6.43$ times	8.0 times
Fixed charge coverage	$\dfrac{\text{income available for meeting fixed charges}}{\text{fixed charges}}$	$\dfrac{50,600}{10,400} = 4.87$ times	5.5 times
Activity			
Inventory turnover	$\dfrac{\text{sales or revenue}}{\text{inventory}}$	$\dfrac{375,000}{54,000} = 6.94$ times	9.0 times
Average collection period	$\dfrac{\text{receivables}}{\text{sales per day}}$	$\dfrac{41,691}{1,417} = 29.4$ days	20 days
Fixed assets turnover	$\dfrac{\text{sales}}{\text{fixed assets}}$	$\dfrac{375,000}{177,249} = 2.11$ times	5.0 times
Total assets turnover	$\dfrac{\text{sales}}{\text{total assets}}$	$\dfrac{375,000}{257,484} = 1.46$ times	2 times
Profitability			
Profit margin on sales	$\dfrac{\text{net profit after tax}}{\text{sales}}$	$\dfrac{37,500}{375,000} = 10\%$	5%
Return on total assets	$\dfrac{\text{net profit after tax}}{\text{total assets}}$	$\dfrac{37,500}{257,484} = 14.6\%$	10%
Return on net worth	$\dfrac{\text{net profit after tax}}{\text{net worth}}$	$\dfrac{37,500}{174,811} = 21.5\%$	15%
Gross margin	$\dfrac{\text{gross profit}}{\text{revenue}}$	$\dfrac{120,000}{375,000} = 32.0\%$	
Operating margin	$\dfrac{\text{Net operating profit before tax}}{\text{revenue}}$	$\dfrac{47,600}{375,000} = 12.7\%$	

Reduced product quality to achieve higher short-term profitability could have serious future effects.

For these reasons and others, a more thorough analysis will involve plotting trends of company operations. Trend lines of current ratio, debt ratio, fixed asset turnover, sales, profit margin on sales, or other ratios discussed, plotted over a 10-year period, may show favorable growth in all areas or may point out directions in which the company is heading that could point up problems.

SOURCES OF INDUSTRY RATIOS

In examining the company for whom you work, a company for whom you might work, a company who is a competitor, or a company whose stock you might wish to buy, you may wish to compare the company with other companies in the same or similar industries. A credit manager may wish to evaluate an industrial customer as a credit risk. In security analysis, the use of ratios as they provide a comparison with industry averages is valuable when the principal focus is on long-run profit potential. Purchasing agents are interested in the financial security of a supplier for assurance of ability to carry through with a supply contract.

There are several sources for industry average ratios. Some are listed below.

Dun and Bradstreet

The industry average ratios compiled by Dun and Bradstreet, Inc., are probably the best known and most widely used of ratio averages. D&B provides 14 ratios calculated for 125 different SIC (Standard Industrial Classification) of industries. The 125 classifications include 74 manufacturing and construction categories, 30 categories of wholesalers, and 24 categories of retailers. Ratios are quoted as median, upper quartile, and lower quartile.

Federal Trade Commission

The Federal Trade Commission (FTC) publishes quarterly financial data on manufacturing companies. An analysis by industry groups, by asset size, and financial statements in ratio form is presented. The reports are issued about 6 months after financial data are available from company financial reports.

Robert Morris Associates

This national association of bank loan officers compiles and publishes a group of useful ratios in its annual *Statement Studies.* Eleven ratios are computed for 125 lines of business and are based on financial statements received by banks by firms applying for loans.

Trade Associations

The financial ratios, along with detailed information on operating expenses, are compiled by trade associations. These are important sources to persons seeking comparative data. The data and averages usually represent some of the best data available and permit a good analysis of the efficiency of firms.

USES OF FINANCIAL RATIOS

Many times an examination of a few calculated ratios will permit the analyst to tell whether a company is very good or very bad. Often it is useful to calculate a number of different ratios and even examine trends over a period of time to determine what changes are occurring in the ratios and in what financial direction the company is headed.

But it must be remembered that, although ratios are good tools, they have limitations. They are constructed from accounting data that may result from different interpretations. Accounting data may even be manipulated. The data are very dependent on methods used in depreciation or in inventory evaluation methods, such as last-in/first-out versus first-in/first-out. Or there may be dead inventory that is still carried as an asset at some finite value. There may be differences in handling bad-debt reserve allowances, pension plan costs, research and development, partially owned subsidiaries, depletions, or any number of specific areas open to some variation in interpretation.

Many times a ratio that varies from the industry median may not be judged good or bad immediately. Further analysis may be required. For example, a fixed asset's turnover ratio may be assessed as low by similar industry standards, which could indeed mean poor utilization of manufacturing assets. It could also mean that the company has recently installed automated devices and has become atypical of its industry classification because of a much higher level of mechanical and computerized automation.

Financial ratios are not good in and of themselves. They must be compared with something before they have value. They may be compared with (1) other firms in the same industry, or (2) the same ratios from the same firm in a trend analysis to see if the firm is improving or deteriorating.

SUMMARY

In this chapter, the reader was introduced to terminology frequently encountered in annual reports and other financial documents. As the scientist or engineer is promoted within industry, he or she will become more involved with the business aspects of the enterprise. Therefore, it is essential that the technical person have a working knowledge of financial terminology and a basic understanding of accounting principles.

The terminology introduced in this chapter will be used throughout the rest of the text. Although there is no standard terminology, the authors have attempted to be consistent insofar as possible.

Suggested Further Readings

1. Copeland, Thomas E., and Weston, J. Fred. *Financial Theory and Corporate Policy.* Reading, Massachusetts: Addison-Wesley Publishing Co.
2. Nickerson, Clarence B. *Accounting Handbook for Nonaccountants.* Boston, Massachusetts: CBI Publishing Co., Inc.
3. Riggs, Henry E. *Accounting: A Survey.* New York: McGraw-Hill Book Co.
4. Weston, J. Fred, and Brigham, Eugene F. *Managerial Finance.* Hinsdale, Illinois: The Dryden Press.

PROBLEMS

1.1 As of December 31, 1984, the balance sheet of the Antique Manufacturing Co. contained a scrambled set of items. Set up the balance sheet in its proper form. Subtotal the current assets and current liabilities, and show the total for assets, liabilities, and net worth.

Mortgage Pay (55,000 due annually)	$165,000	Accrued Wages and Expenses	$ 25,000
Notes Receivable		Earned Surplus	70,000
(due 1 year)	55,000	Notes Payable	
Inventory	300,000	Bank (due 12 months)	55,000
Accounts Payable	65,000	Machinery and	
Goodwill	5,000	Equipment	110,000
Cash	55,000	Accts. Rec., Net	135,000
Preferred Stock	165,000	Prepaid Exp.	40,000
Income Taxes	85,000	Common Stock	225,000
Buildings	190,000	Reserve Dep.—	
		Fixed Assets	110,000
		Land	75,000

1.2 The profit and loss statement of the Antique Manufacturing Co. contains a scrambled set of items for the year ending December 31, 1984. Set up the P&L statement, and determine the net profit after tax for the year.

Sales Commissions	$ 40,000	Office Salaries	$ 60,000
Shipping Expenses	30,000	Cost of Goods	
Sales Discounts and		Manufactured	2,430,000
Returns	100,000	Officer Salaries	70,000
Federal and State		Interest Expense	4,000
Income Tax	37,000	Office Expense	55,000
Advertising	20,000	Depreciation	25,000
Gross Sales	3,000,000		
Office Rent	20,000		

1.3 From the balance sheet constructed in Problem 1.1 and the P&L statement constructed in Problem 1.2, determine the following ratios.

a. Current
b. Quick Ratio
c. Debt Ratio
d. Times Interest Earned
e. Fixed Charge Coverage
f. Inventory Turnover
g. Average Collection Period

h. Fixed Assets Turnover
i. Total Assets Turnover
j. Gross Margin on Sales
k. Profit Margin on Sales
l. Return on Total Assets
m. Return on Net Worth

1.4 Based on the data that follow:
a. Record the transactions by placing their amounts in the appropriate columns.
b. Compute the balance under each heading.
c. Check your work to see if the equation balances.
   An entrepreneur:

1. Deposited $60,000 in the bank as capital to start a business.
2. Purchased a building with $15,000 (from the bank account) and by taking a mortgage for $30,000.
3. Purchased office furniture and supplies for $5,000, placing them on account.
4. Paid $50 cash for advertising.
5. Paid for the office furniture and supplies.
6. Hired a salesperson and paid 2 weeks' salary of $400.
7. Deposited $10,000 more in the bank for the business.

ASSETS		LIABILITIES		OWNER'S EQUITY	
Debits (+)	Credits (−)	Debits (−)	Credits (+)	Debits (−)	Credits (+)

2 FINANCING THE CORPORATE VENTURE

INTRODUCTION

Prior to World War I, most companies were small and were often owned and operated by the founders. Capital expenditures were usually for replacement of obsolete or worn-out equipment and perhaps some modest expansion. The funds for these expenditures were generated from within the company. Between World Wars I and II, industrial growth took place, including mergers with other firms or acquisitions of other enterprises. Internal generation of funds was not sufficient to meet a firm's financial needs, and external sources had to be sought. Established companies that in the past had relied on internal generation of funds were forced to change their financial policy in order to replace equipment and generate growth. External sources had to be obtained, and the sources were banks and investment houses.

In the period since World War II, growth has been one of the major goals of corporate management. For companies to maintain a regular dividend policy and grow, external funds had to be sought. In very recent times, with corporate mergers, joint ventures, and the interest in megadollar projects, external sources of funds were essential for these large-scale projects. Cash generation from internal sources alone could not begin to fund capital-intensive projects.

SOURCES OF FUNDS

The funding for corporate ventures may be derived from internal or external sources.

Internal Sources

The capital a company obtains from its own operation is from retained earnings and from a noncash allowance known as *reserves*.

Retained Earnings. The retained earnings of a firm are the excess of the after-tax net earnings over dividends paid to stockholders. If a company plans no growth, then in theory, all after-tax profits earned could be paid out as dividends. No wise management would do this. A certain part of the profits is retained in the business, while a part is paid as dividends to stockholders. Soule (1954) stated that in the 4-year period, 1947–50, retained earnings accounted for two-thirds of all funds raised by U.S. manufacturing corporations, and noncash charges accounted for one-quarter of the total. The retained earnings then represent a source of internal funding for capital expenditures.

Reserves. In the foregoing paragraph another source of internally generated funds mentioned was derived from reserves. The reserves are to provide for depreciation, depletion, and obsolescence. In actual practice, however, depreciation seldom covers the replacement cost due to improved technology, which means more expensive, sophisticated equipment. Inflation has cut severly into reserves. Even with liberalized depreciation accounting methods, seldom were the reserves adequate for replacement and had to be augmented for other sources. Therefore, with the necessity of providing reasonable dividends to stockholders and inadequate reserves, the only alternative for expansion was to seek external funding.

External Sources

There are three principal sources of external funds: debt, preferred stock, and common stock. These sources will vary widely in the cost to the company and in the risk a company assumes. It is a known fact that the cheapest form of capital is of the least risk to the firm. A general rule in the financial community is that the risker the project, the safer should be the type of capital used. A new venture with small financial requirements would best be funded from common stock. On the contrary, a well-established business area could be financed using principally debt.

Debt. In the following discussion debt will be classified as follows:

current—maturing up to 1 year
intermediate-term—maturing between 1 and 10 years
long-term—maturing beyond 10 years

Current Debt. To illustrate current debt, let's assume a company has the opportunity to purchase a certain raw material at a low price, but the company doesn't have the ready cash. The company wants to repay the debt in 90 days. It has three options available for this transaction. The funds could be obtained from its bank by means of a *commercial loan*.

Another source, providing the company has a good line of credit, would be to borrow in the open market. It would draw a note to the order of the bearer of the note and have it discounted by a dealer in this type of note or by the first purchaser of the note. This type of negotiable note is called *commercial paper.*

The third way would be through what is known as *open-market paper or bankers acceptance.* If the raw material were to be purchased from a single source, this company could sign a 90-day draft on its own bank to the order of the vendor. The company might pay a commission to its own bank to accept in writing on the draft that the company has an unconditional obligation to pay the full amount on the maturity date. Most chemical companies make use of the 90-day note to a commercial bank.

Intermediate Debt.   This form of debt is scheduled for retirement in 1 to 10 years. In terms of the dollar volume of all debt it is usually the smallest. Three types of intermediate debt are the *deferred-payment contract, revolving credit,* and *term loans.*

In the deferred-payment contract, the borrower signs a note for a series of payments over a period of time, say 10 years. The title to the equipment rests with the noteholder until the debt is retired. Banks, insurance companies, and institutional investors are typical lenders.

Revolving credit is an agreement in which a bank or group of banks agrees to loan to a company for a specified time any amount of money up to a specified total. A commission is paid at a stated rate on the unused part of the total credit. This form of credit is to provide variable and recurring demands for credit throughout the specified period. It is not intended for one loan. The duration of these agreements is usually between 1 and 5 years.

Term loans are continuously outstanding in part or all until the maturity date, which may be as long as 10 years. The loans are divided into installments, which are due at specified maturity dates. There is a wide variety of arrangements that can be made, such as monthly, quarterly, semiannual, or annual payments. They may also be paid off prior to maturity, both with and without penalties. Large commercial banks and insurance companies make these loans.

Long-term Debt.   This form of debt is either bonds or notes. Bonds are negotiable certificates that are usually issued at par values of $1,000 and are purchased by the public. There are four types of bonds in the market place today, namely, *mortgage, debenture, income,* and *convertible* bonds.

Mortgage bonds have been used by railroads and public utilities, and they are secured by the pledge of specific assets, usually valuable properties.

Debenture bonds are usually preferred by industrial companies, because they are not secured by specific assets, but by the future earning power of the company. This type of bond then allows the company the freedom to buy and sell the manufacturing plants at any time without being tied to specific assets.

Income bonds differ from the other forms of long-term debt in that the company is obligated to pay no more of the interest charges that have accrued in a certain period than were actually earned in that period. What are the advantages of this type of bond? Income bonds found their use when it was necessary to recapitalize after bankruptcy and the company had uncertain earning power. Interest payments on investment bonds are similar to dividends on preferred stock. Neither need be paid unless dividends are earned.

Convertible bonds are popular in inflationary periods. Suppose a company plans to sell a bond issue when its stock is, say, $90 a share. The company could make the offer in the form of $1,000 bonds, each of which would be convertible into company stock at $100 a share, or 10 shares of stock. There is a stated period of time in which the privilege of conversion into common stock at a specified price is permitted. In inflationary periods, stocks are usually a better investment than bonds.

Stockholders' Equity.   This is the total equity interest that stockholders have in a corporation. There are two broad classes of stock that may be offered by a company: *preferred stock* and *common stock.* There may be several different types or classes of shares issued by a corporation, each class having somewhat different attributes from those of another class.

Preferred Stock.   The word "preferred" means that the people who own preferred stock will receive their dividends before the common stockholders. Also, in the event of company liquidation, preferred stockholders will receive their funds from the assets before common stockholders. Most shares of preferred stock are issued at a par value of $100 at a stated dividend rate, for example, 8%. This means that each share is entitled to $8 dividends a year when dividends are declared by the board of directors. Dividends are paid on these stocks before dividends are paid to the common stockholders. Most preferred stock offered today is *cumulative,* which means, that if in any year the dividend is not paid, it accumulates in favor of the shareholders of preferred stock. The cumulative dividends must be paid before any common stockholders receive dividends. Usually preferred stockholders have no vote in company affairs unless the company fails to pay them dividends at the promised rate. There is a *convertible preferred stock* offered by some companies. This, like a convertible bond, carries for a stated time the privilege of converting preferred stock to common stock. A convertible preferred stock usually pays a lower dividend than ordinary preferred stock.

Common Stock.   Holders of common stock are the suppliers of venture capital for a corporation. As such, they are at the greatest risk, because they are the last to receive dividends for the use of their money. When the company flourishes and earnings are high, they receive the greatest benefits from their investments in the form of dividends. They also have a voice in company affairs, especially at annual meetings called by the board of directors.

Concluding Remarks

In many instances the largest holders of corporate securities are *institutional* investors. Examples of these investors are life insurance, property insurance, fire, marine, casualty, etc., companies. Another class of large investors is educational, philanthropic, and religious organizations. On the rapid increase are the pension funds. All these organizations may purchase the securities on the open market, from investment bankers, or they may purchase all or part of new issues. This last type is called *private placement,* in contrast to the open market, or *public offerings.*

This section has briefly treated the various sources of capital a corporation may elect to use in financing new ventures. As has been pointed out, there are risks involved from both the company's and the investor's position. Each of these capital sources carries a different cost. Management must decide how the capital should be raised for a new venture and what will it cost the firm.

DEBT VERSUS EQUITY FINANCING

Earlier in this chapter, the various options for obtaining funds were presented and discussed. Ultimately, top-level management is confronted with how a venture will be financed. The size of the project may vary from capital requirements of millions to billions of dollars. Large projects tend to develop a corporate life of their own. This characteristic of industrial projects is different from when projects were small in capital requirements compared with the size of the companies undertaking them.

The finance decision is not a simple matter. Significant questions must be answered. Is the state of the economy growing, static, or declining? Is the inflation rate increasing or decreasing? What is the company's indebtedness now? What is the company's cost of capital? What is the cost of financing a new project? Should the company at this time incur more long-term indebtedness, or should it seek venture capital from equity sources by floating a new stock issue? A simple "yes" or "no" answer will not suffice. The financial decision is complex. There are excellent texts on the subject of corporate finance. In this section, a brief discussion of some of the problems associated with funding a venture will be presented.

One consideration is the company's position with regard to leverage. If a company has a large proportion of its debt in bonds and preferred stock, the common stock is said to be highly *leveraged*. The consequence of this position is that should earnings decline by, say, 10%, the dividends available to the common stockholders might be wiped out. The company might also be unable to cover the full interest on its bonds without dipping into accumulated earnings. This is the great danger of a high debt/equity ratio and illustrates the fundamental weakness of companies with a disproportionate amount of debt.

Barna (1981) discusses leverage, risk, and economics. He mentions that when a project is clearly associated with a particular type of financing, a question arises as to what is the correct analysis to use—total capital investment or only on that portion not borrowed, called *return on equity*. Authors of engineering economy texts warn against this approach, but many engineers and managers fail to appreciate the problems. Where low-interest financing may be available, such as the large alternate energy projects, return on equity evaluations is popular. So alternative energy projects have an absolute return that would not normally appear attractive, but suddenly does through municipal bond funding at low interest rates. Such leveraging is tantamount to transferring the money from one pocket to another—or simply you may find yourself borrowing from yourself.

Merrifield (1982) also warns about the pitfalls of high debt/equity ratios. Many capital-intensive industries (steel, chemicals, petroleum, autos, etc.) have debt/equity ratios of 2 or 3 to 1. These industries are often confronted with liquidating their assets in order to survive. One hopes tax laws, inflation, and new technology will not lead to the demise of leading heavy industry companies.

In contrast, a company could reduce its dividend payout or perhaps leverage its assets, that is a 1/1 debt/equity ratio, but then this strategy increases the chance of takeover and does affect the price of the stock.

It is then apparent that strategies for financing depend on a number of factors, some of which may have synergistic affects. Other strategies could doom the corporation to paying high interest through incurring large debts. Still other strategies may be to reduce debt and lower the debt/equity ratio, but invite takeover. The correct strategy for financing a corporate venture has to be evaluated from the standpoint of what is best for the company. The company must attempt to maintain a debt/equity ratio similar to successful companies in the same line of business.

SUMMARY

In this chapter various methods of financing corporate requirements were presented, without becoming enbroiled in the fine technical aspects of finance. Funds generated internally from retained earnings and reserves seldom are adequate for funding today's megadollar projects. Companies have therefore had to seek funds from outside the corporation.

External funds may be obtained from a variety of sources. Management must consider whether debt or equity financing, or a mixture of both, is the best for the company. Debt financing means long-term obligations, perhaps twenty years, for the company. Equity financing is a means of obtaining venture capital by issuing stock.

This chapter concludes with a discussion of the pros and cons of debt and equity financing. In the next chapter, the reader will be introduced to the methods for obtaining an estimate of the capital requirements to fund a project.

REFERENCES

Soule, R. P., and Perry, J. H., eds. *Chemical Business Handbook,* 1st. ed., New York, New York: McGraw-Hill Book Co., Inc., 1954.

Barna, B. A., *Chemtech,* 295–297 (May 1981).

Merrifield, D. B., *Chemtech,* 342–346 (June 1982).

3 CAPITAL INVESTMENT

INTRODUCTION

A company that manufactures a product has funds invested in land, buildings, and equipment. Certain industries have very high capital investments per employee and are said to be *capital-intensive*. Examples of these are mining, petroleum refining, broadcasting, etc. These industries are characterized by a high degree of automatic machinery and automatic control equipment. In contrast to the capital-intensive industries are those that have relatively small investments per employee. This signifies that much of the manufacturing is done by hand. Wearing apparel, appliances, textiles, etc., are examples of labor-intensive industries. *Fortune* magazine (1983) yearly publishes a list of the assets per employee, a sample of which is presented in Table 3.1. Although capital investment is only part of the assets of a company, the list is a measure of capital intensity.

The total funds required to design a plant, purchase the equipment and install it, as well as to bring the facility into operation is called the *total capital investment*. The items comprising the total capital investment are:

    land
    fixed capital investment
    offsite capital
    allocated capital
    working capital
    startup expenses
    other capital items
        interest on borrowed funds prior to startup
        catalysts and other consumable items
        licenses, patents, and royalties

Each of the above items will be discussed in the following sections. In addition, methods of estimating the amount of each capital item will be presented.

Table 3.1   Assets per Employee (1982).

INDUSTRY	$/EMPLOYEE
Petroleum refining	$392,000
Mining crude-oil production	335,000
Chemicals	107,000
Metal manufacturing	100,000
Paper, fiber, and wood products	97,000
Pharmaceuticals	80,000
Soaps, cosmetics	71,000
Motor vehicles	62,800
Office equipment (including computers)	62,500
Food	59,000
Aerospace	53,000
Rubber and plastic products	53,000
Electronics and applicances	48,700
Texiles	34,000
Apparel	24,800
ALL INDUSTRY AVERAGE	67,000

Source: Fortune, 107 (9), 250 (1983)

LAND

Land costs are usually a minor part of the total capital investment. The land may have been purchased some time in the past, but the cost of the land will be allocated to a project by the accounting department when the project is authorized. Some companies feel that the land is a sunk cost and, it being a small part of the total capital investment, omit it from economic evaluation calculations.

To estimate the land costs, a check with the company's real estate department, if it has one, local real estate agents, or local chambers of commerce will produce reasonable up-to-date costs. In the absence of any information, and for preliminary cost estimates only, 3% of the fixed capital cost may be used. Uhl (1979) recommends using 5 acres per million dollars of fixed capital investment. This figure is multiplied by the prevailing price of the land per acre to give the land cost per million dollars of fixed capital investment.

FIXED CAPITAL INVESTMENT

The fixed capital investment for a plant includes the manufacturing or process equipment, piping, ductwork, structures, insulation, painting, site preparation, engineering, contractor's fees, etc. A way to think of fixed investment is that it is the part of the investment pertinent to the manufacture of a product that is "fixed" to the land. It is sometimes referred to as the *manufacturing capital.*

Capital Cost Estimates

Whenever a company considers the manufacture of a product, a capital cost estimate is prepared. This may be done in-house, if the company's engineering staff is large enough, or it may be prepared by an engineering-consulting firm.

Classification of Estimates.   There are two broad classes of estimates— the *grass-roots* and the *battery-limits* estimates. The grass-roots estimate encompasses the entire facility—the manufacturing equipment, utilities, services, office buildings, storage facilities, railroad yards, docks, etc. In other words, this type of estimate starts at the grass roots, and the costs will include all items needed for the facility from the grass roots up. A battery-limits estimate is one in which an imaginary boundary has been drawn around the plant to be estimated. It is assumed that all utilities, raw materials, services, etc., are available at the imaginary boundary in the quality and quantity required to operate the manufacturing facility. Only costs within the boundary are estimated; hence the name battery limits.

Quality of the Estimate.   Capital cost estimation is an art, not a science. A great amount of judgment is required on the part of the estimator. As this person gains experience, the accuracy of the estimate improves. Experience is the best teacher.

Each company has its own method for classifying estimates. As a result, confusion exists over nomenclature. In an attempt to bring order out of chaos, the American Association of Cost Engineers (1983) has classified estimates as follows:

TYPE OF ESTIMATE	ACCURACY
Order-of-magnitude	-30 to $+50\%$
Preliminary	-15 to $+30\%$
Definitive	$- 5$ to $+15\%$

Nichols (1951) prepared a guide for fixed capital investment estimates for the chemical process industries. Similar guides appear throughout the literature. The more information available to prepare the estimate, the greater the accuracy. Of course, the more detail available, the more it costs to prepare an estimate.

Before preparing an estimate, it is advisable to carefully consider the purpose for which the estimate is to be used. An estimate might be used to

prepare feasibility studies
select a process design from a number of alternatives
select an investment opportunity from alternate proposals
appropriate funds for construction
present and select engineering bids

A feasibility estimate would not require the detail that an estimate for the appropriation of funds would. Therefore, before the estimation procedure begins, the purpose and the quality of the estimate must be determined. In the early stages of a project, when planning, screening, and evaluation take place, an order-of-magnitude estimate might be satisfactory. If the results from this study appear promising, a preliminary estimate with bids on selected major equipment items might be prepared. To build a plant, however, detailed engineering and specifications are required for a definitive estimate.

Equipment Cost Data Sources. The foundation of any fixed capital investment estimate is the equipment cost data. From these data, usually through the application of factors or percentages based upon experience, the fixed capital investment estimate is prepared. It is imperative then to have sources of reliable equipment cost data. Kharbanda (1979) surveyed the literature and found over 4,000 references for equipment cost data. Some of the data are of questionable reliability. The engineer preparing an estimate must then exercise good judgment in the selection of the data used. A selected list of such data is found in Table 3.2.

It is essential for an estimator to know the source of the data, the date of the data, the basis, potential errors in the data, and the range over which the data apply. The sources of the data, as shown in Table 3.2, may be journals, texts, or specific data compilations. The date of the data is important, so that a basis for escalating costs is known. Most equipment cost data will clearly state the date, but occasionally textbooks omit this information. If so, by deducting 2 years from the publication date the estimator would be safe in using that date as a basis. The costs refer to purchased, delivered, or installed costs. *Purchased* cost is the price of the equipment FOB at the manufacturer's plant. *Delivered* implies the price of the equipment including delivery charges from the equipment manufacturer's plant to the purchaser's plant FOB. Some costs are reported as *installed*. This usually means that the item, such as a pump, has been purchased, delivered, uncrated, and placed on a foundation in an operating department. It does not include piping,

Table 3.2   Selected Equipment Cost Data Sources.

SOURCE	REFERENCE	BASIS*	COMMENTS
Aries & Newton	1955	FOB plant	Very old data, but historically one of the first compilations
Chilton	1960	Various	Original articles for cost data in this volume
Bauman	1964	Purchased or installed as specified	Installation costs are provided separately. Old but general reference
Page	1984	Purchased	Separate charts for installation labor costs
Popper	1970	Various	Basic articles on cost data and cost engineering techniques
Woods	1970	Various	Extensive tabulation
Guthrie	1969	Purchased	Basic article on modular cost estimation method. Data also summarized in Baasel (1976).
Guthrie	1974	Purchased	Expanded version of previous Guthrie reference
Hall et al.	1982	Purchased	Equipment cost data for 50 items
Richardson	1984	Purchased	Equipment costs for actual equipment

* Basis refers to whether data are purchased price (FOB) manufacturer's plant, delivered price (FOB purchaser's plant), or installed cost.

electrical, insulation, etc., expenses. Perhaps a better name might be *set-in-place* cost.

Presentation of Cost Data.   Equipment costs, whether purchased, delivered, or installed, are correlated as a function of equipment capacity parameters. Typical capacity parameters for selected equipment are presented in Table 3.3.

A convenient, simple means to present cost data is by an equation. Equipment costs are often expressed:

$$C_2 = C_1 \left(\frac{S_2}{S_1}\right)^x \qquad\qquad 3.1$$

Table 3.3 Cost-Capacity Parameters.

EQUIPMENT	CAPACITY PARAMETERS
Heat Exchangers	Surface area, type of exchanger
Pumps	Head, capacity, type of pump
Compressors	Capacity, discharge pressure, number of stages, type of compressor
Filters	Filtration area
Pressure Vessels	Diameter, height, wall thickness, pressure
Distillation and Absorption Towers	Diameter, height, tray type, or packing, pressure

NOTE: The material of construction affects the cost of all equipment.

where C_1 = cost for a capacity, S_1
C_2 = cost for a capacity, S_2
x = an exponent that varies between 0.30 and 1.20, depending on the type of equipment

For most process equipment, the exponent lies between 0.4 and 0.8. Often, when exponential values for equipment items are unknown, an exponent value of 0.6 is used. If all process equipment exponents were averaged, the exponent would be about 0.6. Hence, the equation is frequently called the *six-tenths* rule. A list of typical exponent values is found in Table 3.4. Chase (1970) also published an extensive list. Often equipment cost data are plotted as the logarithm of cost as a function of the logarithm of a capacity factor. Figure 3.1 is a typical plot for leaf-type filters.

When this rule is used, certain precautions should be noted. One should recognize that all data have errors. Any curve drawn to represent cost-capacity data has error limits. If possible, before using any data, it would be advisable to determine how the data were obtained and correlated. The data accuracy may be high over a very narrow range of capacity. It is not advisable to use the data beyond the extremes of the correlation line. In fact, near the ends of such lines the actual data may be skewed. The middle part of the curve is the most accurate. In general, cost-capacity data are reasonably accurate over a small range.

Errors will occur when attempts are made:

to correlate cost with one independent variable when more than one variable affects the cost significantly

Table 3.4   Cost Capacity Exponents for Equipment.

EQUIPMENT	SIZE RANGE	EXPONENT
Blowers	10^3–10^4 ft^3/min	0.59*
Centrifuges	30-in. diameter	1.0
Compressors		
Reciprocating	10–400 ft^3/min @ 150 psig	0.69
Centrifugal	$10^2$$10^3$ ft^3/min @ 150 psig	0.79
Centrifugal, air	100–10,000 hp	1.0
Dryers		
Single Drum, vacuum	10–100 ft^2	0.76
Direct rotary	1,000 ft^2	0.90*
Fan, centrifugal	10^3–10^4 ft^3/min	0.44
Heat Exchanger	100–400 ft^2	0.60
Shell and tube,		
floating head		
Kettles, Jacketed		
Glass-lined	200–800 gal	0.31
316SS clad	1,000 gal	0.40
316SS clad	3,000 gal	0.67
Motors, electric		
220/440, 1800 rpm open	2–30 hp	0.70*
Totally enclosed fan cooled	2–30 hp	0.70*
Explosion-proof	2–30 hp	0.80*
Pumps, centrifugal		
horizontal cast iron	10^4–10^5 (gpm $\times$ psi)	0.33
316 SS	1–15 hp	0.50*
Separator, Centrifugal		
carbon steel	50–200 ft^3	0.49
Tanks, Storage		
Flat head, carbon steel	10^2–10^4 gal	0.57
Horizontal, carbon steel	2×10^3–2×10^4 gal	0.70*
Vertical, carbon steel		0.40*

Sources: Asterisk-marked data are from Jelen (1983). All other data are from Peters and Timmerhaus (1980).

to correlate cost with capacity when pressure and temperature ratings, materials of construction, and design features vary considerably from the base data costs

If no consideration is given to technological advances in equipment or to the "learning curve" in presenting design correlations, errors will also occur.

A sample calculation illustrating the use of the six-tenths rule is found in Example 3.1.

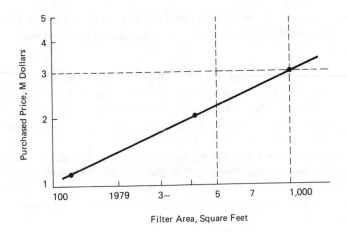

Figure 3.1. Plot of cost-capacity data.

EXAMPLE 3.1

PROBLEM STATEMENT:

A 300-square foot vertical leaf pressure filter was purchased for $1,700 in 1980. What is the estimated cost of a 750-square foot unit of the same design and material of construction in 1980?

SOLUTION:

As no exponential data for the cost-capacity equation is given, a value of 0.6 will be assumed

The cost capacity equation is

$$C_2 = C_1 \left[\frac{S_2}{S_1} \right]^x$$
$$C_1 = \$1,700$$
$$S_1 = 300 \text{ ft}^2$$
$$S_2 = 750 \text{ ft}^2$$
$$x = 0.6$$

3.2

When these values are substituted in the above equation, the cost of the 750-square foot filter is

$$C_2 = \$1,700 \left[\frac{750 \text{ ft}^2}{300 \text{ ft}^2} \right]^{0.6}$$
$$C_2 = \$1,700 \, (1.73) = \$2,941$$

Therefore, the cost of the 750-square-foot leaf filter in 1980 is $2,941. Later in this chapter, methods for escalating this cost to present-day costs will be discussed.

A check with actual cost data (see Fig. 3.2) indicates that the cost calculated by the equation is high. From the figure, it is estimated that the value is $2,600, which indicates a potential error on the high side of 13%. Therefore, the cost-capacity factor for leaf filters is less than 0.6. The exponent is about 0.48, but for preliminary estimates, the 0.6 is satisfactory. When numerous items are estimated using the six-tenths rule, some costs will be high and others low. On the average, however, the errors induced will fall within the range of errors for preliminary estimates. If a detailed estimate is to be prepared, then bids on the equipment must be obtained.

Algorithm Format. With the use of computers in economic evaluations, cost data stored in algorithm format are more efficient than data stored in tabular form. Cost data may be correlated using many equations or equation modifiers to account for pressure, temperature, materials of construction, types of equipment, etc. An example of algorithm for a shell-and-tube heat exchanger is:

$$C_E = C_B \, F_D \, F_{MC} \, F_P \qquad\qquad 3.3$$

where C_E = exchanger cost at a given base date
C_B = base cost of a carbon steel floating-head heat exchanger
F_D = design-type cost factor
F_{MC} = material of construction cost factor
F_P = design-pressure factor
The calculation procedure is as follows:

Compute the surface area of the heat exchanger, and check it against the limits in Table 3.5.
Compute the base equipment cost, C_B, from the data in Table 3.5.
Compute the design-type cost factor, F_D, from the data in Table 3.6.
Compute the material-of-construction cost factor F_{MC}, from data in Table 3.7.
Compute the design-pressure cost factor, F_P, from data in Table 3.8.
Compute the purchased equipment cost at the base date for the heat exchanger by multiplying the base cost, C_B, by the design-type cost factor, F_D, by the material-of-construction cost factor, F_{MC}, and by the design-pressure cost factor, F_P.

Table 3.5 Correlation for Base Cost of Heat Exchanger.

Equation: $\ln C_B = a_1 + a_2 \ln A + a_3 (\ln A)^2$
A = area in m²

Equation limits: 14 to 1,100 m²(150 to 12,000 ft²)
Basis: Floating-head, 100 psig design pressure, carbon steel, sheel-and-tube heat exchanger

Coefficients: $a_1 = 8.202$
$a_2 = 0.01506$
$a_3 = 0.06811$

Date of data: March 1979.
SOURCE: ASPEN (1979).

Table 3.6 Design-Type Cost Correlation.

Equation: $\ln F_D = b_1 + b_2 \ln A$

$(A$ in M²)

Limits: 14 to 1,100 m² (150 to 12,000 ft²)

Type	b_1	b_2	Source
1. Floating-head (base)	0	0	—
2. Fixed-head	−0.9003	0.0906	1
3. Kettle reboiler	0.300	0	2
4. U-tube	−0.7844	0.0830	1

Source: Guthrie (1969).

Other Data Sources. Although numerous equipment data sources are available in the open literature (see Table 3.2) for use in the estimation of fixed capital investment, care must be exercised to find out how the data were obtained and the quality of the data. Comments concerning the use of any cost data information are appropriate. The user must remember that older data sources do not take into account the improvements in equipment design that have occurred in recent years. Also, fabrication techniques have improved. Therefore, it would be difficult to take old equipment cost data projected forward in time using cost indices and compare that cost with current bid prices. The most recent cost data should be used. It is also important to recognize that cost data presented in the open literature have been "smoothed" and do not represent any manufacturer's product.

Guthrie (1969) (1974) presented a considerable amount of equipment cost data for estimating the capital investment of process plants. At the time the articles were published, they contained the most extensive compilation in the open literature. Although the data are satisfactory for preliminary

Table 3.7 Correlation for Material of Construction Cost Factor.

Equation: $F_{MC} = 1 + F_{MCS} + F_{MCT}$
$F_X = g_{1_x} + g_{2_x} \ln A$

where: $X = MC, MCS,$ or MCT

Material	F_{MC}	F_{MCS}	F_{MCTT}
2. Stainless 316 g_1	1.414405	0.4144	0.
g_2	0.232960	0.	0.2330
3. Stainless 304	1.19910	0.1991	0.
	0.159835	0.	0.1598
4. Stainless 347	1.138756	0.1388	0.
	0.221863	0.	0.2219
5. Nickel-200	2.955268	1.9553	0.
	0.608591	0.	0.6086
6. Monel-400	2.329574	1.3296	0.
	0.433770	0.	0.4338
7. Inconel-600	2.410298	1.4103	0.
	0.507644	0.	0.5076
8. Inconel-825	2.366536	1.3665	0.
	0.497059	0.	0.4971
9. Titanium	2.561711	1.5617	0.
	0.429129	0.	0.4291
10. Hastelloy	3.761354	2.7614	1.
	1.517735	0.	1.5177

Source: Guthrie (1969).

Table 3.8 Correlation for Design-Pressure Cost Factor.

Equation: $F_p = 1 + F_{PS} + F_{PT}$
$F_p = h_1 + h_2 \ln A$

Limits: *14 to 1,100 m^2 (150 to 12,000 ft²)*

Pressure Limit, N/m² (psig)	7×10^5 (100)	21×10^5 (300)	42×10^5 (600)	62×10^5 (900)
F_p (total) h_1	1.0	0.8955	1.2002	1.4272
h_2	0.	0.04981	0.07140	0.12088
F_{PS} (0.9) h_1	0.	−0.09407	0.1802	0.3845
h_2	0.	0.04483	0.06426	0.10879
F_{PT} (0.1) h_1	0.	−0.01045	0.0200	0.0427
h_2	0.	0.00498	0.00714	0.01209

Source: Guthrie.
Note: Original data do not separate the shell and tube pressures. The split of 0.9 for the shell and 0.1 for the tube is roughly based on Guthrie (1969).

estimation of small- and medium-sized equipment, the capacity scale is not adequate for large equipment.

Hall, Matley, and McNaughton (1982) published an article in *Chemical Engineering* in which equipment cost data for more than 50 major equipment items were presented. The cost data are presented as plots that show mean costs with accuracies between $\pm 10\%$ and $\pm 25\%$. This is the most recent compilation available in the open literature.

Richardson (1984) has developed a cost estimation system, and each year, for a modest fee, he updates the cost data. His equipment cost data are for specific, yet typical, manufacturer's equipment. Although there are some instances of size limitations and incorrect data, the Richardson data are the most current without requesting bids.

The best source of equipment cost data is from bids, but frequently engineers do not have the time required to obtain this information. Recent equipment manufacturers' price lists or company purchasing records are reliable sources of cost data. Because the estimation of the capital requirements of a venture start with equipment cost data, it is advisable to start with the most reliable information that can be obtained in the time frame allotted for the quality of the estimate required.

Valle-Riestra (1983) warns that, in addition to some of the precautions in using or extending cost data, a reasonable approach should be used for older data. Data up to 10 years old may be used with the proper cost index adjustment. Those data between 10 and 20 years old should be regarded with caution. Standard equipment cost data are probably acceptable, e.g., centrifugal pumps, electric motors, etc. Data over 20 years old are often obsolete. Occasionally, however, cost data may be extended over long periods with results usually satisfactory for preliminary evaluations.

COST INDICES

When the cost of equipment is estimated or quoted, the cost is as of a specific date. Because of inflation and various other economic factors, the value of the dollar is decreasing. This fact is reflected in the cost of purchased equipment items, which generally increases as time passes. All costs must be stated then as of a specified date. The cost data may be adjusted for time through the use of cost indices based upon constant dollars in a base year and actual dollars in any specified year. Usually the base time is the present, but often some cost projections are based upon past data, which must be extended to some future date. Any projection into the near future would have to take into account not only the inflation rate but also short-term estimates of what an index might be. Estimations of inflation rates are at best estimates

Table 3.9 Cost Indices Used in the United States.

YEAR	M-S (1926)	CE (1957–59)	ENR (1913)	NELSON (1946)
1965	245	104	971	261
1970	303	126	1385	365
1971	321	132	1581	406
1972	332	137	1753	439
1973	344	144	1895	468
1974	398	165	2020	523
1975	444	182	2212	576
1976	472	192	2401	616
1977	505	204	2577	653
1978	545	219	2776	701
1979	599	239	2870	757
1980	659	261	3130	823
1981	721	297	3726	903
1982	746	314	3825	977
1983	761	317	4066	1026
1984 (est)	776	322	4161 6/1/84	1049 1/1/84

of what the economy might do. A list of four useful indices is found in Table 3.9.

AVAILABLE COST INDICES

Engineering News Record Index

This is the oldest cost index currently in use. It was established using a base year of 1913, and the index was arbitrarily set to a value of 100. Through the years, as a result of inflation, the index was adjusted twice back to 100, once in 1926 and again in 1949. The 1913 index today is greater than 4,100. In recent times new indices have appeared that are weighted toward specific industries. The *ENR Index* is more useful in the general construction business. It is based upon labor craft rates and the costs of steel, lumber, and other construction materials for a 46-city average. This index does not include an adjustment for labor productivity, and, therefore, it has a tendency to increase more rapidly than other indices. The *ENR Index* may be found weekly in the construction magazine, *Engineering News Record.*

Marshall and Swift Index

In 1926 the *Marshall and Stevens Index* was established with a value of 100. The name of the index was subsequently changed to the *Marshall and*

Swift Index. It is based upon equipment costs in selected process industries. The process industries are cement, chemical, clay products, glass, paint, paper, petroleum products, and rubber. Among the related industries are electrical power, wiring, milling, refrigeration, and steam power. For each related industry, the percentage breakdown is as follows:

ITEM	%
Process Machinery	25
Tankage	24
Piping and Fittings	12
Maintenance Equipment	2
Installation Labor	19
Power	12
Administrative	6
TOTAL	100%

The *Marshall and Swift Index* tracks equipment costs and installation labor. It therefore reflects changes in installed equipment costs. The *M&S Index* does include a correction for changes in labor productivity. This index is found in the first semimonthly issue of *Chemical Engineering* on the page entitled "Economic Outlook."

Chemical Engineering Index

The *Chemical Engineering Index* was established in the early 1960s using a base period of 1957–59 as 100. This index consists of four major components:

COMPONENT	WEIGHT FACTOR
Equipment, machinery, and supports	61%
Construction labor	22%
Building materials and labor	7%
Engineering and supervision	10%
TOTAL	100%

Equipment, machinery, and supports, the dominant component, consists of the following subcomponents: fabricated equipment, process machinery, pipe, valves and fittings, process instruments, pumps and compressors, electrical equipment, structural supports, and miscellaneous items. The *Chemical Engineering (CE) Index* is designed to reflect trends in chemical process equipment plant costs. Originally the index incorporated a 2½% per year productivity improvement in labor and engineering components. In January 1982, the productivity improvement was changed to 1½% per year to reflect recent trends. Like the *M&S Index,* the data for this index may be found in the first semimonthly issue of *Chemical Engineering* on the page entitled "Economic Outlook."

Nelson Refinery Construction Index

This index is published in the first issue each month of the *Oil and Gas Journal,* with quarterly summaries in the January, April, July, and October issues. The *NRCI* was established in 1946 with a base index of 100 and is heavily weighted toward the petroleum and petrochemical industries. The *Nelson Index* is based upon a 40% material and 60% labor distribution as follows:

COMPONENT	PERCENTAGES
Iron and Steel	20%
Nonmetallic Building Materials	8%
Miscellaneous Equipment	12%
Skilled Labor	39%
Unskilled Labor	21%
TOTAL	100%

A detail breakdown of each of the above components is found in an article by Nelson (1956). The *Nelson Refinery Construction Index* does not account for improvements in productivity.

Other Indices

There are several other indices that provide useful information, but these are for special uses.

EPA-STP Treatment Plant Index. This index is for primary and secondary waste treatment facilities. The base period is 1957–59, and the index is 100. Monthly summaries of this index are published in the *Water Pollution Control Foundation Journal.*

Bureau of Labor Statistics. The bureau publishes information on material and labor indices for various industries. The basis for this index is 1926, and these data are published in the *Monthly Labor Review.*

Mining and Metallurgical Indices. A new index for this segment of the industrial complex appeared in *Cost Engineering* (1982). It is very specific to these industries.

OFJ-Morgan Pipeline Cost Index. Every two months this index appears in the *Oil and Gas Journal*. It is specific to the pipeline industry.

Foreign Indices. Chauvel (1981) recently published cost indices that are used in the English, German, and Dutch industries and are found in Table 3.10. A similar index is currently being developed for the French industrial complex.

Company Indices. Those companies that have the manpower, experience, and records should develop their own indices. These will be more realistic when weighted properly to reflect local experience, local labor, and material costs using a national average.

Which Index to Use

The choice of which index one should use is based upon the industry in which a person is employed. If it is general construction, the *ENR Index* would be the best. A person in the petroleum or petrochemical industry might find the *Nelson Refinery Construction Index* more useful. In the chemical process industries the *Chemical Engineering* or the *Marshall and Swift Indices* are adequate. Figure 3.2 is a plot of the *Chemical Engineering* and *Marshall and Swift Indices*. Although they have different bases, the two indices give similar results.

Table 3.10   Cost Indices in Europe and the United States.

YEAR	U.S. CHEM. ENG. (AVG)	U.K. PROC. ENG. (JAN)	W. GERM. CHEM. IND.	NETHERLANDS NEBCI (AVG)
1950	73.9	41.7	53.5	—
1955	88.3	59.4	77.0	—
1956	102.3	68.2	91.4	75
1965	104.2	77.0	108.7	93
1970	125.7	100.0	125.7	119.4
1971	132.3	109.4	135.5	129.2
1972	137.2	118.9	140.0	137.0
1973	144.1	128.0	145.5	144.0
1974	165.4	146.0	156.6	170.0
1975	182.4	190.0	167.4	—
1976	192.1	236.0	—	—

SOURCE: Chauvel (1981).

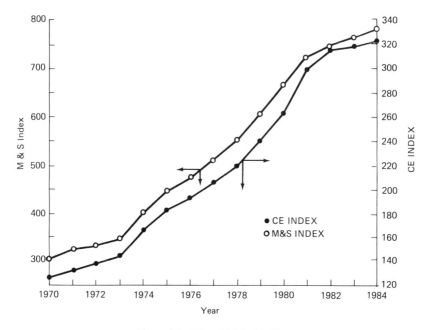

Figure 3.2. CE and M & S indices.

Comments on Cost Indices

All cost indices use a base date, e.g., 1913, 1926, 1946, or 1957–59. These years were selected because they were periods in which inflation did not increase substantially. Therefore, these years serve as bases for cost projections. It should be remembered that cost indices do have accuracy limitations, because they are based upon a statistical treatment. Therefore, they should be used with caution.

Hasselbarth (1967) mentioned that four factors often affect costs, as reflected in the various cost indices. These factors are:

technological development
productivity
process improvement
equipment design

Technological development refers to new and different processes for the manufacture of the same product. In a new process the unit cost of production will be less than in an older process. Any cost index based upon old data should be adjusted to reflect economies obtained as a result of the new process.

Productivity refers to the ability of an employee to work more efficiently. Productivity, when combined with process improvements and technological development, results in reduced manpower requirements and reduced costs with increased production. The net effect of productivity on cost indices is to minimize increases that would be noticed in several published indices.

Process improvement refers to the improvement in existing processes to manufacture a product. The most significant savings are in labor and utilities. The overall objective of process improvement on process improvement is a reduction in production costs. Hasselbarth (1967) mentioned that the effect of process improvement does not show up immediately, but may take many years.

Equipment design improvement is noted when new plants are designed or when new equipment replaces old. Through improved equipment design, it may even be possible to eliminate a process step. Therefore, equipment design may be a significant factor when cost index adjustments are made.

When all the factors mentioned above are taken together, they may not be additive. There may be synergistic effects among the four factors.

Use of a Cost Index

Whatever cost index is used, the procedure for obtaining the cost in a year other than the base year is the same. The following equation is used:

$$\text{Cost at } \theta_2 = \text{Cost at } \theta_1 \left[\frac{\text{Index at } \theta_2}{\text{Index at } \theta_1} \right] \qquad 3.4$$

where θ_1 & θ_2 are two different dates. Example 3.3 illustrates how an index is used.

EXAMPLE 3.3

PROBLEM STATEMENT:

A stainless steel filter cost $8,900 in 1979. What is the cost of this same filter in 1983?

SOLUTION:

For the purpose of this example the *Chemical Engineering Cost Index* will be used:

$$CE \text{ } Index \text{ } 1979 = 238.7$$

$$CE \text{ } Index \text{ } 1983 = 316.9$$

$$\text{Cost (1983)} = \text{Cost (1979)} \left[\frac{CE \; Index \; (1983)}{CE \; Index \; (1979)} \right]$$

$$\text{Cost (1983)} = \$8,900 \left[\frac{316.9}{238.7} \right]$$

$$\text{Cost (1983)} = \$11,800$$

INFLATION AND ESCALATION

Projection of costs into the future is a dangerous and highly speculative exercise, but it is done to estimate investment costs and operating expenses and to develop corporate business plans. Inflation refers to the increase in prices of goods that is usually not accompanied by an increase in productivity. The implication is that there is a tendency for all prices in the economy to increase.

Escalation is a more inclusive term, reflecting price increases due to inflation, supply and demand factors, as well as other such factors as environmental issues and engineering advances. Projected escalation factors are often based upon past and present inflation rates and where these rates might go in the future.

Escalation of costs may be handled in one of several ways. Project costs might be reported in constant dollars as of a given year, with escalation being left to the reader. Another simple but effective way is to assume a constant inflation rate over a short period and multiply the costs by $(1 + f)^n$, where f is the inflation rate per year, expressed as a decimal, and n is the number of years assuming a constant inflation rate each year. A more effective way would be to estimate what the inflation rate might be over a few years, say, 3 or 4, and adjust the rate later as more data are gathered. Initially the cost escalated for a 3-year period might be

$$C = (1 + f')(1 + f'')(1 + f''') \tag{3.5}$$

where f', f'', f''' = varying inflation rates each year.

One major oil company estimates what inflation might be over the next 5 years and then adjusts the estimates every 6 months, based upon immediate past history. In effect, this procedure tends to produce the best guess of the inflation factors.

There will be more complete discussion of inflation in Chapter 5.

Estimation of Fixed Capital Investment

Earlier in this chapter, estimates were classified in three broad categories, namely, order-of-magnitude, preliminary, and definitive, and ranges of accuracy for each were presented. There has been much discussion through the years concerning the number of categories, but with high inflation rates and the fact that estimating methodologies are not well defined, a three-category division is satisfactory.

In this section, the more important and useful estimating methods will be discussed. The methods have been arbitrarily classified by the authors into the three-estimate category.

Order-of-Magnitude Estimating Methods.   At best, the accuracy range is −30% to +50% for this level of estimate. The information available may include a process flowsheet, preliminary material, and energy balances and, perhaps, but not always, major equipment item definition. Although the name for the methods might be misleading, the accuracy is better than the literal interpretation of order-of-magnitude. The results of these methods may be used for screening of processes, rough business estimates, or long-range planning.

Turnover Ratio.   This is the simplest method for obtaining a fixed capital investment, but one of the most inaccurate. The turnover ratio is defined:

$$\text{Turnover Ratio (TOR)} = \frac{\text{Annual Gross Sales in \$}}{\text{Fixed Capital Investment}} \qquad 3.6$$

For chemical processing, the median value of the turnover ratio is 1.0. The statement that it takes "a dollar of capital to generate a dollar of gross annual sales" is frequently heard. Table 3.11 is an early list of turnover ratios complied by Kiddoo (1951). In this table, the ratio may vary widely from 0.21 to 8.30, depending upon processing temperatures and pressures, materials of construction, the amount of equipment required, etc. This method is affected by inflation, because both the numerator and denominator will vary, but not necessarily by the same rate. Although the data in Table 3.11 are old, current annual reports and 10-K data may be used to develop up-to-date turnover ratios.

Financial analysts frequently use the reciprocal of the turnover ratio, called the *capital ratio,* which allows them to compare in a very general way company operations. A sample calculation is presented in Example 3.4.

EXAMPLE 3.4

PROBLEM STATEMENT:

Estimate the fixed capital investment for a 1,000 T/day ammonia plant using the turnover ratio method. The current gross selling price of ammonia is $150/T. The proposed plant is to operate 330 days per year.

Table 3.11 Turnover Ratios.

PROCESS	TURNOVER RATIO
Butadiene ex butane	0.21
Butadiene ex butylenes	0.31
Synthetic ammonia	0.35
Soda ash	0.35
Ethylene dichloride	0.51
Furfural	0.66
Synthetic butanol	0.75
Benzaldehyde via chlorination	0.99
Ethylene ex refinery gases	1.00
Portland cement	1.00
Alcohol ex grain	1.01
Ethylene glycol	1.11
Alcohol ex molasses	1.85
Urea	2.36
Sodium bichromate	3.33
Methyl chlorine ex methanol	3.84
Methyl isobutyl ketone	4.35
Ammonium sulfate	5.55
Ethyl ether	6.16
Chloroform ex acetone	7.18
Phenolic resin	8.30

SOURCE: Kiddoo (1951).

SOLUTION:

From Table 3.11, the turnover ratio for ammonia plants is 0.35.

$$\text{Turnover Ratio (TOR)} = \frac{\text{Annual Gross Sales in \$}}{\text{Fixed Capital Investment}}$$

If this equation is rearranged, the

$$\text{Fixed Capital Investment} = \frac{\text{Annual Gross Sales}}{\text{Turnover Ratio}}$$

Annual Gross Sales = 1,000 T/day $\times$ 330 day/yr $\times$ \$150/T = \$49,500,000

If the appropriate values are substituted in the above equation, then

$$\text{Fixed Capital Investment} = \frac{\$49,500,000}{0.35} = \$141,000,000$$

Fixed Investment per Annual Ton of Capacity. Data expressing the fixed investment per ton of annual production capacity are often quoted in the literature. This is a convenient method of presenting the data, but the user must be careful, because some of the reported information is old. Table 3.12 is a sample of such data. Salem (1981) reported similar information on a limited number of petrochemical processes. Guthrie (1974) presented plots of total plant cost as a function of capacity, from which the fixed capital investment per annual ton of capacity may be calculated. If data of this type are used, one should be certain that the projected plant is to manufacture the same product by the same process. Cost indices also must be applied to bring the fixed investment up to the current date. Example 3.5 demonstrates how the fixed capital investment is calculated using this method.

EXAMPLE 3.5

PROBLEM STATEMENT:

Estimate the fixed capital investment in 1984 for a facility to produce 450 MM lb/yr of butadiene starting with a feed containing butylenes.

Table 3.12 Fixed Investment Per Annual Ton Capacity.

COMPOUND	SOURCE OR ROUTE	TYPICAL PLANT SIZE, TONS/YR	FIXED INVESTMENT PER ANNUAL TON CAPACITY
Acetaldehyde	Ethylene	50,000	70
Ammonia		500,000	32
Carbon dioxide		200,000	12
Butadiene	Butylenes	200,000	350
Cyclohexane		100,000	8
Ethylene	Refinery gases or hydrocarbons	300,000	50
Ethylene oxide	Direct oxidation of ethylene	100,000	90
Maleic anhydride		50,000	360
Methanol	Natural gas	210,000	43
Nitric acid		50,000	100
Phenol		45,000	200
Polyethylene (low-pressure)		50,000	440
Sulfuric acid	Contact process	280,000	8
Vinyl chloride monomer		100,000	20

SOURCE: *Chemical Engineering* (1967).

SOLUTION:

From Table 3.12, $350 of investment is required for a ton of butadiene produced annually in a plant of 200,000-ton capacity per year. Therefore,

$$\text{Fixed Capital Investment (FCI)} = \$350/T \times 200,000T/yr$$
$$FCI = \$70,000,000 \text{ in } 1967$$

The appropriate cost indices must be applied to bring the costs up to 1984. For the purpose of illustration, the *Chemical Engineering Indices* will be used:

CE Index (1967) = 110 est. from Table 3.9
CE Index (1984) = 322 (est.)

$$FCI\ (1984) \quad = FCI\ (1967)\ \frac{CE\ Index\ 1984}{CE\ Index\ 1967}$$

$$FCI\ (1984) \quad = \$70,000,000\ \frac{322}{110}$$

$$FCI\ (1984) \quad = \$205,000,000$$

Seven-tenths Rule. When cost-capacity data for process plants are plotted on logarithmic coordinates, the result is often a straight line with a slope of approximately 0.7. This plot is similar to the six-tenths rule for process equipment. To use this method, the fixed capital investment for a specific plant capacity must be known:

$$\text{Cost Plant } B = \text{Cost Plant } A \left[\frac{\text{Capacity } B}{\text{Capacity } A} \right]^{0.7} \qquad 3.7$$

The exponent will vary between 0.65 and 0.75, with 0.7 being a mean value. Data for a selected few plants are presented in Table 3.13. Like equipment costs, the fixed investment costs may be adjusted for inflation using cost indices. Example 3.6 illustrates the use of the seven-tenths rule.

EXAMPLE 3.6

PROBLEM STATEMENT:

A company is considering the manufacture of ethylene oxide as an intermediate material for its polymer division. The process used involves the direct oxidation of ethylene. The company built a similar unit in 1977, which had a rated capacity of 100,000 tons annually for $23,000,000. The

Table 3.13 Seven-Tenths Rule.

COMPOUND	SOURCE	EXPONENT
Acetaldehyde	Ethylene	0.70
Acetylene	Natural gas	0.70
Ammonia		0.70
Cyclohexane		0.70
Ethyl alcohol	From ethylene by direct hydration or via ethyl sulfuric acid	0.72
Ethylene	Refinery gases or hydrocarbons	0.71
Ethylene oxide	Direct oxiation of ethylene	0.67
Methanol	Natural gas	0.71
Cis-polybutadiene		0.67
Polyethylene (low-pressure)		0.70
Sulfuric acid	Contact process	0.67

SOURCE: *Chemical Engineering* (1967).

projected production is expected to be 150,000 tons annually. Estimate the fixed capital investment required in early 1984 dollars to produce the required ethylene oxide.

SOLUTION:

From Table 3.13, the exponent for the cost-capacity equation is 0.67. In this example the *Chemical Engineering Indices* found in Table 3.9 will be used

$$CE \ Index \ (1977) = 204$$
$$CE \ Index \ (1984) = 322$$

Equation 3.6 will be modified to include the cost indices:

$$Cost_{150}(1984) = Cost_{100}(1977) \left[\frac{Capacity_{150}}{Capacity_{100}} \right]^{0.67} \left[\frac{CE \ Index \ 1984}{CE \ Index \ 1977} \right]$$

$$Cost_{150}(1984) = \$23,000,000 \left[\frac{150,000}{100,000} \right]^{0.67} \left[\frac{322}{204} \right]$$

$$Cost_{150}(1984) = \$23,000,000 \times 1.31 \times 1.58$$

$$Cost_{150}(1984) = \$47,600,000$$

Preliminary Estimates. The purposes of this quality estimate are to screen further processing methods in the research and development stages, to compare in-house technology with purchased technology, to uncover those areas of the process where important design data are missing, and to serve as a basis for the appropriation of funds. The accuracy of the various techniques presented in this section will vary from -15 to $+30\%$.

Because there are more preliminary quality estimates prepared than the others, many proposed methods are found in the open literature. Each method presented in this section has certain advantages and disadvantages, and these will be discussed. The authors found in excess of 30 preliminary methods during a survey of the literature. The methods can be divided broadly into two major groups. One group consists of factors that when applied to purchased or delivered equipment costs will provide a fixed capital cost. The other group is named *functional unit* or *step counting*. Bridgwater (1981) reviewed these methods in considerable detail.

Factored Estimates. These methods may involve the use of a single factor or a series of factors to develop an estimate of the fixed capital investment.

Lang Method. One of the earliest investigators into short-cut methods was Lang (1947)(1948). He related the fixed capital investment to delivered equipment costs by developing factors for battery-limits plants handling primarily solids, solids and fluids, or fluids. These factors are:

TYPE OF PLANT	FACTOR
Solids	3.10
Solids-Fluid	3.63
Fluid	4.74

The delivered equipment costs are multiplied by the respective plant factor to obtain the fixed capital investment. These factors include setting and testing process equipment, instruments, insulation, piping, painting and weatherproofing, electrical components, site preparation, process buildings and control rooms, as well as engineering and contractor costs. No allowance has been made for a contingency factor.

The Lang method is fast, but not particularly accurate. A number of problems emerge when it is used for preliminary estimates. To obtain delivered equipment costs, a detailed flowsheet and equipment specifications must be prepared. No factors are provided to account for materials of construction, so every item has to be reduced to carbon steel equivalent and then the incremental cost for special materials added later. Lang mentioned that one must be careful about throughput and plant size. His factors were developed from data he collected on about 50 plants. There is no compensation for technology or design advances.

For an experienced engineer, the technique can be refined and Lang-type factors developed not only for the process equipment, but also for each of the other items included in his factors. For example, at a given location, it would be possible to develop similar factors for electrical components, foundations, instruments, insulation, etc., if enough data on plants producing similar products were obtained. An illustration of this method is presented in Example 3.7.

EXAMPLE 3.7

PROBLEM STATEMENT:

A small fluid-processing plant is to be constructed adjacent to a larger operating unit in a still large plant site. The present delivered equipment costs are as follows:

EQUIPMENT	DELIVERED COST, $
Distillation Tower	$400,000
Trays and Internals for the Tower	350,000
Receivers	250,000
Accumulation Drums	150,000
Heat Exchangers	500,000
Pumps and Motors	175,000
Instruments	200,000
Miscellaneous Equipment	125,000

Estimate the battery-limits fixed capital investment, assuming a 15% contingency factor.

SOLUTION:

The sum of the delivered equipment costs = $2,150,000.

Because this is a fluid processing plant, a Lang factor of 4.74 will be used.

Fixed Capital Investment = $2,150,000 × 4.74 × 1.15 = $11,700,000

(NOTE: All estimate calculations will be rounded off to three significant figures.)

Hand Method. This is an extension and refinement of the Lang method. It is quick and more accurate. Hand (1958) recommended that equipment be grouped into eight categories and then an appropriate installation factor be used to obtain the battery-limits fixed capital investment. The categories and factors are presented in Table 3.14. Hand states that these equipment multipliers were determined by analyzing several detailed estimates of plants of the same type. It is apparent when comparing the installation of a pump and a compressor that the equipment cost for a compressor is a higher percentage of the total installed cost than for a pump. The Hand factors are 4 for pumps and 2.5 for compressors. Lang's method does not account for such differences, and consequently more accurate estimates are obtained using the Hand method.

To use this method, a process flowsheet is essential, as well as sizes and specifications for equipment. Like the Lang method also, accounting for material of construction differences requires experience. To improve the accuracy of the Hand method, factors must be derived from recent installations or from detailed estimates for a given locale. The Hand method does not include a contingency factor, so the user should apply an appropriate value. The Hand method is demonstrated in Example 3.8.

EXAMPLE 3.8

PROBLEM STATEMENT:

The problem stated in Example 3.1 will be solved for the battery-limits fixed capital investment using the Hand method and a 15% contingency.

SOLUTION:

Distillation Tower and Internals	$= \$750,000 \times 4.0 =$	$3,000,000
Receivers	$= 250,000 \times 2.5 =$	625,000
Accumulator Drums	$= 150,000 \times 2.5 =$	375,000
Heat Exchangers	$= 500,000 \times 3.5 =$	1,750,000
Pumps and Motors	$= 175,000 \times 4.0 =$	700,000
Instruments	$= 200,000 \times 4.0 =$	800,000
Miscellaneous Equipment	$= 125,000 \times 2.5 =$	313,000
	SUBTOTAL	$7,563,000
	or $7,560,000	

Fixed Capital Investment $= \$7,563,000 \times 1.15$

$= 8,694,000$ or $8.700,000$

NOTE: The Hand method results in a lower fixed capital investment.

Wroth Method. A more detailed list of equipment installation factors was published by Wroth (1960). His data were obtained from production

Table 3.14   Hand Factors.

EQUIPMENT	FACTOR
Fractionating columns, pumps, pressure vessels, instruments	4.0
Heat exchangers	3.5
Compressors	2.5
Fired Heaters	2.0
All other equipment	2.5

SOURCE: Hand (1958).

plant, purchasing department, construction accounting, etc., records. The factors he developed are presented in Table 3.15. The factors in this table include the cost of site development, buildings, electrical installations, carpentry, painting, foundations, structures, piping, contractor's fee and rentals,

Table 3.15   Wroth Factors.

EQUIPMENT	FACTOR
Blender	2.0
Blowers and fans (including motor)	2.5
Centrifuges (process)	2.0
Compressors	
Centrifugal	
Motor-driven (less motor)	2.0
Steam turbine (including turbine)	2.0
Reciprocating	
Steam and gas	2.3
Motor-driven (less motor)	2.3
Ejectors (vacuum units)	2.5
Furnaces (package units)	2.0
Heat exchangers	4.8
Instruments	4.1
Motors, electric	8.5
Pumps	
Centrifugal	
Motor-driven (less motor)	7.0
Steam-driven (including turbine)	6.5
Positive displacement (less motor)	5.0
Refrigeration (package unit)	2.5
Tanks	
Process	4.1
Storage	3.5
Fabricated and field-erected (50,000 + gal)	2.0
Towers (columns)	4.0

SOURCE: Wroth (1960).

engineering, overhead, and supervision. The two previous methods both started with delivered equipment costs, but this method starts with purchased equipment costs. Wroth recommended that if an equipment item is not found in the list then "use or modify the factor belonging to a physically similar unit."

Although the Wroth method is not as quick as the Lang and Hand methods, it does produce more accurate results. To the contrary, it does have the same disadvantages with regard to equipment size and materials of construction as the Lang and Hand methods. An example of how to apply this method is presented in Example 3.9.

EXAMPLE 3.9

PROBLEM STATEMENT:

Example 3.7 will be solved for the battery-limits fixed capital investment using the Wroth method. Delivery charges for the equipment are 5% of the purchased equipment cost. A 15% contingency is to be used.

SOLUTION:

From Example 3.8, the delivered equipment costs were:

EQUIPMENT	DELIVERED EQUIPMENT COST, $	PURCHASED EQUIPMENT COST, $
Distillation Tower and Internals	$ 750,000	$ 714,000
Receivers	250,000	238,000
Accumulator Drums	150,000	143,000
Heat Exchangers	500,000	476,000
Pumps and Motors	175,000	167,000
Instruments	200,000	190,000
Miscellaneous Equipment	125,000	120,000
Subtotal	$2,150,000	$2,048,000

EQUIPMENT	PURCHASED EQUIPMENT COST, $[a]	WROTH FACTOR	INSTALLED EQUIPMENT COST, $
Distillation Towers & Internals	$ 714,000	4.0	$2,856,000
Receivers	238,000	3.5	833,000
Accumulator Drum	143,000	3.5	501,000
Heat Exchangers	476,000	4.8	2,285,000
Pumps and Motors	167,000	7.7[b]	1,285,000
Instruments	190,000	4.1	779,000
Miscellaneous Equipment	120,000	4.0[c]	480,000
TOTAL	$2,048,000	FCI =	$9,019,000

[a] Delivered equipment costs were divided by 1.05 to obtain purchased equipment costs.
[b] Average value for pumps and motors.
[c] Assumed a factor of 4.0.

Therefore, the battery-limits fixed capital investment is $9,020,000. Note: The results obtained from the three methods are:

Lang $11,700,000
Hand $ 8,700,000
Wroth $ 9,020,000

The estimate obtained by the Lang method is subject to the greatest error. In general, the Lang method has a tendency to give high results. The fixed capital investment is about $9,000,000.

Bach Method. A method based upon Lang-type factors was developed by Bach (1958) for fluid-processing plants. Factors developed for process, utility, and storage facilities within a battery-limits are:

TYPE UNIT	FACTOR
Process Unit	2.3–4.2
Utility Unit	1.7–2.6
Storage Unit	2.8–4.8

These factors were developed from plant data into an accounting code consisting of 14 items. The 14 items were further subdivided and direct cost factors obtained. Bach cautions the user that the method he proposed does not include services and facilities beyond the battery-limits. Those units would have to be estimated by other means.

The advantage of this method over the methods discussed previously, although limited to fluid-processing plants, is better accuracy. An example will not be presented, because it follows the same general approach mentioned in Examples 3.7, 3.8, and 3.9.

Chilton Method. An extension of the factor methods that requires more experience and judgment on the part of the user is the Chilton method (1960). This method will allow the user to prepare a battery-limits fixed capital investment estimate. It was developed some years ago, and the factors should be modified to reflect current conditions. For many years this was the only method for preliminary cost estimation in the open literature and as a result became popular. We are acquainted with several companies that have expanded on the Chilton concept for their own in-house needs. The Chilton method requires some interpretation to use, which will be presented in the following paragraphs. The reader should look at Table 3.16 while reading the explanation.

Table 3.16   Chilton Method and Factors.

ITEM	FACTOR		% OF ITEM
1. Delivered Equipment Cost	1.0	×	#1
2. Installed Equipment Cost			
(or directly from cost data)	1.43	×	#1
3. Process Piping			
Type of Plant			
Solid	0.07–0.10	×	#2
Solid-Fluid	0.10–0.30	×	#2
Fluid	0.30–0.60	×	#2
4. Instrumentation			
Amount			
None	0.03–0.05	×	#2
Some	0.05–0.12	×	#2
Extensive	0.12–0.20	×	#2
5. Buildings and Site Development			
Type of Plant			
Outdoor	0.10–0.30	×	#2
Outdoor-Indoor	0.20–0.60	×	#2
Indoor	0.60–1.00	×	#2
6. Auxiliaries (Electrical			
power, Steam)			
Extent			
Existing	0	×	#2
Minor Addition	0–0.05	×	#2
Major Addition	0.05–0.75	×	#2
New Facilities	0.25–1.00	×	#2
7. Outside Lines			
Average Length			
Short	0–0.05	×	#2
Intermediate	0.05–0.15 ·	×	#2
Long	0.15–0.25	×	#2
8. Total Physical Plant Costs			
(Σ Items #2 through #7)			
9. Engineering and Construction			
Complexity			
Simple	0.20–0.35	×	#8
Difficult	0.35–0.60	×	#8
10. Contingencies			
Process			
Firm	0.10–0.20	×	#8
Subject to change	0.20–0.30	×	#8
Speculative	0.30–0.50	×	#8
11. Size Factor			
Size of Plant			
Commercial units			
$2 MM or greater	0–0.05	×	#8
Small Commercial Unit			
$0.5 MM to $2.0 MM	0.05–0.15	×	#8
Experimental Unit			
less than $0.5 MM	0.15–0.35	×	#8
12. Total Fixed Capital Investment			
(Items 8 through 11)			

SOURCE: Chilton (1960).

To calculate a fixed capital investment by this method, the user may start with purchased, delivered, or installed equipment costs. If purchased costs are available, then a factor must be applied for delivery charges to obtain the delivered equipment cost, which is Item 1 in the Chilton method. Item 2, the so-called installed equipment cost is obtained by multiplying Item 1 by 1.43. In the equipment cost data section of this chapter, we discussed installed, or set-in-place, costs. Items 3 through 7 then are percentages of the installed cost, Item 2.

Process piping is dependent upon the type of processing unit. The more fluids handled, the greater the factor. In using any of the piping factors, the assumption is made that the piping associated with the equipment is made of the same material as the equipment. For very high pressure and unusually corrosive or erosive conditions in fluid processing plants, the 0.6 factor will approach and occasionally exceed 1.0 times Item 2. Instrumentation estimated by this method has a tendency to be low. No instrumentation is interpreted to mean the process has locally mounted dial thermometers and pressure gauges, but no significant amounts of automatic control equipment. Under the "extensive" category, this is interpreted to mean a highly instrumented and controlled processing unit. We have found that when data loggers, on-line computers, and analyzers are considered a 0.2 factor is not adequate. To circumvent this problem, we recommend that the costs of these sophisticated equipment items be included in Item 2 and that 0.20 to 0.25 be used as extensive instrumentation. Most data loggers have back-up instruments in the control room on the instrument panel.

Buildings and site development depend upon local conditions. Some processes require a minimum of buildings, though others need temperature and/or humidity control to manufacture a product. The terrain will dictate how much clearing and earth moving are required. Most petrochemical and petroleum plants are outdoor structures even in the cold climates. A factor of 0.20 is adequate to allow for superstructures and control rooms for these plants. To manufacture food products, pharmaceuticals, and cosmetics, a building is essential, and the factor may be as high as 1.00 times Item 2.

Auxiliaries, which would include the extension of electrical power, steam, waste disposal, and cooling water facilities, are based upon the extent of the facilities required. If the lines required are minor extensions to the battery limits, then 0.02 to 0.05 times Item 2 is adequate. If new facilities, such as a substation, new cell to a cooling tower, etc., are required then 0.25 to 1.0 is an appropriate factor. Outside process and utility lines sometimes need to be extended to the battery-limits of a plant. Auxiliaries and outside lines require that the user be acquainted with local conditions, as well as company policy and exercise judgment based upon experience.

The sum of Items 2 through 7 Chilton refers to as the *total physical plant costs,* Item 8. The remainder of the categories in this method are factors of Item 8.

Engineering and construction are estimated on the basis of a project's complexity. If it is relatively simple or similar in many respects to plants built previously, then 20 to 35% of Item 8 is reasonable. But if the engineering is difficult, first of its kind or new to the company, a percentage selected from the "difficult" range is appropriate. Contingencies are based upon the process information. If the data are firm and similar to other processes, then 10–20% of Item 8 is satisfactory. If a process is speculative and data are not firm but subject to change, a higher percentage should be used. Small processing plants seem to have a variety of problems that larger plants don't. The "size factor" is included to account for this fact.

Items 8 through 11 are summed to give the total fixed capital investment. If, when using the Chilton method for preliminary estimates, definition is poor for any given item, then an average value is better to use than to select factors that are all at the upper end of a range. If the user is too conservative, it is an easy task to "kill" all potential projects. Sound judgment and experience are essential to estimating. Example 3.9 is an illustration of how the Chilton method is used to prepare a preliminary estimate.

EXAMPLE 3.9

PROBLEM STATEMENT:

A small fluids-processing facility is to be built at an existing plant site. The delivered equipment costs are:

EQUIPMENT	$M	INCREMENTAL COST OF CORROSION RESISTANT MATERIALS, $M
Distillation Towers	$550	$1,100
Receivers	150	250
Small Tanks	400	
Heat Exchangers	600	
Pumps and Motors	165	300
Miscellaneous	135	
Filters	225	

The equipment is to be placed in an outdoor structure. The process is heavily instrumented. Auxiliary services and outside lines are minimal. The process is well defined and is based upon a similar unit built by the company. Estimate the fixed capital investment.

SOLUTION:

ITEM	% OF ITEM	FACTOR	COST, $M
1. Delivered equipment cost	1	1.0	$ 3,875
2. Installed equipment cost	1	1.43	5,541
3. Process piping (piping often is underestimated in a fluids plant)	2	0.60	3,325
4. Instrumentation (extensive)	2	0.20	1,108
5. Buildings and site development (average)	2	0.20	1,108
6. Auxiliaries (minimal)	2	0.02	111
7. Outside lines (minimal)	2	0.02	111
8. Total physical plant costs (Items 2 through 8)			$11,304
9. Engineering and construction (simple)	8	0.30	3,391
10. Contingencies (firm)	8	0.15	1,696
11. Size factor ($2M investment)	8	0.02	226
12. Total fixed capital investment			$16,617

The estimated fixed capital investment by the Chilton method is $16,600,000.

Peters and Timmerhaus Method. A process is categorized according to whether it is a solid, solid-fluid, or fluid processing unit. Peters and Timmerhaus (1980) start with purchased equipment costs and apply factors for 12 direct and indirect costs, as shown in Table 3.17. The authors state that the method applies to an existing plant site and, therefore, have included land. The user must be careful to "back out" the land cost to calculate depreciation. A problem illustrating the use of this method is Example 3.10.

EXAMPLE 3.10

PROBLEM STATEMENT:

The same problem statement found in Example 3.9 will be used in this problem. The fixed capital investment will be estimated using the Peters and Timmerhaus method.

SOLUTION:

The plant in this problem is a fluid-processing unit. Factors for preparing the estimate are found in Table 3.17.

Table 3.17   Peters and Timmerhaus Method.

	SOLID	SOLID-FLUID	FLUID
DIRECT COSTS			
1. Purchased equipment delivered, including fabricated equipment and process machinery	100	100	100
2. Purchased equipment installation	45	39	47
3. Instrumentation and controls (installed)	9	13	18
4. Piping (installed)	16	31	66
5. Electrical (installed)	10	10	11
6. Building (including services)	25	29	18
7. Yard improvements	13	10	10
8. Service facilities (installed)	40	55	70
9. Land (if purchase is required)	6	6	6
10. TOTAL DIRECT PLANT COSTS	264	293	346
INDIRECT COSTS			
11. Engineering and supervision	33	32	33
12. Construction expenses	39	34	41
10. TOTAL DIRECT & INDIRECT COSTS	336	359	420
14. Contractor's fee (about 5% of direct and indirect plant costs)	17	18	21
15. Contingency (about 10% of direct and indirect plant costs)	34	36	42
16. TOTAL FIXED CAPITAL AND LAND	387	413	483

SOURCE: Peters and Timmerhaus (1980).

DIRECT COSTS	FACTOR	COST, $M
1. Purchased equipment delivered	1.00	$ 3,875
2. Equipment installation	0.47	1,821
3. Instrumentation	0.18	698
4. Piping (installed)	0.66	2,558
5. Electrical (installed)	0.11	426
6. Buildings	0.18	698
7. Yard Improvements	0.10	388
8. Service Facilities	0.70	2,713
9. Land (if purchased)	0.06	233
10. TOTAL DIRECT PLANT COSTS		$13,410

DIRECT COSTS	FACTOR	COST, $M
Indirect Costs		
11. Engineering and Supervision	0.33	1,279
12. Construction Expense	0.41	1,589
13. TOTAL DIRECT & INDIRECT COSTS		16,278
14. Contractor's Fee	0.21	814
15. Contingency	0.42	1,628
16. TOTAL FIXED INVESTMENT PLUS LAND		$18,720

Although there are some similarities between the Chilton and Peters and Timmerhaus methods, the results of the estimate in Example 3.9 and 3.10 cannot be compared directly. For example, two items above, land and service facilities are not included in the Chilton Method. In the latter case, if Items 6 and 7 of the Chilton method, which might be interpreted broadly as services, are compared with the service facilities of the Peters and Timmerhaus method, there is about $2,500,000 difference. Also, if land is removed from the latter method, there is $233,000. These two items overburden the Peters and Timmerhaus method by $2,733,000. If this amount is subtracted from Item 16 above, then the figures calculated by both estimating methods are more comparable.

Chilton method	$16,600,000
Peters and Timmerhaus method	$16,000,000

Holland et al. Method. These authors proposed a method that combines some of the features of the Lange and Peters and Timmerhaus methods with those of the Chilton method. In Table 3.18, different equipment installation factors are presented depending upon the type of processing plant. This uses the Lang-Peters and Timmerhaus ideas. The direct and indirect cost factors are modifications of the Chilton method. Example 3.11 is a sample calculation.

EXAMPLE 3.11

PROBLEM STATEMENT:

The problem statement is found in Example 3.9. Estimate the fixed capital investment using the Holland method.

SOLUTION:

The factors for this estimating method are found in Table 3.18.

Table 3.18 Holland Method.

$$C_{fc} = \phi_1 \, \phi_2 \, \phi_3 \, C_{eq}$$

C_{fc} = fixed capital cost of plant

C_{eq} = major process equipment cost (delivered)

ϕ_1 = 1.45 for solids processing

ϕ_1 = 1.39 for mixed solids-fluid processing

ϕ_1 = 1.47 for fluid processing[23]

$\phi_2 = 1 + f_1 + f_2 + f_3 + f_4 + f_5$

$\phi_3 = 1 + f_6 + f_7 + f_8$

The process piping factor ranges are

  f_1 = 0.07 to 0.10 for solids processing

  f_1 = 0.10 to 0.30 for mixed solids-fluid processing

  f_1 = 0.30 to 0.60 for fluid processing

The instrumentation factor ranges are

  f_2 = 0.02 to 0.05 for little automatic control

  f_2 = 0.05 to 0.10 for some automatic control

The buildings factor ranges are

  f_3 = 0.05 to 0.20 for outdoor units

  f_3 = 0.20 to 0.60 for mixed indoor and outdoor units

  f_3 = 0.60 to 1.00 for indoor units

The facilities factor ranges are

  f_4 = 0 to 0.05   for minor additions

  f_4 = 0.05 to 0.25 for major additions

  f_4 = 0.25 to 1.00 for a new site

The outside lines factor ranges are

  f_5 = 0 to 0.05   for existing plant

  f_5 = 0.05 to 0.15 for separated units

  f_5 = 0.15 to 0.25 for scattered units

The engineering and construction factor ranges are

  f_6 = 0.20 to 0.35 for straightforward plants

  f_6 = 0.35 to 0.50 for complex plants

The size factor ranges are

  f_7 = 0 to 0.05   for large plants

  f_7 = 0.05 to 0.15 for small plants

  f_7 = 0.15 to 0.35 for experimental plants

The contingency factor ranges are

  f_8 = 0.10 to 0.20 for a firm process

  f_8 = 0.20 to 0.30 for a process subject to change

  f_8 = 0.30 to 0.50 for a tentative process

SOURCE: Holland et al. (1974).

Delivered Equipment Costs = $3,875,000

ϕ, is used to convert delivered equipment costs to "installed" equipment costs. In this case, ϕ = 1.47; therefore

Installed Equipment Costs = $3,875,000 × 1.47 = $5,696,000

$$\phi_2 = 1 + f_1 + f_2 + f_3 + f_4 + f_5$$

For this problem

f_1 — process piping = 0.60
f_2 — instrumentation = 0.15
f_3 — buildings = 0.20
f_4 — facilities = 0.02
f_5 — outside lines = 0.02
$\phi_2 = 1 + 0.60 + 0.15 + 0.20 + 0.02 + 0.02$
$\phi_2 = 1.99$
$\phi_3 = 1 + f_6 + f_7 + f_8$
  f_6 — engineering and construction = 0.30
  f_7 — size factor (large plant) = 0.20
  f_8 = contingency (price) = 1.65
$\phi_3 = 1 + 0.30 + 0.20 + 0.15 = 1.65$

Therefore

Delivered Equipment Costs $\times \phi_1 \times \phi_2 \times \phi_3 =$
Total Fixed Capital Investment

$$\$3,875,000(1.47)(1.99)(1.65) = \$18,700,000$$

The estimate obtained by this method gives a higher result than the Chilton or Peters and Timmerhaus methods.

Happel Method. Another preliminary method for estimating the fixed capital investment was developed by Happel (1958) for fluid processing plants only. The factors are presented in Table 3.19, and Example 3.12 shows how to apply these factors.

EXAMPLE 3.12

PROBLEM STATEMENT:

The problem statement is found in Example 3.9. Estimate the fixed capital investment using the Happel method.

SOLUTION:

The factors and equations for this method are found in Table 3.19.

Table 3.19   Happel Method.

DELIVERED EQUIPMENT COSTS	I_E
ADDITIONAL DIRECT COSTS AS A FRACTION OF I_E	
Labor for installing major equipment	0.10–0.20
Insulation	0.10–0.25
Piping (carbon steel)	0.50–1.00
Foundations	0.03–0.13
Buildings	0.07
Structures	0.05
Fireproofing	0.06–0.10
Electrical	0.07–0.15
Painting and cleanup	0.06–0.10
f_i	1.09–2.05
TOTAL DIRECT COST $(1 + f_i)\,I_E$	
INDIRECT COSTS AS FRACTION OF DIRECT COSTS	
Overhead, contractor's costs, and profits	0.30
Engineering fee	0.13
Contingency	0.13
$f_I = (1 + 0.56) = 1.56$	
TOTAL COST $I_F = (1 + f_i)f_I I_E = (3.1\text{–}4.8)^I E$	

SOURCE: Happel (1958).

Delivered Equipment Costs $= I_E =$ \$3,875,000
Direct Costs, Fraction of I_E
Labor for installing equipment   0.20

Insulation	0.18
Piping (Carbon Steel)	0.60
Foundations	0.08
Buildings	0.07
Structures	0.05
Fireproofing	0.08
Electrical	0.11
Painting and Cleanup	0.08
f_i	1.45

TOTAL DIRECT COSTS $= (1 + f_i)I_E =$ \$3,875,000 $\times$ 2.45 $=$ \$9,494,000

Indirect Costs as Fraction of Direct Costs

Overhead, Contractor's Costs	0.30
Engineering Fee	0.13
Contingency	0.13
	0.56

TOTAL INDIRECT COSTS $= f_I = 1 + 0.56 = 1.56$

TOTAL COST $= I_F = (1 + f_i)f_I I_E$

TOTAL COST $= I_F = \$3,875,000 \times 2.45 \times 1.56 = \$14,800,000$

The reader will note that when there was a choice to be made, we chose average values, and the result was lower than the other methods. Certainly, the Chilton, Happel, and the Peters and Timmerhaus methods when modified give similar results. The results fall within $\pm 7\%$ of their mean value. If the Holland method is included, the results are within $\pm 11\%$ of their mean. For this quality estimate, these are close results.

Hirsch and Glazier Method. One of the earliest attempts at estimating by gathering equipment into groups or quasi modules and applying factors was developed by Hirsch and Glazier (1960). The user starts with purchased equipment costs, applies various factors, also expressed in equation form, and ultimately the calculation terminates in a battery-limits fixed capital investment. The definitions and equations are presented in Table 3.20.

Guthrie Method. One of the problems that repeatedly occurs in cost estimation is consistency. This is particularly important when alternate processes are to be compared. Guthrie (1969) developed a method based upon a "modular" concept using data from 42 plant projects. All major cost elements are grouped into six modules:

Chemical processing
Solids handling
Site development
Industrial buildings
Offsite facilities
Project indirects

There are five direct and one indirect modules.

In the chemical processing module, there are 7 primary cost elements and 14 secondary cost elements. These are listed in Table 3.21. A module represents a group of cost elements that have similar characteristics and relationships. Each module is combined at the material and labor level, provided all costs are on a consistent basis. Each chemical process module consists of a cost-capacity plot for a given equipment item, as well as factors for the other direct and indirect cost items in Table 3.21. For example, there is a module for shell-and-tube heat exchangers, which includes the bare equipment cost-capacity plot, adjustment factors for design pressures, and materials

Table 3.20   Hirsch and Glazier Method (1960).

$$I = E\,A(1 + F_L + F_P + F_M) + B + C$$

where

I = total battery-limits investment, \$

A = total purchased equipment cost FOB less incremental cost for corrosion-resistant alloys, \$

B = cost of all equipment estimated on an erected basis, such as furnaces, tanks, cooling towers, etc., (company-erected equipment)

C = incremental cost of alloy materials used only for their corrosion-resisting properties, \$

E = indirect factor for contractor's overhead and profit, engineering, supervision, and contingencies (normally 1.4)

F_L = cost of field labor; $F_L A$ is the total field labor costs, less supervision and excluding the labor charges in item B

F_M = cost factor of miscellaneous item; $F_M A$ includes material cost for insulation, instruments, foundations, structural steel, buildings, wiring, painting, and the cost of freight and supervision

F_P = cost factor for piping materials; $F_P A$ is the total cost of piping materials, including pipe, fittings, valves, hanger, and support, but excluding insulation and installation charges

   The F_L, F_M, and F_P factors are not simple ratios, but are defined by equations

$$\log F_P = 0.635 - 0.154 \log A_0 - 0.992\,\frac{e}{A} + 0.506\,\frac{f}{A}$$

$$\log F_P = -0.266 - 0.014 \log A_p - 0.156\,\frac{e}{A} + 0.556\,\frac{p}{A}$$

$$F_M = 0.344 + 0.033 \log A_0 + 1.194\,\frac{t}{A}$$

where $A_0 = \dfrac{A}{1,000}$, express in \$M

e = total heat exchanger cost, less incremental cost of alloy, \$

f = total cost of field-fabricated vessels, less incremental cost of alloy, \$. (vessels larger than 12 ft in diameter are usually field-erected)

p = total pump plus driver cost less incremental cost of alloy, \$

t = total cost of tower shells less incremental cost of alloy, \$

   The total cost equation will handle both purchased equipment on an FOB basis or completely installed cost.

   In the article there are plots for

$$\log F_L = f\left(\frac{e}{A}, \frac{f}{A}\right)$$

$$\log F_P = f\left(\frac{e}{A}, \frac{p}{A}\right)$$

$$F_M = f\left(A_0, \frac{t}{A}\right)$$

SOURCE: Hirsch and Glazier (1960).

Table 3.21 Chemical Process Module.

Equipment FOB Cost, E
    Piping
    Concrete
    Steel
    Instruments
    Electrical
    Insulation
    Paint
Auxiliary Material, M
Direct Material, $M = E + m$
    Material erection
    Field installation (equip.)
Direct Field Labor, L
Direct M & L Cost $(E + M + L)$

SOURCE: Guthrie (1969).

of construction, as well as piping, concrete, steel, instruments, electrical, insulation, paint, material erection, equipment setting, freight, insurance, taxes, and other indirect costs. When these costs are summed, the resultant is a bare module cost. The first publication (1969) included 10 chemical equipment cost modules. In a later publication (1974), the number was increased considerably.

The solids-handling module was structured like the chemical-processing module and consisted of items shown in Table 3.22. Table 3.23, 3.24, and 3.25 are lists of the items to obtain the site development, industrial buildings, and offsite facilities costs, respectively. Guthrie presents tabular data and factors for each of these three cost modules.

At this point in the method, a lumped indirect cost factor may be applied to each of the aforementioned modules or indirect cost factors may be calculated from a project indirect cost factor module. The items in this module are presented in Table 3.26. To the sum of each bare module cost, the indirect costs are added, as well as contingency and contractor's fees to give the total module cost.

Because a process consists of a group of equipment items, each being a module, then when all total module costs are summed, the fixed capital investment results. Baasel (1976) illustrates the Guthrie method using data on a polyvinyl chloride plant.

Other Factor Methods. Miller (1965) expanded the Lange factor method and included a procedure for calculating minimum, most likely, and maximum

Table 3.22 Solids-Handling.

Ball Mills
Blenders
Centrifuges
Conveyors
Crushers
Dryers
Evaporators
Filters
Hydraulic Presses
Screens
Weigh Scales
Hoppers
    Piping
    Concrete
    Steel
    Instruments
    Electrical
Auxiliary Material (M)
Estimate to direct M & L cost
Solids-Handling M & L Cost

SOURCE: Guthrie (1969).

Table 3.23 Site Development.

Land, surveys, and fees
Dewatering and drainage
Site clearing
Excavation
Grading
Underground sewers
Piling
Roads, walkways, and paving
Parking lots
Landscaping
Fencing
Fire protection facilities
(Estimate to direct M & L cost)
Site Development M & L Cost

SOURCE: Guthrie (1969).

fixed plant investment. Cran (1981) proposed a factor method for preliminary cost estimating and analyzed the results statistically.

Functional or Step-Counting Methods.   Early attempts to prepare preliminary estimates by analogy can be traced to Hill (1956) and Zevnik and Buchanan

Table 3.24 Industrial Buildings.

Administration offices
Laboratory
Medical
Warehouses
Maintenance shops
Garages
Cafeterias
Steel structures
(Estimate to direct M & L cost)
Buildings M & L Cost

SOURCE: Guthrie (1969).

Table 3.25 Offsite Facilities.

Steam generation and distribution system
Power generation and distribution system
Cooling towers and CW distribution system
Fuel oil/fuel gas systems
Blowdown and flare
Pollution control facilities
Fireloops and hydrants
Separators and ponds
Yard lighting and communications
Receiving storage, shipping
    Automotive
    Railroads
    Docks and wharfs
    Tankage
(Estimate to direct M & L cost)
Offiste Facilities M & L Cost

SOURCE: Guthrie (1969).

(1963). Hill's method identified major equipment items as being equivalent to one of two "units." Simple items, like carbon steel exchangers, were classified as single units, and more expensive or complex items were two units. Factors for installation and other direct and indirect costs were used to obtain a grass-roots investment. Zevnik and Buchanan proposed a method identifying functional units and process complexity. Factors were applied for pressure, temperature and materials of construction to obtain a grass-roots investment. Stallworthy's method (1970) is similar to Zevnik and Buchanan's, but it changes functional units into process steps. Stallworthy's equation for a battery-limits investment is

Table 3.26 Plant Indirect Costs.

Sales and other taxes
U.S. freight, packing, insurance
Ocean freight
Marine insurance
Import duties
Freight, insurance, taxes
    Fringe benefits
    Labor burden
    Field supervision
    Temporary facilities
    Construction equipment
    Small tools
    Miscellaneous field costs
Construction overhead
    Project engineering
    Process engineering
    Design and drafting
    Procurement
    Home office construction
    Office overhead
Contractor engineering costs
Indirect cost

SOURCE: Guthrie (1969).

$$I_f = \frac{0.0075}{A} \sum_{1}^{s} NF_M F_P F_t R \qquad\qquad 3.8$$

where S = number of main and process side streams
    R = ratio of the stream to main stream
    N = number of significant process steps in the main stream or process
       side stream
    F_m = factors for specific materials of construction
    F_p = factors for design pressure
    F_t = factors for design temperature
    A = size factor for the capacity of the plant required
    I_F = fixed capital investment (battery-limits)

Stallworthy's method attempted to account for the affect of side streams and recycles. F_m varies between 1.0 and 2.0, F_p between 1.0 and 1.3, and F_t between 1.0 and 1.5. As a basis, 1.0 is for "mild steel" plant operating at a normal temperature of 100°C and pressure of 100 psi. A chart is presented for the cost size factor A. Wilson (1971) combined the Lange factors of

Miller with some of Stallworthy's ideas to obtain a battery-limits investment expression

$$I_F = f N_m (AUC) F_t F_p F_m \qquad\qquad 3.9$$

where f = investment factor
$\quad N_m$ = number of main-plant items
$\quad AUC$ = average unit cost of main-plant items
$\quad F_t, F_p, F_m$ = Stallworthy's factors
$\quad I_f$ = fixed capital investment (battery-limits)

Allen and Page (1975) used some of the Wilson parameters and included a complexity figure, throughput factor, charge to the unit, flow factor, phase factor, and an average weighted exponent for equipment capacity cost. Viola (1981) started with a flowsheet and broke it into major operating steps. Like the preceding methods, his introduces a plant complexity factor, corrections for pressure level and materials of construction, and input/output ratio. Viola also accounted for the percentage of the operating steps employing solid-fluid mixtures. All these are lumped into a complexity factor K, and a plot of K as a function of estimated capital cost for various parametric production rates permits an estimator to obtain a battery-limits fixed capital investment.

Definitive Estimates. This quality estimate is required for the appropriation of funds to build a plant. It is a firm definition of the process upon which a contractor can bid. With these methods an estimate accuracy of -5% to $+10$–15% is possible. Detailed flowsheets, equipment and instrument specifications, etc., must be available. The Nichols chart (1951) shows the exact information required to prepare this level estimate. Because of the vast amount of detail required, the cost of preparing the estimate increases considerably over that for a preliminary estimate.

Richardson Rapid Estimation System. There are several commercial estimation systems available. They range from volumes of manuals for hand calculators to sophisticated computer-oriented systems. One such system was developed and marketed by Richardson Engineering Services (1984). In the entire system there are seven volumes of data, as described in Table 3.27. Equipment cost data are actual purchased costs from manufacturers. The manufacturers are identified, and the equipment model numbers are included. By following the instructions in the manuals, one can calculate a definitive estimate of the fixed capital investment.

Customized Cost Estimation Systems. There are numerous firms in the business of preparing definitive cost estimates for customers. For those companies

Table 3.27 Richardson Rapid Method (1984).

The Richardson system is presented in seven volumes that cover all the detailed estimating elements:

Civil Engineering Work	—Excavation, backfill, and earthmoving
Concrete	—Forming, pouring, reinforcing, equipment foundations, treatment plants, etc.
Structural Steel	—Building, process equipment supports, platforms, handrails, stairs, and ladders
Electrical Work	—Conduit, wire, switchgear for buildings, process equipment, power distribution, etc.
Mechanical Work	—Piping, instrumentation, plumbing
Process Equipment	—Pressure vessels, tanks, compressors, motors, freight
Indirect Costs	—Jobsite and home office overhead, supervision, rental equipment, and tools

A detailed fixed capital investment may be prepared from the volumes for the cost of a process plant. The cost data are updated annually

that do not have the staff or the engineers available, this is a means of obtaining detailed estimates. Some of the firms in this business prepare the estimates entirely by computers. Estimates from these design-construction companies are expensive, but in the long term may be more practical and economical for a company to consider.

Company Methods. Because of the sensitivity of proprietary information, companies frequently prepare their own definitive estimates using in-house techniques. All follow a detailed code of accounts, similar to the one in Table 3.28. Hackney (1965) discusses the establishment of a code. It must be detailed enough to allow the appropriate costs to be categorized, but not so detailed as to be burdensome and difficult to retrieve information at later date. A code of accounts serves as a checklist so that no item is overlooked in the estimating step. It is also used in the construction phase of a project for cost-control purposes. If the code is established properly, then estimated versus actual costs can be compared at a company audit after the process has started. Hackney suggests that once a code of accounts has been established, live with it for a while. Changing codes requires re-education of those who use it.

Some companies have developed in-house factor methods for each item in the code of accounts, similar to the Lang factors. These are based upon local conditions and local factors. This approach can be useful, especially when the same type of processing is used.

Table 3.28 Code of Accounts.

NUMBER	DIRECT CAPITAL COST ACCOUNTS
01	Equipment Items
02	Instrument Items
03	Set & Test Equipment
04	Set & Test Instruments
05	Piling
06	Excavation
07	Foundations
08	Structural Steel
09	Building Items
10	Fire Protection
11	Piping
12	Ductwork
13	Wiring
14	Land
15	Sewers & Drains
16	Underground
17	Yards & Roads
18	Railroads
19	Insulation
20	Painting
21	Fence
Contractor's Overhead & Fee	
22	Temporary Facilities
80	Indirect Charges (Engineering)
81	Construction Stores
82	Temporary Construction Equipment
83	Accounts Receivable
84	Contractor's Retention
85	Premium Wages
Owner's Overhead	
90	Indirect Charges
91	Temporary Construction Stores
92	Temporary Construction Equipment
93	Owner's Miscellaneous
94	Relocation and Modification Expense

OFFSITE CAPITAL

Offsite capital investment refers to the utilities equipment and service facilities that are not included within the boundary of the battery-limits plant. Utilities offsite investment might include:

steam-generating and distribution equipment
electrical-generating and distribution equipment

fuel gas distribution system
pumping stations and distribution systems for river water, well water, cooling tower water, and city water
plant refrigeration systems
plant air systems
waste disposal facilities

The service facilities might include:

railroad spurs
service roads
fire- and security-protection systems
blowdown and flare equipment
warehouse facilities
raw materials and/or finished goods storage
auxiliary buildings

The offsite investment is frequently difficult to estimate. Errors often occur through omission. According to Jelen (1983), the cost of offsite facilities may be estimated as a percentage of the fixed capital investment of the battery-limits plant. Ranges and median percentage are presented in Table 3.29.

Table 3.29 Offsite Facility Costs as a Percentage of Fixed Capital Investment.

ITEM	RANGE, %	MEDIAN, %
Auxiliary Building	3.0–9.0	5.0
Steam Generation	2.6–6.0	3.0
Water-Supply Cooling and Pumping	0.4–3.7	1.8
Process Waste Systems	0.6–2.4	1.5
Electric Main Substation	0.9–2.6	1.3
Raw Material Storage	0.3–3.2	1.1
Finished Product Storage	0.7–2.4	1.5
Steam Distribution	0.2–2.0	1.0
Electrical Distribution	0.4–2.1	1.0
Water Distribution	0.1–2.0	0.9
Fire Protection	0.3–1.0	0.7
Railroads	0.3–0.9	0.6
Yards and Fence Lighting	0.1–0.3	0.2
Water Treatment	0.5–2.1	1.3
Safety Installations	0.2–0.6	0.4

Source: Jelen (1983).

Table 3.30   Offsite Capital Costs as a Percentage of Fixed Costs.

FACILITY	PROCESS $1 MM	UNIT $10 MM	COST $100 MM
Storage	14.8%	12.0%	10.5%
Site preparation	6.8	4.4	3.2
Utilities	6.0	4.2	3.8
Buildings	5.2	3.5	2.0
Piping, offsite	3.4	2.7	2.4
Auxiliaries	2.0	1.6	0.8
TOTAL	38.2%	28.4%	22.7%

Source: Kharbanda (1979).

For preliminary estimates, Kharbanda (1979), like Jelen, suggested that offsite capital investment be a percentage of the processing unit's fixed investment. Table 3.30 is a tabulation of his data. A detailed breakdown of unit costs with minimum, normal, and maximum values for offsite investment was published by Guthrie (1969).

ALLOCATED CAPITAL

An earlier part of this chapter classified estimates broadly as *grass-roots* or *battery-limits*. As the name grass-roots implies, the plant is estimated, designed, and constructed assuming that the only item of total capital investment available is the land upon which the plant is to be located. Boiler and electrical facilities, plant laboratories and offices, as well as raw material storage and warehouses for finished goods, would have to be included in the estimate. In a battery-limits estimate, however, it was assumed that all utilities, services, and storage facilities were present in the quantity and quality at the battery limits. In the latter case, if a new project is to use these facilities, then a percentage of the fixed capital investment of the facilities is allocated to the battery-limits plant.

Allocated capital may consist of contributions from:

intermediate production facilities
utilities
services
sales, administration, research, and engineering

The sum of these four items, if necessary, is called the *total allocated capital.*

Intermediate Production Facilities

At a large integrated production site, a product made in Department A might be sold on the open market. If another product is proposed for Department X, which would use a part of the total output of Department A, then the company would probably use that intermediate product from A to manufacture X. If so, then product from A is sent to Department X at the manufacturing cost plus any transportation charges, but, in return, Department X must assume an amount of Department A's fixed capital investment as allocated capital. The proportion of the fixed capital allocated is based upon the percentage of the output of Department A that Department X will use. From an accounting standpoint, Department A's fixed investment against which it must earn a return is reduced by the proportionate amount, and Department X's total capital investment against which it must earn a return is increased. This allocated capital is sometimes called *back-up* capital or *proportionate share of existing facilities*.

Department A benefits from this procedure by having a captive outlet for its production, and also the investment against which it earns a return is reduced. Overall, this should improve the profitability of Department A. Nevertheless, Department A earns no profit on that proportion of its output going to Department X.

Department X obtains raw materials at manufacturing cost plus some minor transportation and handling charges. This is less expensive than purchasing the raw material, if available, on the open market. But Department X's total capital investment increases by the amount of allocated capital assumed. It is advisable, when considering a project in which back-up capital is possible, to calculate the "costs and benefits" of assuming a proportionate share of the existing facilities or to buy the raw material on the open market and pay for the profit.

Utilities

Utilities are frequently treated in the same fashion, depending upon how utility charges are calculated. The capital investment charges, for example, may be included with the fuel, labor, etc., for generating steam. If so, no proportionate share of the utilities capital is considered as allocated capital. As an alternate, a share of the utilities investment may be allocated to a proposed project depending upon the proportion of the utilities capacity to be consumed. The charges to Department X in this case are then the "operating expenses" for the utility at no profit.

Service and SARE Investment

Service facilities, for example, cafeterias, change houses, maintenance buildings, plant offices, and laboratories are proportioned on a percentage use basis. Plant accounting departments can be of assistance in calculating the proportion to be used. Sales, administration, research, and engineering (SARE) capital investment is also proportioned to departments using their facilities or services.

Any one or all four of the items constituting total allocated capital may be included in any project. Example 3.13 is an illustration of how allocated capital is determined.

EXAMPLE 3.13

PROBLEM STATEMENT:

LAX Petrochemicals, Inc., is considering the manufacture of 18MM lb/yr of a chlorinated product. In the process, it is estimated that 4.0 MM lb/yr of chlorine will be required. LAX has a chlorine-caustic soda plant at the same location that produces 200 T/day, and the fixed capital investment of this old facility is $20 MM. Calculate the amount of allocated capital to be charged to the chlorinated product department if the required amount of chlorine is to be transferred from the existing chlorine-caustic soda plant. It may be assumed that both plants operate 330 days per year.

The new facility is estimated to consume the following utilities:

UTILITY	USAGE BY DEPARTMENT	UTILITY RATED CAPACITY	FIXED CAPITAL INVESTMENT
Steam	3,000 lb/hr	600 PSIG, 750°F 400,000 lb/hr	$25 MM
Cooling Tower Water	900 gal	15,000 gal	$ 0.6 MM
Electricity	500 KW	20,000 KW	$15 MM

The accounting department has provided the following data:

ITEM	DEPARTMENTAL	FIXED CAPITAL INVESTMENT
Service Facilities	3%	$ 8,000,000
SARE	1%	$18,000,000

SOLUTION:

Intermediates

$$\text{The chlorine required} = 4,000,000 \text{ lb/yr} \times \frac{\text{Ton}}{2,000 \text{ lb}} = 2,000 \text{ T/yr}$$

Yearly capacity $= 100 \text{ T/day} \times 330 \text{ day/yr} = 33,000 \text{ T/yr}$

Therefore, the proportion of the chlorine facility capital allocated to the chlorinated hydrocarbon department is

$$\frac{2,000 \text{ T/yr}}{33,000 \text{ T/yr}} \times \$20,000,000 = \$1,212,000$$

Utilities

Steam

$$\frac{3,000 \text{ lb/hr}}{400,000 \text{ lb/hr}} \times \begin{array}{l} \$25 \text{ MM} = \$187,500 \\ \text{say } \$188,000 \end{array}$$

Cooling Tower Water

$$\frac{900 \text{ gal}}{15,000 \text{ gal}} \times \$0.6 \text{ MM} = \$36,000$$

Electricity

$$\frac{500 \text{ KW}}{20,000 \text{ KW}} \times \$15 \text{ MM} = \$375,000$$

Service Facilities

$$\$8 \text{ MM} \times 0.03 = \$240,000$$

SARE

$$\$18 \text{ MM} \times 0.01 = \$180,000$$

TOTAL ALLOCATED CAPITAL:

Intermediates	$1,212,000
Utilities	
Steam Plant	188,000
Cooling Tower	36,000
Electrical Facilities	375,000
Service Facilities	240,000
SARE	180,000
TOTAL ALLOCATED CAPITAL =	$2,231,000

The alternative to the concept of proportionate share is the *profit center*. This means that each operating unit is a profit generator for the company and as such will exist depending upon its ability to meet company profitability criteria. If the facility doesn't, it is either modified or shut down. One petroleum company carries the profit center concept even to the utilities that have different criteria to meet, compared with a department producing salable products.

Which approach should one use? The answer to this question is that there are successful companies operating with either the proportionate share or the profit center approach. Management of a firm will determine which concept is to be applied.

WORKING CAPITAL

Working capital is a very important aspect of company operations, especially for new processes and/or new products. A company needs an adequate amount of working capital to conduct the normal day-to-day business, but in the case of new ventures, adequate amounts of working capital are essential until sales generate enough revenue for a venture to be self-sustaining. Often small businesses fail due to a shortage of working capital. At times when interest rates are high, a small business operation may have difficulty borrowing sufficient money so the venture won't fail.

Working capital has been defined in Chapter 1 as current assets minus current liabilities. This is the classic definition used by accountants. In reality, this is net working capital. Some economists call current assets "working capital" but in this text, the accounting definition will be used and the word *net* dropped from use.

Although the initial input of working capital for a new project comes from the company's financial resources, it is regenerated from the sale of products and services. If a project is considered, working capital is continuously liquidated and regenerated and represents the "working" funds necessary to conduct normal day-to-day business.

Several methods are available for estimating an adequate amount of working capital for a proposed venture. The methods may be divided into two broad categories:

percentage methods
inventory methods

Let's consider each category and the variations in estimating techniques.

Percentage Methods

For quick, order-of-magnitude or preliminary estimates, these methods are adequate. Working capital requirements are estimated based upon annual sales or upon capital investment.

Percentage of Sales. The estimation of working capital for specialty products is often based upon a percentage of annual sales. Specialty products might include cosmetics, flavors, condiments, food additives, perfumes, etc., to name a few. Let's consider the manufacture of perfumes. The essences and alcohols used in the preparation of a perfume are high-cost items. The cost of the capital equipment to produce and package the perfume is relatively small compared with, say, petrochemical operations. Therefore, a perfume manufacturer may have considerable amounts of money tied up in raw materials and finished goods with only a modest fixed capital investment. Therefore, it would be more reasonable to base the amount of working capital for day-to-day operations on sales. According to Wessel (1953), the percentage of sales may vary between 15 and 40% of the annual sales, with 30% being a reasonable mean value. If a person wishes to determine more closely the percentage figure for a specialty product, the annual and 10-K reports for a company engaged in that business will give enough information to calculate the percentage.

EXAMPLE 3.14 PERCENTAGE-OF-SALES METHOD

PROBLEM STATEMENT:

A flavor additive is to be made by a specialty chemical company. The annual sales are expected to be $7,000,000 for this product. Estimate the amount of working capital required for this project.

SOLUTION:

This is a specialty product, and as such the working capital may be estimated as a percentage of annual sales. The range is 15 to 40% of sales, with a mean value of 30%.

Annual Sales = $7,000,000
Estimated Working Capital = $7,000,000 × 0.30 = $2,100,000

Percentage of Capital Investment. Frequently, the working capital requirements are estimated on the basis of either the fixed or total capital investment. If a company produces and sells a product at a uniform annual rate, then 10 to 20% of the total capital investment is an adequate amount for preliminary evaluations. If the basis selected is fixed capital investment, 15 to 25% percent of that investment would be satisfactory. Some businesses, however, are seasonal. For example, fertilizers, herbicides, and fungicides are produced often in multipurpose equipment and then stored at distribution centers in agricultural areas. If this is the case, then 20 to 40% of the total capital investment might be used as a working capital estimate to account for the large inventories that must be maintained.

EXAMPLE 3.15 PERCENTAGE-OF-CAPITAL-INVESTMENT METHOD

PROBLEM STATEMENT:

A company is considering a new product venture. The engineering department has estimated the battery-limits fixed capital investment at $9.8 MM. Land allocated for the plant is valued at $200,000, and startup expenses are estimated at $800,000. The company normally uses 15% of the total capital investment as an estimate of working capital. Determine the amount of working capital required.

SOLUTION:

As the problem is stated, there are four elements of the total capital investment present, namely, land, working capital, fixed capital investment, and startup expenses. All are known except the working capital. If it is 15% of the total capital investment, then land, fixed capital investment, and startup expenses constitute 85%.

Land	$ 200,000
Fixed Capital Investment	9,800,000
Startup Expenses	800,000
Subtotal	$10,800,000

Therefore, the total capital investment is

$$\frac{\$10,800,000}{0.85} = \$12,700,000$$

Working capital = total capital investment minus subtotal
$$= \$12,700,000 - \$10,800,000 = \$1,900,000$$

The $1,900,000 working capital is 15% of the total capital investment.

Inventory Methods

Net working capital was defined earlier in this section as current assets minus current liabilities. Inventory is one of the items in the definition, as are cash, accounts receivable, and accounts payable. Aries and Newton (1954) present three variations on the inventory method for estimating working capital, but all seem to have the common thread of inventory. The following method is one that represents the major elements of working capital.

Raw Materials Inventory. An adequate supply of raw materials must be available to cover, for example, delays in delivery. The inventory level is controlled by the rate of consumption, availability of raw materials, sources, storage requirements, value, and delivery times. For continuous production a 2-weeks' supply is adequate.

Goods-in-Process Inventory. The amount of goods being processed varies widely depending upon the type of process—batchwise or continuous around the clock. Goods-in-process inventory is a function of the equipment size and the overall length of the processing cycle. To estimate the amount this item contributes, one-half of the total manufacturing cost occurring during a period equivalent to the total process cycle is a reasonable figure. This calculation is based upon the assumption that material at the beginning of the process has just begun to be converted, while that at the end is nearly completed.

Finished Goods Inventory. The amount of finished goods retained as inventory will vary considerably depending upon the end-use of the product. Some products are made and sold uniformly over the year, but others are made and sold on a seasonal basis. Still other products may have peculiar shelf-life characteristics and cannot be stored for long periods. The amount of finished goods inventory must be determined for each product. In the case of uniformly continuous production of a product with no unusual shelf-life problems, 2 to 3 weeks of inventory is adequate.

Stores-and-Supplies Inventory. This item includes inventories of spare parts for items too small in value to be capitalized—operating supplies, maintenance materials, office supplies, chart paper, etc. A reasonable estimate would be 10% of the annual maintenance expense, if the plant is located in any area easily serviced by railroads, truck companies, and barge lines. If the plant is in a remote area and experiences long delivery times, 20% of the annual maintenance expense might be reasonable.

Cash. An adequate amount of cash on hand is necessary to pay for wages, salaries, raw materials, and other operating expenses. Most authorities agree that cash on hand should amount to 1 month's manufacturing expense at rated capacity.

Accounts Receivable. A certain amount of capital is required to cover the credit extended to customers who have not yet paid for the product. The amount may vary greatly depending upon the type of business and the company's credit policies. In the chemical-process industries, the average length of time for outstanding accounts receivable is 45 days. Most authorities, however, recommend 1 month of sales to cover accounts receivable.

Accounts Payable. This item is the amount a firm owes its creditors for raw materials, supplies, etc. One month at manufacturing cost of the product is considered adequate.

The sum of the above seven items will give an estimate of the working capital required for a venture. It is used for preliminary or detailed estimates of capital investment, but rarely for order-of-magnitude estimates, because the inventory method is more detailed than needed.

Concluding Remarks

If the percentage methods are used to estimate working capital, the estimator should be aware that annual sales forecasts and fixed or total capital investment figures are preliminary at best and subject to error. Several factors affecting working estimates are:

Seasonal variations in project operations or product demands,
Accuracy of sales forecasts and investment estimates,
Firmness of raw material and finished goods price structures,
Low yield or low conversion processes require large volumes of raw materials,
Inventory is critical for those processes in which the product has a high dollar value.

Example 3.16 is an example of the calculation of working capital by the inventory method.

EXAMPLE 3.16

PROBLEM STATEMENT:

A company is considering the manufacture of a bioherbicide. It is expected to sell 10,000,000 lb/yr at 65 cents/lb. In the manufacture of this product, all raw materials except one are delivered by pipeline from a plant in the vicinity. The only onsite storage would be for an acid. It costs 18 cents/pound and is consumed at a rate of 500,000 pounds per month. The total manufacturing expense is expected to be 30 cents per pound of product. Goods-in-process amounts to about $300,000 because of several large hold tanks in the process. The fixed capital investment for the plant was estimated to be $8 MM. Maintenance for the company has averaged 6%/year of the fixed capital investment over the past few years. Estimate the amount of working capital required using the inventory method presented in this chapter.

SOLUTION:

Raw Materials Inventory:

Two week supply of inorganic acid =

$$500,000 \text{ lb/mo} \times \frac{14}{30} \text{ days} = 233,000 \text{ lb of acid}$$

Raw Material Inventory = 233,000 lb × $0.18/lb = $42,000

No other raw materials are stored on the plant site, as they are delivered by pipeline.

Goods-in-Process Inventory = $300,000

Finished Product Inventory:

$$\text{Two weeks supply} = 10,000,000 \text{ lb/yr} \times \frac{2 \text{ weeks}}{52 \text{ weeks/yr}}$$
$$= 385,000 \text{ lb}$$

Value of product inventory = 385,000 lb × $0.65/lb
= $250,000

Stores-and-Supplies Inventory:

Assume 10% of the annual maintenance cost

Maintenance expense per year = $8,000,000 × $0.06 = $480,000/yr
10% of annual maintenance expense − $48,000

Cash:

One month's manufacturing expense

10,000,000 lb/yr × 1 yr/12 mo × $0.30/lb = $250,000

Accounts Receivable:

One month of sales

$$10,000,000 \text{ lb/yr} \times \frac{1 \text{ mo}}{12 \text{ mo/yr}} \times \$0.65/\text{lb} = \$542,000$$

Accounts Payable:

Same as cash = $250,000

SUMMARY

ITEM	AMOUNT
Raw Materials Inventory	$ 42,000
Good-in-Process Inventory	300,000
Finished Goods Inventory	250,000
Stores-and-Supplies Inventory	48,000
Cash	250,000
Accounts Receivable	542,000
Accounts Payable	250,000
Total Estimated Working Capital	$1,182,000

It is good practice to check the working capital as a percentage of the total capital investment

$$\frac{\$1,182,000}{\$8,000,000 + 1,182,000} \times 100 = 12.9\%$$

This result compares favorably with working capital determined by the percentage method.

STARTUP EXPENSES

When a process is brought on-stream, there are a number of expenses associated with this activity. Equipment deficiencies, design errors, and construction mistakes must be corrected. The actual time when startup begins is not easy to pinpoint; however, management in conjunction with the accountants will determine when salable product is produced and when startup expenses are charged to the project.

These expenses usually include the following:

training the operating labor

training and instructing the maintenance labor in the repair and care of new and nonstandard equipment

constructing temporary facilities to be used during startup only

training laboratory personnel in new analytical procedures

calibrating and adjusting equipment and instruments for normal operations

water-batching operations or pressure-testing process equipment for leaks and proper operation

operator errors

The length of time that this activity lasts depends upon agreements between the manufacturing and engineering personnel concerning satisfactory performance. In most instances, the termination of startup occurs when salable product is manufactured. If the engineering and construction have been performed by an outside contractor, then there is a contractual agreement stating when a plant is considered acceptable. If the engineering and construction are performed in-house, the exact time when startup occurs is more nebulous.

The estimation of startup expenses is a difficult task. There is a dearth of information concerning the estimation of startup expenses and what data do exist are fragmentary. Bauman (1960), McCallister (1971), Gans (1976), and Derrick and Sutor (1977) present estimation methods based on a percentage of the fixed capital investment. The lack of cost information on startup expenses is understandable, because the time frame during which startup occurs is not well defined, and also the information is often proprietary.

Peters and Timmerhaus (1980) recommend 8 to 10% of the fixed capital investment as satisfactory for preliminary estimates. Baasel (1976) suggests that startup expenses vary between 5 and 20% of the fixed capital investment. Most authorities, however, agree that for a battery-limits plant the startup expenses rarely exceed 10% of the fixed capital investment. If the plant is a retrofit or an addition to an existing operation, startup expenses may be up to 30% of the fixed investment (1984).

The best source of information may be company files on a process similar to the one proposed, but sometimes the true costs are buried in the total plant costs. Frequently, local factors, e.g., labor productivity, may be a dominant factor in startup expenses.

In the absence of local information and for preliminary estimates, two methods are proposed for estimating startup expenses:

Single-factor method—The startup expense is computed by multiplying the fixed capital investment by a factor as follows:

FIXED CAPITAL INVESTMENT (FCI)	% OF FCI
$100 MM or greater	6%
$ 10 MM to 100 MM	8%
$ 10 MM	10%

Multiple-factor method—This method is based upon three components:
labor
commercialization expense
inefficiency

Earlier in this section, the expenses associated with startup were influenced by the above three components. The labor component is based upon 2 months' training and 3 months' startup for each laborer. Therefore, 5 months of operating labor and maintenance labor expenses are computed.

Commercialization expenses are estimated as a percentage of the fixed capital investment. This expense is related to temporary construction, calibration of instruments and equipment, etc. For estimation purposes, 5% of the purchased equipment cost is satisfactory.

Startup inefficiency depends upon mechanical breakdowns, operator errors, and the inability of the process to maintain continued production. Four percent of the annual manufacturing expense is a reasonable estimate.

The sum of the three components is the startup expenses.

EXAMPLE 3.17

PROBLEM STATEMENT:

An aluminum trim piece is to be manufactured in a new facility that has an estimated fixed capital investment of $1.5 MM. The purchased equipment cost is $400,000. To operate this facility, three operating laborers and two maintenance men are required. Their annual wages are $28,000 and $26,000, respectively. The annual manufacturing expense for this new facility is expected to be $2.3 MM. Calculate the startup expenses using both the single-factor and multiple-factor methods.

SOLUTION:

Single-factor method

For plants with fixed capital investments less than $10 MM, 10% of the fixed capital investment is recommended.

Therefore,

$$\text{Startup expenses} = \$1,500,000 \times 0.10 = \$150,000$$

Multiple-factor method

Labor component

$$\text{Operating labor} = \$28,000 \times \frac{5}{12} \times 3 = \$35,000$$

$$\text{Maintenance labor} = \$26,000 \times \frac{5}{12} \times 2 = \$21,700$$

$$\text{Total Labor Component} = \$56,000$$

Commercialization expense

Use 5% of the purchased equipment cost

$$\$400,000 \times 0.05 = \$20,000$$

Startup inefficiency

Use 4% of annual manufacturing expense

$$\$2,300,000 \times 0.04 = \$92,000$$

The total startup expenses are the sum of the labor component, commercialization expense, and startup inefficiency by the multiple-factor method are:

Labor component	= $ 56,700
Commercialization expense	= 20,000
Startup inefficiency	= 92,000
Total startup expense	= $168,700

OTHER CAPITAL ITEMS

There are three more components of the total capital investment that may be involved in any project.

Interest on Borrowed Funds

If funds required for a new venture are generated by borrowing, for example from the sale of bonds, then the interest on these bonds during construction is usually capitalized. After the facility becomes operable, then the interest on borrowed funds becomes an operating expense. The federal regulations governing interest on borrowed funds change frequently; therefore, it is recommended that company accountants be consulted for the proper procedure.

Catalysts and Other Consumable Items

Chemical processes may require an initial charge of catalysts. Some of these contain platinum, rhodium, palladium, or other very expensive materials. Still other processes may require a one-time filling of equipment to initiate the process. If these materials have a life of 1 year, the cost is capitalized. If not, then the expenses are entered on the manufacturing cost sheet. The cost may be calculated from knowing the amount of material required and its unit cost.

Licenses, Patents, and Royalties

Technical process information may be purchased by royalty or licensing agreements. The purchase of technical expertise is considered a replacement for process research and development. Royalties are classified broadly into *paid-up* or *running* royalties. If the agreement is a paid-up royalty, a one-time expenditure is made, and the cost is entered as part of the total capital investment. In contrast, if a running royalty agreement is executed, then a charge for the technical information is made based upon the amount and cost per pound of product manufactured. This expense then is entered on the manufacturing cost sheet as a direct operating expense. There is no known method for estimating this item. The information would have to be obtained from the licensor.

COMPUTER-PREPARED CAPITAL COST ESTIMATES

This chapter has presented the essentials for the preparation of capital cost estimates. In the past 20 years large simulation programs have been developed, most of which included economic evaluation modules. In the evaluation modules were simple capital cost estimation programs. These simulation programs were extensive and required the use of large mainframe computers. Frequently, most of the effort in the development of the simulation programs went into the process modeling and very little into the economics. As a result the economic evaluation modules were simplistic and not in keeping with modern business practices. Some of the large programs were constructed so that it was difficult to use the economic packages.

With the advent of the microcomputer, programs dedicated to the economics have been developed that allow the user to consider many cases in a short time without the associated expense of using large computers. Most engineers and scientists have personal computers at their desks.

Need for Computers in Cost Estimation

In recent years, there has been a literature explosion throughout the world. In no area has the impact been felt more than in cost estimation and cost control. An enormous amount of data has been published concerned with only capital costs. Kharbanda (1979) stated that most of the cost data were published in the United States and some in the United Kingdom. The British data were based upon the American data with a conversion factor.

The massiveness of the cost data information and estimating techniques dictates the need for computers. The person preparing the estimate then is confronted with the enormous task of screening and evaluating a plethora of information. This step can be performed only by an experienced person. Once the screening and evaluating have been completed, the useful cost data can be stored in files, tapes, diskettes, etc., for ready access. The data might include equipment cost algorithms, cost indices, labor rates, labor productivity, etc., that can be updated and retrieved when needed.

The extent of the usage by industry varies from one company to another, as well as, within large corporations, from one plant to another. The manner in which programs have been developed, especially for the microcomputers, makes them *user-oriented.* This means the user does not have to be a computer expert to operate the programs. With the large-scale computers, however, the user did have to have some computer expertise. Concurrent with the movement from the large computers to the mini- and microcomputers, companies have streamlined their economic evaluation techniques.

Advantages of Using Computers

There are many reasons for using computers to prepare capital cost and operating expense estimates. In addition to saving a large amount of time in doing repetitive calculations, computers reduce mathematical errors. An estimator may use time more effectively making decisions and judgments that require technical skills, rather than spending time on data gathering and clerical tasks. If the data are gathered and stored properly in a uniform data base, then fewer errors will be present.

Computers with electronic spreadsheets allow the user to examine changes in costs not only as a function of time, but for various proposed cases. Also, sensitivity analysis, which examines the sensitivity of variables to some economic guideline, for example, return on investment, is easily performed on a computer. Sensitivity analyses performed using a hand calculator require a considerable amount of engineering time.

In capital cost estimating, certain trends are emerging as a result of computer use. There is less use of factor-type multipliers based upon flimsy data that are subject to errors. Correlations are developed such that multiple-factored estimates are becoming more accurate. Computers have allowed the estimator to have access to greater amounts of stored data. These data are not only more extensive, but also more reliable. When manual estimates are prepared, the engineer frequently uses heuristics, or rules of thumb, because of their simplicity. With the computer, more elaborate and often more accurate mathematical models are used, resulting in more accurate estimates.

Disadvantages of Using Computers

Of course, the old adage "garbage in = garbage out" still applies. One must be certain of the accuracy, source, and date of the data in any computer program. With the advent of the microcomputer, simple, less costly data banks and evaluation programs are becoming available. Whether a user should purchase a program or develop one to fit the requirements of the company requires careful consideration. Although advertising for packaged programs is not intentionally misleading, these programs may not be what the user wants. Nonetheless, it is very expensive and time consuming to develop a program for a specific use, if a purchased program can be modified to the user's needs.

SUMMARY

In this chapter, the items essential for the preparation of the Total Capital Investment were presented and discussed. For any given project, not all of the items are included. The quality of the desired estimate affects the amount of detail required to prepare the Fixed Capital Investment. The methods for preparing this Fixed Investment are those frequently used by practising engineers. Allocated Capital, Working Capital and Startup Expenses may be estimated by equations or by assuming a percentage of the Fixed or Total Capital Investment. Reasonable guidelines were discussed.

The remaining items such as Land, Off-Site Capital and Other Capital Items are usually obtained as dollar amounts supplied perhaps from sources other than the person preparing the estimate.

The chapter concludes with a short discussion of the role that computers have taken in the preparation of capital cost estimation. There are various commercial capital cost programs available for large main-frame computers, minicomputers and microcomputers. These programs include cost modules for commonly-used equipment. For specialty equipment or for unusual processing conditions, it may be advisable for the user to develop his or her own computer programs.

In the next chapter, the estimation of operating expenses is presented. The methodology for operating expenses is not as well developed as for capital cost estimation.

PROBLEMS

3.1. Using the sales prices listed below, calculate the fixed capital investment by the turnover ratio method for chemical plants manufacturing the following products:

    a. maleic anhydride: $0.55 per pound
    b. sulfuric acid: $73.00 per ton
    c. acetone: $0.24 per pound
    d. carbon black: $0.32 per pound
    e. butyl alcohol: $0.36 per pound
    f. butadiene: $0.34 per pound

3.2. You read in a trade journal that a competitor that, like your company, is basic in fertilizer manufacturing has announced plans for a $5 million expansion to increase urea production. The article gave no information concerning how much this expansion would increase production. Your immediate supervisor asks you to estimate the increase in annual production, if urea is currently selling for $150/ton.

3.3. The following chemical market prices were obtained from a current issue of the *Chemical Marketing Reporter:*

alcohol, butyl, drms., c.l.	$0.36/pound
butadiene, tank	$0.34/pound

Estimate the fixed capital investment required for the following plants:

    a. A plant to manufacture 30 tons/day of butyl alcohol, assuming 330 days per year stream time.
    b. A plant to produce 150,000 tons/year of butadiene from butylenes.
    c. How do the results in b compare with the results obtained in Problem 3.1?

3.4. The purchased prices of glass-lined steel reactors with an agitator, thermwell, and baffle are given below:

GALLONS	PURCHASED PRICE, FOB FACTORY
500	$ 45,690
750	49,900
1,000	55,300
1,500	65,350
2,000	70,500
3,000	90,500
4,000	101,700

a. Construct a graph of purchased price as a function of size on a log-log plot.

b. Determine whether the six-tenths rule applies to this equipment.

c. Derive an equation for the purchase price as a function of size.

3.5. A 100,000 gal carbon steel storage tank was purchased for $50,000 in 1978.

a. Estimate the purchased price of a 300,000-gallon tank in that same year.

b. Estimate the purchased price of a 500,000-gallon tank in 1984.

3.6. A shell-and-tube heat exchanger of 200-square feet surface area was purchased for $4,000 in 1980.

a. Estimate the cost of a similar exchanger of 500-square feet area using the six-tenths rule.

b. What is the estimated cost of the 500-square foot exchanger in 1984?

The literature reported that the cost-capacity exponent for this type exchanger is 0.81 in the range of 400 to 2,000 square feet.

c. Using this exponent, what was the difference in purchased price in 1984 compared with that obtained by the six-tenths rule?

3.7. In January 1978, a steel vertical leaf filter press with a filtering surface of 150 square feet was purchased for $3,500. Production has increased so that a 400-square foot press will be needed. The current filter press has shown some corrosion, so it has been recommended that the new press be made of 304SS, which is 1.45 times more expensive than steel. Estimate the purchased price of the new unit in January, 1986, assuming a 5% inflation rate during 1985.

3.8. Estimate the fixed capital investment for an alkylation unit listed below using the:

a. Lang method,

b. Hand method, and

c. Chilton method.

d. Compare and discuss the results of your calculations.

ITEM	NO. REQUIRED	DESCRIPTION
Charge Pump	1 + 1 spare	730 gpm at 50-ft head, high-silicon iron
Product Pump	1 + 1 spare	300 gpm at 50-ft head, high-silicon iron
Alkylators	5	Each reactor is 10 ft dia. × 60 ft long. Use storage tank for alkylator, carbon steel.
Agitators	40	Turbine, dual impeller, carbon steel, 100 rpm 50 hp each
Settlers	5	13 ft dia. × 40 ft long, carbon steel tank
Compressor	1	30,000 SCFM, 4-stage, axial compressor, 2000 hp

3.9. Ajax Petrochemical is considering the manufacture of an organic aldehyde in the amount of 20,000,000 pounds per year. In the manufacturing process, 4,000,000 pounds per year of chlorine will be consumed. It may be obtained from the company's on-site chlorine plant, which has a rated capacity of 100 tons per day. The fixed capital investment of the chlorine plant, as carried on the company books, is $20,000,000. The engineering department estimates that the total fixed capital investment of the aldehyde unit is $5,000,000 in 1984 dollars. Land for the new plant is evaluated at $80,000.

The company uses the proportionate share method for determining allocated capital. Working capital may be taken as 12% of the total capital investment. Startup expenses may be assumed to be 6% of the fixed capital investment. Prepare a statement of the total capital investment.

3.10. A small fluid-processing unit is to be constructed adjacent to a larger operating unit in a multiproduct chemical plant. The purchased equipment costs, FOB the vendor's plant, are:

NUMBER REQUIRED	EQUIPMENT	TOTAL PURCHASED PRICE
1	Tower & Internals	$300,000
2	Accumulators	150,000
3	Receivers	400,000
6	Heat Exchangers	600,000
5	Pumps & Motors	165,000
–	Miscellaneous	135,000

If the delivery charges are 5% of the purchased price, estimate the battery-limits fixed capital investment using the Hand and Wroth methods.

3.11. Recently, the Corporate Planning Committee of Luray Chemicals, Inc., met to consider plans for capital expenditures in the near future. It was decided that a capital cost estimate should be prepared for the new plasticizer, XBC, which is in the research stage. From the equipment list below, prepare the total capital requirements for a battery-limits plant.

The following guidelines are used:

a. Preliminary fixed capital investment estimates are made using the Lang and Chilton methods. Use the 1984 *CE Cost Index.*

b. As the plant is a fluid-processing unit, a considerable amount of piping is required.

c. The company policy is to minimize labor wherever possible, so extensive instrumentation is to be used.

d. The plant is to be constructed outdoors with only a modest amount of capital for auxiliaries and outside lines.

e. The company has built similar plasticizer plants, and the engineering is simple.

f. Working capital is to be estimated as follows:

1. Raw Materials Storage (average)

    Alcohol—10,000 gallons at $1.10/gallon
    POCl₃— 1,000 gallons at $0.40/pound

2. Finished Goods Storage (average)

    5,000 gallons at $4.00/gallon

3. Accounts Receivable—$100,000
4. Cash   —$400,000
5. Stores and Supplies —1% of fixed capital investment

g. Land for this project is $100,000.

h. Startup expenses are 8% of the fixed capital investment.

EQUIPMENT LIST

ITEM NO.	ITEM NAME	DESCRIPTION
101	Alcohol Storage Tank	Vertical Cylindrical Vessel, 15,000 gal, 304 SS
102	Alcohol Transfer Pump	Horizontal Centrifugal Pump, Single Stage, 50 gpm, 50 ft. Head, Duriron, 1.5 hp, TEFC Motor, 1800 rpm
103	POCl₃ Head Tank	Vertical Cylindrical Vessel, 1,500 gal, 304 SS

ITEM NO.	ITEM NAME	DESCRIPTION
104	Reactor	Vertical Cylindrical Vessel, 2,000 gal, 304 SS
105	Agitator	Six-bladed Turbine, 304 SS, 20 hp, TEFC Motor, 1,150 rpm
106	Reactor Circulating Pump	Horizontal Centrifugal Pump, Single Stage, 100 gpm, 150 ft. Head, Duriron, 5 hp, TEFC Motor, 1,800 rpm
107	Reactor Cooler	Horizontal Shell-and-Tube Heat Exchanger, U-Tube, 100 psig, 1,000 ft.^{2}, 304 SS
108	Distillation Column	6-ft. Dai. $\times$ 40 ft. Str. Side, 25 Sieve Trays, 100 psig, 316 SS
109	Reboiler	Kettle Reboiler, 100 psig, 1,500 ft.^{2}, 304 SS
110	Bottoms Pump	Horizontal Centrifugal Pump, Single Stage, 50 gpm, 75 ft. Head, 304 SS, 3 HP, TEFC Motor, 1,800 rpm
111	Bottoms Receiver	Vertical Cylindrical Tank, 1,500 gal, 304 SS, ATM. Press.
112	Condenser	Horizontal Shell-and-Tube Heat Exchanger, 100 psig, U-Tube, 1,200 ft.^{2}, 316 SS
113	Accumulator	Horizontal Cylindrical Tank, 1,500 gal, 316 SS
114	Recycle Pump	Horizontal Centrifugal, 2-Stage Pump, 300 gpm, 200-ft. Head, 25 hp, TEFC Motor, 316 SS
115	Product Receiver	Vertical Cylindrical Tank, 3,000 gal, 316 SS, ATM. Press.

REFERENCES

Lang, H. J. *Chem. Eng.* 54(10), 117 (1947).
Stevens, R. W. *Chem. Eng.* 54(6), 124–126 (1947).
Lang, H. J. *Chem. Eng.* 55(6), 112 (1948).
Kiddoo, G. *Chem. Eng.* 58(10), 145–148 (1951).
Nichols, W. T. *Ind. Eng. Chem.* 43(10), 2295 (1951).
Wessel, H. E. *Chem. Eng.* 60(1), 168–171 (1953).
Aries, R. S., and Newton, R. D. *Chemical Engineering Cost Estimation.* New York: McGraw-Hill Book Co., 1955.

Nelson, W. L. *Oil and Gas J.* 54(74), 110–111 (1956).

Bach, N. G. *Chem. Eng.* 65(18), 155–159 (1958).

Hand, W. E. *Pet. Ref.* 37(9), 331 (1958).

Bauman, H. C. *Ind. Eng. Chem.* 52(3), 51–52A (1960).

Chilton, C. H., ed. *Cost Estimation in the Process Industries.* New York: McGraw-Hill Book Co., 1960.

Hirsch, J. H., and Glazier, E. M. *Chem. Eng. Progr.* 56(12), 37–43 (1960).

Wroth, W. F. *Chem. Eng.* 67(10), 204 (1960).

Arnold, T. H., and Chilton, C. H. *Chem. Eng.* 70(4), 143–152 (1963).

Hackney, J. W. *Control and Management of Capital Projects.* New York: John Wiley & Sons, 1965.

Miller, C. A. "Factor Estimating Refined for Appropriation of Funds." AACE Bulletin 7 (Sept. 1965).

Hasselbarth, J. E. *Chem. Eng.* 74(25), 214 (1967).

Guthrie, K. M. *Chem. Eng.* 76(6), 114–142 (1969).

Chase, J. D. *Chem. Eng.* 77(7), 114–118 (1970).

Popper, H. *Modern Cost Engineering Techniques.* New York: McGraw-Hill Book Co., 1970.

Stallworthy, E. A. *The Chemical Engineer.* 238, 182–189 (1970).

McAllister, R. A. *Oil and Gas J.* 69(26), 72 (1971).

Wilson, G. T. *Brit. Chem. Eng. and Proc. Tech.* 16(10), 931–934 (1971).

Perry, R. H., and Chilton, C. H., eds. *Chemical Engineers Handbook,* 5th ed. New York: McGraw-Hill Book Co., 1973.

Guthrie, K. M. *Process Plant Estimating, Evaluation and Control.* Solana Beach, California: Craftsman Book Co., 1974.

Holland, F. A., Watson, F. A., and Wilkinson, J. D. *Introduction to Process Economics.* New York: John Wiley & Sons, 1974.

Allen, D. H., and R. C. Page *Chem. Eng.* 82(5), 142–150 (1975).

Happel, J., and Jordan, D. G. *Chemical Process Economics,* 2 ed., New York: Marcel Dekker, Inc., 1975.

Baasel, W. D. *Preliminary Chemical Engineering Plant Design.* New York: American Elsevier Publishing Co., Inc., 1976.

Gans, M. *Chem. Eng.* 83(6), 72 (1976).

Derrick, G. C., and Sutor, W. L. *AACE Bull.* 19(3), C-2.300 (1977).

Kharbanda, O. P. *Process Plant and Equipment Cost Estimation.* Solana Beach, California: Craftsman Book Co., 1979.

Uhl, V. W., *A Standard Procedure for Cost Analysis of Pollution Control Procedures.* Research Triangle, North Carolina: U.S. Environmental Protection Agency Report, Jan. 1979.

Peters, M. S., and Timmerhaus, K. D. *Plant Design and Economics for Chemical Engineers,* 3rd ed. New York: McGraw-Hill Book Co., 1980.

Chauvel, A. *Manual of Economic Analysis of Chemical Processes,* trans. by R. Miller and E. B. Miller. New York: McGraw-Hill Book Co., 1981.

Cran, J. *Chem. Eng.* 88(7), 65–69 (1981).

Salem, A. B. *Hydro. Proc.* 60(9), 199–200, 1981.

Viola, J. L. *Chem. Eng.* 88(7), 80–86 (1981).

Hall, R. S., Matley, J., and McNaughton, K. J. *Chem. Eng.* 89(7), 80–116 (1982).

_____. *Cost Engineers' Notebook.* Morgantown, West Virginia: American Association of Cost Engineers, 1983.

_____. *Fortune* 107(7), 250 (1983).

Jelen, F. C., and Black, J. H. *Cost and Optimization Engineering,* 2nd ed. New York: McGraw-Hill Book Co., 1983.

Valle-Riestra, J. K. *Project Evaluation in the Chemical Process Industries.* New York: McGraw-Hill Book Co., 1983.

————. *Engineering News Record* 212(23), 51 (1984).

————. Private communication (1984).

————. *Richardson Rapid System, Process Plant Construction Estimating Standards,* vol. 4. San Marcos, California: Richardson Engineering Services, 1984.

Bauman, H. C. *Fundamentals of Cost Engineering in the Chemical Industry,* Reinhold Publishing Corp., New York, 1964.

Page, J. C. *Conceptual Cost Estimation,* Gulf Publishing Co., Houston, TX, 1984.

Woods, D. R. *Financial Decision Making in the Process Industry,* Prentice-Hall Inc., Englewood Cliffs, NJ, 1975.

Bridgwater, A. V. Cost Engineering, 23(5), 293–302 (1981).

———— ASPEN PROJECT, Twelfth Quarterly Report, MIT, Cambridge, MA March 1, 1979–May 31, 1979.

Happel, J., *Chemical Process Economics,* J. Wiley & Sons, New York, 1958.

Hill, R. D. *Pet. Ref.,* 35(8), 106–110 (1956).

Zevnick, F. C. and R. C. Buchanan. *Chem. Eng. Progr.,* 59(2), 70 (1963).

4 OPERATING EXPENSE

INTRODUCTION

Operating expenses are those recurring expenses which are related to the manufacture of a product. They are unlike capital expenditures which occur once during the life of a project. Operating expenses significantly affect the cash flow and profitability of a venture. In Chapter 7, the relationship between operating expenses and cash flow will be presented.

In Chapter 4, those items that constitute the operating expenses will be presented along with methods for obtaining estimates of these expenses. A list of the total operating expenses is presented in Fig. 4.1.

TERMINOLOGY

Certain terms are used in preparation of an operating expense report which will require definition and explanation:

Unit cost is the cost of an item based upon either a mass or volume unit, e.g., dollars per pound, dollars per gallon, dollars per cubic foot, dollars per barrel, etc.

Direct expenses are those directly associated with the manufacture of a product, e.g., utilities, labor, and operating supplies. These expenses vary nearly in direct proportion to the production rate. On a unit-cost basis, that is on the basis of a production unit, they tend to remain constant irrespective of the amount of material produced.

Indirect expenses are those that tend to remain constant with respect to the production rate. Examples of these expenses are ad valorem taxes, depreciation and a group of miscellaneous expenses such as fire and safety protection, expenses associated with yards, docks, plant roads, plant cafeterias, change houses, etc. On a unit-cost basis, indirect expenses will tend to decrease with increasing production, since their cost is constant or varies slightly with the production rate.

Raw Materials
By-Product Credits
  Net Materials
Utilities
Operating Labor
Supervision
Maintenance
Payroll Charges
Laboratory Charges
Operating Supplies
Miscellaneous Direct Expenses
  Total Direct Expenses
  Total Direct Manufacturing Expenses
Depreciation
Plant Indirect Expenses
  Total Indirect Expenses
  Total Manufacturing Expense
Packaging, Loading, and Shipping Expense
  Total Product Expense
General Overhead Expense
  Total Operating Expense

Figure 4.1. Total operating expense.

Variable expenses vary in approximately direct proportion to the production rate. Examples are utilities, operating supplies, etc. Like direct expenses, they tend to remain constant on a unit-cost basis as the production rate varies.

Fixed expenses are as the name implies, that is, they remain constant as the production rate changes. Depreciation, insurance, ad valorem taxes, etc., are examples. On a unit-cost basis, they tend to decrease as the production rate increases.

Semivariable expenses tend to decrease as the production rate decreases, but are not zero at zero production rate. Examples are maintenance, supervision, and sometimes operating labor.

A company when establishing its accounting procedures will select either direct-indirect or variable-fixed-semivariable nomenclature. Once it has been established, then the nomenclature is used throughout the company.

MANUFACTURING COST SHEET

A typical manufacturing cost sheet is presented in Fig. 4.2. The sheet has four distinct sections. At the top is the *heading*, which identifies the name of the product, the production capacity, operating hours per year, plant location, fixed capital investment, etc.

The next section of the manufacturing cost sheet includes the raw materials and any by-products produced. It lists each raw material or by-product;

LOCATION:_____ DEPT. NO:_____ PRODUCT:_____
Mfg. Capital_____ Design:_____ per Yr. (_____Hr.)
Yields:_____ Prod:_____ per Yr. (_____Hr.)

RAW MATERIALS	UNIT	QUANTITY	$/UNIT	$/YEAR
	GROSS R.M. COST			

BY-PRODUCT CREDIT

	TOTAL CREDIT			

NET MATERIAL COST

DIRECT EXPENSE	UNIT	QUANTITY	$/UNIT	
Steam	MM Btu			
Electricity	KWH			
Water - CT	M Gal			
– Filt.	M Gal			
– Sea	M Gal			
Fuel Gas	MM Btu			
Comp. Air	MCF			
Steam Condensate	M Gal			
	TOTAL UTILITIES			
Labor				
Supervision				
Payroll Charges				
Factory Supplies				
Laboratory				
Product Control				
Technical Service				
Royalty				

TOTAL DIRECT CONVERSION EXPENSE
TOTAL DIRECT MFG. COST (DIRECT EXPENSE plus NET MATERIAL)
INDIRECT EXPENSE
   Depreciation
   Factory Indirect Expense
TOTAL INDIRECT CONVERSION COST
TOTAL MANUFACTURING COST
   * Indicates negative quantity, or credit.

Figure 4.2. Manufacturing cost sheet.

the unit, such as pounds, gallons, etc.; the quantity of material consumed annually; the unit price of the material; and the total annual cost. Sometimes raw material and by-products are moved from storage within the plant site to the manufacturing department. If this should happen, then a *handling charge* might also be assessed. All the raw material expenses are summed to give the *gross* raw material expenses. In like manner, the by-products are listed separately, and the total *by-product credit* is calculated. If the total by-product credits are subtracted from the gross raw material expenses, the *net* material expense is obtained.

Some companies prefer to include raw materials as part of the direct expenses. Others separate raw material costs from direct expenses. This is an arbitrary decision but there is some justification for doing so. It is to emphasize how much of the total manufacturing expense is related to raw material costs.

The third section of the manufacturing cost sheet is the direct expenses. All direct expenses are listed, starting with the utilities, which are given by unit, quantity consumed, cost per unit, and annual expense. If there is a credit for a utility, such as recovered or generated steam, it is also included. Although Fig. 4.2 is a very detailed manufacturing cost sheet, not all items may apply in any given process. Labor, supervision, etc., are listed as single entry items.

The last section of the cost sheet includes the indirect expenses. Two major items constitute this entry—depreciation and plant indirect expenses. These expenses are listed as single entry items.

In summary, then, the four sections of a manufacturing cost sheet are:

the heading
raw materials and by-products
direct expenses
indirect expenses

MANUFACTURING COST ITEMS

Raw Materials

The raw materials required are calculated for a specified production rate from a material balance or experience. The price of each raw material may be obtained from the purchasing department, sales personnel of the company manufacturing the raw material, or from price listings in technical magazines or newspapers. Most companies, however, enter into contracts with a raw material supplier at well below costs stated in the technical literature. For chemicals, if the information is not readily available from a supplier, the *Chemical Marketing Reporter* is a good alternate source of information. Raw material prices listed in the *Reporter* are market prices not contract prices. It should also be remembered that prices vary depending upon the

form of the raw material—powder, flake, solution, etc.
grade of the material—reagent, industrial, etc.
quantity purchased
mode of delivery—barge, rail, truck
containers in which the product is shipped—drums, carboys, etc.

After the unit price is obtained and the annual material requirements are known, multiplying these two quantities will yield the annual raw material expense.

By-Products

These materials are treated in the same fashion as raw materials. The unit prices are obtained at market price less any purification, packaging, marketing, and transportation expenses. In some operations, if by-products are intermediates for which no immediate market is available, they may be credited at their net value to downstream or subsequent manufacturing operations at a value equivalent to their value as a replacement.

Utilities

The utility requirements for a process are obtained from material and energy balances around the operation. Utility unit prices may be obtained from the company accountants, plant utilities supervisors, or local utility company. Typical 1984 utility costs in the Gulf Southwest area are:

UTILITY	PRICE
Steam	$3.00–4.00/M1b*
Electricity	3.0–4.5¢/KWH
Natural Gas	$3.50–4.00/MM Btu
Cooling Tower Water	3.5–6.0¢/M gal
City Water	$0.25–0.45/M gal

* Standard nomenclature used in quoting utility prices: M is 1,000 units, MM is 1,000,000 units.

Operating Labor

Labor on a manufacturing cost sheet refers to operating labor. Maintenance labor is usually considered part of the maintenance expense. Labor is one of the more significant manufacturing expenses. The most reliable way to determine operating labor requirements is to prepare a table of round-the-clock coverage, including weekends and vacations. Hourly wage rates may be obtained from the union contract, company accountants, the company labor relations lawyer, the Bureau of Labor Statistics publications, or from the magazine *Engineering News Record*. In the Gulf Southwest the average chemical plant operator's annual base salary is between $25,000–$30,000 excluding fringe benefits in 1985.

An alternate approach to obtaining labor requirements for preliminary estimates is the Wessel method (1952). He correlated the operating labor man-hours with the number of processing steps for plant capacities between 2 and 2,000 tons/day. The equation is

$$\log_{10} Y = -0.783 \log_{10} X + 1.252 \, B \qquad 4.1$$

where Y = operating labor in man-hours per ton per processing step
X = plant capacity in tons/day
B = a constant that has the following values:
+0.132 for multiple units or where the process is operated batchwise
0 for average chemical processing plants
−0.167 for large plants with process control or those that are continuous and process fluids only

A processing step might be a unit operation wherein physical changes take place, such as a filtration step consisting of a feed tank, pump, filter, and receiver tanks. A processing step may include several equipment items. The number of processing steps can be counted using a flowsheet. It should be mentioned that the Wessel equation does account for improvement in operating labor productivity as the plant size increases. This equation may also be used to extrapolate manpower requirements to plants of greater or lesser capacity. In our experience, the Wessel equation is conservative. Although other methods (1957, 1962) have been proposed, either the schedule or Wessel method is to be preferred.

Although much concern is expressed today over labor productivity, it is a difficult quantity to measure. Productivity in the classical sense is the output of product divided by input in labor man-hours. What studies have been reported are concerned with construction or maintenance labor, but there have been no quantitative data for plant operating labor.

Supervision

Supervisory personnel are the nonunion, salaried employees who have overall responsibility for a department's operation. These are the department supervisor, foremen, and clerks. If the type of position and salaries can be identified, then these values should be used in the estimation process. As an alternate, 20 to 30% of the annual operating labor expense is a reasonable figure.

For batchwise operation, the higher percentage is more realistic. The lower figure would be for processes that are continuous and have considerable automatic control.

Payroll Charges

These expenses include workmen's compensation, group life and medical insurance premiums, paid vacations and holidays, social security, unemployment taxes, pension plans, profit-sharing, thrift plans, etc., and an ever-increasing list of fringe benefits paid by the company. A decade ago these expenses amounted to 20–25% of the operating labor and supervision expense. Today, they have increased to 45–50% of the same base.

Maintenance

There are two major cost components of maintenance—materials and labor. Little published information is available. On the average about 40% of the maintenance charge is for materials, and 60% for labor. A company's maintenance expense records are the best source of information, because these records will take into account local cost factors. For preliminary cost estimates, a percentage of the fixed capital investment is used. *Chemical Week* (1983) reports annual maintenance expenses based upon fixed investment for approximately 30 companies. A reasonable percentage for estimating purposes may be 6 to 10% of the fixed capital investment. A percentage at the upper end of the range should be used for processes that have a preponderance of rotating or moving equipment, extreme conditions of temperature and/or pressure, or extremely corrosive or erosive conditions. A percentage at the lower end of the range would represent maintenance in plants that operate at or near ambient conditions with few corrosion or erosion problems. Hackney (1961) presented simple equations for maintenance expenses in paper and pulp mills and coke, cement, petroleum, and electrolytic plants. He related the maintenance expenses empirically to the fixed plant investment and the number of years the plant was in operation.

The above percentage figures are based upon plants operating at or near capacity production. If the production is reduced, the maintenance expenses are not in direct proportion. For example, if a plant's production were reduced to half its rated capacity, the maintenance expenses might be 70–80% of those at full capacity.

Operating Supplies

This expense item might include control charts, computer paper, mops, brooms, etc. Company records for similar operations should be an excellent source of information. If this information is not available, then approximately 6% of the operating labor would be satisfactory for a preliminary estimate.

Laboratory Expenses

As more on-line analytical equipment is developed and proven rugged enough for production line use, laboratory expenses as an item in the manufacturing cost sheet will decrease. Many products, however, still must be subjected to various quality-control tests in a laboratory. The expenses for laboratory tests are increasing, but for estimation purposes $40–60 per laboratory hour or 10–20% of the operating labor are reasonable estimates. These figures include amortization of equipment, laboratory supplies, and personnel salaries.

Clothing and Laundry

In the production of food-grade products, pharmaceuticals, toxic chemicals, and high-technology microelectronics, companies will provide clothing and laundry service for the manufacturing employee. This expense will vary considerably depending upon the type of product made and the manufacturing facility. Company records for similar operations are a good source of information, but if no information is available, then 10% of the operating labor expense may be used for estimating purposes.

Technical Service

In some companies, this is a budgeted expense item to spread the cost of maintaining technical and/or engineering assistance to a manufacturing facility. These technical people are concerned with minor process or production improvements in quality and quantity of the product manufactured, as well as the addition of new equipment. It is recommended that about 25% of a new engineer's or technician's salary be allocated. The 25% figure is based on the assumption that the new engineer might have about four such projects for which he is responsible.

Royalty

This expense item will apply if the company buys technology. There are many different ways in which a royalty agreement may be drawn. The royalty charge on the manufacturing cost sheet refers to one type of agreement known as the *running royalty*. For every unit of product manufactured there is a charge assessed, for example, a fraction of a cent per pound of product manufactured.

Waste Disposal

Wastes from manufacturing operations must be disposed of in a safe manner. The expense associated with the disposal is borne by the producing department. Some companies contract with other firms to dispose of these wastes for a fee. Some companies may have their own facilities, but no matter how the wastes are handled there is a fee. The magazine *Chemical Engineering* (1982) published some waste disposal costs, which are presented in Table 4.1.

Total Direct Expense

This expense is the sum of all expenses in Fig. 4.1, beginning with the utilities and ending with waste disposal.

Total Direct Manufacturing Expense

When the net material expense is added to the total direct expense, the result is the total direct manufacturing expense.

Table 4.1 Waste Disposal Costs.

TYPE OF WASTE MANAGEMENT	TYPE OR FORM OF WASTE	COST (1981) $/METRIC TON
Landfill	Drum	168–240
Landfill	Bulk	55–83
Land Treatment	All	5–24
Incineration+	Relatively clean liquids, high BTU value	13–53
Incineration	Liquids	53–237
Incineration	Solids, highly toxic liquids	395–791
Chemical Treatment	Acids, alkalines	21–92
Chemical Treatment	Cyanides, heavy metals, highly toxic wastes	66–791
Resource Recovery	All	66–264
Deep-Well Injection	Oily wastewaters	16–40
Deep-Well Injection	Toxic rinse waters	132–264

+ Some cement kiln operators and light-aggregate manufacturers are now paying for wastes.

Depreciation

According to the Internal Revenue Service (1962), depreciation is a "reasonable allowance for the exhaustion, wear and tear, and normal obsolescence of a property used in the trade or business." It is not a cash expenditure or a cash transfer as some textbooks would have the reader believe. It is a paper transfer that is established by a set of rules set forth by Congress. Periodically, the methods of calculating this allowance are revised. It is a noncash charge that appears on manufacturing cost sheets and cash flow analyses. The net effect is to allow a company to charge off the investment over a specified time. On the manufacturing cost sheet, the straight-line depreciation method is used. The fixed capital investment divided by the allowable depreciation life is entered as an indirect or fixed expense. Irrespective of the amount of material produced, the depreciation remains constant. If the fixed capital investment is $1,000,000 and the allowable depreciation period is 5 years, then $200,000 per year is entered on the manufacturing cost sheet each year for five years. A more detailed discussion will be presented in Chapter 6.

Plant Indirect Expense

There are a large number of minor expenses at a plant site that are shared by many operating departments. These expenses might include fire insurance premiums on the plant and equipment; plant security and fire protection; maintenance of yards, roads, and docks; cafeteria and office building expenses; ad valorem taxes, etc. The company's accountants usually have developed factors for each plant site. The factors are often fixed percentages of labor, equipment, or both. One method for estimating this expense is to use 2 to 3% of the fixed capital investment per year. Hackney (1961) proposed a method that involves both labor and investment components; it is presented in Table 4.2. An example of the application of the Hackney method is given in Example 4–1. From this example, the plant indirect expenses are about 4–6% of the fixed capital investment. In general, the Hackney method tends to be conservative, but is satisfactory for preliminary estimates.

EXAMPLE 4.1

A small-capacity heavy chemical plant has a fixed capital investment of $10 million. The operating labor for this plant has been estimated at $125,000 per year. Calculate the plant indirect expenses by the Hackney method.

$$\text{Investment Part} - \$10,000,000 \times 0.04 = \$400,000/\text{year}$$
$$\text{Labor Part} - \$125,000 \times 0.45 = \underline{\quad 56,250/\text{year}}$$
$$\text{Plant Indirect Expenses} = \$456,250/\text{year}$$

Table 4.2   Plant Indirect Expense Factors.*

PLANT TYPE	INVESTMENT FACTOR, %	LABOR FACTOR, %
Heavy Chemical (large capacity)	1.5	45
Power	1.8	75
Electrochemical	2.5	45
Cement	3.0	50
Heavy Chemical (small capacity)	4.0	45

* Hackney (1961).

Total Indirect Expense

The sum of the depreciation and plant indirect expense is the total indirect expense.

Total Manufacturing Expense

This item includes the total direct and indirect manufacturing expenses. A product has been manufactured, but must be made ready for shipping to the customer.

Packaging, Loading, and Shipping Expense

A product may be shipped in a wide variety of packages or containers. Packaging includes not only the container cost, but also the labor required. The product must then be loaded onto a barge, ship, truck, or rail car. There is the labor expense of moving the packaged product from the manufacturing department to the transporting vehicle. Under some circumstances, dunnage is required to prevent the manufactured product from moving inside the vehicle. The third expense, shipping, may be absorbed by the manufacturing firm or may be charged to the customer. If the manufacturer assumes the expense, then it is part of the total operating expenses.

The best source of these cost data is company records or products of similar characteristics. Most companies maintain good cost control data on warehousing costs. The cost of containers may be obtained from the company's purchasing agent or from local vendors. If the company is large and it manufactures a variety of products, perhaps it has a materials handling specialist. This person would be an excellent source of information. Gases or liquids are frequently shipped by pipelines.

Transportation charges are obtained from a company specialist or from

Table 4.3 Transportation Rates.*

TRANSPORTATION MEANS	$/TON MILE*
Pipeline	$0.003–0.005
Barge and Tanker	0.004–0.010
Railroad	0.02 –0.05
Truck	0.03 –0.10

*Private communication.

local barge, shipping, rail, or truck companies. Typical large-volume, long-haul (over 250 miles) rates are presented in Table 4.3.

Total Product Expense

This expense is the sum of the manufacturing, loading and shipping, and handling costs.

General Overhead Expense

The expenses of maintaining sales offices in various locations, staff engineering and research department staffs, and administrative offices are included in this item. All products are expected to share in these overhead burdens, so a charge is made for each product. Companies often develop formulas or percentage factors based upon sales to be used for this expense. If factors are used they may vary between 6 and 15% of the annual sales revenue. The percentage is affected by the amount of customer service provided.

Total Operating Expense

This expense is the sum of the manufacturing, packaging, loading, and shipping expenses, as well as the general overhead expense. The operating expenses for any venture may include any or all of the foregoing components. Example 4.2 illustrates the preparation of annual manufacturing and total operating expenses for a petrochemical plant. The same general procedure in preparing these estimates may be used for any manufacturing operation.

EXAMPLE 4.2

PROBLEM STATEMENT:

The Acme Petrochemical Co. of Gopher Gulch, Texas, is considering the possibility of producing plasticizer M. The engineering department has estimated that a fixed capital investment of $8 million will be required to produce 15 million pounds per year of product. Plasticizer M is expected to sell for 62 cents per pound.

The net material expense will be 22 cents per pound of product. It is estimated that three men per shift will be required. The process is semicontinuous and is assumed to operate at 90% stream time. Other costs and/or usages are:

UTILITIES	USAGE/LB PRODUCT	COST
Steam	4.0 lb	$3.50/M lb
Electricity	0.25 KWH	3.5¢/KWH
Cooling Water	6.0 gal	4.0¢/M gal
City Water	5.0 gal	$0.30/M gal

Maintenance—6%/year of the fixed capital investment
Average Operating Labor Expense—$25,000/year/man
Supervision—$3,000/month
Payroll Charges—45% of operating labor plus supervision
Supplies—$250/month
Clothing and Laundry—$500/month
Laboratory Charges—40 hours per month at $50 per hour
Packaging, Loading, and Shipping Charges—0.5 cent per pound of product
Other Direct Expenses—$1,000 per month
Depreciation—straight-line for 5 years
Plant Indirect Expenses—3% of the fixed capital investment per year
General Overhead Expense—6% of the annual net sales

a. Prepare an annual manufacturing cost based upon full production.
b. Calculate the total annual operating expense

SOLUTION:

ANNUAL SALES

$$\frac{15,000,000 \text{lbs}}{\text{yr}} \times \frac{\$0.62}{\text{lb}} = \$9,300,000$$

MANUFACTURING COST SHEET

Net Material Expense:

$$\frac{15,000,000 \text{lbs}}{\text{yr}} \times \frac{\$0.22}{\text{lb}} = \$3,300,000$$

LOCATION: GOPHER Gulch, TX   DEPT. NO:_____ PRODUCT: Plasticizer M
Mfg. Capital $8,000,000   Design: 15,000,000 _____ per Yr. (8,320 Hr.)
Yields:_____   Prod:_____ per Yr. (_____Hr.)

RAW MATERIALS	UNIT	QUANTITY	$/UNIT	$/YEAR
		GROSS R.M. COST		

BY-PRODUCT (CREDIT

		TOTAL CREDIT		

NET MATERIAL COST			3,300	3,300
DIRECT EXPENSE	UNIT	QUANTITY	$/UNIT	
Steam	M lbs	60,000	$3.50	210
Electricity	KWH	3,750,000	0.035	131
Water - CT	M Gal	90,000	0.04	4
– Filt.	M Gal			
– City	M Gal	75,000	$0.30	23
Fuel Gas	MM Btu			
Comp. Air	MCF			
Steam Condensate	M Gal			
		TOTAL UTILITIES		368
Labor				315
Supervision				36
Payroll Charges				158
Maintenance				480
Factory Supplies				3
Laboratory				24
Clothing and Laundry				6
Technical Service				
Other D.E.				12

TOTAL DIRECT CONVERSION EXPENSE	1,402
TOTAL DIRECT MFG. COST (DIRECT EXPENSE plus NET MATERIAL)	4,702
INDIRECT EXPENSE	
Depreciation	1,600
Factory Indirect Expense	240
TOTAL INDIRECT CONVERSION COST	1,840
TOTAL MANUFACTURING COST	6,542

*Indicates negative quantity, or credit.

Figure 4.3. Example 4.2 Manufacturing cost sheet.

DIRECT EXPENSES

Utilities

Steam:

$$\frac{15,000,000\text{lbs product}}{\text{yr}} \times \frac{4\text{lb steam}}{\text{lb product}} \times \frac{\$3.50}{1000\text{lb steam}} = \$ \quad 210,000$$

Electricity:

$$\frac{15,000,000\text{lb product}}{\text{yr}} \times \frac{0.25\text{KWH}}{\text{lb product}} \times \frac{\$0.035}{\text{KWH}} = \quad 131,000$$

Cooling Water:

$$\frac{15,000,000\text{lb product}}{\text{yr}} \times \frac{6.0\text{gal}}{\text{lb product}} \times \frac{\$0.04}{1000 \text{ gal}} = \quad 4,000$$

City Water:

$$\frac{15,000,000\text{lb product}}{\text{yr}} \times \frac{5.0 \text{ gal}}{\text{lb product}} \times \frac{\$0.30}{1000 \text{ gal}} = \$ \quad 23,000$$

Total Utilities = $ 368,000

Labor:

$$\frac{4.2 \text{ men} \times 3 \text{ men}}{\text{shift}} \times \frac{\$25,000}{\text{yr}} = \$ \quad 315,000$$

Maintenance:

$$\frac{0.06}{\text{yr}} \times \$8,000,000 = \quad 480,000$$

Supervision:

$$\frac{\$3,000}{\text{month}} \times \frac{12 \text{ months}}{\text{yr}} = \quad 36,000$$

Payroll Charges:

$$0.45 \, (\$315,000 + \$36,000) = \quad 158,000$$

Supplies:

$$\frac{\$250}{\text{month}} \times \frac{12 \text{ months}}{\text{yr}} = \quad 3,000$$

Clothing and Laundry:

$$\frac{\$500}{\text{month}} \times \frac{12 \text{ months}}{\text{yr}} = \quad 6,000$$

Laboratory Charges:

$$\frac{40 \text{ hours}}{\text{month}} \times \frac{12 \text{ months}}{\text{yr}} \times \frac{\$50}{\text{hour}} = \quad 24,000$$

Other Direct Expenses:

$$\frac{\$1,000}{\text{month}} \times \frac{12 \text{ months}}{\text{yr}} = \quad 12,000$$

TOTAL DIRECT EXPENSES = $1,402,000

TOTAL DIRECT MANUFACTURING EXPENSES = $4,702,000

INDIRECT EXPENSES

Depreciation:

$$\frac{\$8,000,000}{5 \text{ yr}} = \$1,600,000$$

Plant Indirect Expenses:

$$\frac{\$0.03}{\text{yr}} \times \$8,000,000 = \underline{\quad 240,000}$$

TOTAL INDIRECT MANUFACTURING EXPENSES $= \$1,840,000$

TOTAL MANUFACTURING EXPENSES $= \$6,542,000$

Packaging, Loading and Shipping Expenses:

$$\frac{15,000,000 \text{ lb}}{\text{yr}} \times \frac{\$0.005}{\text{lb}} = \underline{\quad 75,000}$$

TOTAL PRODUCT EXPENSE $= \$6,617,000$

General Overhead Expenses:

$$\$9,300,000 \times 0.06 = \underline{\quad 610,000}$$

TOTAL OPERATING EXPENSES $= \$7,227,000$

OPERATING EXPENSE SCALE-UP

The manufacturing expense of a product discussed previously consists of three major items—raw materials expense and direct and indirect expenses. The latter two expenses are roughly related to investment, labor, and utility costs. They are sometimes referred to as *conversion expenses.* For example, maintenance and depreciation are a percentage of the fixed capital investment, whereas supplies, supervision, and payroll charges are labor-related.

Holland et al. (1976) have developed an expression for the rapid estimation of the conversion expenses based upon investment, labor, and utility expenses. In Chapter 3 investment was shown to vary as the capacity of the plant, according to the following cost-capacity equation:

$$C_2 - C_1 \left(\frac{Q_1}{Q_2}\right)^x \qquad\qquad 4.2$$

where $Q_1 =$ capacity of a plant or equipment

$C_1 =$ cost of a plant or equipment at Q_1

$Q_2 =$ capacity of a plant or equipment at another rate

$C_2 =$ cost of a plant or equipment at capacity Q_2

$x =$ exponent that depends upon the type of plant or equipment

A fixed plant investment, C_{FC1}, for a given production rate, R_1, the labor requirements, N_L, and the utility expenses, U_1, related according to the following equation:

$$A_1 = mC_{FC\,1} + nc_L N_1 + pU_1 \qquad\qquad 4.3$$

where m, n, and p = constants

$C_{FC\,1}$ = fixed capital investment at capacity 1

c_L = cost of labor in dollars/man/shift

N_1 = annual labor requirements in men/shift/year at capacity 1

U_1 = utility expenses at capacity 1

A_1 = annual conversion expenses at capacity 1

If the Qs in Eq. 4.2 are changed to Rs, and if Eq. 4.2 is combined with Eq. 4.3, the annual conversion expenses may be estimated at another capacity:

$$A_2 = mC_{FC\,1}\left(\frac{R_2}{R_1}\right)^{0.7} + nc_L N_1 \left(\frac{R_2}{R_1}\right)^{0.25} + pU_1\left(\frac{R_2}{R_1}\right) \qquad 4.4$$

where R_1 = production rate at capacity Q_1

R_2 = production rate at capacity Q_2

A plot of the conversion expenses as a function of the production rate on log-log coordinates is a straight line. Figure 4.4 is an example of such a plot for the manufacture of a pharmaceutical product. This plot may be used to estimate the conversion expenses at interpolated production rates. Extrapolation beyond a threefold range in production rate is not advised because errors will become significant.

The Holland procedure is used to estimate the conversion expenses. The other items in the total operating expenses must be estimated individually to determine what effect changes in production rate will have. The Holland method is satisfactory for preliminary estimates, but for more accurate esti-

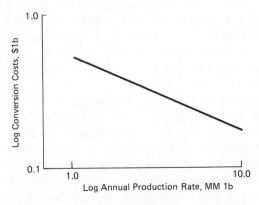

Figure 4.4. Conversion costs as a function of production rate.

mates, an item-by-item consideration of each expense component must be undertaken. This procedure eliminates the possibility of overlooking an expense item that might have a significant effect on the operating expenses.

Management frequently requires the operating expenses at rates other than design capacity. For example, requests might be made for these expenses at 0, 50, and 75% capacity. Operating expenses must be computed for each case, considering the effect of reduced operating rate on each item of operating expenses. It is not correct to say that these expenses at 50% of capacity are one-half of those expenses at 100% rate. Linear proportioning is not possible, because there are certain fixed and semivariable expenses that are not zero at zero rate. It is advisable to prepare the expenses at the reduced capacity cases while preparing the 100% rate case. Reflection on each item at that time brings out various factors that might be overlooked if the reduced capacity expenses are deferred until a later date.

The operating expense estimates developed for all cases are frequently used for the preparation of break-even charts, which will be discussed in Chapter 10.

OPERATING EXPENSE ESTIMATES USING MICROCOMPUTERS

With the development of electronic spreadsheets, manufacturing or operating expense estimates can be prepared quickly. An electronic spreadsheet may be thought of as a large worksheet. There are numerous spreadsheets available on the market today bearing such names as VISICALC, SUPERCALC, MULTIPLAN, and LOTUS 1, 2, and 3, to name a few.

The worksheet is organized as a large grid of rows and columns of information. In general, letters designate the column and numbers designate the row. One version has 127 columns and 9,999 rows, making possible about 1,270,000 entries available. Indeed, this is a large worksheet. To find one's way around the spreadsheet, the location of data is given as before F26. This means the data may be found in the F column at row 26. The findings are similar to locating a city on a map. A typical grid is found in Fig. 4.5. The number 45,000 is located at C5.

One particularly attractive feature of the spreadsheet is that a manufacturing cost estimate may be prepared for not only a base case but for several others, the data for each case being displayed next to each other. Another feature of most spreadsheets is the ability to insert equations into the grid for preparing a cost sheet. Figure 4.6 shows a sample of the equation form. Then through a series of instructions for a specific spreadsheet, the equations are stored in the program and underlie the worksheet. As data are entered into the spreadsheet, the calculations begin. At any time the underlying equa-

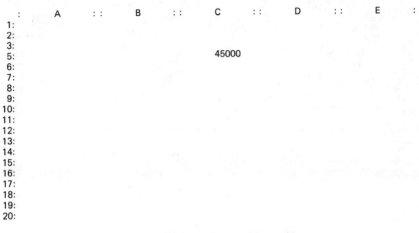

:	A	: :	B	: :	C	: :	D	: :	E	:
1:										
2:										
3:										
5:					45000					
6:										
7:										
8:										
9:										
10:										
11:										
12:										
13:										
14:										
15:										
16:										
17:										
18:										
19:										
20:										

Figure 4.5. Electronic spreadsheet grid.

TOTAL OPERATING EXPENSES
==
PRODUCT: PLASTICIZER X
TOTAL SALES ($/YR):   7200000
RATED CAPACITY (MM LBS/YR):   12
LOCATION:
FIXED CAPITAL INVESTMENT: 800000
LAND   25000
WORKING CAPITAL   120000
OPERATING HOURS (HR/YR):
DATE:
BY:

RAW MATERIALS:				
MATERIAL	UNIT	ANNUAL QUANTITY	$/UNIT	$/YEAR
A AND B	LB	12000000	.23	C17‡D17
				C18‡D18
				C19‡D19
				C20‡D20
GROSS MATERIAL EXPENSE				SUM(E17:E20)

BY-PRODUCTS:	UNIT	ANNUAL QUANTITY	$/UNIT	$/YEAR
				C24‡D24
				C25‡D25
BY-PRODUCT CREDIT				SUM(E24:E25)

NET MATERIAL EXPENSE   E21-E26 E28

DIRECT EXPENSES:				
	UNIT	ANNUAL QUANTITY	$/UNIT	$/year
UTILITIES:				
steam, low pressure				C33‡D33
steam, medium pressure				C34‡D34
steam, high pressure	LB	60000000	3/1000	C35‡D35
GROSS STEAM EXPENSE				SUM(E33:E35)
STEAM CREDIT				SUM(B37:D37)
NET STEAM EXPENSE				E36-E37
electricity	KWH	.25‡12000000	3.5/100	C39‡D39
cooling water	GALLONS	6‡12000000	.045/1000	C40‡D40
fuel gas				C41‡D41
other:				C42‡D42
city water	GALLONS	30‡12000000	.2/1000	C43‡D43
TOTAL UTILITIES COST				SUM(E36:E43) E44

Figure 4.6. Typical equation format for electronic spreadsheet.

LABOR:		
men per shift	4	SUM(B46:D46)
annual labor rate per shift	25000	SUM(B47:D47)
TOTAL LABOR COSTS		E46≋E47 E48
SUPERVISION:		
% total of labor expense		M(B50:D50))/100
SUPERVISION EXPENSE=		1500≋12 E51
PAYROLL CHARGES, FRINGE BENEFITS:		
% total of labor, supervision	40	M(B53:D53))/100
PAYROLL EXPENSE		E53≋(E51+E48) E54
MAINTENANCE		
% of fixed capital investment	8	M(B56:D56))/100
MAINTENANCE EXPENSE		E56≋B8 E57
SUPPLIES:		
% of operating labor		M(B59:D59))/100
SUPPLIES EXPENSE		150≋12 E60
LABORATORY:		
laboratory hours per year	75≋12	SUM(B62:D62)
cost per hour	30	SUM(B63:D63)
WASTE DISPOSAL:		
tons per year		SUM(B67:D67)
waste charge per ton		SUM(B68:D68)
WASTE DISPOSAL EXPENSE		E67≋E68 E69
OTHER:		
laundry	500≋12	SUM(B71:D71) E71
TOTAL DIRECT EXPENSE		SUM(F38:F71)
TOTAL DIRECT + NET MATERIAL COSTS		E73+E28
INDIRECT EXPENSES:		
DEPRECIATION		
% of fixed capital investment	100	M(B78:D78))/100
life of project (yrs)	12	SUM(B79:D79)
DEPRECIATION		(E78≋B8)/E79 E80
PLANT INDIRECT EXPENSES		
% of fixed capital investment	5	M(B82:D82))/100
PLANT INDIRECT EXPENSES		E82≋B8 E83
TOTAL INDIRECT EXPENSES		SUM(F76:F83)
TOTAL MANUFACTURING EXPENSE:		E74+E85
PACKAGING, SHIPPING EXPENSE		
rated capacity per year	12000000	SUM(B89:D89)
dollars per unit	.005	SUM(B90:D90)
PACKAGING AND SHIPPING EXPENSE		E89≋E90
TOTAL PRODUCTION EXPENSE		E87+E91
GENERAL OVERHEAD EXPENSES		
percent of annual sales	5	M(B94:D94))/100
GENERAL OVERHEAD EXPENSES		B5≋E94
TOTAL OPERATING EXPENSE		E92+E95

Fig. 4.6. (*Continued*)

tions may be called up onto the screen, modified if necessary, and then returned to memory. As quickly as the data are entered, the final answer for the manufacturing cost sheet or operating expense estimate is displayed. The resulting total operating expense estimate for the equations in Fig. 4.6 may be found in Fig. 4.7.

Microcomputers relieve the user of tedious hand calculations, generate answers more quickly and eliminate simple arithmetic errors. Further, with the proper amount of planning, the expense sheets can be designed to be included in a report directly.

TOTAL OPERATING EXPENSES
==

PRODUCT:	PLASTICIZER X
TOTAL SALES ($/YR):	7200000
RATED CAPACITY (MM LBS/YR):	12
LOCATION:	
FIXED CAPITAL INVESTMENT:	800000
LAND	25000
WORKING CAPITAL	120000
OPERATING HOURS (HRS/YR):	
DATE:	
BY:	

RAW MATERIALS:	UNIT	ANNUAL QUANTITY	$/UNIT	$/YEAR
MATERIAL				
A AND B	LB	12000000	.23	2760000
				0
				0
				0
GROSS MATERIAL EXPENSE				2760000

BY-PRODUCTS:	UNIT	ANNUAL QUANTITY	$/UNIT	$/YEAR
				0
				0
BY-PRODUCT CREDIT				0

NET MATERIAL EXPENSE				2760000

DIRECT EXPENSES:	UNIT	ANNUAL QUANTITY	$/UNIT	$/year
UTILITIES:				
steam, low pressure				0
steam, medium pressure				0
steam, high pressure	LB	60000000	.003	180000
GROSS STEAM EXPENSE				180000
STEAM CREDIT				0
NET STEAM EXPENSE				180000
electricity	KWH	3000000	.035	105000
cooling water	GALLONS	72000000	.000045	3240
fuel gas				0
other:				0
city water	GALLONS	360000000	.0002	72000
TOTAL UTILITIES COST				540240
LABOR:				
men per shift	4			4
annual labor rate per shift	25000			25000
TOTAL LABOR COSTS				100000
SUPERVISION:				
% total of labor expense				0
SUPERVISION EXPENSE=				18000
PAYROLL CHARGES, FRINGE BENEFITS:				
% total of labor, supervision	40			.4
PAYROLL EXPENSE				47200
MAINTENANCE				
% of fixed capital investment	8			.08
MAINTENANCE EXPENSE				64000
SUPPLIES:				
% of operating labor				0
SUPPLIES EXPENSE				1800

Figure 4.7. Total operating expense on an electronic spreadsheet.

LABORATORY:
laboratory hours per year	900	900
cost per hour	30	30
TOTAL LABORATORY EXPENSE		27000
ROYALTIES		0

WASTE DISPOSAL:
tons per year		0
waste charge per ton		0
WASTE DISPOSAL EXPENSE		0

OTHER:
laundry	6000	6000

TOTAL DIRECT EXPENSE	804240
TOTAL DIRECT + NET MATERIAL COSTS	3564240

INDIRECT EXPENSES:
DEPRECIATION
% of fixed capital investment	100	1
life of project (yrs)	12	12
DEPRECIATION		66667

PLANT INDIRECT EXPENSES
% of fixed capital investment	5	.05
PLANT INDIRECT EXPENSES		40000

TOTAL INDIRECT EXPENSES	106667

TOTAL MANUFACTURING EXPENSE:		3670907

PACKAGING, SHIPPING EXPENSE
rated capacity per year	12000000	12000000
dollars per unit	.005	.005
PACKAGING AND SHIPPING EXPENSE		60000
TOTAL PRODUCTION EXPENSE		3730907

GENERAL OVERHEAD EXPENSES
percent of annual sales	5	.05
GENERAL OVERHEAD EXPENSES		360000
TOTAL OPERATING EXPENSE		4090907

Fig. 4.7. (*Continued*)

SUMMARY

In this chapter, the reader was introduced to the terminology and items essential for the development of an operating expense report. Each item was defined and sources as well as methods for estimating each entry were presented. An example illustrating the preparation of an operating expense report is given.

Often an engineer or scientist is confronted with scaling up or scaling down the operating costs to another proposed production level. A method for doing this was suggested.

Lastly, the use of an electronic spreadsheet to prepare an operating expense report was discussed and an example given.

In Chapter 3, the methods for estimating the capital investment were discussed. In this chapter methods for determining operating expenses for a venture were presented. In subsequent chapters, the reader will learn how the capital investment and the operating expenses are related to the financial success (or failure), namely, the profitability of a project.

PROBLEMS

4.1 A division of a petroleum company is interested in producing 40 million pounds per year of a plasticizer. L. Jones & Co. has a proprietary manufacturing process for this product, but charge $225,000 a year for royalty. Other pertinent costs are:

Fixed Capital Investment	$6,800,000
Natural Gas	100,000/yr
Raw Materials	250,000/yr
Steam	563,000/yr
Solvent Inventory	53,000
Cooling Water	85,000/yr
Solvent Make-up	54,000/yr
Electricity	18,000/yr
Labor	200,000/yr
General Overhead	25,000/yr
Supplies Inventory	269,000
Depreciation	680,000/yr
Cash	600,000
Real Estate	30,000
Interest on Loan	260,000/yr
Local Taxes and Insurance	134,000/yr

From the information given above, prepare a statement of the total capital investment and an estimate of the total operating expenses.

4.2 A company is considering the possibility of manufacturing a metal insert for a plastic part used in automobile parts. A total fixed capital investment of $800,000 has been estimated by the company's engineering department. This plant produces 10,000,000 pounds per month of metal inserts. The land on which the facility is to be located costs $25,000, and working capital necessary for this venture is $120,000. The part sells for 60 cents/pound. The operating labor requirements are four men/shift around the clock. Assume that this operation has a stream time of 90%.

The total raw materials cost 23 cents/pound of product, and the packaging and shipping costs are 0.5 cents/pound of product. Other usages and costs are:

UTILITY	USAGE/LB OF PRODUCT	COST
Steam	5.0 lb	$3.00/Mlb
Electricity	0.25 KWH	$3.50/100KWH
Plant Water	6.0 gal	$0.045/M gal
City Water	30.0 gal	$0.20/M gal

Repairs—8%/yr of the fixed capital investment
Depreciation—straight line over 5 years

Miscellaneous indirect expenses—5%/year of the fixed capital investment
Average labor rate—$25,000/operation/year
Supervision—$2,000/month
Payroll charges—50% of labor plus supervision charges
Supplies—$150/month
Clothing and Laundry—$500/month
Laboratory hours—75 hours/month at $30/hour

Calculate:

a. The total product cost at the rated capacity.
b. If the general overhead expenses are 5% of the annual sales, what are the total annual operating expenses?

4.3 A company built a plant to produce 10 million pounds per year of dichloroethane in 1978 at $3 million (fixed capital investment). The plant is operating at full capacity and cannot meet the sales demand. Management has decided to build a second plant and have it on-stream as quickly as possible. The target date is late 1986. This plant will be a 12 million pounds per year battery limits unit identical to the existing plant.

Dichloroethane is produced by the gas-phase reaction of ethylene and chlorine:

$$C_2H_4 + Cl_2 = C_2H_4Cl_2$$

The reaction is 100% complete with respect to chlorine, but only 90% complete with respect to ethylene. The excess ethylene is sent to the boiler house as fuel gas. The cost of chlorine is $5.62/1,000 SCF, and the cost of ethylene is $0.36/1,000 SCF. The value of the ethylene in the fuel gas is $0.20/1,000 SCF, and by-product credit may be taken for this excess ethylene.

Other operating costs per 1000 pounds of products are:

Utilities	$10.00
Labor	$17.50
Repairs	$ 8.00
All Other Direct Expenses	$20.00
Depreciation	5-yr straight line
All Other Indirect Expenses	$ 5.00

The general overhead expenses may be taken as 8% of sales. The estimated sales price is $0.41/pound.

Provide a total operating expense in dollars per year for the new plant.

4.4 Excalibar Plastics, Inc., is currently producing a resin for the toy market, which is centered in the New York–New Jersey area. The present batch reactors are old. New reactors must be purchased in the near future to replace the old equipment. To meet market demands, 10,000 pounds/day of resin must be produced. Batch reactors similar to the ones currently in operation are estimated to have an installed cost of $15,000 each. A typical batch reactor is a stainless-steel-jacketed, agitated vessel with a temperature recorder, a pressure recorder, and manual control valves. The heating medium used is Dowtherm vapor. One batch kettle has a capacity of 1,000 pounds resin per 10-hour polymerization cycle, but it takes 2 hours between batches for discharging, cleaning, and recharging the reactor. The labor cost is estimated to be 5 cents per pound of resin produced. Raw material and other direct charges are estimated to be 12 cents per pound of resin. Other fixed costs are $15.00 per batch reactor per day of operation, assuming 340 operating days per year.

The Gelt Equipment Company of Hottentot, New Jersey, offers for sale a continuous reactor package with automatic controls at an installed cost of $50,000 each. This reactor is stainless steel and is capable of producing 2,500 pounds of resin per 24-hour day. The labor costs are expected to be 2 cents per pound of resin produced. Raw material and other variable charges are expected to be 12 cents/pound of resin, which you will note is the same as for the batch reactors. The other fixed costs on each continuous reactor are expected to be $20 per day of operation.

Interest on the capital borrowed for the reactors must be considered as a cost item in the initial selection of new production equipment. Invested money is worth 10% per year to the company. Depreciation is taken as 5-year straight line. Project life is 10 years.

Summarize the solution using a basis of 1 day of operation.

DAILY PRODUCTION	BATCH	CONTINUOUS
Variable Costs		
Labor Costs		
Labor Costs		
Depreciation		
Fixed Costs		
Interest on Capital		
Total Cost of Operation		
Cost per Pound of Resin		
Total Investment Required		
Number of Reactors Required		

REFERENCES

The references and recommended readings are "classics" in the operating expense literature.

Wessel, H. E. *Chem. Eng.* 59(7), 209–210 (1952).

Haines, I. *Chem. Eng. Progr.* 53, 556–562 (1957).

Wobus, R. S. *Chem. Eng. Progr.* 53, 581–585 (1957).

Hackney, J. W. *Control and Management of Capital Projects.* New York: John Wiley & Sons, Inc. 1961.

O'Connell, F. P. *Chem. Eng.* 69(4), 150 (1962).

———. Internal Revenue Service, U.S. Treasury Department, *Depreciation Gudielines and Rules, Revenue Procedure 62–61.* Publication No. 456 (issued 1962; revised August 1964).

Holland, F. A., Watson, F. A. and Wilkinson, J. K. *Chem. Eng.* 81(11), 91–96 (1976).
———, *Chem. Eng.* 89(18), 54 (1982).
———. *Chem. Week* 129(3), 32 (1983).

RECOMMENDED READINGS

Guthrie, K. M. *Chem. Eng.* 77(13), 140 (1970).
Jenckes, L. C. *Chem. Eng.* 77(27), 168 (1970).
Jenckes, L. C. *Chem. Eng.* 78(1), 168 (1971).
Liebson, I., and Trischman, C. A. *Chem. Eng.* 78(12), 69 (1971).

5 TIME VALUE OF MONEY

INTRODUCTION

Interest is the term that refers to the cost of renting money. It is the amount charged by financial institutions for the use of money. Because scientists and engineers may be involved in the presentation or evaluation of projects requiring the investment of money, it is important that the time value of money be properly applied in analyzing these projects. This chapter is concerned with the development and use of the formulas in the time value of money.

INTEREST RATE

The rate of interest is the ratio of the interest payable or chargeable at the end of a period (usually a year or less) to the amount of money owed at the beginning of that period. For example, if $10 of interest is payable at the end of a year on a debt of $100, the interest rate is $10/$100 or .10 per year. This is usually described as an interest rate of 10%. It is usually understood the interest rate is per year or per annum unless otherwise stated.

Interest is frequently payable more often than once per year. Ten percent per year, 5% payable semiannually, 2½% payable quarterly, or 0.833% payable monthly all refer to 10% nominal annual interest rates.

There are several types of interest, a few of which are explained below.

Simple Interest

In *simple interest,* interest is paid on the original loan regardless of whether the interest has been paid on prior years. Table 5.1 illustrates simple interest.

Note that interest is not charged on the unpaid balance, only on the original loan. Though as a concept it still exists, it is seldom if ever used.

Compound Interest

In financial institutions, loans or deposits are made at *compound interest.* If $1,000 were invested or loaned at 10% interest compounded annually,

Table 5.1 10% Simple Interest on $100.

END OF YEAR	INTEREST OWED AT END OF EACH YEAR, $	TOTAL AMOUNT OWED, $
0	–	100
1	10	110
2	10	120
3	10	130
4	10	140

Table 5.2 10% Compound Interest on $1000.

YEAR	AMOUNT OWED AT BEGINNING OF YEAR	INTEREST ACCRUED DURING YEAR	AMOUNT OWED AT END OF YEAR
1	$1,000.00	$1,000.00 × .10 = 100.00	$1,000 × 1.10 = $1,100.00
2	$1,100.00	$1,100.00 × .10 = 110.00	$1,000 × (1.10)^2 = $1,210.00
3	$1,210.00	$1,210.00 × .10 = 121.00	$1,000 × (1.10)^3 = $1,331.00
4	$1,331.00	$1,331.00 × .10 = 133.10	$1,000 × (1.10)^4 = $1,464.10
5	$1,464.10	$1,464.10 × .10 = 146.41	$1,000 × (1.10)^5 = $1,610.51

then at the end of one year, $1100 would be on deposit or owed. The $1,100, if left on deposit or owed for another year at 10%, would earn $110 interest, so the amount on deposit would be $1,100 plus the $110, or $1,210. This is continued for illustrative purposes in Table 5.2.

Nominal Interest

Whether the 10% annual interest paid or calculated at 10% compounded annually, 10% compounded semiannually (or 5% payable every 6 months), 10% compounded quarterly (or 2½% payable quarterly), or 10% compounded monthly (or 0.8333% payable monthly), it is called 10% *nominal interest.* Thus nominal interest is the annual interest rate without considering the effect of any compounding during the year.

COMPOUND INTEREST FACTORS

To facilitate calculations, a series of interest formulas will be developed using the following notation:

i = interest rate per period expressed as a decimal, e.g., 10% is expressed as .10

n = number of interest periods
P = a present sum of money
F = a future sum of money, n periods hence
A = a single payment in a series of n equal payments, made at the end of each interest period n

Moving money forward in time is referred to as *compounding*. Moving it backward is referred to as *discounting*. This is shown in Fig. 5.1.

The calculations shown in Table 5.2 are not difficult, but they are time consuming, particularly as the number of compounding periods becomes large. Formulas or factors for handling interest are developed and illustrated, which reduce the tedium in interest calculations. In the discussion of interest, the interest rate per period must conform to the periods involved. Though initially the periods will be years and interest per annum, later in this chapter compounding periods shorter than a year will be discussed. Initially, also, only end-of-the-period cash flows are considered, a widely used convention.

Single Payment Compound Amount Factor

Examining Table 5.2, one can see that the amount owed at the end of each year is:

$$F = P\,(1 + i)^n \qquad\qquad 5.1$$

For example, at the end of 4 years, the amount due is:

$$F = 1000\,(1 + 0.10)^4 = 1000\,(1.4641) = \$1464.10$$

This factor, $(1 + i)^n$ is known as the *single payment compound amount factor* and is designated in the Appendix and text as $(F/P,i,n)$, which is

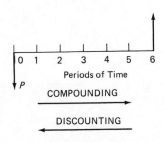

Figure 5.1. Compounding and discounting.

expressed as the F, given P factor at i interest and n periods of time. Accordingly,

$$(F/P,i,n) = (1 + i)^n \qquad 5.2$$

EXAMPLE 5.1

If $2,500 were invested at 9% compounded annually for 7 years, what would the balance be in the account at the end of 7 years?

Please refer to Fig. 5.2. This figure is referred to as a *time diagram*, or a *dollar/time diagram*. It shows the $2,500 desposit as an arrow down, or paid out. The value of F, to be found, is shown with an arrow upward and is available to be received.

To find F using Eq. 5.1,

$$F = P(1 + i)^n = \$2500\ (1.09)^7 = 2500\ (1.8280)$$
$$= \$4570.10$$

Or the value of $(F/P\ 9\%,7)$ could have been located in Appendix A

$$F = P(F/P\ i,n) = \$2500\ (F/P\ 9\%,7) = 2500\ (1.8280)$$
$$= \$4570.10$$

Single Payment Present Worth Factor

This factor is the inverse of the single payment compound amount factor and is

$$(P/F\ i,n) = \frac{1}{(1 + i)^n} \qquad 5.3$$

and a full equation may be written

$$P = F(P\ i,n) = F(1 + i)^{-n} \qquad 5.4$$

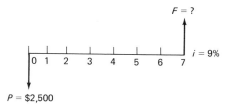

Figure 5.2. Figure to illustrate Example 5.1.

EXAMPLE 5.2

If \$5,000 were needed 4 years from now to meet a certain payment, how much would have to be deposited at 8% interest compounded annually to have the \$5,000 in 4 years (Fig. 5.3)?
From Eq. 5.4,

$$P = F(1+i)^{-n} = \$5000\,(1.08)^{-4}$$
$$= \$5000\,(0.7350) = \$3675.15$$

Or, from Appendix A, where $i = 8\%$,

$$P = F(P/F\,i,n) = 5000\,(P/F\,8\%,4)$$
$$= \$5000\,(0.7350) = \$3675.15$$

In Example 5.1 it should be recognized that \$2,500 at the present time is equivalent to \$4,570.10 7 years hence when deposited at 9% interest. Their equivalence is valid only as long as 9% is the interest and 7 years is the time period. Similarly, in Example 5.2 \$5,000 in 4 years at 8% interest discounted to today is equivalent to \$3,675.10. It is obvious that these respective pairs of numbers are not equal, but they are equivalent under specified conditions.

Uniform Series Compound Amount Factor

Frequently in the economic analysis of alternatives, a series of equal receipts or payments occurs at the ends of each of a successive series of periods. This is shown in the dollar/time diagram of Fig. 5.4.

Allowing A to represent each of the uniform amounts at the end of each period, then the future amount, F, occurring at the end of n years, could be calculated as follows.

$$F = A(1+i)^{n-1} + A(1+i)^{n-2} + A(1+i)^{n-3} \ldots + A(1+i)^0 \qquad 5.5$$

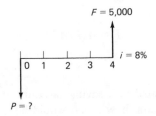

Figure 5.3. Figure to illustrate Example 5.2.

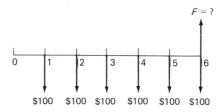

Figure 5.4. Figure to illustrate Example 5.3.

Uniform payments could be handled in this manner, but it would become time consuming and tedious. Equation 5.5 can be simplified with a few steps. Multiplying Eq. 5.5 by $(1 + i)$ will yield:

$$F(1 + i) = A(1 + i)^n + A(1 + i)^{n-1} + A(1 + i)^{n-2} \ldots + A(1 + i) \quad 5.6$$

Subtracting Eq. 5.5 from Eq. 5.6 gives

$$F(1 + i) - F = A(1 + i)^n - A \quad 5.7$$

Rearranging Eq. 5.7 will yield

$$F = A \left[\frac{(1 + i)^n - 1}{i} \right] \quad 5.8$$

The term in brackets is referred to as the *uniform series compound amount factor* and is designated $(F/A \ i,n)$ and

$$(F/A \ i,n) = \left[\frac{(1 + i)^n - 1}{i} \right] \quad 5.9$$

and

$$F = A(F/A \ i,n) \quad 5.10$$

EXAMPLE 5.3

If $100 were deposited in a savings account at 7% interest at the end of every year for 6 years, how much would be in the account at the end of the 6 years?

The dollar/time diagram is shown in Fig. 5.4. Substituting in Eq. 5.8,

$$F = A \left[\frac{(1+i)^n - 1}{i}\right] = \$100 \left[\frac{(1.07)^6 - 1}{.07}\right]$$
$$= \$100 (7.1533) = \$715.33$$

The concept of waiting for a year to start the annual deposits may seem illogical. However, the end-of-the-year convention, used when discrete payments are assumed, follows the logic that the amounts of money are accumulated during the period to be moved at period end. If, in specific cases it is desired to start the uniform payments at time period 0, then all payments can be moved up one period by multiplying by an F/P factor where n is equal to 1 year, as in the following:

$$F = A(F/P \ 7\%,1)(F/A \ 7\%,6)$$
$$= \$100 (1.07)^1(7.1533) = \$765.40$$

This is the first instance of our using the product of two factors, which is perfectly correct as long as it makes sense.

Uniform Series Sinking Fund Factor

This factor represents the uniform series amount that would have to be sunk into a fund to achieve a specified future amount for a given number of periods at a specified interest rate. The uniform series sinking fund factor is the reciprocal of the uniform series compound amount factor:

$$(A/F \ i,n) = \frac{i}{(1+i)^n - 1} \qquad 5.11$$

thus,

$$A = F(A/F \ i,n) = F\left[\frac{i}{(1+i)^n - 1}\right] \qquad 5.12$$

EXAMPLE 5.4

If in the need for \$5,000 in 4 years in Example 5.2, it were decided to deposit an equal amount at the end of every year for 4 years at 8% instead of a single sum at time period 0, then what would that annual amount be (Fig. 5.5)?

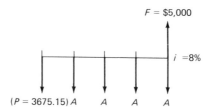

Figure 5.5. Figure to illustrate Example 5.4.

From Eq. 5.12

$$A = F\left[\frac{i}{(1+i)^n - 1}\right] = \$5000\left[\frac{0.08}{(1.08)^4 - 1}\right]$$

$$= \$500\,(0.2219) = \$1109.60$$

Thus we have found, between Examples 5.2 and 5.4, that a present sum of $3675.15, a uniform series of $1109.60, and a future sum of $5000 are all equivalent as long as n is four periods and i is 8% per period.

Uniform Series Present Worth Factor

This factor is a product of two previously developed factors, $(F/A\ i,n)$ and $(P/F\ i,n)$. That is,

$$(P/A\ i,n) = (F/A\ i,n)(P/F\ i,n) \qquad 5.13$$

$$= \left[\frac{(1+i)^n - 1}{i}\right]\left[\frac{1}{(1+i)^n}\right] = \left[\frac{(1+i)^n - 1}{i(1+i)^n}\right] \qquad 5.14$$

Thus

$$P = A\,(P/A\ i,n) = A\left[\frac{(1+i)^n - 1}{i(1+i)^n}\right] \qquad 5.15$$

EXAMPLE 5.5

A man wanted to borrow as much money as possible today with an annual payment of $100 at the end of each year for 6 years. If he were to be charged 7% interest, how much could he borrow?

This corresponds to the dollar/time diagram of Fig. 5.4, but the value of P is desired instead of F.

From Eq. 5.15

$$P = A \left[\frac{(1+i)^n - 1}{i(1+i)^n} \right] = \$100 \left[\frac{(1.07)^6 - 1}{0.07(1.07)^6} \right]$$
$$= \$100[4.7665] = \$476.65$$

Uniform Series Capital Recovery Factor

This is the factor that would be used by a lender to determine the annual payments to be made by a borrower to permit the lender to recover his capital with interest. It is the reciprocal of the uniform series present worth factor:

$$(A/P\, i,n) = \frac{1}{(P/A\, i,n)} = \left[\frac{i(1+i)^n}{(1+i)^n - 1} \right] \qquad 5.16$$

thus,

$$A = P(A/P\, i,n) = P \left[\frac{i(1+i)^n}{(1+i)^n - 1} \right] \qquad 5.17$$

EXAMPLE 5.6

A person desiring to borrow $10,000 now to be paid back over 10 years at 12% compounded annually would be required to pay back how much annually for the 10-year period (Fig. 5.6)

From Eq. 5.17,

$$A = P \left[\frac{i(1+i)^n}{(1+i)^n - 1} \right] = 10,000\, (0.176984)$$
$$= \$1769.84$$

This is the uniform annual amount required to retire the loan. An examination of Table 5.3 will indicate that at the first payment, over two-thirds of

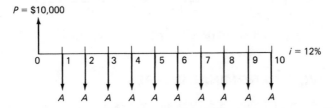

Figure 5.6. Figure to illustrate Example 5.6.

Table 5.3   Detailed Illustration of Example 5.6.

YEAR	AMOUNT OWED AT BEGINNING OF PERIOD	INTEREST DUE FOR PERIOD @ 12%	AMOUNT PAID ON PRINCIPAL	BALANCE OF PRINCIPAL OWED AFTER PAYMENT
0				
1	$10,000.00	$1,200.00	$569.84	$9,430.16
2	9,430.16	1,131.62	638.22	8,791.94
3	8,791.94	1,055.03	714.81	8,077.13
4	8,077.13	969,25	800.59	7,276.54
5	7,276.54	873.18	896.66	6,379.88
6	6,379.88	765.59	1,004.25	5,375.63
7	5,375.63	645.07	1,124.77	4,250.86
8	4,250.86	510.10	1,259.74	2,991.12
9	2,991.12	358.94	1,410.90	1,580.22
10	1,580.22	189.63	1,580.22	0
		$7,698.41	$10,000.00	

the payment is required to pay the interest. But with the constant payment of $1,769.84, the annual interest amount is slowly reduced as the outstanding principal is reduced. The total payments against the principal were $10,000, of course, and $7,698.41 was paid in interest, at this interest rate and with a time horizon of 10 years.

It is a more common experience to have monthly payments rather than annual payments for a home mortgage or an automobile loan. Industrial loans may be payable monthly, quarterly, semiannually, or annually.

EXAMPLE 5.7

Suppose an automobile buyer desired to borrow $8,000, agrees to pay a monthly interest rate of 1% compounded monthly, and agrees to retire the debt in 42 months. How much will his monthly payments be? From Eq. 5.17

$$A = P \left[\frac{i(1+i)^n}{(1+i)^n - 1} \right] = \$8000 \left[\frac{0.01(1.01)^{42}}{(1.01)^{42} - 1} \right]$$

$$= \$8000 \ (0.029276) = \$234.21/\text{month}$$

EFFECTIVE AND NOMINAL INTEREST

In the problem of Example 5.7 the interest rate was 1% per month. This would be equivalent to 12% nominal annual interest compounded monthly (this is many times referred to by loan agencies or merchants dealing with the consumer as simple interest). But if the 1% is compounded 12 times in a year, the effective annual interest would be greater than 12%.

Nominal interest rates are always annual. Effective interest rates may be the effective rate for any period. As in Example 5.7, the effective monthly interest rate was 1%. Annual effective interest rates will reflect the effect of compounding at the end of every period. To calculate effective annual interest rate, I_{eff}.

$$I_{\text{eff}} = \left(1 + \frac{r}{m}\right)^m - 1 \qquad 5.18$$

where r = nominal interest and
  m = number of compounding periods in the period for which the effective interest is desired

The ratio r/m is, of course, the period interest rate. And in our example above

$$I_{\text{eff}} = \left(1 + \frac{0.12}{12}\right)^{12} - 1$$
$$= (1.01)^{12} - 1$$
$$= 0.126825 \text{ or } 12.6825\%$$

Thus the 1% monthly interest rate which was a nominal interest rate of 12% is an effective annual interest of 12.68%. If we let i be the period interest rate, then Eq. 5.18 becomes

$$I_{\text{eff}} = (1 + i)^m - 1 \qquad 5.19$$

which can be expressed as

$$I_{\text{eff}} = (F/P\ i,m) - 1$$

and the tables of Appendix A can be used. It will be noted that in the table for $i = 1\%$, discrete compounding, the F/P factor at an n value of 12 is 1.1268, which gives the I_{eff} value of 12.68%.

EXAMPLE 5.8

A man borrows $1,000 for 30 months and agrees to pay $39.50 per month. Determine the monthly interest rate, the nominal interest rate, and the effective annual interest rate.

From Eq. 5.17

$$A = P(A/P \, i,n) = P \left[\frac{i(1+i)^n}{(1+i)^n - 1} \right]$$

The solution for i would be a trial-and-error solution, but the tables from Appendix A can save a lot of time.

$$\$39.50 = 1000(A/P \, i, 30)$$

so

$$(A/P \, i, 30) = \frac{39.50}{1000} = 0.0395$$

Scanning the tables in Appendix A at $n = 30$

if $i = 1\%$, $A/P = 0.0387$
if $i = 1\frac{1}{2}\%$, $A/P = 0.0416$

Our values lies

$$\frac{0.0395 - 0.0387}{0.0416 - 0.0387} = \frac{0.0008}{0.0029} = 0.2756$$

of the distance between 1 and $1\frac{1}{2}\%$, so

$$0.2756 \times \frac{1}{2}\% + 1\% = 1.138\%$$

Thus the monthly interest rate by interpolation is 1.138%. The nominal interest rate is

$$12 \times 1.138 = 13.66\%$$

and the effective annual interest rate is

$$\left(1 + \frac{0.1366}{12} \right)^{12} - 1 = 0.1454 \text{ or } 14.54\%$$

There are occasions in which the compounding periods and the payments or receipts are not the same. In these instances it is required to convert the given interest rate to an effective annual rate and then to a period rate that corresponds to the payment or receipt period.

EXAMPLE 5.9

A man deposits $900 each quarter into an account that pays 12% compounded monthly. How much money will be in the account at the end of 4 years?

Because the deposits are quarterly and the compounding is monthly, the monthly interest must be converted to an effective quarterly interest by first finding the effective annual interest using Eq. 5.18.

$$I_{eff} = \left(1 + \frac{0.12}{12}\right)^{12} - 1 = 0.1268 = 12.68\%$$

This can be converted to the quarterly rate using Eq. 5.18.

$$0.1268 = \left(1 + \frac{r}{4}\right)^{4} - 1$$

$$(1.1268)^{1/4} = 1 + \frac{r}{4}$$

$$r = [(1.1268)^{1/4} - 1]4 = 12.12\% \text{ compounded quarterly}$$

and thus the quarterly rate is

$$\frac{0.1212}{4} = 0.0303 = 3.03\% \text{ effective quarterly interest rate}$$

When compounding periods are more frequent than payments or receipts, the effective period interest can also be calculated directly as follows where $n = 3$ months.

$$(1 + i)^{n} - 1 = (1.01)^{3} - 1 = 0.030301 = 3.0301\%$$

and

$$F = A(F/A \ i,n)$$

$$= 900(F/A \ 3.30301,16)$$

$$= 900 \left[\frac{(1.030301)^{16} - 1}{0.030301}\right]$$

$$= 900(20.2048) = \$18,184.30$$

Where payments are more frequent than compounding periods, the longer calculation must be used, as illustrated in Example 5.10.

EXAMPLE 5.10

A man deposits $900 each quarter into an account that pays 12% compounded semiannually. How much money will be in the account at the end of 4 years?

Because the deposits are quarterly and the compounding is semiannual, the semiannual interest must be converted to an effective annual interest using Eq. 5.18:

$$I_{eff} = \left(1 + \frac{0.12}{2}\right)^2 - 1 = 0.1236 = 12.36\%$$

This can be converted to the quarterly rate using Eq. 5.18:

$$0.1236 = \left(1 + \frac{r}{4}\right)^4 - 1$$

$$(1.1236)^{1/4} = 1 + \frac{r}{4}$$

$$r = [(1.1236)^{1/4} - 1]4 = 0.118252 = 11.83\%$$

and

$$F = A(F/A \; i,n)$$

$$= 900 \left(F/A \; \frac{11.83}{4}, 4(4)\right)$$

$$= 900 \left[\frac{(1.02956)^{16} - 1}{0.02956}\right]$$

$$= 900(20.0875) = \$18,078.80$$

CHANGING INTEREST RATES

In all discussions to this point we have assumed that interest rates were constant from period to period. Certainly the experience of the last decade has taught us that interest rates may change appreciably over time. As an example, consider a single sum of money, $5,000, placed in a CD (certificate of deposit) for three 3-year periods where the interest was 12.53%, 13.03%,

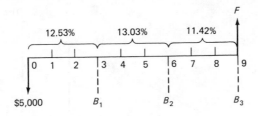

Figure 5.7. Figure to illustrate changing interest rates.

and 11.42% for each of the 3-year periods, respectively. The time diagram is shown in Fig. 5.7.

Letting B_1 indicate the balance on deposit at the end of the third year at 12.53% interest.

$$B_1 = \$5000(F/P\ 12.53\%,3) = 5000(1.1253)^3 = \$7124.84$$

and B_2, the balance at the end of the third year at 13.03% interest.

$$B_2 = \$7124.84(F/P\ 13.03\%,3) = 7124.84(1.1303)^3 = \$10,288.60$$

and B_3, the balance at the end of the third year at 11.42% interest.

$$B_3 = \$10,288.60(F/P\ 11.42\%,3) = 10,288.60(1.1142)^3$$
$$= \$14,231.33$$

which is the value of F in Fig. 5.7.

ARITHMETIC GRADIENT SERIES OF CASH FLOWS

The gradient series of cash flows is shown in Fig. 5.8. In the gradient series, the first cash flow occurs at the end of the second period, and each successive cash flow increases by an amount G.

The size of the cash flow at the end of period k is given by

$$A_k = (k-1)G \qquad (k = 1, \ldots, n) \qquad\qquad 5.20$$

The arithmetic gradient series may be used whenever the individual cash flows differ from their preceding cash flows by a constant, G. The present worth equivalent, P, of a gradient series is obtained by recalling

$$P = \sum_{k=1}^{n} A_k (1+i)^{-k} \qquad\qquad 5.21$$

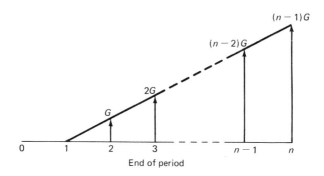

Figure 5.8. Cash flow diagram of the arithmetic gradient series of cash flows.

Substituting Eq. 5.20 into Eq. 5.21 yields

$$P = \sum_{k=1}^{n} (k-1)G(1+i)^{-k} \qquad 5.22$$

or

$$P = G\sum_{k=1}^{n} (k-1)(1+i)^{-k} \qquad 5.23$$

This summation reduces to

$$P = G\left[\frac{1-(1+ni)(1+i)^{-n}}{i^2}\right] \qquad 5.24$$

Converting this to interest factors already developed yields

$$P = G\left[\frac{(P/A,\,i,n)-n(P/F\,i,n)}{i}\right] \qquad 5.25$$

or

$$P = G\left[\frac{(1+i)^n-1}{i}-n\right]\left[\frac{1}{i\,(1+i)^n}\right] \qquad 5.26$$

or

$$P = G(P/G\,i,n) \qquad 5.27$$

where $(P/G\ i,n)$ is the arithmetic gradient, present worth factor and can be found in Appendix A.

Multiplying Eq. 5.25 by the $(A/P\ i,n)$ factor will yield

$$A = G\left[\frac{1}{i} - \frac{n}{i}\ (A/F\ i,n)\right] \qquad 5.28$$

or

$$A = G\left[\frac{1}{i} - \frac{n}{(1+i)^n - 1}\right] \qquad 5.29$$

or

$$A = G(A/G\ i,n) \qquad 5.30$$

where $(A/G\ i,n)$ is the arithmetic gradient uniform series factor.

EXAMPLE 5.11

The amount of $1,150 is deposited at 9% interest in a special savings account at the end of year 1. Each year thereafter the amount deposited in the account is increased by $150. At the end of 10 years, how much will be in the account?

Figure 5.9a shows the time diagram of the problem as stated, Fig. 5.9b shows the uniform annual amount without the annual increase, and Fig. 5.9c shows the annual increase G, which starts at the end of the second year.

Converting the gradient and the uniform annual amount into a total uniform annual amount may be done by adding the two:

$A_{\text{total}} = A_1(\text{uniform amount}) + A_2(\text{equivalent to gradient amount})$
$A_{\text{total}} = A_1 + G[A/G\ i,n]$

This can be calculated from Eq. 5.29 or can be found in Appendix A. Using Eq. 5.29,

$$A_{\text{total}} = \$1150 + 150\left[\frac{1}{0.09} - \frac{10}{(1.09)^{10} - 1}\right]$$
$$= \$1150 + 150(3.7978) = \$1719.70$$

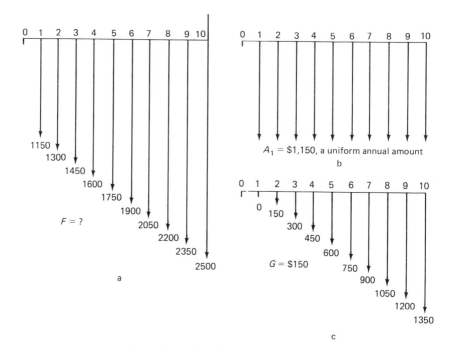

Figure 5.9. Arithmetic gradient, Example 5.11.

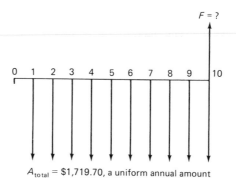

Figure 5.10. Uniform amount equivalent to Figure 5.9.

Thus the time diagram of Fig. 5.9 is converted into an equivalent uniform annual amount as shown in Fig. 5.10.

The value of the deposits in the bank account after 10 years at 9% interest, the value of F, would be

$$F = A_{total}(F/A\ i,n) = \$1719.70\ (15.1929) = \$26,127.30$$

which could be expressed as a total equation

$$F = [1150 + 150\ (A/G\ 9\%,10)]\ (F/A\ 9\%,10) = \$26,127.30$$

SUMMARY OF COMPOUND INTEREST FACTORS

Table 5.4 summarizes the discrete compound interest factors developed on the previous pages. It also gives the formulas for each factor at the limiting values of the interest, i, at 0% and of the number of periods, n, at infinity. These values will be useful when examining returns on investment to determine if revenue is equal to investment with zero time value of money (that is, to assure that i is not negative) or when the invested capital produces an asset that may have an infinite life, such as a tunnel through a mountain or when an endowment is established to provide period payments forever.

COMPARISON OF ALTERNATIVES

The economic evaluation of cash flow alternatives usually involves comparing the receipt and/or disbursement of funds, which will be different between alternatives at each period examined. The initial total capital cost, P, of each will probably be different. And the revenue and costs or their net will also probably be different for each period in the economic life, n. Thus, it is necessary to compare and evaluate alternatives on common ground. This may be done in several ways:

1. By discounting all cash flows back to their present value and comparing the present values of the alternatives.
2. By compounding all cash flows forward to their future value and comparing the future values of the alternatives.
3. By converting all cash flows into equivalent uniform annual costs or annual worths and comparing the equivalent annual costs or worths.
4. By determining the rate of return obtained for each alternative by equating investment or capital cost, P, to the revenue or savings achieved and determining that interest, i, or rate of that which makes them equal. Then the alternatives can be compared on the basis of the rates of return.

EXAMPLE 5.12

Consider the cash flows of Table 5.5. The negative cash flow at the end of year 0 is the investment for each alternative. The positive values

Table 5.4   Summary of Discrete Compound Interest Factors.

	FACTOR	FIND	GIVEN	DISCRETE COMPOUNDING	DISCRETE PAYMENTS	LIMITING FACTORS $i=0$	LIMITING FACTORS $n=\infty$
Single Payment	Compound Amount	F	P	$F = P(1+i)^n$	$P(F/P,i,n)$	1	∞
Single Payment	Present Worth	P	F	$P = F\dfrac{1}{(1+i)^n}$	$F(P/F,i,n)$	1	0
Uniform Series	Compound Amount	F	A	$F = A\left[\dfrac{(1+i)^n - 1}{i}\right]$	$A(F/A,i,n)$		∞
Uniform Series	Sinking Fund	A	F	$A = F\left[\dfrac{i}{(1+i)^n - 1}\right]$	$F(A/F,i,n)$	$\dfrac{1}{n}$	0
Uniform Series	Present Worth	P	A	$P = A\left[\dfrac{(1+i)^n - 1}{i(1+i)^n}\right]$	$A(F/A,i,n)$	n	$\dfrac{1}{i}$
Uniform Series	Capital Recovery	A	P	$A = P\left[\dfrac{i(1+i)^n}{(1+i)^n - 1}\right]$	$P(A/P,i,n)$	$\dfrac{1}{n}$	i
Arithmetic Gradient	Present Worth	P	G	$P = G\left[\dfrac{(1+i)^n - 1}{i}\right]\left[\dfrac{1}{i(1+i)^n}\right]$	$P = G(P/G,i,n)$	$\dfrac{n-1}{2}$	
Arithmetic Gradient	Uniform Series Equivalent	A	G	$A = G\left[\dfrac{1}{i} - \dfrac{n}{(1+i)^n - 1}\right]$	$A = G(A/G,i,n)$		$\dfrac{1}{i}$

Table 5.5   Data for Example 5.12.

	ALTERNATIVES	
END OF YEAR	A	B
0	−$40,000	−$42,000
1	+ 6,000	+ 8,000
2	+ 6,000	+ 8,000
3	+ 6,000	+ 8,000
4	+ 6,000	+ 8,000
5	+ 9,000	+ 8,000
6	+ 9,000	+ 8,000
7	+ 9,000	+ 8,000
8	+ 9,000	+ 8,000

are the net of receipts less disbursements. Suppose the interest rate were 8%. Which is the better alternative?

1. By discounting each alternative back to present worth (also referred to as *net present value*)

$$PW_A(8\%) = \overset{3.3121}{\$6,000\,(P/A\ 8\%,4)} + \overset{3.3121}{\$9,000\,(P/A\ 8,4)}\overset{0.7350}{(P/A\ 8\%,4)}$$
$$- \$40,000$$
$$= \$19,873 + \$21,910 - \$40,000$$
$$= +\$1,783$$

$$PW_B(8\%) = \overset{5.7466}{\$8,000\,(P/A\ 8\%,8)} - \$42,000$$
$$= \$45,973 - +\$42,000 = + \$3,973$$

Based on the present worth analysis, alternative B, which shows a higher net present value, is the preferred alternative. It should be noted that each present worth is positive. This means that in both cases the initial investment of $40,000 and $42,000, respectively, returned the 8% interest plus an additional amount over the 8 years.

2. By compounding all cash flows forward to their future values

$$F_A(8\%) = \overset{1.8509}{-\$40,000\,(F/P\ 8\%,8)} + \overset{4.5061}{\$6,000\,(F/A\ 8\%,4)}\overset{1.3605}{(F/P\ 8\%,4)}$$
$$+ \overset{4.5061}{\$9,000\,(F/A\ 8\%,4)}$$
$$= -\$74,037 + \$36,783 + \$40,555 = +\$3,301$$

$$F_B(8\%) = \overset{1.8509}{-\$42,000\,(F/P\ 8\%,8)} + \overset{10.6366}{\$8,000\,(F/A\ 8\%,8)}$$
$$= -\$77,738 + \$85,093 = +\$7,355$$

Based on the future worth, alternative B, which shows a higher future worth, is the preferred alternative.

3. By converting all cash flows into equivalent uniform annual costs or worths

$$
\begin{array}{cc}
& 0.17401 \qquad\qquad\quad 3.3121 \quad\ 0.17401 \\
AW_A (8\%) = & -\$40,000\ (A/P\ 8\%,8) + \$6,000\ (P/A\ 8\%,4)\ (A/P\ 8\%,8) \\
& \qquad\qquad\quad 4.5061 \quad\ 0.094015 \\
& +\ \$9,000\ (F/A\ 8\%,4)\ (A/F\ 8\%,8) \\
& = -\$6,960 + \$3,458 + \$3,813 = \$310
\end{array}
$$

$$
\begin{array}{c}
\qquad\qquad\qquad\quad 0.17401 \\
AW_B (8\%) = -\$42,000\ (A/P\ 8\%,8) + \$8,000 \\
\qquad\quad = -\$7,308 + \$8,000 = \$692
\end{array}
$$

4. By determining the rate of return for each alternative

$$
PW_{(\text{investment in A})} = PW_{(\text{return on A})}
$$
$$
\$40,000 = \$6,000\ (P/A\ i,4) + \$9,000\ (P/A\ i,4)(P/F\ i,4)
$$

at 8%, as we have seen,

$$
\$40,000 \neq \$41,783;\ \text{diff} = +\$1,783
$$

at 9%,

$$
\begin{array}{cc}
& 3.2397 \qquad\qquad 3.2397 \quad\ 0.7084 \\
\$40,000 = & \$6,000\ (P/A\ 9\%,4) + \$9,000\ (P/A\ 9\%,4)\ (P/F\ 9\%,4) \\
\$40,000 = & \$19,438 + 20,655 \\
\$40,000 \neq & \$40.093;\ \text{diff} = +\$93
\end{array}
$$

at 10%

$$
\begin{array}{cc}
& 3.1699 \qquad\qquad 3.1699 \quad\ 0.6830 \\
\$40,000 = & \$6,000\ (P/A\ 10\%,4) + 9,000\ (P/A\ 10\%,4)\ (P/F\ 10\%,4) \\
\$40,000 = & \$19,019 + \$19,485 \\
\$40,000 \neq & \$38,504;\ \text{diff} = -\$1,496
\end{array}
$$

By interpolation:

$$
\left(\frac{93}{93 + 1496}\right)(1\%) + 9\% = 9.06\%
$$

$$PW_{(\text{investment in B})} = PW_{(\text{return on B})}$$
$$\$42{,}000 = \$8{,}000 \ (P/A \ i\%,8)$$

at 8%, as we have seen

$$\$42{,}000 \neq \$45{,}973; \text{ diff} = \$5{,}973$$

at 10%,

$$5.3349$$
$$\$42{,}000 = \$8{,}000 \ (P/A \ 10\%,8)$$
$$\$42{,}000 \neq \$42{,}679; \text{ diff} = +\$679$$

at 11%,

$$5.1461$$
$$\$42{,}000 = \$8{,}000 \ (P/A \ 11\%,8)$$
$$\$42{,}000 \neq \$41{,}169; \text{ diff} = -\$831$$

By interpolation:

$$\frac{679}{679 + 831} \ (1\%) + 10\% = 10.45\%$$

Thus, on the basis of return on investment (ROI), the return for alternative B is better than A.

Reviewing the results of Example 5.12, several observations should be made. Though the actual numbers achieved by methods 1, 2, and 3 were different, the ratios of alternative B and alternative A appear to be about the same. And indeed they are. That is, the ratio of the present worth results is equal to the ratio of the annual worth results, which is equal to the ratio of their future worth results:

$$\frac{PW_B}{PW_A} = \frac{FW_B}{FW_A} = \frac{AW_B}{AW_A}$$
$$\frac{3973}{1783} = \frac{7355}{3301} = \frac{692}{310} = 2.23$$

This states that the return over 8% was 2.23 times as great for alternative B as it was for alternative A by any one of the three methods used.

In each method we started with the basic data. It would have been just as accurate if, once one set of comparative values was obtained, the other values were calculated from that value. Thus

$$FW_A\,(8\%) = PW_A\,(8\%)(F/P\ 8\%,8)$$
$$= \$1783(1.8509) = \$3301$$

and

$$FW_B\,(8\%) = 3973(1.8509) = \$7355$$

and

$$AW_A = PW_A\,(A/P\ 8\%,8) = FW_A\,(A/F\ 8\%,8)$$
$$\$310 = \$1783(0.17401) \quad = \$3301(0.094015)$$
$$\$310 = \qquad \$310 \qquad = \qquad \$310$$

and

$$AW_B = PW_B\,(A/P\ 8\%,8) = FW_B\,(A/F\ 8\%,8)$$
$$\$692 = \$3973(0.17401) \quad = \$7355(0.094015)$$
$$\$692 = \qquad \$692 \qquad = \qquad \$692$$

Multiple Interest Periods within 1 Year

Table 5.6 shows the resulting effective interest rate at a nominal interest rate of 12% with an increasing number of interest periods per year. The effective rates were calculated using Eq. 5.18.

TABLE 5.6 Effect of Compounding Periods per Year on Effective Interest Rates.

NUMBER OF COMPOUNDING PERIODS PER YEAR	COMPOUNDING PERIOD	EFFECTIVE ANNUAL INTEREST, %
1	Year	12
2	Semiannual	12.36
4	Quarter	12.55
12	Month	12.68
52	Week	12.73
365	Day	12.75

CAPITALIZED COST

A capitalized cost is a present worth analysis where the economic life is assumed to be indefinitely long. Railroad roadbeds and tunnels, canals, dams, interstate highway roadbeds, and aquaducts are all installations that could be considered to have indefinitely long lives and thus could be considered to last until infinity. Table 5.4 listed the values of the various factors when it can be assumed that n is equal to infinity. The application can best be illustrated by the following example.

EXAMPLE 5.13

An interstate roadbed for a given stretch of highway through the rough terrain of the Ozark Mountains can be built for $1 million. Due to the steep angle of slope back to the natural terrain, maintenance costs were anticipated to be $130,000 per year. An alternative design with a less steep angle of slope of the sides of the roadbed would cost $1,500,000, but the maintenance cost would be reduced to $80,000 per year. With a minimum acceptable rate of return of 6½%, which is the less expensive design?

SOLUTION

First design:

$0\downarrow \qquad A = 130,000 \quad n = \infty$
$P = \$1,000,000$

Alternative design:

$0\downarrow \qquad A = 80,000 \quad n = \infty$
$P = \$1,500,000$

Capitalized cost for first design:

$$PW = 1,000,000 + 130,000 \, (P/A \, 6\tfrac{1}{2}\%, \infty)$$

$$= 1,000,000 + 130,000 \left(\frac{1}{i}\right)$$

$$= 1,000,000 + 130,000 \left(\frac{1}{0.065}\right)$$

$$= \$3,000,000$$

Capitalized cost of the alternative design:

$$PW = 1,500,000 + 80,000 \ (P/A \ 6\tfrac{1}{2}\%, \ \infty)$$

$$= 1,500,000 + 80,000 \left(\frac{1}{0.065}\right)$$

$$= \$2,731,000$$

Thus the alternative design is less expensive by a quarter of a million dollars.

Occasionally the analyst may be required to compare two alternatives where both lives are not infinite.

EXAMPLE 5.14

Water supply is required by an industrial plant. A wooden caisson can be erected at a stream on higher ground with a wooden flume to the plant at a cost of $56,000. So designed, it is expected to last 10 years. A concrete dam, as an alternative design with concrete pipes, would be more expensive, but would last indefinitely. It would require an investment of $150,000. Maintenance on the wooden structure would cost $10,000/year, and maintaining the concrete installation would cost only $6,000/year. At a MARR of 10%, which alternative is better?

Annual cost of wooden installation:
$$\$56,000 \ \overset{0.16275}{(A/P \ 10\%, \ 10)} + \$10,000 = \$19,113.70/\text{year}$$

Annual cost of concrete installation:
$$\$150,000 \ \overset{0.10}{(A/P \ 10\%, \ \infty)} + 6000 = \$21,000/\text{year}$$

Thus, if the industrial plant expects to need the water for at least 10 years, the wooden design has the advantage. For an indefinite period, the wooden design has the advantage if we assume that every time we replace the wooden installation the costs will be the same as they are now.

To find that cost of the wooden structure x that would make the choices equal, we can equate the two equations above.

$$\$x \ (A/P \ 10\%, 10) + \$10,000 = \$150,000 \ (A/P \ 10\%, \ \infty) + \$6000$$

from which

$$x = \frac{21,000 - 10,000}{0.16275} = \$67,588$$

Or at the same installation cost, if the maintenance costs increase by $1,886.30 to $11,866.30/year, there would be no advantage to either alternative.

CONTINUOUS INTEREST FACTORS

The natural extension of Table 5.6 is continuous compounding. And in many organizations, transactions occur daily or even hourly, and this cash flow is put to work immediately. As one banking establishment has said, "We compound your savings every time your heart beats." To account for such frequent compounding, continuous compounding is used. In continuous compounding each year is divided into an infinite number of periods.

Single Payment Compound Amount Factor

The single payment compound amount factor is given by

$$\lim_{m \to \infty} \left(1 + \frac{r}{m} \right)^{mn} = e^{rn}$$

where n is the number of years, m is the number of interest payments per year, r is the nominal annual interest rate, and e is the base for Naperian logarithms. Thus given P, r, and n, the value of F under continuous compounding is:

$$F = Pe^{rn} \qquad 5.31$$

or

$$F = P(F/P \; r,n)_{\infty} \qquad 5.32$$

where $(F/P \; r,n)_{\infty}$ indicates the continuous compounding, single payment compound amount factor. The subscript ∞ denotes that continuous compounding is being used. Interest tables for continuous compounding are given in Appendix B.

Effective Interest with Continuous Compounding

The effective interest rate using continuous compounding is obtained using the relation

$$i_{\text{eff}} = e^r - 1 \qquad 5.33$$

Thus at the 12% nominal interest used for Table 5.5, the effective interest rate under continuous compounding is 12.74969%, as compared with the figure for daily compounding of 12.74745% carried out to the same number of significant figures. Equation 5.33 can also be expressed as

$$i_{eff} = (F/P\ r, 1)_\infty - 1 \qquad 5.34$$

Thus from Appendix B, if the nominal interest rate is 10% and interest is compounded continuously, then the effective interest rate is

$$i_{eff} = (F/P\ 10\%, 1)_\infty - 1$$
$$= (1.1052) - 1 = 10.52\%$$

Single Payment Present Worth Factor

This is the inverse of the single payment present worth factor

$$(P/F\ r, n)_\infty = \frac{1}{e^{rn}} \qquad 5.35$$

or

$$P = F(P/F\ r, n)_\infty = F\left(\frac{1}{e^{rn}}\right) \qquad 5.36$$

Uniform Series Compound Amount Factor

If each single payment in the uniform series is considered individually, the future amount is

$$F = A[1 + e^r + e^{2r} + \ldots + e^{r(n-1)}]$$

The geometric progression with a common ratio of e^r reduces to the sum of n terms as

$$\frac{e^{rn} - 1}{e^r - 1} \qquad 5.37$$

and

$$F = A\left[\frac{e^{rn} - 1}{e^r - 1}\right] = A\ (F/A\ r, n)_\infty \qquad 5.38$$

This represents the uniform series compound amount factor.

EXAMPLE 5.15

a. If $1,000 is deposited in a savings account at 6.0% compounded continuously, the amount in the account at the end of 8 years would be what?

$$F = P(F/P\ r,n)_\infty \qquad = Pe^{rn}$$
$$F = \$1,000\ (1.6161)^* = \$1,000\ e^{.06 \times 8}$$
$$\qquad = 1,616.10 \qquad\quad = 1,000\ (1.61607)$$
$$\qquad = 1,616.10 \qquad\quad = 1,616.07$$

* From Appendix B

b. If $100 is deposited every year at the end of the year in a savings account that pays 6.0% compounded continuously, how much would be in the account at the end of 8 years?

$$F = A(F/A\ r,n)_\infty \qquad = A\left[\frac{e^{rn}-1}{e^r-1}\right]$$

$$= \$100\ (9,9630)^* = \$100\left[\frac{e^{0.48}-1}{e^{0.06}-1}\right]$$

$$= \$996.30 \qquad\quad = \$100\left[\frac{0.61607}{0.061836}\right]$$

$$= \$996.30 \qquad\quad = \$100[9.9628] = \$996.28$$

* From Appendix B

EXAMPLE 5.16

If $100 is deposited each quarter into an account that pays 6% compounded continuously, how much would be in the account at the end of 8 years?

$$F = A(F/A\ r,n)_\infty$$

$$= \$100\left[F/A\ \frac{6}{4};8(4)\right]_\infty$$

$$= \$100[F/A\ 1\tfrac{1}{2},32]_\infty$$

$$= \$100[40.7644]$$

$$= \$4076.44$$

or using the algebraic expression from Eq. 5.38

$$F = A\left[\frac{e^{rn}-1}{e^r-1}\right] = A\left[\frac{e^{.06/4\ 8(4)}-1}{e^{.06/4}-1}\right] = A\left[\frac{e^{.48}-1}{e^{.015}-1}\right]$$

$$= \$100\left[\frac{0.6160744}{0.0151131}\right] = \$100(40.76436)$$

$$= \$4076.44$$

Uniform Series Sinking Fund Factor

This factor is the inverse of the uniform series compound amount factor.

$$(A/F \ r,n)_\infty = \left[\frac{e^r - 1}{e^{rn} - 1}\right] \qquad 5.39$$

and

$$A = F(A/F \ r,n)_\infty = F\left[\frac{e^r - 1}{e^{rn} - 1}\right] \qquad 5.40$$

Uniform Series Present Worth Factor

A combination of $(F/A \ r,n)$ and $(P/F \ r,n)$ factors will yield the $(P/A \ r,n)$ factor and is equal to

$$(P/A \ r,n)_\infty = \frac{e^{rn} - 1}{e^{rn}(e^r - 1)} \qquad 5.41$$

and

$$P = A(P/A \ r,n)_\infty = A\left[\frac{e^{rn} - 1}{e^{rn}(e^r - 1)}\right] \qquad 5.42$$

Uniform Series Capital Recovery Factor

This factor is the inverse of the uniform series present worth factor

$$(A/P \ r,n)_\infty = \left[\frac{e^{rn}(e^r - 1)}{e^{rn} - 1}\right] \qquad 5.43$$

and

$$A = P(A/P \ r,n)_\infty = P\left[\frac{e^{rn}(e^r - 1)}{e^{rn} - 1}\right] \qquad 5.44$$

EXAMPLE 5.17

If \$1,000 were deposited in an account now at an interest rate of 10% compounded continuously, and it was desired to withdraw 10 equal annual payments so that the fund was depleted in 10 years, what would be the amount of each of the equal annual withdrawals?

Using the tables in Appendix B:

$$A = P(A/P\ r,n)_\infty = \$1000\ (A/P\ 10\%,10)$$
$$= 1000\ (0.16638) = \$166.38$$

Using the formula from Eq. 5.43

$$A = P \left[\frac{e^{rn}(e^r - 1)}{e^{rn} - 1} \right] = \$1000 \left[\frac{e^{0.10(10)}(e^{0.10} - 1)}{e^{0.10(10)} - 1} \right]$$
$$= 1000\ (0.166378) = \$166.38$$

The factors and formulas given above involve discrete payments assumed to occur at the end of the defined periods. The time period of interest in continuous interest compounding, r, as quoted is 1 year. If cash flows are more frequent, that is, for shorter periods, the annual nominal interest is divided by the number of periods of cash flows per year. And n, representing the number of periods of cash flows, is the product of the number of years and the number of cash flow periods per year.

It should be recognized that tables of interest factors for continuous compounding are tabulated on two different methods. One indexes the tables by nominal annual interest rates. That is the basis used in Appendix B. The other method is based on the effective annual interest rate. There is considerable difference. A nominal interest rate of 10% is an effective annual rate of 10.52% (Eq. 5.33), and an effective rate of 10% is a nominal rate of only 9.53%.

CONTINUOUS CASH FLOW FACTORS

Up to this point all cash flows have been considered discrete, occurring at the end of the periods involved. There are instances when the cash flows are essentially continuous throughout the periods, and it may be desirable to consider them on that basis. They are referred to as *continuous cash flows* and are represented by $\bar{A}$. Whenever continuous cash flows are used, continuous compounding is assumed. The factors and formulas for continuous cash flow, continuous compounding are given in Table 5.7.

When necessary to convert from continuous cash flows to discrete cash flows, a conversion factor may be used. The relationship is expressed by the equation

$$A = \bar{A} \left[\frac{e^r - 1}{r} \right] \qquad\qquad 5.45$$

Table 5.7 Continuous Compounding—Discrete and Continuous Cash Flows.

FACTOR		FIND	GIVEN	DISCRETE CASH FLOWS — CONTINUOUS COMPOUNDING		FIND	GIVEN	CONTINUOUS CASH FLOWS — CONTINUOUS COMPOUNDING	
Single Payment	Compound Amount	F	P	$F = P(e^{rn})$	$P(F/P\,r,n)_\infty$				
	Present Worth	P	F	$P = F(e^{-rn})$	$F(P/F\,r,n)_\infty$				
Uniform Series	Compound Amount	F	A	$F = A\left[\dfrac{e^{rn}-1}{e^r-1}\right]$	$F(F/A\,r,n)_\infty$	F	$\bar{A}$	$F = \bar{A}\left[\dfrac{e^{rn}-1}{r}\right]$	$\bar{A}(F/\bar{A}\,r,n)_\infty$
	Sinking Fund	A	F	$A = F\left[\dfrac{e^r-1}{e^{rn}-1}\right]$	$F(A/F\,r,n)_\infty$	$\bar{A}$	F	$\bar{A} = F\left[\dfrac{r}{e^{rn}-1}\right]$	$F(\bar{A}/F\,r,n)_\infty$
	Present Worth	P	A	$P = A\left[\dfrac{e^{rn}-1}{e^{rn}(e^r-1)}\right]$	$A(P/A\,r,n)_\infty$	$\bar{P}$	$\bar{A}$	$\bar{P} = \bar{A}\left[\dfrac{e^{rn}-1}{re^{rn}}\right]$	$\bar{A}(P/A\,r,n)_\infty$
	Capital Recovery	A	P	$A = P\left[\dfrac{e^{rn}(e^r-1)}{e^{rn}-1}\right]$	$A(P/A\,r,n)_\infty$	$\bar{A}$	P	$\bar{A} = P\left[\dfrac{re^{rn}}{e^{rn}-1}\right]$	$P(\bar{A}/P\,r,n)_\infty$

The factor, $(e^r - 1)/r$, is called the *fund-flow conversion factor*. Rewriting Eq. 5.44,

$$\frac{(e^r - 1)}{r} = \frac{A}{\bar{A}} \qquad\qquad 5.46$$

Because the value of A, a discrete annuity at the end of the year, will be greater than $\bar{A}$ at any interest rate, the funds flow conversion factor is always greater than unity. The value of the funds flow conversion factor at various values of r is given in Table 5.8.

EXAMPLE 5.18

a. What are the present worth and future worth equivalents of a uniform series of cash flows of $10,000 per year for 8 years at 12% interest compounded continuously?

Table 5.8 Funds-Flow Conversion Factors.

r	$\dfrac{e^r - 1}{r}$ $\dfrac{A}{\bar{A}}$	r	$\dfrac{e^r - 1}{r}$ $\dfrac{A}{\bar{A}}$
.01	1.005017	.21	1.112753
.02	1.010067	.22	1.118531
.03	1.015151	.23	1.124348
.04	1.020269	.24	1.130205
.05	1.025422	.25	1.136102
.06	1.030609	.26	1.142039
.07	1.035831	.27	1.148017
.08	1.041088	.28	1.154035
.09	1.046381	.29	1.160095
.10	1.031709	.30	1.166195
.11	1.057073	.31	1.172339
.12	1.062474	.32	1.178524
.13	1.067911	.33	1.184752
.14	1.073384	.34	1.191022
.15	1.078895	.35	1.197336
.16	1.084443	.40	1.229562
.17	1.090029	.45	1.262916
.18	1.095652	.50	1.297443
.19	1.101314	.60	1.370198
.20	1.107014	.70	1.448218

$$P = \$10,000 \ (P/\bar{A} \ 12,8)_\infty = \$10,000 \ (5.14256)$$
$$= \$51,425.6$$
$$F = \$10,000 \ (F/\bar{A} \ 12,8)_\infty = \$10,000 \ (13.43080)$$
$$= \$134,308$$

b. What is the annual discrete amount, A, that would be equivalent to $10,000 as a uniform series as in (a) above?
From Eq. 5.46,

$$\frac{A}{\bar{A}} = \frac{e^r - 1}{r} = \frac{e^{0.12} - 1}{0.12} = 1.0624738$$

which agrees with Table 5.8 and then

$$\$10,000 \ (1.0624738) = \$10,624.74$$

This would not change the values of either the present worth or future worth as illustrated by using the discrete cash flow factor

$$P = A \ (P/A \ r,i)_\infty = \$10,624.74 \ (P/A \ 12\%,8)_\infty$$
$$= \$10,624.74 \ (4.840175) = \$51,425.60$$

SUMMARY

In Chapter 5, the reader was introduced to the concept of the time value of money and how it affects business transactions. Interest, or the cost of renting money, is a business fact of life of which everyone should have a working knowledge. The different types of interest—simple, discrete, and continuous compounding—were presented along with simple illustrative examples. The pronounced effect of interest upon an investment or financial transaction is evident. The use of interest in the management decision-making process will again occur in Chapter 8, "Profitability Measures." Therefore, in this chapter the techniques for calculating interest were introduced and these same principles will be applied to problems of larger scope in Chapter 8.

Suggested Further Readings

1. DeGarmo, E. Paul, Sullivan, William G., and Canada, John R. *Engineering Economy*, 7th ed. New York: Macmillan Publishing Company.
2. Grant, Eugene L., Ireson, W. Grant, and Leavenworth, Richard S. *Principles of Engineering Economy*. New York: John Wiley & Sons.

3. Taylor, George E., *Managerial and Engineering Economy.* 3rd Edition. New York: D. Van Nostrand Co.
4. Thuesen, H. G., Fabrycky, W. J., and Thuesen, G. J. *Engineering Economy,* 5th edition. Englewood Cliffs, N.J.: Prentice-Hall, Inc.
5. White, John A., Agee, Marvin A., and Case, Kenneth A. *Principles of Engineering Economic Analysis,* 2d ed. New York: John Wiley & Sons.

PROBLEMS

5.1 If a man invests $6,000 at 10% interest compounded annually, how much will the investment be worth in 10 years? How much total interest will he have earned?

5.2 If a man borrows $6,000 at 10% interest and pays it back with equal annual payments in 10 years, how much will each payment be? How much interest will he have paid in the 10-year period?

5.3 If a woman borrows $6,000 at 10% interest and pays it back in equal monthly payments in 10 years, how much will each payment be? How much interest will she have paid in the 10-year period?

5.4 If a person wanted to have $6,000 in the bank in 6 years and certificates of deposit were paying 12% interest compounded monthly, how much should be invested in CDs?

5.5 In Problem 5.4, how much would have to be deposited monthly in the 6 years to have the $6,000 in 6 years?

5.6 If $125 per month were put into a credit union that paid 8% interest, how much would be in the account at the end of 12 years?

5.7 What is the effective interest rate of Problem 5.3?

5.8 What is the effective interest rate of Problem 5.4?

5.9 A couple takes a $50,000 mortgage on a house at 11.3% interest and agrees to pay it off in 20 years with monthly payments.

    a. How much are the monthly payments?
    b. How much will be left to pay after the 100th payment?

5.10 If $1,616.50 is paid back at the end of 6 years for $1,000 borrowed 6 years ago, what interest compounded annually was paid?

5.11 How many years will it take to double a sum of money at an 8% interest rate compounded annually?

5.12 A person is contemplating depositing an amount in a savings account. Various interest rates are listed below. Which is best for the depositor?

    a. 7% compounded annually
    b. 6.9% compounded semiannually
    c. 6.8% compounded quarterly
    d. 6.75% compounded continuously?

5.13 A revolving charge account charges 1½% on the unpaid balance. What is the effective annual interest if charges are monthly?

5.14 What is the uniform annual amount that is equivalent to the following series of cash flows at the end of each year if the interest rate is

    a. 10% compounded annually

    b. 10% compounded continuously?

END OF YEAR	AMOUNT
0	$5,000
1	1,000
2	1,200
3	1,400
4	1,600
5	1,800
6	2,000
7	2,200
8	2,400

5.15 If $10,000 were borrowed at 10.3% compounded continuously for 6 years, what would be the quarterly payments?

5.16 A man places $5,000 in a CD account for 3 years paying 13.4% compounded monthly. At the end of the 3 years, he withdraws one-third of the money and leaves the remainder in a 3-year CD at 11.3%. How much is in the CD account at the end of the 6th year?

5.17 A debt of unknown amount is entered into at time 0. The debtor has agreed to pay $5,000 at the end of year 1, $4,000 at the end of year 2, $3,000 at the end of year 3, $2,000 at the end of year 4, and $1,000 at the end of year 5. The debt will be fully settled at that time. At 10% interest compounded annually, how much was borrowed at time 0?

5.18 Dorothy invests $3,000 in a money market account at 11.6% compounded monthly. At the end of the 12th month she deposits $100 into the account and continues to do so every month for 3 years, making 37 such monthly deposits. At the end of 5 years from time 0, assuming a constant interest rate, how much money is in the account?

5.19 What is the equivalent at the end of year 5 of the following set of annual cash flows, assuming the interest is 6% compounded monthly?

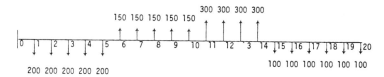

All cash flows are in dollars.

6 DEPRECIATION, OBSOLESCENCE, INVESTMENT CREDIT, AND INCOME TAXES

INTRODUCTION

In Chapter 4, one item constituting Total Operating Expenses was depreciation. Of all the expenses listed, it was the only noncash item. Depreciation was introduced in the early 1930's in the United States and the method of calculating this item has been revised many times since its introduction. Depreciation is tied directly to income taxes; therefore when major tax revisions have occurred, so have the methods of calculating depreciation.

Most engineers and scientists accept the concept of *obsolescence*, for they see the effect of obsolescence in the form of new equipment, new processes, and new techniques being developed which are more efficient and less costly than existing methods. *Depreciation*, on the other hand is a bit more elusive but is an important consideration in operating expenses and cash flow analysis. Therefore, the scientist or engineer must be conversant with depreciation accounting, taxation, and tax credits to fully understand a company's strategy in funding projects. Chapter 6 is a brief treatment of depreciation accounting and taxation. The methodologies learned in this chapter will be applied in subsequent chapters, especially Chapter 8, "Profitability Measures."

DEPRECIATION

Depreciation and taxes are important in financial and economic analysis. In an earlier chapter we discussed accounting in terms of generating financial statements. Accounting is the recording of financial events of an enterprise to provide managers with information to be used in decision-making and to comply with certain legal requirements. In this chapter a very important aspect of accounting, namely, accounting for depreciable fixed assets, will be studied. Depreciable fixed assets include machinery, equipment, buildings, and structures. Land is not a depreciable asset.

Depreciation is the amortization of fixed costs and has been defined by the Internal Revenue Service as: "A reasonable allowance for the exhaustion, wear and tear, and normal obsolescence of property used in the trade or business." Such property must have a determinable useful life of more than 1 year. Different depreciation rates may be used within the same accounting entity for the same asset, based on whether the accounting is being done for computing state and federal income taxes or for preparing financial reports. For tax purposes accelerated depreciation rates are generally employed to delay payment of taxes and to maximize cash flow in the early years. Accelerated depreciation will not change the total tax paid, however. This will be shown in examples later. Financial reports may be based on straight-line depreciation, which presents a more conservative financial statement. Certain selections must be made to determine a depreciation schedule: the tax life of the equipment, the type of depreciation to be used, and the salvage value at the end of the tax life. As suggested by the IRS definition above, obsolescence may play a major factor in terminating the useful life of an asset.

Obsolescence may indeed be a significant factor in determining the useful life of an asset. With rapidly expanding technology, obsolescence becomes a factor of greater importance, and this is particularly true in the process and electronics industries. Obsolescence may occur due to obsolescence of product, process, equipment, or capacity, and there are many examples of each. It is impossible in most cases to forecast obsolescence.

TAX LAWS

The history of tax laws is one of periodic change. Since passage of the first modern income tax law in 1913, tax laws and regulations have been modified to accommodate the concept of the tax life of assets having some relationship to the useful life of the particular asset. Bulletin F, issued in 1934 and revised in 1942, allowed an average write-off of 19 years and classified about 5,000 separate items. Treasury Decision 6183, issued in 1954, reduced the average write-off to 15 years and placed equipment in about 75 broad categories. Again in 1962 (with a 1964 revision) the average life was reduced, this time to 13 years. And in 1971 with a Class Life Asset Depreciation Range System, assets were placed in 143 asset categories with a permissible 20% deviation from the specified tax life permitted.

It is this Asset Depreciation Range (ADR) table that determined the tax life of most items being depreciated on the accountants' books today. But the ADR table was replaced by the latest tax act in 1981, the Accelerated Cost Recovery System (ACRS). In this act, all eligible depreciable assets have statutory recovery periods of 3, 5, 10, or 15 years for tax purposes.

The 3-year class consists of a few short-lived items such as cars, light-duty trucks, and much research and development equipment. Most depreciable assets were placed in the 5-year category, including most machinery and equipment, furniture and fixtures, and transportation equipment. The 10-year class is mostly public utility property that under the ADR system had been in the 18- to 25-year class. There are two 15-year classes: certain public utility property previously assigned lives of over 25 years, and depreciable real property, such as buildings and structures.

Different yearly depreciation schedules were assigned, depending on the date purchased, permitting a transition into the schedule which was to apply to 1986 and thereafter, as tabulated in Table 6.1. However, Parts B and C of Table 6.1 were eliminated by Congress.

Annual percentages were specified similarly for the 3-, 5-, 10-, and 15-year classes. For all depreciable assets the annual depreciation allowances are to be calculated as if all salvage values were zero. If on retirement of the asset an actual net salvage value is realized that is greater than the book value of the asset for income tax purposes, there would be a "gain on disposal" that would be taxable as ordinary income. With these new accelerated depreciation schedules employing vastly shortened tax lives, the older conventional methods of calculating accelerated depreciation are not as desirable and will not be used. The new law does permit straight-line depreciation over extended periods for any company that may expect higher incremental tax rates in years after the new tax life periods. With certain restrictions, taxpayers may elect to use straight-line depreciation over the same or certain stipulated longer lives. For example, in the 5-year category, which includes almost everything except automobiles and light trucks, certain public utility property, and depreciable real property, such as buildings and structures, the taxpayer could elect straight-line depreciation for 5, 12, or 25 years. Land has never been considered depreciable under previous tax laws nor is it under the ACRS method.

For all classes of property, the optional straight-line depreciation recovery periods under ACRS rules are as follows:

In the case of	The taxpayer may elect a recovery period of
3-year property	3, 5, or 12 years
5-year property	5, 12, or 25 years
10-year property	10, 25, or 35 years
15-year public utility property	15, 35, or 45 years

DEPRECIATION METHODS

Although these are certainly the schedules to be used for depreciable assets installed this year or in the future, there are depreciable assets currently on the tax books that are depreciated by the methods permitted up until

Table 6.1 Percentage Depreciation by Years for ACRS Schedule.

IF THE RECOVERY YEAR IS:	THE APPLICABLE PERCENTAGE FOR THE CLASS OF PROPERTY IS:			
	3-YEAR	5-YEAR	10-YEAR	15-YEAR PUBLIC UTILITY
A. For Property Placed in Service, 1981–84				
1	25	15	8	5
2	38	22	14	10
3	37	21	12	9
4		21	10	8
5		21	10	7
6			10	7
7			9	6
8			9	6
9			9	6
10			9	6
11				6
12				6
13				6
14				6
15				6
B. For Property Placed in Service in 1985				
1	29	18	9	6
2	47	33	19	12
3	24	25	16	12
4		16	14	11
5		8	12	10
6			10	9
7			8	8
8			6	7
9			4	6
10			2	5
11				4
12				4
13				3
14				2
15				1
C. For Property Placed in Service after 1985				
1	33	20	10	7
2	45	32	18	12
3	22	24	16	12
4		16	14	11

Table 6.1 (*continued*)

IF THE RECOVERY YEAR IS:	THE APPLICABLE PERCENTAGE FOR THE CLASS OF PROPERTY IS:			
	3-YEAR	5-YEAR	10-YEAR	15-YEAR PUBLIC UTILITY
5		8	12	10
6			10	9
7			8	8
8			6	7
9			4	6
10			2	5
11				4
12				3
13				3
14				2
15				1

the tax changes of 1981. Accordingly, a limited amount of space will be used to explain these methods.

As brought out at the beginning of the chapter in the quoted definition of depreciation accounting, it is the cost of tangible assets, less prospective salvage value, that is permitted to be written off in the account books. What was intended was that the cost of capital was considered a prepaid expense that was recovered by apportionment over a number of years so that at the end of the specified time, or tax life, the cost of the asset would be recovered, permitting reinvestment of those recovered monies in new equipment to replace the worn out. This theory worked well in a static economy, but as inflation moved into double-digit annual figures in the late 1970s, it became apparent that replacement of assets employed only 7 years or less required a capital investment of twice the original cost or more. As a result there have been strong petitions to the federal government to permit some alteration of the depreciation regulations to acknowledge the effects of inflation. It is probable that the 1981 laws are a result.

Prior to the 1981 tax law revisions, the most generally used methods for determining annual depreciation charges were:

1. straight-line method
2. sum-of-the-years digits method
3. declining balance method
4. combination of declining balance and straight-line methods
5. sinking fund method
6. units of production method

Straight-Line Depreciation

The straight-line method of depreciation provides for the uniform annual write-off of a depreciable asset. The depreciation taken at the end of the tth year, D_t, is constant during the asset's tax life and is given by:

$$D_t = \frac{P - S}{N} \qquad 6.1$$

where P is the asset's original installed cost, S is the net salvage value, and N is the tax life in years. The undepreciated *book value, B_t,* at the end of each year is given by:

$$B_t = P - \left(\frac{P - S}{N}\right) t \qquad 6.2$$

where t is the number of years the asset has been depreciated.

EXAMPLE 6.1

We purchased a minicomputer in 1980 at a total cost of $60,000 with a salvage value after 10 years of $5,000 and a tax life of 10 years. The straight-line depreciation and resulting book value for each year are given in Table 6.2.

The straight-line method, as stated earlier, is used by most companies for their financial accounts (as opposed to income tax accounts) to present a more conservative financial picture in their periodic reports. The Internal

Table 6.2   Straight-Line Depreciation.

END OF YEAR, t	DEPRECIATION, D_t	BOOK VALUE, B_t
0		$60,000 = P
1	$ 5,500	54,500
2	5,500	49,000
3	5,500	43,500
4	5,500	38,000
5	5,500	32,500
6	5,500	27,000
7	5,500	21,500
8	5,500	16,000
9	5,500	10,500
10	5,500	5,000 = S
	$55,000	

Revenue Service also permits straight-line depreciation accounting for tax purposes at the taxpayer's option. In addition, it has been common to switch to straight-line depreciation in the latter years of the life of an asset that was initially depreciated under an accelerated method.

Sum-of-the-Years Digits Depreciation

The sum-of-the-years digits method of depreciation has been one of two popular methods of accelerated depreciation. It provides higher than average depreciation amounts over the early years of the asset's life and less than average amounts over the latter years of the asset's life. The sum-of-the-years digits name comes from the fact that SOYD (sum-of-years-digits)

$$1 + 2 + \ldots + N - 1 + N = \frac{N(N+1)}{2} \qquad 6.3$$

is used directly in the computation of yearly depreciation. The allowance for depreciation for any year t is given by:

$$D_t = \frac{N - (t - 1)}{SOYD_N} (P - S) \qquad 6.4$$

and the book value at the end of each year t is given by

$$B_t = P - \frac{(P - S)}{SOYD_N} \left[SOYD_N - \frac{(N - t)(N - t + 1)}{2} \right] \qquad 6.5$$

EXAMPLE 6.2

The same minicomputer in Example 6.1 where $P = 60,000$, $S = 5,000$, and $N = 10$, if depreciated by the sum-of-the-years digits, would yield the results shown in Table 6.3.

Sum-of-the-years digits accelerated depreciation was used for income tax purposes with tangible assets having a tax life of only 3 years or more and where the original use began with the current taxpayer.

Declining-Balance Depreciation

The other of the two popular methods of accelerated depreciation is the declining balance method. In this method, the depreciation allowed for any year t is a constant fraction f of the book value at the end of the previous year. To accelerate depreciation over the straight-line rate, some percentage

Table 6.3 Sum-of-the-Years Digits Depreciation.

END OF YEAR, t	DEPRECIATION, D_t	BOOK VALUE, B_t
0		$60,000 = P$
1	$10,000	50,000
2	9,000	41,000
3	8,000	33,000
4	7,000	26,000
5	6,000	20,000
6	5,000	15,000
7	4,000	11,000
8	3,000	8,000
9	2,000	6,000
10	1,000	5,000 = S
	$55,000	

between 100 and 200% is taken of the straight-line rate, which was $1/N$, and that rate is multiplied by the book value at the end of the previous year. Salvage value is not considered in calculating annual depreciation in the declining-balance method. Double-declining balance, which yields the most accelerated depreciation and was permitted by law, is the most commonly used. In the previously used example of the $60,000 minicomputer, $200\% \times 1/10$ would yield an f value of 20% as the constant fraction, and thus the first year's depreciation D_1 would be .20 ($60,000) = $12,000. In the second year the allowance would be .20 ($60,000 - $12,000) = $9,600, and so forth. The formulas used for depreciation allowance in double-declining balance depreciation are:

$$f = 2.0/N \qquad 6.6$$

$$B_t = P(1-f)^t \qquad 6.7$$

$$D_t = f(B_{t-1}) = (B_{t-1} - B_t) = fP(1-f)^{t-1} \qquad 6.8$$

EXAMPLE 6.3

The double-declining balance method, if applied to our previous examples in this chapter, where $P = $60,000$, $S = $5,000$, and $N = 10$ years, would give the results shown in Table 6.4

Double Declining Balance Switch to Straight Line

It will be noted in Table 6.4 that the book value at the end of the 10th year, $6,442, did not equal the desired salvage value. This is the normal

Table 6.4   Double Declining Balance Depreciation.

END OF YEAR, t	DEPRECIATION, D_t	BOOK VALUE, B_t
0		$60,000 = P$
1	$12,000	48,000
2	9,600	38,400
3	7,680	30,720
4	6,144	24,576
5	4,915	19,661
6	3,932	15,729
7	3,146	12,583
8	2,517	10,066
9	2,013	8,053
10	1,611	6,442
	$53,558	

result. To be able to arrive at a book value equal to the salvage value, a switch to straight-line depreciation is permitted whenever the book value B_t for the end of a year less the salvage value divided by the number of years remaining $(N - t)$ yields a depreciation D_{t+1} equal to or greater than the depreciation D_{t+1} determined by the double-declining balance method.

In Example 6.3 the book value at the end of the 5th year was $19,661. The value of $(P - S)$ is $14,661 divided by $(N - t)$ or 5 years is equal to $2,932 which is less than D_{t+1}, which is $3,932. At the end of year 6, the book value is $15,729, less S is $10,729 and divided by $(N - t)$, or 4, is $2,682, which is less than $3,146 shown for D_t at year 7. In tabular form these results are shown in Table 6.5, where the depreciation used is underlined.

Table 6.5   Double Declining Balance Switch to Straight Line.

END OF YEAR, t	B_t	ALTERNATIVE, STRAIGHT LINE $D_t = (B_{t-1} - S)/(N - t)$	DDB (FROM EX. 6.2), D_t	
5	$19,661		$4,915	
6	15,729	$ 2,932	3,932	
7	12,583	2,682	3,146	
8	10,055	2,528	2,517	SWITCH POINT
9	7,527	2,528	2,013	
10	5,000	2,527	1,611	
		$55,000		

It will be noted that at the end of year 7 the depreciation for the remaining 3 years as calculated by straight line with a value of $2,528, which is greater than the $2,517 calculated by the double declining balance method. This, then, is the depreciation used for the last 3 years to bring the book value to the salvage value at the end of year 10.

If a switch were not made from double declining balance to straight line, then, as we found in Example 6.3, a book value at the end of 10 years of $6,442 would have been reached. If the useful life of the minicomputer were over, and if indeed it were sold for a net salvage value of $5,000, then a loss on sale of fixed assets would be recorded on the books for that year for the difference between $5,000 and $6,442.

Sinking Fund Depreciation

This method was at one time widely used for economy studies for governmental agencies and regulated public utilities, but has largely fallen into disuse. It is calculated by determining from interest tables how much annual payment would be required to place into a sinking fund to accumulate at a given interest rate i for a period of years N an amount of money equal to the difference between the first cost of the asset P and its salvage value S ($P - S)(A/F\ i,N)$. That quantity of money is the depreciation D_1 for the first year. For the second year, the depreciation would be $D_1(1 + i)^1$, for the third year $D_1(1 + i)^2$, and so forth. The model assumes that the depreciable assets depreciate at an increasing rate. So if the declining balance model and the sum-of-the-years digits model are considered accelerated depreciation, then sinking fund depreciation must be considered decelerated depreciation. It is assumed that the method was used earlier by governmental agencies because of little concern for the cost of money expressed as an interest rate, for they paid no interest on money. It was free. It came from taxes. With more review of government expenditures and broader realization that an alternative to governmental expenditures is reduction of debt and thus a finite opportunity cost, governmental attitudes have changed.

Units of Production Method

This method of computing depreciation allows equal depreciation for each unit of output, regardless of the elapsed time involved. The depreciation allowance for any year would be equal to the depreciable amount $(P - S)$ times the ratio of the units U_t produced in the year t to the total units that are estimated to be produced during the useful life of the producing asset U_T, which may be expressed as

$$D_t = (P - S)\frac{U_t}{U_T} \qquad\qquad 6.9$$

DEPRECIATION UNDER NEW TAX LAWS

Having reviewed depreciation models in use until the 1981 tax law discussed earlier in this chapter, we would do well to try our problem under the new tax law.

EXAMPLE 6.5

Using the Accelerated Cost Recovery System (ACRS), let us examine our minicomputer costing $60,000 with an estimated salvage of $5,000 and an estimated useful life of 10 years. You will recall that salvage value is ignored in the ACRS method. The depreciation and book value for each year are given in Table 6.6. The schedule of depreciation percentages shown in Table 6.1A, has been used in the calculations.

Table 6.7 compares the three methods of accelerated depreciation and straight-line depreciation. The book values resulting from these depreciation rates are shown in Fig. 6.1.

SINGLE-ASSET AND MULTIPLE-ASSET ACCOUNTING

Depreciable assets have in the past been depreciated on the basis of individual items, or depreciation accounts may have been set up for a group of items that fit in specified groups or classifications. Publications of the U.S. Internal

Table 6.6   ACRS Depreciation Method.

END OF YEAR, t	ALLOWED % DEPRECIATION	DEPRECIATION, D_t	BOOK VALUE, B_t
0			$60,000
1	15	$ 9,000	51,000
2	22	13,200	37,800
3	21	12,600	25,200
4	21	12,600	12,600
5	21	12,600	0
6	0	0	0
7	0	0	0
8	0	0	0
9	0	0	0
10	0	0	0

Table 6.7 Comparison of Depreciation Charges by Four Methods of Depreciation Accounting.

Asset has a first cost of $60,000, an estimated salvage value of $5,000, and an estimated life of 10 years

DEPRECIATION ALLOWANCE FOR YEAR

END OF YEAR	STRAIGHT LINE	SUM-OF-YEARS DIGITS	DECLINING BALANCE*	ACRS
0				
1	$ 5,500	$10,000	$12,000	$ 9,000
2	5,500	9,000	9,600	13,200
3	5,500	8,000	7,680	12,600
4	5,500	7,000	6,144	12,600
5	5,500	6,000	4,915	12,600
6	5,500	5,000	3,932	0
7	5,500	4,000	3,146	0
8	5,500	3,000	2,528**	0
9	5,500	2,000	2,528	0
10	5,500	1,000	2,527	0
Total	$55,000	$55,000	$55,000	$60,000

END OF YEAR BOOK VALUE

END OF YEAR	STRAIGHT LINE	SUM-OF-YEARS DIGITS	DECLINING BALANCE*	ACRS
0	$60,000	$60,000	$60,000	$60,000
1	54,500	50,000	48,000	51,000
2	49,000	41,000	38,400	37,800
3	43,500	33,000	30,720	25,200
4	38,000	26,000	24,576	12,600
5	32,500	20,000	19,661	0
6	27,000	15,000	15,729	0
7	21,500	11,000	12,583	0
8	16,000	8,000	10,055	0
9	10,500	6,000	7,527	0
10	5,000	5,000	5,000	0

* Switching to straight-line.
** Switch point.

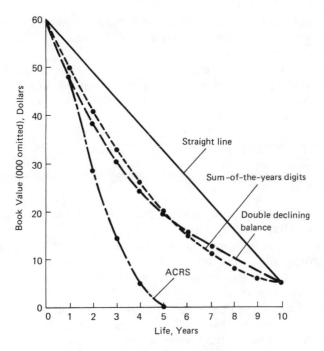

Figure 6.1. Book values of $60,000 minicomputer.

Revenue Service have defined three general types of multiple-asset accounts as follows:

1. Group Accounts—Similar depreciable assets having the same average life may all be put into the same account. Though in actual life span some of these individual items may have longer or shorter average lives, as determined by experience and as listed in the tax bulletins, statistically the life span will average the same as the listed group age and can be depreciated together. Examples of assets falling into groups could be passenger cars, typewriters, office desks, machines, lathes, and punch presses.

2. Classified Accounts—As described in 1962 and revised in 1964 in guide-line classes, certain assets may be segregated without regard to useful life. For example, machinery and equipment in the same functional classification, office furniture, and transportation equipment may be put into classified accounts.

3. Composite Accounts—This is a broader grouping where the assets may be included in the same account regardless of their character or useful lives. For example, all the assets of a definable single business entity

might be put in the same composite account and consist of machinery, furniture, fixtures, and transportation equipment.

Usually, however, single items of relatively large value are required to be treated separately and be depreciated throughout their lives as separate, distinguishable items.

VALUE OF DEPRECIATION DEDUCTIONS

Midyear Convention

One year is the standard accounting period for both business accounting and for computing taxable income. And, of course, assets are placed in use at irregular intervals throughout the accounting year. If the depreciation charge were based on the ratio of the time remaining in the year to the total year, each new asset would have a different depreciation percentage, and appreciable expensive clerical labor would be required. This is avoided by the use of some type of averaging convention. The most commonly used convention has been to charge all newly placed assets with half a year's depreciation regardless of the time of year they are placed in service.

With the new tax law passed in 1981, this has all changed. The grouping of all assets into four ages—3, 5, 10, or 15 years—greatly simplifies recordkeeping. The percentage depreciation for the first year, incorporated into each of these schedules, allows a liberal average convention for all assets in each class. It will be noted that in ACRS schedules for the 5-year assets listed that the first year is appreciably less than the second year. In 1981 and after, the depreciation by years is: 15, 22, 21, 21 and 21%. Examining this as an arithmetic series, one would have expected the first year to be 30%. Instead, to allow for a first-year, average, placed-in-service time, the depreciation is cut in half to 15%.

The reader certainly appreciates at this point in the chapter that accelerated depreciation schedules in effect before 1981 are, after 1981, only of historical significance. All future accounting and economic analyses involving after-tax cash flows will use the new depreciation schedules. We have felt that since scientists or engineers looking into depreciation schedules of existing equipment would encounter the older methods, they should be explained.

The Government as a Partner

It is well to consider the government as a partner in business. As a partner it made no cash contribution to the formation of the business, nor is it a stockholder in the venture, but it shares in the profit of the venture. The tax rates on corporate income are listed in Table 6.8.

In 1982 the 17% rate for the first bracket from $0 to $25,000 dropped to 16%, and the second bracket from $25,000 to $50,000 dropped from 20% to 19%. And for 1983 these two brackets are reduced to 15 and 18%, respectively. Thus in 1983, corporate taxable income over $100,000 is taxed $25,750 plus 46% of the corporate taxable income over $100,000. The net result is a reduction of $1,000 in corporate tax for corporations having a taxable income in excess of $100,000.

Combined Federal and State Taxes

Thus most corporations face an incremental federal tax rate of 46% or face a tax rate of 46% on their incremental net profit. In addition, most states have a corporate state income tax, which is also stepwise. But because state tax is deductible before figuring federal tax, they cannot be directly added. T_s represents the incremental state tax rate, and if T_f represents the incremental federal tax rate, with both rates expressed as decimals, then the combined incremental tax rate $= T_s + (1 - T_s)T_f$.

For example, if the incremental rate on the federal tax is 46% and the incremental state rate is 7%, then the combined incremental rate is .07 + $(1 - .07).46 = .4978$ or 49.78%. If $1,000 of income is earned, the corporation is liable for a combined tax of $497.80. The last increment of net income is split. Therefore 7%, or $70, goes to the state government, $(1 - .07).46 \times $1,000$, or $427.80, goes to the federal government, and $502.20 is retained by the corporation to pay dividends to its stockholders or reinvest in the corporation's business.

Table 6.8   Federal Tax Rate Schedules on Incomes of Corporations in the United States.

TAXABLE INCOME	TAX, PRIOR TO 1982	TAX, 1982	TAX, 1983 AND BEYOND
Less than $25,000	17%	16%	15%
Over $25,000 but less than $50,000	$4,250 plus 20% over $25,000	$4,000 plus 19% over $25,000	$3,750 plus 18% over $25,000
Over $50,000 but less than $75,000	$9,250 plus 30% over $50,000	$8,750 plus 30% over $50,000	$8,250 plus 30% over $50,000
Over $75,000 but less than $100,000	$16,750 plus 40% over $75,000	$16,250 plus 40% over $75,000	$15,750 plus 40% over $75,000
All over $100,000	$26,750 plus 46% over $100,000	$26,250 plus 46% over $100,000	$25,750 plus 46% over $100,000

Cash Flow

It is important to recognize that income taxes are a negative cash flow, or another disbursement of funds to add to those for operations, maintenance, selling costs, and so forth. Depreciation, however, is not a negative cash flow, because it is not paid to anyone. Depreciation is Internal Revenue Service approved amortizations of previous capital expenditures. As such, it is deducted from income before tax. After the tax calculations have been made, the depreciation expense that was deducted may be added back to net profit after tax to get cash flow after tax. An example might well be used to illustrate.

EXAMPLE 6.6

A company's skeleton tax and cash flow might be as follows:

Net Sales Revenue	$2,000,000
Less Cost of Goods Manufactured	1,000,000
Gross Profit	1,000,000
Less G & A & Selling Expense	400,000
Less Depreciation for the Year	200,000
Net Profit before Tax	400,000
Less 7% State Sales Tax	28,000
Net Profit before Federal Tax	372,000
Less 46% Federal Tax	171,120
Net Profit after Tax	200,880
Add Back Depreciation Expense	200,000
After-tax cash flow—to be used for stockholder dividends or reinvestment in the company	400,880

For most examples in this book we will use a combined income tax rate of 50% unless we want to make a specific point, in which case we might calculate state and federal taxes separately.

Availability of Capital

Technological progress is generally the principal contributor to a high standard of living. Obstacles to capital formation and technological development are obstacles to improvement in the standard of living. High tax rates, both corporate and personal, are deterrents to capital investment and, combined with depreciation rates to be taken over a long period of time, are an even greater deterrent. Four different types of government actions have aimed to offset part of the effects of high tax rates. One step taken was to shorten tax lives and provide for accelerated depreciation during this shortened life. This permits the return of capital spent more rapidly and its resultant reuse earlier. The second step has been a campaign within the federal government to reduce bureaucratic control and reporting required over all facets of industrial operations.

The third step has been declared as intended, but only time will tell whether it can be accomplished within current federal legislative mentality. This is the reduction in government expenditures and the elimination of deficit spending to reduce the competition for borrowed funds, which drives the cost of money or interest rates upward.

OTHER TAX CONSIDERATIONS

Investment Tax Credit

The fourth step made by government action has been the establishment of an *investment tax credit.* Like much tax reformation, this was initiated in 1962. Where accelerated depreciation is the delaying of taxes to be paid, investment tax credit actually reduces the total amount of income taxes paid.

Additional First-Year Depreciation

A number of years ago, as an aid to small businesses, a tax law passed by Congress allowed an additional first-year depreciation on certain qualifying property for income tax purposes. In 1980, the deduction of 20% of the cost of qualifying assets could be deducted in addition to regular depreciation, up to a limit of $10,000 on a separate return or $20,000 on a joint return. For example, a $100,000 investment by a couple filing a joint tax return and depreciating the property over 10 years could take the special depreciation of 20%, or $20,000, in the first year and, in addition, the standard deduction for the first year. If this deduction were by the straight-line method over 10 years, then ($100,000 − $20,000)/10 years would be an additional $18,000, for a total of $38,000 of depreciation in the first year. A 10% investment credit could also be taken in 1980.

The tax act of 1981 eliminated this provision in favor of a limited permission for 100% write-off of $5,000 of selected assets in the year of purchase. Assets written off in this manner are not eligible for investment tax credit. The $5,000 limit applies to years 1982 and 1983. The limit is increased to $7,500 in 1984 and 1985 and to $10,000 in all subsequent years.

In 1975 the rules for the investment tax credits were greatly liberalized, and in 1981 the rules were further liberalized. Table 6.9 indicates the levels

Table 6.9   Investment Tax Credit.

BEFORE 1981		AFTER 1981	
TAX LIFE	INVESTMENT TAX CREDIT, %	TAX LIFE	INVESTMENT TAX CREDIT, %
Less than 3 years	None		
3 to 4 years	$3\frac{1}{3}$	3 years	6
5 or 6 years	$6\frac{2}{3}$	5 years	10
7 or more years	10	10 and 15 years	10

of investment credit available. The credit could be used to offset tax liability up to the first $25,000 and up to 50% of the tax liability in excess of $25,000. If more credit is available than can be used, the credit can be carried forward for 7 years or back for 3 years. Nor does it reduce the amount to be depreciated.

Under the 1981 tax act, the 10% investment tax credit applies to eligible assets in the 5-, 10- and 15-year classes. This was no appreciable change in the 10- and 15-year categories, but the 5-year category was changed from $6\frac{2}{3}$% to the full 10% tax credit. Eligible assets in the new 3-year category now are allowed a 6% investment tax credit.

In any given year the investment credit cannot exceed the tax liability. The investment tax credit can be taken as 100% of the calculated credit up to $25,000 of tax liability. Above $25,000 of investment credit against a tax liability, only 90% of the tax liability can be taken as investment credit. Assume that a company has a tax liability of $50,000 for a given year and has invested in the following assets:

Amount	Expected Life	ACRS Life
$300,000	10 years	5 years
100,000	5 years	5 years
150,000	4 years	3 years

The calculated investment tax credit is:

$$\begin{array}{r} \$300,000 \times 10\% = \$30,000 \\ 100,000 \times 10\% = 10,000 \\ 150,000 \times\ \ 6\% = \underline{\ \ \ 9,000} \\ \$45,000 \end{array}$$

The firm's maximum allowable credit is:

$$\$25,000 + 90\% \ (\$45,000 - \$25,000) = \$43,000$$

And the firm's tax liability after investment credit is:

$$\$50,000 - \$43,000 = \$7,000$$

The first-year expense deduction is referred to as the Section 179 expense deduction. If it is elected to be used, expense deduction must be used in the year the property is placed in service. If used, the first year's depreciation must be subtracted from the capital invested before calculating the investment credit. In addition, the remaining depreciable value of the asset must be reduced by 5%. Assuming an asset value of $110,000, the Section 179 allowable deduction would be $10,000, reducing the value of the asset for investment credit to $100,000. The investment credit would be 10% ($100,000), or $10,000, to be taken in year 1. The remaining value of $100,000 is then reduced by 5% to bring the value of the asset for depreciation to $95\% \times 100,000 = \$95,000$.

It is apparent that the value of the additional expense deduction was designed to be of value only to the small company. It is not used in any of the examples and is not expected to be used in any of the problems.

Because the legislators frequently change the tax laws in regard to incentives for investment, it is recommended that the analyst check with tax experts before using investment credit or additional first year depreciation in an economic analysis.

Effect of Depreciation Method on Tax

It would be well to illustrate the effect of accelerated depreciation on cash flow by an example or two. In our minicomputer problem of Example 6.1, let us assume a $20,000 positive cash flow before taxes and straight-line depreciation. With a first cost of $60,000 and a salvage value of $5,000, the after-cash tax profile could be developed as in Table 6.10.

If double-declining balance accelerated depreciation had been used, as it was in Examples 6.3 and 6.4, Table 6.11 would show the effect on cash flow.

Note that the total tax paid over the 10-year period is the same whether straight-line depreciation or accelerated depreciation is used. Ultimately your partners, the federal government and the state government, will get their shares of the profits. But given this choice, most businessmen would select the cash flow provided by the accelerated depreciation method, because it provides more money in the earlier years. The quantitative justification for this preference will be described later.

Table 6.10   After-Tax Cash Flow Profile with Straight-Line Depreciation.

END OF YEAR A	BEFORE-TAX CASH FLOW B	DEPRECIATION STRAIGHT-LINE C	TAXABLE INCOME B-C D	TAX D (.50) E	AFTER-TAX CASH FLOW B-E F
0	−$60,000			−$6,000*	−$54,000
1	+20,000	$ 5,500	$ 14,500	7,250	12,750
2	+20,000	5,500	14,500	7,250	12,750
3	+20,000	5,500	14,500	7,250	12,750
4	+20,000	5,500	14,500	7,250	12,750
5	+20,000	5,500	14,500	7,250	12,750
6	+20,000	5,500	14,500	7,250	12,750
7	+20,000	5,500	14,500	7,250	12,750
8	+20,000	5,500	14,500	7,250	12,750
9	+20,000	5,500	14,500	7,250	12,750
10	+20,000	5,500	14,500	7,250	12,750
10**	5,000				5,000
Totals	$145,000	$55,000	$145,000	$66,500	$78,500

* Investment tax credit of 10%.
** Asset sold at book value.

Table 6.11   After-Cash Flow Profile with Double-Declining Balance Depreciation.

END OF YEAR A	BEFORE-TAX CASH FLOW B	DEPRECIATION DOUBLE DECLINING BALANCE C	TAXABLE INCOME B-C D	TAX D (.50) E	AFTER-TAX CASH FLOW B-E F
0	−$60,000			−$6,000*	−$54,000
1	+20,000	$12,000	$ 8,000	4,000	16,000
2	+20,000	9,600	10,400	5,200	14,800
3	+20,000	7,680	12,320	6,160	13,840
4	+20,000	6,144	13,856	6,928	13,072
5	+20,000	4,915	15,085	7,543	12,457
6	+20,000	3,932	16,068	8,034	11,966
7	+20,000	3,146	16,854	8,427	11,573
8	+20,000	2,528	17,472	8,736	11,264
9	+20,000	2,528	17,472	8,736	11,264
10	+20,000	2,527	17,473	8,736	11,264
10**	5,000				5,000
Totals	$145,000	$55,000	$145,000	$66,500	$78,500

* Investment credit.
**Asset sold at book value.

If the Accelerated Cost Recovery System (ACRS) depreciation, permitted in the tax act of 1981 and calculated in Example 6.5, were used, the cash flow developed in Table 6.12 would result. If cash flows in the early years of a project are important (later it will be shown that they are), then the last table utilizing ACRS depreciation provides the earliest high cash flow years. It permits in this specific problem, with the given cash flows, very low tax is due in the second year.

It should be noted in Tables 6.10 and 6.11 using straight-line and double-declining balance, respectively, that $55,000 total depreciation is taken. This is the difference between installed price and net salvage value. It should be noted in Table 6.12, where the ACRS accelerated depreciation is used, salvage value was ignored and $59,550 was depreciated which according to ACRS is 95% of the depreciable investment. Under ACRS, if the Investment Tax Credit is taken, then only 95% of the investment may be depreciated. However, it must be assumed that, though the asset is depreciated to zero book value, the asset would have actually the same real value as it did in the two earlier tables. Assuming then that the asset was indeed sold, there would be a gain on the sale that would be taxable. In the two earlier tables, it was also assumed that the asset was sold. In these cases the asset was sold at its book value, so no tax was involved.

Table 6.12 After-Cash Flow Profile with the 1981 ACRS Accelerated Depreciation.

END OF YEAR A	BEFORE-TAX CASH FLOW B	DEPRECIATION ACRS C	TAXABLE INCOME B-C D	TAX D (.50) E	AFTER-TAX CASH FLOW B-E F
0	−$60,000			−$6,000*	−$54,000
1	+20,000	$ 8,550	$11,450	5,725	14,275
2	+20,000	13,200	6,800	3,400	16,600
3	+20,000	12,600	7,400	3,700	16,300
4	+20,000	12,600	7,400	3,700	16,300
5	+20,000	12,600	7,400	3,700	16,300
6	+20,000		20,000	10,000	10,000
7	+20,000		20,000	10,000	10,000
8	+20,000		20,000	10,000	10,000
9	+20,000		20,000	10,000	10,000
10	+20,000		20,000	10,000	10,000
10**	5,000		5,000	2,500	2,500
Totals	$145,000	$59,550	$145,000	$66,725	$78,275

* Investment credit.
** By the ACRS method, the asset is depreciated to zero book value. Thus when it is sold, the sale is a gain and is taxed as ordinary income.

As a result, the total taxes paid by any of the three depreciation methods is about the same. It is only the timing of the taxes that differs. With accelerated depreciation, income taxes are delayed until later in the life of the asset. Expressed as a percentage, only 28% of the taxes in Table 6.12, using the ACRS accelerated depreciation, was paid in the first half of the life of the asset. If the investment credit is added to the calculations as a negative tax at the beginning of year 1, then only 21% of the total taxes for the 10 years were paid in the first half of the life of the asset.

In economic analysis of capital expenditures, the time value of money must be acknowledged. In the examples developed thus far, the annual after-tax cash flows have been developed, and we have pointed out that accelerated depreciation yielded higher after-tax cash flows in the early years of the asset life. To complete the comparison of results with different depreciation methods, the annual cash flows are discounted back to a present value. This has been done in Table 6.13, in which the after-tax cash flow has been listed by each of three depreciation methods taken from Tables 6.10, 6.11, and 6.12. Then the discount factor $(P/F \ 10,n)$ for different values of n has been tabulated. The last three columns represent the product of the after-tax cash flows and the discount factor to give the discounted cash flow for each depreciation method.

It will be noted that the totals of each column represent positive cash flows. That is, the $54,000 net investment returned 10% plus the amount shown. The ACRS method had the largest excess over 10%. The rate of return calculated by trial and error gave a value of 20.1% for the straight-line method of depreciation, 21.7% for the double declining balance method, and 24.1% for the ACRS method. This is a significant difference in return on investment and may help to encourage investment.

Depletion Allowance

Depletion is the gradient removal or reduction of natural resources, such as metal ores, gas, oil, timber, and other natural deposits. From the standpoint of recovering an asset that was consumed or used up, depletion is related to depreciation. The depleted asset loses value by being removed, while the depreciated asset loses value by wear and obsolescence. In theory, the money recovered through the depletion allowance would be used to discover and develop new depletable assets.

In corporate financial accounting for depletion, costs are usually kept on a unit-of-production basis. But for income tax purposes, U.S. tax laws permit depletion charges to be taken by one of two methods. Similar to most tax-related matters, the law, as it relates to royalties, sales, lessor and lessee, is complicated, many times requiring expert help to stay on safe ground.

Table 6.13 After-Tax Cash Flows Discounted Back to the Present.

END OF YEAR	AFTER-TAX CASH FLOW DEPRECIATION METHOD			DISCOUNT FACTOR AT $i = 10\%$ $(P/F\ i,n)$	ANNUAL CASH FLOW DISCOUNTED TO PRESENT VALUE BY DEPRECIATION METHOD		
	STR.-LINE	DDB	ACRS		STR.-LINE	DDB	ACRS
0	−$54,000	−$54,000	−$54,000	0	−$54,000	−$54,000	−$54,000
1	12,750	16,000	14,275	.90909	11,591	14,545	12,977
2	12,750	14,800	16,600	.82645	10,537	12,281	13,719
3	12,750	13,840	16,300	.75131	9,579	10,398	12,246
4	12,750	13,072	16,300	.68301	8,708	8,928	11,133
5	12,750	12,457	16,300	.62092	7,917	7,735	10,121
6	12,750	11,966	10,000	.56447	7,197	6,754	5,645
7	12,750	11,573	10,000	.51316	6,543	5,939	5,132
8	12,750	11,264	10,000	.46651	5,948	5,255	4,665
9	12,750	11,264	10,000	.42410	5,407	4,770	4,241
10	12,750	11,264	10,000	.38554	6,844	6,271	4,819
10*	5,000	5,000	2,500				
TOTAL	$78,500	$78,500	$78,275		$26,241	$28,876	$30,698

* Salvage Value.

191

The cost method is the generally used method for calculating depletion allowances for tax purposes. This depletion allowance is equal in any year to the ratio of the total cost of the property, C, to the total units of product contained in the property, U_T, multiplied by the number of units sold for the year being studied U_t:

$$\text{Depletion allowance} = \frac{C}{U_T} \times U_t \qquad\qquad 6.10$$

This depletion figure is subtracted from the before-tax cash flow, just as depreciation was in earlier examples, to calculate taxable income.

The percentage depletion method provides for calculating depletion allowance by taking a percentage of gross income produced by the property in the year. These percentages are assigned in the appropriate tax law and relate to the material being depleted. Typical of such percentages are: oil and gas, 22%; sulfur, mica, graphite, bauxite, asbestos, uranium, and certain ores, such as chromite, cadmium, cobalt, lead, mercury, nickel, tin, and zinc, 22%; silver, gold, copper, iron ore, and oil shale, 15%; various clays, diatomaceous earth, granite, and certain metals not listed above, 14%; coal, lignite, perlite, and sodium chloride, 10%; clay and shale used for sewer pipe and bricks, 7½%; and sand, gravel, pumice, and peat, 5%. The allowance for oil and gas and possibly others may change in the next few years. The depletion allowance calculated by percentage depletion may not be less than that calculated by the cost method, but may not otherwise exceed 50% of the taxable income before depletion allowance.

EXAMPLE 6.7

A small company has purchased oil rights, drilled, and developed an oil well, which has a total recoverable oil resource of 660,000 barrels at a cost of $3,300,000. As a result of increased difficulty in recovering the oil as the oil field is depleted, the operating costs start at $7.00 per barrel and increase by $.50 each year, reaching $12.00 per barrel in the 11th year. Geological experts estimate that the 660,000 barrels of oil in the field will be of such a nature that 110,000 barrels can be removed the first year, with the quantity diminishing by 10,000 barrels each year over the previous year. Each barrel sold will have a net sales value of $20.00. By the cost method, $3,300,000/660,000 barrels gives a ratio of $5.00/barrel for a depletion allowance.

If the qualifications for a small producer are met, then a 22% depletion allowance could be made by the percentage depletion method. In Table 6.14 the year's depletion allowance is calculated by both methods, and

Table 6.14 Depletion Allowance, Tax, and After-Tax Cash Flows for Oil Well Example (in $M)

END OF YEAR	BARRELS SOLD	GROSS INCOME	OPERATING COST	BEFORE-TAX CASH FLOW	50% OF NET INCOME	COST DEPLETION @ $5.00/ BARREL 5 (B)	% DEPLETION @ 22% OF GROSS INCOME .22 × C	TAXABLE INCOME E-MAX[G,H]	INCOME TAX 0.5 (I)	AFTER-TAX CASH FLOW E-J
A	B	C	D	E	F	G	H	I	J	K
0		−$3,300		−$3,300						−$3,300
1	110	2,200	$770	$1,430	$715	$550	$484	$880	$440	990
2	100	2,000	750	1,250	625	500	440	750	375	875
3	90	1,800	720	1,080	540	450	396	630	315	765
4	80	1,600	680	920	460	400	352	520	260	660
5	70	1,400	630	770	385	350	308	420	210	560
6	60	1,200	570	630	315	300	264	330	165	465
7	50	1,000	500	500	250	250	220	250	125	375
8	40	800	420	380	190	200	176	180	90	290
9	30	600	330	270	135	150	132	120	60	210
10	20	400	230	170	85	100	88	70	35	135
11	10	200	120	80	40	50	44	30	15	65

tax and after-tax cash flows are calculated. Note that in every year the cost depletion method, column G, gives a larger depletion allowance than column H, the percentage depletion allowance. This is not always true. Note also that in years 10 and 11 the percentage depletion method gives an allowance larger than 50% of the before-tax cash flow, which would have exceeded the allowable allowance if the percentage depletion numbers had been used. They were not used because the cost depletion figures were higher.

Carry Forward and Carry Back

Both as a result of previous tax laws and certain liberalizations made in 1981, corporations losing money in a given year have two options. First, as a result of the liberalized tax laws of 1981, losses for a given year can be carried forward 15 years (this has been increased from 7 years) or carried back 3 years. Thus if a loss occurs in 1984, that loss can be carried back, and the books for 1981, 1982, and 1983 reopened and the loss applied to one or more of those years. Or the loss could be carried forward to reduce taxable income in any year until 1999. Thus in our treatment of incomes, we will continue to treat them as incremental, assuming that they are incremental to a profit earned somewhere in that 18-year interval.

Secondly, the government, by its investment credit concept, has shown that it wants to encourage expansion of the economy. But the investment credit has no value to a company with no positive income. That is, if new investments in assets are entitled to new accelerated depreciation deductions and to investment tax credits, then those investments have a so-called tax benefit, because the deductions and credits reduce taxes that would have had to be paid otherwise. Business enterprises that are then not paying income taxes currently, because they are not earning taxable income, have no immediate tax benefits from the proposed investments and must wait until some indefinite time in the future to reap benefits of investment now.

Transfer of Deductions and Credits

Thus the Congress in the conception of the 1981 tax law saw it to be in the public interest for enterprises losing money to have incentive for technological improvements and to make investments that would improve productivity. Thus the laws were liberalized, as they governed the tax aspects of leasing, to permit, under a complex set of restrictions, the depreciation deductions and investment credits to be transferred to a profitable corporation that would finance the lease of the new asset. So business enterprises losing money are permitted to peddle their entitlements to deductions and credits for cash or

advantageous leases. Once transferred, the depreciation deductions and investment tax credits are not available to the lessee for that asset later when his
operations become profitable.

Capital Gains Treatment

The treatment of capital gains and losses in the internal revenue laws is
more difficult to understand and apply than any other IRS laws. Any assets
that can receive capital treatment are important for tax purposes because
of the preferential treatment they receive, in that they are taxed at a lesser
rate than ordinary income. It was the original intent of Congress to reduce
the impact of ordinary income tax on gains that resulted from an appreciation
in the value of items held under a certain amount of risk over a period of
time. Over a period of years imaginative taxpayers have found ways of getting
certain items classed as eligible for the capital gains privilege. And as these
loopholes were plugged, the tax provisions increased in complexity. As a
result, any uncertainty should be clarified by legal counsel or reference to
a reliable up-to-date tax publication.

As stated by the Internal Revenue Service, a capital asset is any property
held by a taxpayer *except:*

a. Stock in trade or other property included in inventory or held for sale
   to customers.
b. Accounts or notes receivable you received for services in the ordinary
   course of your trade or business or from the sale of any property described in (a) or for services you performed as an employee.
c. Depreciable property used in a trade or business, even if it was fully
   depreciated.
d. Real property used in a trade or business.
e. A copyright, literary, musical, or artistic composition, letter, memorandum, or similar property
   1. Created by your personal efforts, or
   2. Prepared or produced for you (in the case of a letter, memorandum
      or similar property), or
   3. That you received from a taxpayer mentioned in (1) or (2) in such
      a way (such as a gift) that entitled you to the labor of the previous
      owner.
f. U.S. Government publications (including the *Congressional Record*) that
   you received from the government other than by purchase at the normal
   sales price or that you got from another taxpayer who had received it
   in a similar way, if your basis is determined by reference to the previous
   owner.

g. Certain government obligations acquired before June 1981, as a discount, payable without interest, and maturing at a fixed date not more than 1 year from the date of issue.

The amount of time an asset has been held to qualify as a long-term capital gain (or loss) has changed over the years and until quite recently was 6 months. For 1982, the time required to permit capital treatment was 1 year or more. Thus, two requirements must be met—the nature of the asset, and the time held—to qualify for the reduced tax afforded capital gains. But before applying gains (or losses) on disposal of capital assets, a balancing of short-term and long-term gains and losses is required. A net short-term gain or loss is the sum of short-term gains minus short-term losses. And similarly, a net long-term gain or loss is the sum of long-term gains minus long-term losses.

If there is a net short-term gain (and no net long-term gain or loss), the gain is taxed as ordinary income. If there is a net short-term loss (and no net long-term gain or loss), the loss may be carried back or forward. If there is a net long-term gain (and no net short-term gain or loss), the gain is taxed as capital gain. If there is a net long-term loss (and no net short-term gain or loss), then net capital loss may be carried over. If there is a net long-term gain and a net short-term gain, the long-term gain is taxed as capital gain, and the short-term gain is taxed as ordinary income. But if there is a net capital gain, after a net long-term gain is reduced by a net short-term loss, the net capital gain is taxed as capital gain.

If there is a net long-term loss and net short-term gain resulting in a net loss, the loss may be carried back or forward. If the result is a net capital gain, it is taxed as ordinary income.

If both net long-term and net short-term are losses, then the total net capital loss may be carried back or forward.

SUMMARY

In this chapter, the techniques concerning depreciation and taxation accounting were introduced. With each revision to the United States tax laws are revisions in the methods for calculating the depreciation allowance, taxes, and tax credits. Scientists and engineers need to have a working knowledge of the principles presented in this chapter so that they have a better understanding of the effect which revisions in the taxation laws have upon the financial operations of a company.

In subsequent chapters, depreciation accounting principles will be applied to more complex economic analysis problems than were encountered in this chapter.

PROBLEMS

6.1 A minicomputer has been acquired by a firm at an initial installed cost of $24,000. With an estimated economic life of five years, it is estimated to have a salvage value of $4,000 at that time. Find the first year's depreciation charge based on:
  a. Straight line depreciation
  b. Sum-of-the-years digits
  c. Double declining balance
  d. ACRS for years 1986 and beyond

6.2 Find the book value at the end of the second year for the minicomputer of Problem 6.1.

6.3 A company purchased a site for a new plant which consisted of 100 acres at $10,000 per acre. It erected a manufacturing and office building of 150,000 square feet at an average cost of $35 per square foot. The total cost therefore was six and a quarter million dollars. The facility was depreciated over 15 years using straight line depreciation assuming a zero salvage value. What was the book value after 10 years?

6.4 A company in the plastics business is planning on getting into the thermoforming of plastic sheet to make margarine cups. The machine will cost $105,000 installed. They forecast an economic life of 15 years. Revenue from the machine is forecast at $50,000/year and operating, maintenance, and raw material costs of $24,000/year. Their corporate tax rate is 50%. The minimum acceptable rate of return is 18%. Determine the present worth of the after-tax cash flow in the following manner.
  a. Using straight line depreciation over 15 years with a $7,500 salvage at that time.
  b. Using a straight line depreciation over 5 years, depreciating it to its salvage value at the end of 15 years, its economic life.
  c. Using the ACRS depreciation schedule applicable to assets placed in service in 1986 and beyond.

6.5 A company plans to install a small computer to facilitate better inventory control in their warehousing operations. The economic life is expected to be 6 years with a salvage value of $7,000 at that time. First cost will be $49,000. The operating cost will be $24,000/year. The method of depreciation for tax and profit calculations is ACRS for 1986. The tax rate is 50%. Determine the present worth of their commitment to buy if their MARR is 18% after tax.

Recommended Further Reading

1. DeGarmo, E. Paul, Sullivan, William G., and Canada, John R. *Engineering Economy.* New York: Macmillan Publishing Co.
2. Grant, Eugene L., Ireson, W. Grant, and Leavenworth, Richard S. *Principles of Engineering Economy,* 7th ed. New York: John Wiley & Sons.
3. *Handbook on the Economic Recovery Act of 1981.* Englewood Cliffs, N.J.: Prentice-Hall, Inc.
4. White, John A., Agee, Marvin H., and Case, Kenneth E. *Principles of Engineering Economic Analysis,* 2nd ed. New York: John Wiley & Sons.

7 THE CASH FLOW CONCEPT

INTRODUCTION

In recent times, the term *cash flow* has come into common use in the news media and in company financial statements. Much confusion has arisen over the definition and use of cash flow. The term is usually defined as the net income after taxes plus depreciation and depletion. Accountants use the concept of *funds* or *money flow* which include cash flow and other *noncash items*. Nevertheless cash flow is an important concept and is used by financial and engineering cost analysts.

For the cost analysis of a venture or project, it is necessary to identify the sources, flow, and disposition of monies. A simple diagram analogous to the flow of materials through a process may be used to illustrate the cash flow concept. This diagram will be presented and discussed in the following section; it is called the *cash flow model*.

CASH FLOW MODEL

In any industrial process raw materials are charged into a plant and finished products exit. Figure 7.1 is a graphical representation of this process. A similar diagram may be drawn to illustrate the flow of money. Revenues from sales are fed into an operation, and, if the cash operating expenses are deducted, the operating income results. Figure 7.2 illustrates this process.

In an industrial process, it is necessary to have a supply of funds available to meet the demands of current expenses. These funds, called *working capital*, are used to purchase raw materials and to pay wages and salaries and other day-to-day expenses. Although working capital is initially charged into an operation at startup, it is replenished from sales. Over a period of time, the net flow of working capital into and out of an operation is zero, with none of it going into net annual operating expense or operating income. Figure 7.3 depicts the effect of working capital on a proposed venture.

If the above concept is expanded to include a company's operation, a money flow diagram can be constructed to demonstrate the source of cash

198

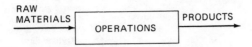

Figure 7.1. Process flow diagram. [Uhl and Hawkins (1971)]

Figure 7.2. Flow of money. [Uhl and Hawkins (1971)]

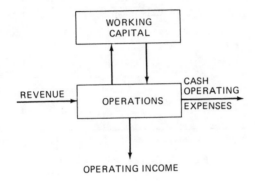

Figure 7.3. Money flow diagram with working capital. [Uhl and Hawkins (1971)]

flow. Of course, one should recognize that the money flow diagram, shown in Fig. 7.4, has been idealized. Let's look more closely at this money flow model.

The difference between revenue from sales and/or services and the cash operating expenses is usually called the *operating income*. If depreciation is deducted from the operating income, the gross profit results. Depreciation is handled as an annual operating expense prescribed by tax laws and appears as an expense item on annual operating expense sheets. Notice that depreciation is considered an internal cost and is retained in the company. It is customary to separate depreciation from net income after taxes, since a part of the net income may leave the company.

Depletion, which is an allowance for the consumption of such exhaustible natural resources as timber, sand, gravel, minerals, etc., is handled similarly.

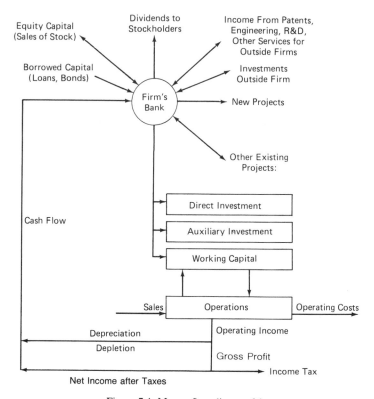

Figure 7.4. Money flow diagram.[2,3]

The gross profit is the result when depreciation and depletion are subtracted from the operating income. Next the income taxes are deducted from the gross profit to yield the net income after taxes. When the depreciation and depletion are added to the net income after taxes, the result is cash flow.

With the exception of revenues, cash operating expenses, and income taxes, all other funds flow into or out of the company through a fictitious company bank. The funds may be used to repay borrowed capital, purchase equity stock, pay dividends, purchase patents or technology, or invest in other companies, new projects, or other existing projects. Funds flow into the bank from borrowed capital, sale of stock income from patents and technology, income from outside investments, and cash flow generated by existing projects.

Part of the net income after taxes is used to pay dividends of the common stockholders, and part is retained; together with depreciation, it is used to meet the capital requirements of the company.

The firm's bank may be regarded as the part that decides how to invest, expand operations, etc. In this respect, it is similar to the operation of a commercial bank.

The lower section of the money flow diagram contains the definition of cash flow. Figure 7.5 isolates this part of the money flow diagram. Let's take 1 year of operation as a basis. If the annual cash operating expenses, C, are subtracted from the annual revenue, R, the operating income is $R - C$. Depreciation, D, is then subtracted from the operating income to yield the gross profit, $R\text{-}C\text{-}D$. If an income tax rate, t, is applied to the gross profit, then income taxes are $t(R\text{-}C\text{-}D)$. The net income (profit) becomes $(1 - t)(R\text{-}C\text{-}D)$. Cash flow, by definition, is net income after taxes plus depreciation and depletion. We shall assume that there is no depletion in this case. Therefore,

$$\text{Cash flow} = CF = D + (1 - t)(R\text{-}C\text{-}D) \qquad (7.1)$$

This equation may be rearranged to give:

$$CF = tD + (1 - t)R - (1 - t)C \qquad (7.2)$$

The term tD is the contribution to cash flow from depreciation and $(1 - t)R$ and $(1 - t)C$ are the contributions to cash flow from the revenues and cash operating expenses, respectively.

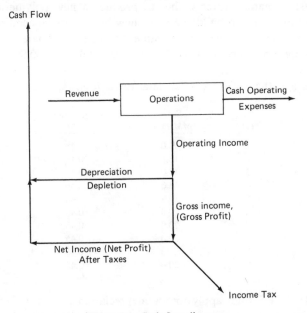

Figure 7.5. Cash flow diagram.

Equation (7.2) may be modified for use when comparing two cases. The modification involves differences:

$$\Delta CF = t\,\Delta D + (1-t)\,\Delta R - (1-t)\,\Delta C \qquad (7.3)$$

where

ΔCF = difference in cash flow, \$
ΔD = difference in depreciation, \$
ΔR = difference in revenue, \$, and
ΔC = difference in cash operating expenses, \$

In some instances, revenue may be unaffected by a process change. If that is so, then $\Delta R = 0$. An example of this would be to compare two processes for making the same product. The amount of product produced would be the same by either process; therefore $\Delta R = 0$.

An example of how the cash flow model may be used will be considered. We have found it advisable to draw the cash flow model, label the streams, and then proceed with the problem solution in tabular form.

EXAMPLE 7.1

A plastics manufacturer wishes to produce a new polymeric material for household use. To build the plant new land must be acquired, valued at \$200,000. The fixed capital investment has been estimated by a design-construction firm to be \$7,000,000. Approximately, \$1,300,000 of working capital will be required initially. The product is expected to have a 10-year life, and the projected sales data are as follows:

Year	Sales, MM lb/yr	Sales Price, $/lb
1	16.0	0.48
2	16.5	0.48
3	17.0	0.47
4	18.0	0.46
5	19.9	0.46
6	20.0	0.45
7	20.0	0.45
8	20.0	0.45
9	20.0	0.45
10	20.0	0.45

The 1981 ACRS rules apply for the depreciation of this equipment, and a 48% federal income tax rate may be assumed. Calculate the cash flow from sales each year of this venture (Table 7.1).

Table 7.1 Solution to Example 7.1.

YEAR	SALES MMLB/YR	SALES PRICE $/LB	ANNUAL SALES MM	TOTAL OPER. EXP.	DEP.	CASH OPER. EXP.	OPER. INCOME	DEP.	GROSS PROFIT	48% TAX	NIAT	DEP.	CASH FLOW
1	16.0	$0.48	$7.68	$4.96	$1.05	$3.91	$3.77	$1.05	$2.72	$1.31	$1.41	$1.05	$2.46
2	16.5	0.48	7.92	5.11	1.54	3.57	4.35	1.54	2.81	1.35	1.46	1.54	3.00
3	17.0	0.47	7.99	5.20	1.47	3.73	4.26	1.47	2.79	1.34	1.45	1.47	2.92
4	18.0	0.46	8.28	5.27	1.47	3.80	4.48	1.47	3.01	1.44	1.57	1.47	3.04
5	19.0	0.46	8.74	5.30	1.47	3.83	4.91	1.47	3.44	1.65	1.79	1.47	3.26
6	20.0	0.45	9.00	5.52	–0–	5.52	3.48	–0–	3.48	1.67	1.81	–0–	1.81
7	20.0	0.45	9.00	5.52	–0–	5.52	3.48	–0–	3.48	1.67	1.81	–0–	1.81
8	20.0	0.45	9.00	5.52	–0–	5.52	3.48	–0–	3.48	1.67	1.81	–0–	1.81
9	20.0	0.45	9.00	5.52	–0–	5.52	3.48	–0–	3.48	1.67	1.81	–0–	1.81
10	20.0	0.45	9.00	5.52	–0–	5.52	3.48	–0–	3.48	1.67	1.81	–0–	1.81

SUMMARY OF CAPITAL REQUIREMENTS

FCI	= $7,000,000
LAND	= 200,000
WC	= 1,300,000
TCI	= $8,500,000

203

In the foregoing example, the decrease in cash flow is significant between the 5th and 6th year, because depreciation is not considered beyond the 5th year under the ACRS depreciation rules.

COMPARISON OF ALTERNATIVES

The cash flow diagram, Fig. 7.6, is especially helpful for envisioning how cash flows in a project. This diagram can also be used very effectively when comparing alternative proposals. Uhl and Hawkins (1971) have developed the methodology. Example 7.2 will be used to illustrate the utility of this diagram.

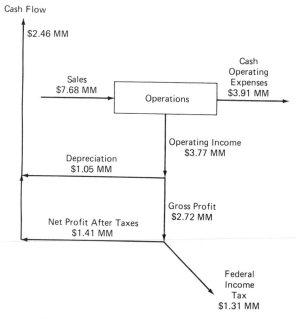

Figure 7.6. Cash flow diagram for Example 7.1—first year of operation.

EXAMPLE 7.2

PROBLEM STATEMENT:

A manufacturer of automobile springs finds that to debottleneck the operation, a new piece of equipment will be required. Two local vendors have presented the following information:

	VENDOR A	VENDOR B
Cost of Installed Equipment	$87,000	$110,000
Cash Operating Expenses (Annual)	10,650	9,850

The equipment is to be depreciated over a 5-year period by straight-line depreciation. The federal income tax rate is 46%. Which alternative should the manufacturer install, based upon a cash flow analysis?

SOLUTION:

Consider Case A (Vendor A) first by drawing a cash flow diagram.

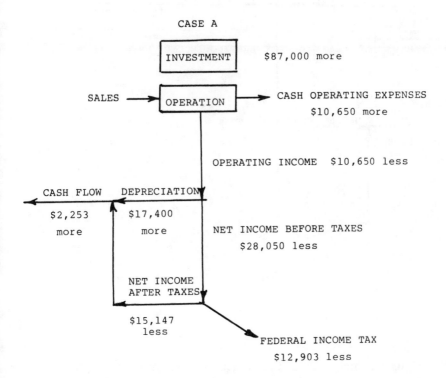

A basic assumption underlying this problem is that either Vendor A's or Vendor B's equipment will provide the same service. From the statement of the problem, $87,000 would have to be installed for Case A compared with the present. If this is done, then $10,650 more cash operating expenses are incurred. This results in $10,650 less operating income. If the equipment is installed, then $17,400 more depreciation may be claimed. The net income before taxes then becomes $28,050 less. The federal income tax (46%) is $12,903 less and the net income after taxes is $15,147 less. As cash flow is the algebraic sum of depreciation and net income after taxes, it becomes $2,253 more.

Next, let's consider Vendor B's proposal:

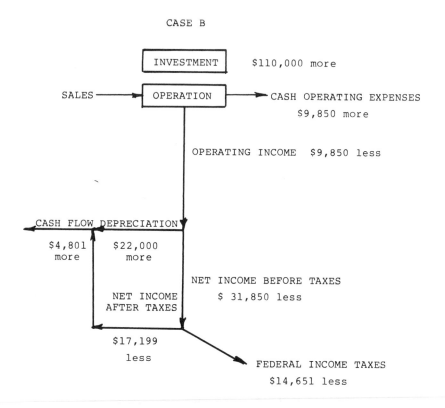

CASE B

INVESTMENT $110,000 more

SALES → OPERATION → CASH OPERATING EXPENSES $9,850 more

OPERATING INCOME $9,850 less

CASH FLOW DEPRECIATION

$4,801 more | $22,000 more

NET INCOME BEFORE TAXES $ 31,850 less

NET INCOME AFTER TAXES

$17,199 less

FEDERAL INCOME TAXES $14,651 less

Using the same analysis, Case B generates $4,801 more cash flow.

The problem may also be solved using the differences in cash flow between Cases A and B. For the resultant numbers to be positive, the larger investment should be compared to the smaller, or Case B versus Case A. Let's draw the cash flow diagram for the difference or incremental values.

By the difference method, $2,548 more cash flow is generated when Case B is considered versus Case A. This is exactly the same answer obtained by subtracting the cash flow generated by Case A, $2,253, in the first diagram, from the cash flow generated by Case B, $4,801. In the second diagram, therefore, Case B is preferred.

This "more-less" or "difference" analysis is particularly useful for small plant investment problems involving replacing or adding equipment.

CASE B VERSUS CASE A

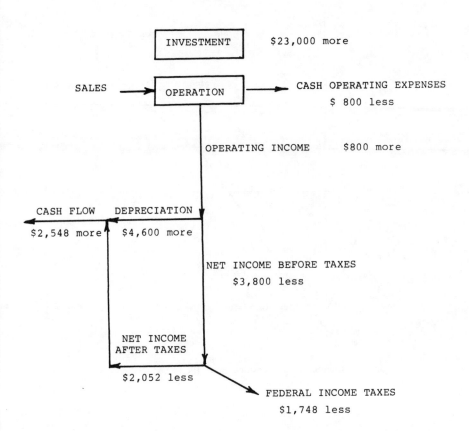

CASH POSITION CHART

Often we are interested in the flow of funds for a single project and not the entire enterprise. The expenditures for capital items as well as cash flow generated from revenues may be shown over the project's life on a diagram known as the *cumulative cash position chart.*

The selection of time zero is arbitrary. Usually, time zero is considered to be when the plant first produces salable products or provides service. Of course expenditures are made prior to time zero for the acquisition of land, the purchase of manufacturing equipment and buildings, and for working capital. The flows of cash from the project for these purposes are assigned a negative sign and, with the exception of working capital, occur at negative time, prior to time zero. Working capital is assumed to be charged to the

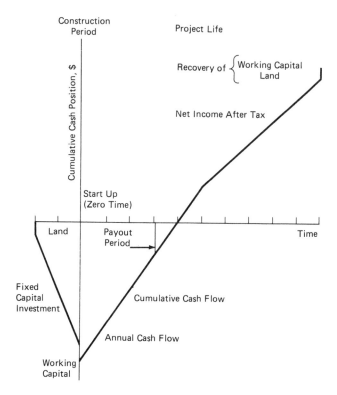

Figure 7.7. Cumulative cash position chart. [Perry and Chilton (1973)]

project at time zero. As the project begins and revenues are generated, positive cash flows begin to occur. Figure 7.7 represents the historical flow of cash into and out of a project. It also shows the cumulative effect of cash flow in the project. This chart is the cumulative cash position chart.

In the foregoing paragraph, time zero was an arbitrary choice. Sometimes it is more convenient to take time zero when the first funds are expended. This approach is used in those cases where equipment or expansions to an already existing operating unit take place. The selection of either time base is satisfactory for economic analysis, as long as consistency is maintained.

When the project terminates, adjustments are made for the recovery of land and working capital.

To illustrate the use of the cumulative cash position chart, an expansion of Example 7.1 will be used.

EXAMPLE 7.3

PROBLEM STATEMENT:

Reread Example 7.2. It is assumed that the fixed capital investment of $7,000,000 will be purchased and installed over a period of 2 years prior to startup. Land and working capital will be recovered at the end of the project life. With this information and the data from Example 7.2, prepare a cumulative cash position table and chart (Table 7.2).

SOLUTION:

A cumulative cash position chart for Example 7.3 is presented as Fig. 7.8. Land is charged to the project instantaneously 2 years prior to startup. The company may have purchased the land at that time or it may have owned the land for some time prior to the project's conception. In either case, the purchase price of the land is transferred to the project essentially instantaneously by the accountants. The fixed capital investment is purchased over 2 years prior to startup. Equipment is actually purchased and installed nonuniformly over that period in a fashion similar to that shown in Fig. 7.9. For simplicity, the cash outflow shall be considered to be uniform with

Table 7.2   Cumulative Cash Position Table.

| | CASH FLOWS IN $M | | |
TIME PERIOD	INVESTMENT	REVENUE	CUMULATIVE CASH POSITION
−2 yr at start	$ −200	–	−$ 200
−2 yr during			
−1 yr at start	−7,000	–	−7,200
−1 yr during			
0	−1,300	–	−8,500
1st yr	–	+$2,460	−6,040
2nd yr	–	3,000	−3,040
3rd yr	–	2,920	−120
4th yr	–	3,040	+2,920
5th yr	–	3,260	+6,180
6th yr	–	1,810	+7,990
7th yr	–	1,810	+9,800
8th yr	–	1,810	+11,610
9th yr	–	1,810	13.420
10th yr	–	1,810	15,230
End of 10th yr	+1,500	–	16,730

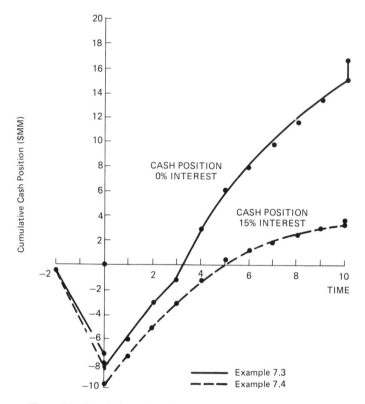

Figure 7.8. Cumulative cash position chart for Examples 7.3 and 7.4.

time. From an economic analysis standpoint, the simplification does not normally affect the decision, although the absolute value of the cash flow will vary when it is considered to be nonuniformly or uniformly dispensed.

At startup, working capital is charged to the project. The cash inflows from depreciation and sales begin to reduce the negative cumulative cash position, as can be seen in Table 7.2. The yearly cash flows are added, and a cumulative total is calculated for each project year. In the 5th year, the total investment has been paid off, and a net profit begins to accrue. In the 6th year, the depreciation part of cash flow is zero; therefore the net income of the taxes is the only element of cash flow. At the end of the 10th year, the land and working capital are recovered and are entered in the investment cash flow column. The value of the land and working capital are the last entry in the cumulative cash position table and chart.

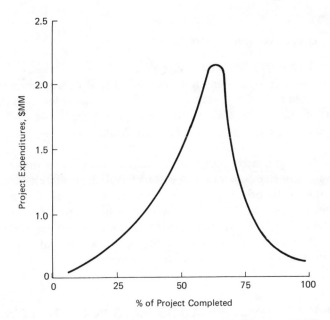

Figure 7.9. Typical cash flow pattern for a project. [Bauman (1961)]

Payout period, a measure of profitability, can be determined from the cumulative cash position chart. It is defined as the fixed capital investment divided by cash flow. At first glance, one might consider the payout period to occur where the cumulative cash position line crosses the time axis. This is not correct, because, as is apparent from Fig. 7.7, land and working capital have been included. To find the correct payout period, the sum of the ordinates for land and working capital must be subtracted. Therefore, the correct payout period lies to the left of the intersection of the cumulative cash position line and the time axis.

EFFECT OF THE TIME VALUE OF MONEY ON THE CASH POSITION CHART

Up to this point, we have not considered the time value of money, i.e., interest. In today's economy, this is a fact of life. Therefore, let's consider how the effect of interest changes the cash position chart in Example 7.3.

We suggest that the calculations be placed in tabular format. Such a procedure organizes the calculations and provides for quick review. To illustrate the methodology, Example 7.3 will be used but modified.

EXAMPLE 7.4

PROBLEM STATEMENT:

Reread Example 7.3. The company uses 15% continuous interest for present worth computations (discrete end-of-year or midyear convention could be used instead of continuous interest. The methodology is the same). Prepare a cumulative cash position table and cumulative cash position chart using 15% continuous interest (see Appendix).

Table 7.3 is the cumulative cash position table with 15% continuous interest. The cumulative cash position chart showing the results in Examples 7.3 and 7.4 is Fig. 7.8. The net effect of including interest in cash flow calculations is that the payout period is increased and the final cumulative cash position is less. There is a positive terminal present worth for this project of $3,767,000 when a 15% continuous interest rate is used. The lower the interest rate, the higher the project's terminal cash position. In Chapter 8, we will discuss the case when the terminal cash position is zero.

USE OF ELECTRONIC SPREADSHEETS IN CASH FLOW ANALYSIS

The development of electronic spreadsheets for use on microcomputers has reduced the amount of hand calculations, brought about quick cash flow

Table 7.3 Cumulative Cash Position Table.

TIME PERIOD	INVESTMENT	CASH FLOW $M	INTEREST FACTOR	PRESENT WORTH	CUMULATIVE CASH POSITION
−2 yr at start	$− 200	–	1.350	$− 270	$− 270
−2 yr during	$−7,000		1.166	−8,162	−8,432
−1 yr at start					
−1 yr during					
0	$−1,300		1.000	−1,300	−9,732
1		$+2,460	0.929	+2,285	−7,447
2		3,000	0.799	2,397	−5,050
3		2,920	0.688	2,009	−3,041
4		3,040	0.592	1,800	−1,241
5		3,260	0.510	1,663	+422
6		1,810	0.439	795	1,217
7		1,810	0.378	684	1,901
8		1,810	0.325	588	2,489
9		1,810	0.280	507	2,996
10		1,810	0.241	436	3,432
end 10	+1,500		0.223	335	3,767

analyses, and allowed studying many cases using the "what-if" approach. Examples of the electronic spreadsheets available are VISICALC, SUPER-CALC, MULTIPLAN, LOTUS 1, 2, and 3, and PERFECTCALC, to name a few of the more popular ones. Each of these spreadsheets has certain advantages and disadvantages, but all will readily perform cash flow analyses. The spreadsheet selected will depend to some extent upon the hardware and the user's personal preference.

The use of the electronic spreadsheet for cash flow analysis will be illustrated using Example 7.5.

EXAMPLE 7.5

PROBLEM STATEMENT:

R-J, Inc., is interested in investing in the manufacture of plastic bags. A fixed capital investment of $2,200,000 will be required to meet the projected demand. Land for this project is evaluated at $200,000, and $424,000 working capital will be required to launch the project. It will take 2 years to prepare the land site and erect the equipment. At the end of the project, land and working capital are recovered. For this 10-year project, the following income and cash operating expenses have been estimated:

Year	Income, $M	Cash Operating Expenses, $M
1	$3,000	$2,800
2	4,000	3,200
3	4,500	3,400
4	5,000	3,700
5	5,500	3,800
6	5,000	3,800
7	5,000	4,000
8	4,500	3,800
9	4,200	3,600
10	4,000	3,500

Assume that the 5-year ACRS depreciation rules are in effect and that the federal income tax rate is 46%. Using an electronic spreadsheet, develop a cash flow summary and a cash position chart for this project.

PROBLEM SOLUTION:

A cash flow summary (see Table 7.4) contains all the major elements of a cash flow analysis. Across the top of the sheet are the project years, starting with construction period at −2 years prior to startup to the end of the proposed project life at 10 years. A possible modification would

Table 7.4 Cash Flow Summary for Example 7.5.

YEAR	-2	-1	0	1	2	3	4	5	6	7	8	9	10	END 10
Investment														
Land	-200													
Fixed Capital Investment	-500	-1700												
Offsite Capital														
Allocated Capital														
Working Capital			-424											
Startup Expenses														
Interest														
Catalysts and Chemicals														
Licenses, Patents, Etc.														
Total Capital Investment	-700	-1700	-424											
Profit-Loss Statement														
Income				3000	4000	4500	5000	5500	5000	5000	4500	4200	4000	
Expenses														
Cash Operating Expenses				2800	3200	3400	3700	3800	3800	4000	3800	3600	3500	
Depreciation				330	484	462	462	462	0	0	0	0	0	
Total Operating Expenses				3130	3684	3862	4162	4262	3800	4000	3800	3600	3500	
Operating Income				200	800	1100	1300	1700	1200	1000	700	600	500	
Net Income Before Taxes				-130	316	638	838	1238	1200	1000	700	600	500	
Federal Income Taxes				0	145	293	385	569	552	460	322	276	230	
Net Income After Taxes				-130	171	345	453	669	648	540	378	324	270	
Cash Flow				200	655	807	915	1131	648	540	378	324	270	
Capital Recovery														624
Cumulative Cash Flow	-700	-2400	-2824	-2624	-1969	-1162	-247	882	1530	2070	2448	2772	3042	3666

All figures in table are in $M

be to include the calendar year above or below these numbers. In the upper left corner of the spreadsheet is the total capital investment summary. Not every study will include all the items constituting capital investment, but the template has been set up to provide the necessary flexibility to include all the items. Beneath the capital investment is the profit-loss (P&L) statement. Again, on the left side the significant items are listed as part of the template. At the bottom left are the items cash flow, capital recovery, and cumulative cash flow.

Systematically, the various numbers in Example 7.5 are entered at the appropriate places on the spreadsheet. With certain software, a similar template may be constructed that contains the equations used for calculating each numerical entry in the spreadsheet. The user may think of this template as underlying, beneath, or behind Table 7.4. Each spreadsheet requires certain commands to generate the template, and the respective software instructional manual should be consulted.

If the microcomputer is equipped with a graphics card, then, by following the software instructions, it is a simple task to generate a cumulative cash flow chart like Fig. 7.10 from the data in Example 7.5.

One of the major advantages of the electronic spreadsheet is that, once the base case for a venture is entered, including the required equations, the various entries may be changed and new cash flow patterns developed.

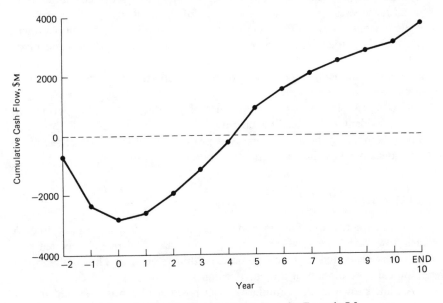

Figure 7.10. Cumulative cash flow diagram for Example 7.5.

Also, equations may be modified quickly. Therefore, many cases can be studied, printed, or plotted in a matter of minutes, whereas hand calculations could take hours. Further, management can inspect the results of a what-if study.

EFFECT OF CASH FLOW ON PROJECT OPERATIONS

In this chapter, we have described the movement and timing of cash with respect to a project. The *Cost Engineers' Notebook* (1961) defines cash flow as "the net flow of dollars into and out of a project." Why is cash flow so important to an operation? Jelen and Yaws (1978) discuss the subject of cash flow with respect to project investments, citing examples.

If the company is considering a new venture, it is essential to have sufficient cash flow in the early years to prevent the project from floundering. In these early years, markets may not have developed as projected, so sales and ultimately the cash flow generated might be less than expected. There is the possibility that manufacturing expenses were higher than estimated. Therefore, an adequate amount of cash flow is essential to ameliorate the two problems cited.

One of the major constituents of cash flow is depreciation. Accelerated depreciation methods help to increase substantially the cash flow in the early years of a project, allowing management flexibility to meet price competition, to reduce operating expenses, and to stabilize production. Of course, one of the reasons for accelerated depreciation is to recover the fixed investment earlier in the project life. Revisions to the depreciation methods have occurred historically whenever there has been a slowdown in the economy. These accelerated methods were instituted, in part, to stimulate the economy by stimulating investment.

Although cash flow is not a measure of profitability, it is important, as will be evident in succeeding chapters, in evaluating profitability. It is a way of comparing the attractiveness of projects Allen (1967). Further, many companies have as their objective the increase of cash flow.

SUMMARY

In this chapter, the definition and concept of cash flow were presented. A cash flow model was developed for a general case. This model depicted how cash was generated and how it flows within a project. The model was a graphical presentation of tabulated numbers.

A plot, known as the cumulative cash position plot was prepared from a cumulative cash flow chart, listing all the cash inflows and cash outflows.

The cumulative cash position plot is particularly useful since it provides the reader quickly how cash accumulates over the life of a project.

In subsequent chapters, the reader will find a use for the cash flow model and the cumulative cash position chart, especially those problems concerned with feasibility studies and choice between alternative investments.

This chapter concluded with an illustration of how electronic spreadsheets can be used effectively for presenting cash flow over the life of a project. With a graphic card in the microcomputer cumulative cash position charts may be prepared for cash flow spreadsheets.

Lastly, the movement and timing of cash flows with respect to a project were described. Although cash flow is not a measure of profitability, it is essential to have an adequate amount during the early life of a venture when markets are developing, operating expenses are high and new product acceptance is low. On the other hand, an inadequate amount of cash flow limits the growth of a company. This means that new projects should generate cash flow and not deplete the existing cash flow. So those ventures that can meet this objective are looked upon with favor.

With the cash flow, management often invests in other ventures to stimulate more cash flow. In this way companies meet "the growth" objective. This aspect of cash flow will be considered in Chapter 11. Bankers and investment houses consider cash flow essential when financing a venture. An excellent article on this subject has been written by Castle (1978).

PROBLEMS

7.1. Complete the cash flow table in Table 7.5.

7.2. To remedy a dust problem in the bulk packaging area of a fertilizer plant, two alternative wet-scrubbing systems have been proposed. The data are as follows:

	A	B
Installed Equipment Cost	$157,000	$230,000
Annual Cash Operating Expenses	32,000	28,000

Depreciation on the equipment is by the straight-line method over 5 years. The federal income tax rate is 46%. Compare the cash flows for each proposal, and indicate which alternative is to be preferred on the basis of cash flow. What conclusion or conclusions can you draw from this analysis? (Hint: It is suggested that Case B be compared with Case A. Use cash flow diagrams in your analysis).

7.3. A small manufacturing company is considering expanding its plastics operation.

Table 7.5

YEAR	NET SALES	CASH OPERATING EXPENSES	OPERATING INCOME	DEPRECIATION	NET INCOME BEFORE TAXES	FEDERAL INCOME TAXES (46%)	NET INCOME AFTER TAXES	DEPRECIATION	CASH FLOW	CUMULATIVE CASH FLOW
1	$100,000	$32,000		$30,000				$30,000		
2	125,000	38,000		44,000				44,000		
3	210,000	41,000		42,000				42,000		
4	240,000	50,000		42,000				42,000		
5	265,000	52,000		42,000				42,000		
6	300,000	55,000		0				0		
7	290,000	53,000		0				0		
8	265,000	54,000		0				0		
9	275,000	56,000		0				0		
10	255,000	55,000		0				0		

To meet sales demands, a new molding machine must be installed. An economic analysis based upon cash flow will have to be made using the following data:

	MACHINE A	MACHINE B
Installed Fixed Investment	$285,000	$197,000
Cash Operating Expenses/Year	42,000	38,000
Depreciation (Straight-line)	5 years	5 years

The federal income tax rate is 46%.
Determine the following:
  a. Cash flow difference for the installation of Machine A.
  b. Cash flow difference for the installation of Machine B.
  c. Using the difference method, compare Machine A with Machine B.
  d. On the basis of cash flow, which machine is to be preferred? Why?
Use cash flow diagrams in the analysis.

7.4. The Star Chemical Co. manufactures specialty products. The land for a proposed expenditure may be considered negligible, but the fixed capital investment is estimated to be $6,000,000. An adequate amount of working capital is estimated at $1,000,000. The equipment is to be purchased and installed over an 18-month period prior to startup. For this project time zero may be assumed at startup. It is assumed that the ACRS 5-year depreciation rules apply. The projected sales, selling price, and cash operating expenses are tabulated below. If the federal income tax rate is 46%, provide the following for management's consideration:
  a. a tabulated cash flow summary
  b. a cumulative cash position chart, labeling all lines on the chart
  c. the cumulative cash position at the end of the project (10 years)
How would the above change had time zero been selected as the beginning of construction? (Compare the numerical results of both.)

PROJECTED SALES

YEAR	SALES, LB/YR	SELLING PRICE, $/LB
1	15,000,000	$0.28
2	17,000,000	0.28
3	19,000,000	0.26
4	20,000,000	0.27
5	20,000,000	0.28
6	20,000,000	0.29
7	18,000,000	0.30
8	17,000,000	0.30
9	15,000,000	0.28
10	13,000,000	0.28

CASH OPERATING EXPENSES

YEAR	CASH OPERATING EXPENSE, $/LB
1	$0.16
2	0.16
3	0.15
4	0.15
5	0.15
6	0.16
7	0.17
8	0.17
9	0.18
10	0.18

7.5. A small electronics firm needs an inert as generator to provide an inert atmosphere for part of its silicon electronics manufacturing equipment. The generator can be purchased outright for $2,500,000 as a packaged unit from one manufacturer or leased from another for $300,000 per year. If the company decides to purchase the unit, its annual cash operating expenses are $600,000, but if it elects to lease the equipment, the lease charge is considered to be an operating expense. The company uses the 5-year ACRS depreciation rules and is subject to a 46% federal income tax rate. Develop a cash flow analysis for both cases. With the information provided above, discuss the advantages of leasing or purchasing the equipment, presenting both sets of figures to justify your analysis.

7.6. M and J Enterprises, Inc., a small "mom-and-pop" company, must purchase a new piece of equipment costing $500,000 installed to stay in full production. This new equipment will generate after-tax cash flows as follows:

Year	After-Tax Cash Flow
1	$ 75,000
2	80,000
3	90,000
4	100,000
5	82,000
6	76,000
7	72,000
8	69,000

At the end of the 3rd year, new bearings must be installed at $30,000 and again at the end of the 6th year for $40,000. Using the cumulative cash flow diagram, and assuming that time zero occurs when the equipment is purchased, show how the cash flows into and out of this venture are affected if the bearings are considered as

a. capital investment
b. operating expenses over 1 year

This company uses 5-year straight-line depreciation and is subject to a 46% federal income tax rate.

7.7. Farout Ventures is considering manufacturing a machine part. The fixed capital investment for the plant is estimated to be $8,000,000, and the construction period is expected to be 2 years. A market survey for the proposed 10-year project is:

Year	Sales Volume Units/Yr	Sales Price $/Unit
1	4.0	$0.68
2	5.0	0.66
3	7.0	0.65
4	8.0	0.64
5	8.5	0.64
6	8.7	0.63
7	9.0	0.62
8	8.5	0.64
9	8.2	0.65
10	7.8	0.70

Cash operating expenses are estimated as follows:

Year	Cash Operating Expenses
1	$2.0 MM
2	2.5
3	2.7
4	2.8
5	3.0
6	3.1
7	3.3
8	3.4
9	3.4
10	3.5

Depreciation is calculated according to the 1981 ACRS rules, using a 5-year life.

During the first year of construction, $3 million of the fixed investment is expended, and $4 million during the second year of construction, which is the year before startup, and during the startup year $1 million. At startup, $1 million of working capital is obtained. This company qualifies for a 10% investment tax credit. If the federal income tax rate is 46%, prepare a cash flow analysis for each year of the project life and a cumulative cash flow diagram. From your analysis, discuss the following:

a. your opinion of this proposed venture, backing all statements with numbers
b. the effect of the investment tax credit upon this venture

7.8. Rover Products, Inc., manufactures an intermediate that will be sold to two large pharmaceutical companies for processing into a vitamin supplement. Land for the project is $300,000, and startup expenses are estimated to be $500,000. The fixed capital investment for the project is $10,000,000, and a working capital of $2,000,000 is required. The company uses the 5-year ACRS depreciation rules and is subjected to a federal income tax rate of 46%. The Economic Projection Group has provided the following information:

PROJECTED SALES

YEAR	SALES, LB/YR	SELLING PRICE, $/LB
1	6,000,000	$0.86
2	6,500,000	0.87
3	7,000,000	0.87
4	8,000,000	0.88
5	10,000,000	0.88
6	10,000,000	0.88
7	10,000.000	0.88
8	9,000,000	0.89
9	7,000,000	0.88
10	6,000,000	0.87

CASH OPERATING EXPENSES

YEAR	CASH OPERATING EXPENSES, $/LB
1	$0.30
2	0.31
3	0.31
4	0.33
5	0.33
6	0.35
7	0.35
8	0.36
9	0.35
10	0.35

Management requests the following information:
  a. A cash flow summary at 0 and 15% continuous interest.
  b. A cumulative cash position chart at 0 and 15% continuous interest. Label all segments of this chart.

NOTE: It is recommended that Problems 7.4, 7.7, and 7.8 be solved with and without the use of an electronic spreadsheet.

REFERENCES

Uhl, V. W., and Hawkins, A. W. "Technical Economics for Engineers," AIChE Continuing Education Series #5. New York: American Institute of Chemical Engineers, 1971.

Cummings, L. W. T. "Economic Evaluation of New Ventures," Wharton School, University of Pennsylvania, 1963.
Rudd, D. F., and Watson, C. C. *Strategy in Process Engineering.* New York: John Wiley & Sons, Inc., 1968.
Perry, R. W., and Chilton, C. W., eds. *Chemical Engineers' Handbook,* 5th ed. New York: McGraw-Hill Book Co., 1973.
Bauman, H. C. *Ind. Eng. Chem.* 53 (8), 49–50A (1961).
American Association of Cost Engineers. *Cost Engineers' Notebook,* AA-4.000, May 1981.
Jelen, F. C., and Yaws, C. L. *Hydrocarbon Processing,* March 1978, pp. 77–81.
Allen, D. H. *Chem. Eng.* 74(14), 75–78 (1967).
Castle, G. R. *Hydrocarbon Processing,* March, 1978, pp. 90–98.

8 PROFITABILITY MEASURES

INTRODUCTION

In Chapter 5 we developed the concept of the time value of money and derived algebraic equations to move single amounts of money or uniform amounts of money from uniformly spaced periods forward or backward in time. The comparison of alternatives was discussed in one example by discounting cash flows to their present value, compounding to future values, determining equivalent uniform annual amounts, and by comparing internal rates of return on invested capital. In this chapter we will further discuss the measures of merit for decision-making between alternatives.

MINIMUM ACCEPTABLE RATE OF RETURN

Almost every business enterprise has limitations of total capital available for investment in a given period. For this reason, between an analysis of funds projected as available for a coming year and an analysis of its long-term position on sources of funds, a firm decides on an amount available for the coming year. It then evaluates the projects it has received. Table

Table 8.1 Projects Submitted to Budget Committee.

ITEM	COST $	RETURN %
A	20,000	24
B	20,000	18
C	40,000	29
D	30,000	32
E	60,000	22
F	16,000	14
G	10,000	20
H	42,000	10
Total	238,000	

8.1 lists what could be an annual submission of projects where some projects could be groups of similar items at the same rate of return.

The requests for appropriation could be placed in order of reducing return on investment and plotted as in Figure 8.1. If $170,000 were the maximum available for capital expenditure, then the dashed horizontal line of Figure 8.1 at 19% return would be the minimum acceptable rate of return (MARR). The total of projects proposed that have a greater return than the 19% is $160,000 and safely under the $170,000 maximum available.

The firm may take an additional step and rate the projects in terms of risk, e.g., high, medium, and low risk. The projects submitted, A through H, are rated on this basis in Table 8.2. On the basis of risk, the lowest acceptable rate might be modified as follows:

High-risk	22%
Moderate-risk	19%
Low-risk	17%

Examining Table 8.2 and using these criteria, projects G, F, and H would be ruled out, leaving D, C, A, E, and B, for a total of $170,000, which is equal to the funds projected to be available. Thus the minimum acceptable rate of return would be set. But that return must be greater than the average and the incremental cost of money to the organization.

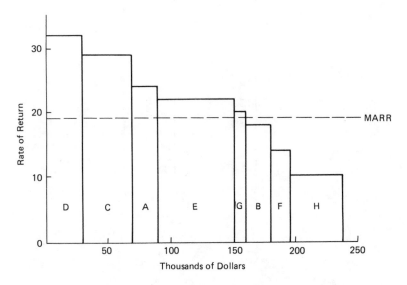

Figure 8.1. Projects in order of return.

Table 8.2 Projects Rated According to Risk Categories.

	HIGH-RISK			MEDIUM-RISK			LOW-RISK	
PROJECT	INVEST-MENT $	RATE OF RETURN %	PROJECT	INVEST-MENT $	RATE OF RETURN %	PROJECT	INVEST-MENT $	RATE OF RETURN %
D	30,000	32	C	40,000	29	E	60,000	22
G	10,000	20	A	20,000	24	B	20,000	18
			F	16,000	14	H	42,000	10

Establishing the Minimum Acceptable Rate of Return

The minimum acceptable rate of return may vary within a company from year to year and even within a given year. The basis of establishing the MARR varies widely from company to company within an industry and even more widely with firms in different industries. Methods of establishing the MARR include:

1. Use different rates of return, depending on degree of risk (as developed earlier in this chapter).
2. Develop risk factors based on such things as technological risk, market risk, obsolescence risk, and add the total risk factor to the firm's average cost of capital.
3. Use different rates for replacement and cost-reduction expenditures from new venture expenditures.
4. Use different rates for different magnitudes of capital investment.
5. Use the average cost of equity capital or expected stockholders' return for industries in similar businesses.
6. Add a fixed percentage to the cost of borrowed money.
7. Use different rates from as low as reasonable to as high as 60% to encourage or discourage capital investment requests, depending on whether the company is in good or poor financial position.
8. Use a rate that is based on the past actual rate of return for a prescribed period or an amount equal to that average.
9. Some companies establish their rates on a before-tax or before-depreciation-and-tax cash flow, though others set a rate after income taxes and allowances for investment credit.

And there are other methods and combinations of methods used today based on custom in the type of industry. The basis for establishing the MARR also varies with investment per sales dollar, capital intensity (investment per employee), economic life, economic forecast, and on and on. Suffice it to say there will probably never be a great deal of agreement.

AVERAGE COST OF CAPITAL

There are fundamentally two sources of capital to a private company or corporation: equity capital and borrowed money. Borrowed money may take the form of debentures, bonds, or bank mortgage money, but, in essence, borrowed money by these or other names are notes secured by some type of tangible assets that can be claimed if loan repayments are in default. The term of the loan may be as long as 30 years or as short as a few months.

Based on the soundness of a company, the interest rate on the loans can be as low as the quoted prime rate or several points above. It is not unusual for a small, relatively young company to be required to pay several points above the prime rate, depending on the marketability of its securities. Mature firms may have outstanding loans anywhere from 5% to as high as 15%, depending on the age of the loan. If new loans are involved in the source of capital to finance the projects proposed, then the new rate should be used as a factor in determining the average cost of capital.

The other source of capital is equity capital or retained earnings. Most companies have several shares of common stock held by the company, but approved by the board of directors. These treasury shares may be released to secure capital funds. And, of course, a company will use retained earnings to the extent of their availability. Retained earnings are generally recognized to have the same cost as equity capital raised through sale of common stock.

Though there are many formulas for the cost of equity capital, most of them can ultimately be simplified to the required rate of return on common equity, k_r, being equal to the expected dividend being paid at year end, d_1, divided by the current market price of the common stock, P_0, plus the growth rate of the company, g:

$$k_r = \frac{d_1}{P_0} + \text{expected } g \qquad 8.1$$

To illustrate, if a company's stock were selling at $20 per share, and the dividend were expected to total $2.00 for the year, and the annual growth rate of 5% were expected to continue, then the cost of the equity capital or retained earnings would be:

$$k_r = \frac{2.00}{20.00} + 5\% = 15\% \qquad 8.2$$

If the dividend were reduced, to put more capital back into the company to accelerate growth, then, although the ratio of the dividend to stock price would be reduced, the growth g would be larger.

There is an element of risk in investing in any company, because any number of things could happen to reduce the earning power or put a company in a tight financial position. Recognizing this risk, investors require a higher rate of return than they would in government bonds or certificates of deposit in a bank.

Consider a company that has decided to spend $170,000 and to fund the capital required by borrowing $90,000 at 13% interest and to make available $80,000 from retained earnings; the cost of capital to that company is developed in Table 8.3. Because interest is deductible before figuring tax, the after-tax cost of borrowing is important. With a combined federal and state tax of, say, 49%, and annual interest of 13%, the interest charge is .13 × 90,000, or $11,700. This $11,700 reduces the income tax to be paid by 49% of $11,700, or $5,733, resulting in a savings of $5,733. Therefore the after-tax net cost of the interest is $11,700 − $5,733, or $5,967, and the after-tax interest cost if $5,967 ÷ $90,000, or 6.63%.

However, the retained earnings are subject to income taxes and must be debited for the full cost of equity capital. As a result, the before-tax cost of $170,000 is 13.94%, and the after-tax cost is 10.57%. The overall return on the $170,000 total for five projects is $42,800, or 25.18% before tax. So the margin between the cost of money and the return on the projects is 25.18% −13.94%, or 11.24%, which amounts to $19,100 per year. This is an adequate margin for the MARR over the company's cost of capital money.

It should be recognized that a corporation must keep a balance between borrowed money, which is cheaper after tax and equity capital. If too much capital is borrowed, the debt/equity ratio becomes too high and the times/interest coverage ratio becomes too low. This will cause lenders to raise their interest rates, and purchasers of stock will worry about the soundness of the company and require higher potential earnings on the riskier stock, thus driving stock prices down, making equity financing more expensive.

If equity financing is relied on too heavily, the average cost of capital increases and stock is diluted, reducing the stock price. Thus a company looks at companies in similar businesses, recognizing that lending institutions as well as investors will compare the debt ratio (total debt divided by total assets) to other companies in the same industry and become suspicious if the ratio becomes too high. Conversely, if the debt ratio becomes too low compared with others in the same industry, a concern may develop that

Table 8.3 Average Cost of Capital and Effect of Income Taxes.

1. Amount required	$170,000
2. Amount from retained earnings and cash flow	80,000
3. Amount to be borrowed at 13%	90,000
4. Before-tax interest cost [(3) × .13]	11,700
5. After-tax interest cost [(4) × (1 − .49)]	5,967
6. Cost of equity [(2) × .15]	12,000
7. Total cost before taxes [(4) + (6)]	23,700
8. Total cost after taxes [(5) + (6)]	17,967
9. Average rate before taxes [(7) ÷ (1)]	13.94%
10. Average rate after taxes [(8) ÷ (1)]	10.57%

management may not be using good judgment in not taking advantage of leverage.

NET CASH FLOWS FOR INVESTMENT OPPORTUNITIES

All economic analysis decisions require some basis for comparison that measures the significant differences between investment opportunities and alternatives. The alternatives must be reduced to a common base so that a quantitative comparison can be made with consideration for the time value of money.

The common bases for comparison most usually used are the present-worth amount, the annual equivalent amount, the future-worth amount, and the rate of return. Payout period and payout period with interest are other bases sometimes used.

In an investment opportunity there are disbursements or costs. These are indicated as negative (−) because they are paid out. There are also receipts or revenue. These are indicated as positive (+) because they are income. At the same period we can take the algebraic sum of the positive and negative cash flows to show a net cash flow for that specific period.

Table 8.4 illustrates the concept of net cash flows. In this illustration an investor deposits $6,000 in the bank at time period 0. At the end of each year an additional $1,000 is invested in the account; $3,000 is withdrawn at the end of the 3rd year and $8,000 is withdrawn at the end of the 5th year. To the investor, a deposit in the bank is a negative number, and the

Table 8.4   An Illustration of Net Cash Flows.

a. As it appears to the investor

END OF YEAR	RECEIPTS	DISBURSEMENTS	NET CASH FLOW
0	0	−6,000	−6,000
1	0	−1,000	−1,000
2	+3,000	−1,000	+2,000
3	0	−1,000	−1,000
4		−1,000	−1,000
5	+8,000	−1,000	+7,000

b. As it appears to the banker

END OF YEAR	RECEIPTS	DISBURSEMENTS	NET CASH FLOW
0	+6,000	0	+6,000
1	+1,000	0	+1,000
2	+1,000	−3,000	−2,000
3	+1,000	0	+1,000
4	+1,000	0	+1,000
5	+1,000	−8,000	−7,000

All figures in table are in dollars.

withdrawal, or receipt, is a positive number. To the banker each cash flow is opposite in sign.

Equivalence

Just to review the concept of equivalence presented in Chapter 5, assume the interest paid at the bank of Table 8.4 was 5%. From the investors' standpoint the following equation could be written for the annual worth AW:

$$AW = -1000 - 6000 \, (A/P \; 5\%, \, 5 \; \text{yr}) + 3000 \, (P/F \; 5,2)(A/P \; 5,5)$$
$$+ \; 8000 \, (A/F \; 5,5)$$
$$= -1000 - 6000(0.2310) + 3000(0.9070)(0.2310) + 8000(0.1810)$$
$$= -\$309.45$$

The future worth FW of the series of cash flows would be determined by the equation:

$$FW = -6000(F/P \; 5,5) - 1000(F/A \; 5,5) + 3000(F/P \; 5,3) + 8000$$
$$= -6000(1.276) - 1000(5.526) + 3000(1.158) + 8000$$
$$= -1710.45$$

The present worth PW of the series of cash flows would be determined by the equation:

$$PW = -6000 - 1000(P/A \; 5,5) + 3000(P/F \; 5,2) + 8000(P/F \; 5,5)$$
$$= -1340.18$$

The three answers are equivalent. That is, with a 5-year period and 5% interest, $1,340.18 today is equivalent to $1,710.45 in 5 years, which is equivalent to $309.45 a year for the 5 years and

$$\$309.45/\text{yr} = \$1710.45(A/F \; 5,5) = \$1340.18(A/P \; 5,5) = AW$$

and

$$\$309.45(F/A \; 5,5) = \$1710.45 = \$1340.18(F/P \; 5,5) = FW$$

and

$$\$309.45(P/A \; 5,5) = \$1710.45(P/F \; 5,5) = \$1340.18 = PW$$

It will be noted that in all three solutions the results are negative, because the value of the money withdrawn is less than the value deposited. Thus the depositor has a balance in the bank at the end of the 5 years worth $1,710.45.

PRESENT WORTH

Thus from equivalence we have learned that for any given cash flow and specified interest rate there is an equivalent cash flow at any other period. So it is possible to convert any series of cash flows to a single value at a point in time and compare that value with another series of cash flows converted to a single value at the same point in time. Then by comparing these two alternative cash flows, the better alternative can be selected.

If the cash flows are brought to the present or to time zero, the analysis is called a *present-worth analysis.* That value obtained represents the equivalent value of a cash flow that, at a specified interest rate, either exceeds or fails to equal that interest rate desired.

EXAMPLE 8.1

A person with $5,000 to invest wanted at least a 10% return on his investment. The two alternatives of Table 8.5 were available. The *present worth* of Alternative A can be expressed in several ways, typical of most series of cash flows, but they all yield the same value

$$PW_A = -5,000 + 1,500(P/A\ 10,5) \overset{3,791}{} - 500(P/F\ 10.1) \overset{0.9091}{} = \$232$$

or

$$PW_A = -5,000 + 1,000(P/A\ 10,5) + 500(P/A\ 10,4)\overset{3.170}{}(P/F\ 10,1)$$
$$= \$232$$

Table 8.5 Alternatives for Investment for Example 8.1.

END OF YEAR	ALTERNATIVE A $	ALTERNATIVE B $
0	−5,000	−5,000
1	+1,000	+2,500
2	+1,500	+1,000
3	+1,500	+1,000
4	+1,500	+1,000
5	+1,500	+1,500

And Alternative B

$$PW_B = -5,000 + 2,500(P/F\ 10,1) + 1,000(P/A\ 10,4)(P/F\ 10,1) \\ + 500(P/F\ 10,5) = \$465$$

or

$$PW_B = -5,000 + 1,000(P/A\ 10,5) + 1,500(P/F\ 10,1) + 500(P/F\ 10,5) \\ = \$465$$

Alternative B yields 10% return on the $5,000 invested and returns $465 in addition, and Alternative A returns $232 beyond the 10%, so Alternative B is the better investment.

From a simple tabulation of cash flows, let us look at the evaluation of a more complicated opportunity in Example 8.2.

EXAMPLE 8.2

Your company is considering buying a robot for spot-welding in the sheet metal assembly shop. The installed cost consists of the following:

Robot purchase price FOB Erie, Pa.	$63,515
Freight	915
Electrical power and welding contacts	836
Base table for robot	315
Table for securing various sheet metal assemblies in programmed spots	1,119
Training maintenance personnel	250
Training operating personnel	110
	$67,060

The installation will increase productivity and result in uniform quality, increased sales, and reduced cost. The economic life has been estimated at 10 years, at which time the robot will have a value of $7,500. The net profit per year for each of the 10 years is shown in Table 8.6. The net profit figures are a result of forecast changes in labor cost and a cyclic market. The minimum acceptable rate of return is 20%. As shown in Table 8.6, the profit fails to meet the required MARR by $974 of present worth.

Example 8.2 may be typical of the level of analysis required by some corporations at the plant level. In companies that require that level of analysis at the plant level, additional financial considerations are added back at the

Table 8.6   Data and Calculations for Example 8.2.

EOY	NET PROFIT	(P/F 20%,10)	PRESENT WORTH
0	−$67,060	1.00000	−$67,060
1	+ 13,008	0.83333	10,840
2	+ 15,011	0.69444	10,424
3	+ 16,491	0.57870	9,544
4	+ 15,891	0.48225	7,663
5	+ 15,419	0.40188	6,197
6	+ 15,449	0.33490	5,174
7	+ 16,126	0.27908	4,500
8	+ 16,943	0.23257	3,940
9	+ 17,983	0.19381	3,485
10	+ 19,242	0.16151	3,108
Salvage	+ 7,500	0.16151	1,211

$$\sum_{t=0}^{n} F_t (P/F\ 20\%,t) = -974$$

corporate offices. For those technical people who are asked to make the economic analysis at the headquarters office or for those who may do it at the plant level, the calculation of after-tax cash flow will change the analysis appreciably. This can be seen in Example 8.3, which is a continuation of Example 8.2.

EXAMPLE 8.3

The robot installation described in Example 8.2 is to be depreciated by the ACRS method over 5 years using the 1986 allowed rates. The company buying the robot is at a federal incremental tax rate of 46% and a state tax rate of 7%. The after-tax cash flow is required with allowance for investment credit.

Solution:

The combined tax rate is

$$T_s + (1 - T_s)T_f = 0.07 + (1 - 0.07)0.46 = 0.4978 \text{ or } 49.78\%$$

where T_s is the state tax, and T_f is the federal tax rate (see Chapter 6). The investment tax credit is 10% of the initial investment, or $6,706. Details of the calculation are shown in Table 8.7.

In Example 8.3 on a cash flow basis after tax there is a return of 20%, and in addition there is additional cash generated equivalent to $14,439 on

Table 8.7 Data and Calculations for Example 8.3.

EOY	DEPRECIATION[a]	BTCF[b]	TAXES[c] $	AFTER-TAX CASH FLOW[d]	DISCOUNTED TO PRESENT WORTH[f]
0	—	−67,060	−6,706 ⎤[e]	−67,060	−67,060
1	13,412	+26,420	6,475 ⎦	+26,651	+22,209
2	21,459	+36,470	7,472	+28,988	+20,138
3	16,094	+32,585	8,209	+24,376	+14,106
4	10,730	+26,621	7,911	+18,710	+ 9,023
5	5,365	+20,784	7,676	+13,108	+ 5,268
6		+15,449	7,691	+ 7,758	+ 2,598
7		+16,126	8,028	+ 8,098	+ 2,260
8		+16,943	8,434	+ 8,509	+ 1,979
9		+17,983	8,952	+ 9,031	+ 1,750
10		+19,242	9,579	+ 9,663	+ 1,560
10		+ 7,500	3,734	+ 3,766	+ 608
					+14,439

[a] Based on ACRS 1986 allowed rate.
[b] The sum of net profit from Table 8.6 and column a.
[c] 49.78% of the net profit column of Table 8.6.
[d] BTCF minus taxes ($b - c$).
[e] The negative tax assumes the firm has a tax due from which the tax credit can be deducted.
[f] At MARR of 20%.

a present-worth basis. In other words, the investment of $67,060 had a return in terms of cash flow generated after tax of 20% and in addition generated $14,439 as a present-worth equivalent.

EXAMPLE 8.4

The company buying the robot decided to borrow $35,000 from the bank at 13% interest, making annual payments every year for 8 years to retire the debt in that time. How would that affect the return?

Solution:

The annual bank payment is

$$A = P \left[\frac{i(1+i)^n}{(1+i)^n - 1} \right] = 35,000 \left[\frac{0.13(1.13)^8}{(1.13)^8 - 1} \right]$$
$$= 35,000[0.208387] = \$7,293.54$$

The breakdown between principal and interest for each payment is shown in Table 8.8. The interest paid every year is deductible from income before calculating taxes owed. Thus our economic analysis must be redone as shown in Table 8.9.

In Table 8.9 the taxable income is the cash flow before tax (net profit plus depreciation) less depreciation and interest payments. The cash flow after tax (CFAT) (column 7) is the cash flow before tax (column 1) less the taxes (column 5) and the loan payment to the bank (column 6). The cash flow at time 0 is the cost of the robot, less the tax credit of 10% and less the proceeds of the bank loan, reflecting the out-of-pocket cost to the company of $32,060. The present worth of the cash flow after tax

Table 8.8 Principal and Interest Payments for Example 8.4.

EOY	PRINCIPAL OWED BEGINNING OF PERIOD	INTEREST PAYMENT	PRINCIPAL PAYMENT	PRINCIPAL OWED AFTER PAYMENT
			$	
1	35,000.00	4,550.00	2,743.54	32,256.46
2	32,256.46	4,193.34	3,100.19	29,156.27
3	29,156.27	3,790.32	3,503.22	25,653.05
4	25,653.05	3,334.90	3,958.64	21,694.41
5	21,694.41	2,820.27	4,473.26	17,221.15
6	17,221.15	2,238.75	5,054.79	12,166.36
7	12,166.36	1,581.63	5,711.91	6,454.45
8	6,454.45	839.08	6,454.45	0

Table 8.9 Data and Calculations for Example 8.4.

EOY	1. CASH FLOW BEFORE TAX[a]	2. DEPRECIATION[b]	3. INTEREST ON LOAN[c]	4. TAXABLE INCOME $1-(2+3)$	5. TAXES @ .4978	6. LOAN CASH FLOW	7. CASH FLOW AFTER TAX $1-5+6$	8. PRESENT WORTH OF CFAT
0	−67,060				−6,706	+35,000	−32,060	−32,060
1	+26,420	13,412	4,550	8,458	4,210	− 7,294	21,622	+18,018
2	+36,470	21,459	4,193	10,818	5,385	− 7,294	23,791	+16,522
3	+32,582	16,094	3,790	12,698	6,321	− 7,294	18,967	+10,976
4	+26,621	10,730	3,335	12,556	6,250	− 7,294	13,077	+ 6,306
5	+20,784	5,365	2,820	12,599	6,272	− 7,294	7,218	+ 2,901
6	+15,449		2,239	13,210	6,576	− 7,294	1,579	+ 529
7	+16,126		1,582	14,544	7,240	− 7,294	1,592	+ 444
8	+16,943		839	16,104	8,017	− 7,294	1,632	+ 380
9	+17,983			17,983	8,952		9,031	+ 1,750
10	+19,242			19,242	9,579		9,663	+ 1,561
10	+ 7,500			7,500	3,733		3,767	+ 608
								+27,935

[a] From Table 8.7.
[b] From Table 8.7.
[c] From Table 8.8.
[d] All figures are in $.

237

is the yearly cash flow multiplied by $(P/F\ 20\%,t)$, where t is the year of the cash flow. The result indicates a 20% return on the $32,060 invested by the company plus $27,935.

Example 8.4, beyond illustrating how to analyze an investment after tax where borrowed money is involved, also indicates the effect of leverage. The company borrowed money at 13% while using a MARR for its own investment of 20%. Thus it reduced its own investment and increased its dollar profit over the 20% return.

Examples 8.2, 8.3, and 8.4 illustrated a discounted cash flow analysis of an investment opportunity. In the examples, the same MARR of 20% was used in both Example 8.2 and 8.3. This is not a realistic comparison for two reasons: the depreciation was not included in Example 8.2, and the MARR would be set differently for after-tax analysis and before-tax analysis. Recognize that Example 8.4 may be criticized for charging the project with the interest on borrowed money. This is usually done on a corporate basis where the need and advantages for borrowing money on a corporatewide basis can be better analyzed by financial people. But for the small company such an analysis may be a valid one, particularly as an example of financial leverage.

In all examples presented to this point it has been assumed that the initial investment is all made at time zero. In larger projects 2, 3, or, in extreme cases, 5 or more years may be involved in the engineering, governmental approvals where needed, procurement, building of a facility, and startup. In these cases the expenditures made in the $-1, -2, \ldots, -t$ years are compounded forward to time zero in accordance with respect for the time value of money.

In our examples we have generally used discrete cash flows occurring at year end with discrete compounding (or discounting) occurring at year end. Since of course cash flows occur essentially continuously during the year, some companies adjust for this continuous flow by using the midyear convention, assuming that all cash flows as a discrete amount in the middle of the year. Tables have been prepared similar to the appendix in this book, but which are based on discrete midyear cashflows.

To achieve greater accuracy some analysts have adopted a practice of using continuous flow, continuous compounding factors in their calculations. Most analysts, however, feel the general lack of accuracy in the estimated investment, revenue, and disbursement figures does not justify the refinement.

Present-Worth Index

The present-worth evaluation developed in the foregoing examples yields a final answer, which is a number of dollars above or below the required rate of return. To compare projects some expression of the size of the investment needs to be involved in the single measure of merit. This has been done by dividing the numerical value of the present worth by the present worth of the investment to give a ratio called the *present-worth index:*

$$PWI = \frac{\text{Net present worth of all positive and negative cash flows}}{\text{Present worth of the capital investment}}$$

For Example 8.3 the values would be (from Table 8.7)

$$PWI = \frac{\$14,439}{\$67,060} = 0.215$$

For Example 8.4 (from Table 8.9)

$$PWI = \frac{\$27,935}{\$67,060} = 0.417$$

The present-worth index, where used, is used by corporations where a large number of projects are examined in competition for capital building funds.

ANNUAL WORTH

The equivalent uniform annual worth or annual cost (frequently abbreviated EUAW or EUAC) is popular because many people, even decision-makers, are unfamiliar with present worth (discounting), future worth (compounding), or even rate of return. Thus if all the variations in cash flow from year to year can be eliminated, and an investment can be said to result in an equivalent uniform annual flow of a certain number of dollars per year over (or under) the MARR, it is easily understood.

Investment Costs

In the analysis of the robot investment in Examples 8.2 to 8.4, there was a first investment of $67,060, a time horizon of 10 years, a salvage value of $7,500, and a MARR of 20%. If the investment cost were spread uniformly over 10 years and credit were given for the salvage value, the resulting equation for this or any other investment would be:

$$EUAC = P(A/P\ i,n) - S(A/F\ i,n) \qquad 8.3$$

but

$$(A/F\,i,n) = (A/P\,i,n) - i \qquad\qquad 8.4$$

thus

$$\begin{aligned}
\text{EUAC} &= P(A/P\,i,n) - S[(A/P\,i,n) - i] \\
&= P(A/P\,i,n) - S(A/P\,i,n) + S(i) \qquad\qquad 8.5 \\
&= (P - S)(A/P\,i,n) + S(i)
\end{aligned}$$

and the *investment cost* of the robot would be:

$$\begin{aligned}
& \qquad\qquad\qquad 0.23852 \\
\text{EUAC} &= (\$67,060 - \$7,500)(A/P\ 20\%,10) + \$7,500(0.20) \\
&= \$14,206 + \$1,500 = \$15,706 \text{ per year each year}
\end{aligned}$$

This then is the equivalent uniform annual cost for every year of the economic life. The annual receipts or savings must exceed the disbursements by this amount, or the 20% return will not be achieved. Equation 8.5 is referred to as the *capital recovery investment cost.*

By using a different statement of Eq. 8.4,

$$(A/F\,i,n) + i = (A/P\,i,n) \qquad\qquad 8.6$$

and substituting it in Eq. 8.4, we would get the following equation:

$$\begin{aligned}
\text{EUAC} &= P[(A/F\,i,n) + i] - S(A/F\,i,n) \\
&= P(A/F\,i,n) + Pi - S(A/F\,i,n) \qquad\qquad 8.7 \\
&= (P - S)(A/F\,i,n) + P(i)
\end{aligned}$$

This is referred to as the *sinking fund investment cost,* and it will give the same answer as the *capital recovery investment cost.* In our robot investment cost Eq. 8.7 would give:

$$\begin{aligned}
& \qquad\qquad\qquad 0.03852 \\
\text{EUAC} &= (\$67,060 - \$7,500)(A/F\ 20\%,10) + \$67,060(0.20) \\
&= \$2,294 + \$13,412 = \$15,706
\end{aligned}$$

The advantage of either equation over Eq. 8.4 is that only one factor need be looked up in the tables or calculated.

Annual Worth Analysis

An examination of Table 8.6 would indicate that the net profit before tax in only 4 years is below the figure of $15,706 and in 6 years is above. If we were to develop the uniform equivalent annual worth of the annual net profit figures of Table 8.6, they cannot be averaged. Instead each annual profit must be transferred by appropriate factor to either year 0 or year 10 and from there spread forward with an $(A/P\ 20\%,10)$ factor or spread backward with an $(A/F\ 20\%,10)$ factor.

Collecting the discounted values back at time zero was done in Table 8.6. If, in the present worth column of Table 8.6, we had left out the investment and salvage values, the total annual profits discounted individually to time 0 would be $63,485. Now, instead of handling each one separately, we can spread the total of all the yearly discounted values over the 10 years uniformly with an $(A/P\ 20\%,10)$ factor:

$$\overset{0.23852}{\text{EUAW} = \$64,875(A/P\ 20\%,10) = \$15,474}$$

This is less than the investment cost developed earlier of $15,706. Thus the total of net profit annually does not equal the investment cost of $15,706 − $15,474, or $232 per year. Alternatively stated, the investment has failed to achieve the 20% return on investment by $232 per year. The $232 on an annual-worth basis is equivalent to the $973 on a present-worth basis. That is,

$$\overset{0.23852}{\$973(A/P\ 20\%,10) = \$232}$$

and

$$\overset{4.1925}{\$232(P/A\ 20\%,10) = \$973}$$

In any economic analysis, unless the annual costs, or worths, for each year are equal (and in an actual problem they will not be), each cash flow is discounted back and collected as a present-worth value, and then the sum of all these values is converted to equivalent uniform annual values. They could, of course, as easily be compounded forward to a future worth at time n and then be discounted back to equivalent uniform annual values. The calculation of present worth from which the annual cost is obtained is more popular probably because present worth as a measure of merit or basis of comparison has been more popular than the future worth.

Analysis with No Positive Cash Flows

The analysis of the robot investment involved positive cash flows, or revenue. Occasionally cost reduction alternatives are proposed where no positive cash flow exists.

EXAMPLE 8.5

Consider the costs involved in a hand operation requiring three workers on day shift only at an annual cost of $39,000/year. One alternative would require spending $30,000 to reduce the labor cost by $\frac{1}{3}$ from $39,000/ year to $26,000/year. Another alternative would require spending a total of $50,000 and would cut labor costs by an additional $5,500. A third alternative would require spending $60,000, but would cut costs to $17,000 per year. Let the do-nothing case be Alternative A and the others be B, C, and D, respectively. With a 6-year period the three alternatives are described in Table 8.10.

Alternative A is the do-nothing alternative. Alternative B requires spending $30,000. Subtracting Alternative A from B would give the following cash flow:

EOY	CASH FLOW ALTERNATIVE B — ALTERNATIVE A
0	−$30,000
1	+ 13,000
2	+ 13,000
3	+ 13,000
4	+ 13,000
5	+ 13,000
6	+ 13,000

Table 8.10   Cash Flow Profiles for Three Investment Proposals with No Positive Cash Flows.

EOY	ALTERNATIVE A	ALTERNATIVE B	ALTERNATIVE C	ALTERNATIVE D
			$	
0	0	−30,000	−50,000	−60,000
1	−39,000	−26,000	−20,500	−17,000
2	−39,000	−26,000	−20,500	−17,000
3	−39,000	−26,000	−20,500	−17,000
4	−39,000	−26,000	−20,500	−17,000
5	−39,000	−26,000	−20,500	−17,000
6	−39,000	−26,000	−20,500	−17,000

If the MARR is 18% and if the expenditure of $30,000 yields this return or better, Alternative B is approved:

$$AW_{18\%}(B - A) = \overset{0.2859}{-\$30,000(A/P\ 18\%,6)} + \$13,000 \qquad 8.8$$
$$= -\$8,577 + \$13,000 = +\$4,423$$

Alternative B over Alternative A shows a return of $4,423 per year over the 18% MARR, so it is adopted. Alternative C is then compared with Alternative B by subtracting B from C, yielding the following cash flow:

EOY	CASH FLOW ALTERNATIVE C − ALTERNATIVE B
0	−$20,000
1	+ 5,500
2	+ 5,500
3	+ 5,500
4	+ 5,500
5	+ 5,500
6	+ 5,500

If the MARR of 18% is met or exceeded, then Alternative B is discarded and Alternative C adopted:

$$AW_{18\%}(C - B) = -\$20,000(0.2859) + \$5,500 \qquad 8.9$$
$$= -\$5,718 + \$5,500 = -\$218$$

The 18% MARR is not reached; thus Alternative B is retained, and Alternative C is discarded.

Next Alternative B is compared with Alternative D by subtracting B from D, yielding the following cash flow:

EOY	CASH FLOW ALTERNATIVE D − ALTERNATIVE B
0	−$30,000
1	+ 9,000
2	+ 9,000
3	+ 9,000
4	+ 9,000
5	+ 9,000
6	+ 9,000

Evaluating Alternative D as an increment of investment over Alternative B,

$$AW_{18\%}(D - B) = -\$30,000(0.2859) + \$9,000$$
$$= -\$8,577 + \$9,000 = +\$423 \qquad 8.10$$

So D is the selected alternative.

Incremental Analysis

Example 8.5 is an example of incremental analysis. Though it was used on an example without positive cash flows in the alternatives, it may also be used in analyses with positive and negative cash flows. It should be noted in the incremental study of Example 8.5 that Alternative C was discarded because the $20,000 incremental investment of Alternative C over B did not return the required 18% in its savings in labor over Alternative B. However, if Alternative C were compared with Alternative A, the following cash flow could be developed by subtracting A from C:

EOY	CASH FLOW ALTERNATIVE C − ALTERNATIVE A
0	−$50,000
1	+ 18,500
2	+ 18,500
3	+ 18,500
4	+ 18,500
5	+ 18,500
6	+ 18,500

From this cash flow the following equation can be written:

$$AW_{18\%}(C - A) = -\$50,000(0.2859) + \$18,500$$
$$= -\$14,295 + \$18,500 = +\$4,205 \qquad 8.11$$

which indicates that the required rate of 18% is exceeded. However, most of the return of Alternative C is achieved by spending the first $30,000 instead of the $50,000. The $30,000 of Alternative B has the required return, but the additional $20,000 that would be invested to implement Alternative C instead of Alternative B is not justified.

RATE OF RETURN

Table 8.11 indicates that in the incremental analysis the investment of $30,000 in Alternative B over the base case A met the required rate of return plus

Table 8.11 Summary of the Incremental Analysis of Example 8.5.

	CASH FLOW ALTERNATIVE B − ALTERNATIVE A $	CASH FLOW ALTERNATIVE C − ALTERNATIVE B $	CASH FLOW ALTERNATIVE D − ALTERNATIVE B $
Incremental investment	30,000	20,000	30,000
Incr. investment A.C.			
$P(A/P\ 18\%,6)$	8,577	5,718	8,577
Net annual revenue	13,000	5,500	9,000
EUAW @ 18%	+ 4,423	− 218	+ 423

$4,423 per year. So the rate of return is better than 18%, but how much better? In most cases the answer to that question would require a trial-and-error solution, i.e., pick a higher interest rate and calculate the equivalent uniform annual worth until that interest rate is determined that will equate the investment cost with the net receipts. In Eq. 8.6 restated

$$\text{AW}_{i\%}(\text{B} - \text{A}) = -\$30,000(A/P\ i\%,6) + \$13,000 = 0 \qquad 8.12$$

we want to equate the annual worth to zero by finding the interest rate i that is high enough to produce a capital recovery factor that, when multiplied by $30,000, will equal $13,000. Rearranging Eq. 8.12,

$$(A/P\ i\%,6) = \frac{\$13,000}{\$30,000} = 0.43333 \qquad 8.13$$

From Appendix A,

I	VALUE OF FACTOR	VALUE OF EQ. 8.10
20%	0.30071	+$3,978
30%	0.37839	+ 1,648
40%	0.46126	− 838

These data are plotted in Fig. 8.2. Linear interpolation will give the approximate rate of return:

$$\frac{40\% - 30\%}{i\% - 30\%} = \frac{1648 - (-838)}{1648 - 0}$$

$$i\% = \frac{10\%(1648)}{2486} + 30\%$$

$$= 30\% + 6.63\% = 36.63\%$$

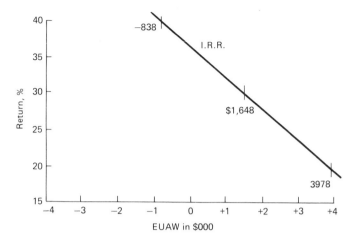

Figure 8.2. Interpolation for the internal rate of return for Example 8.5.

This would give an EUAC of +$15. Further refinement would divulge the answer 36.69%. This is the internal rate of return on the expenditure of $30,000 that saved $13,000 per year in labor costs, at an economic life of 6 years. For the internal rate of return for spending another $20,000 to install Alternative C and return $5,500, we restate Eq. 8.9

$$AW_{i\%}(C - B) = -\$20,000(A/P\ i\%,6) + \$5,500 = 0 \qquad 8.14$$

or

$$(A/P\ i\%,6) = \frac{\$5,500}{\$20,000} = 0.275 \qquad 8.15$$

I	VALUE OF FACTOR	VALUE OF EQ. 8.14
18%	0.28591	−$218
16%	0.27139	+ 72

By interpolation similar to that resulting from Fig. 8.2,

$$i\% = \frac{72}{290}(2\%) + 16\% = 16.5\%$$

This value is less than the minimum acceptable rate of return and was rejected. Similarly, the rate of return for Alternative D compared with Alternative B can be calculated. Restating Eq. 8.10,

$$\mathrm{AW}_{i\%}(\mathrm{D} - \mathrm{B}) = -\$30{,}000(A/P\,i\%,6) + \$9{,}000 = 0$$

$$(A/P\,i\%,6) = \frac{\$9{,}000}{\$30{,}000} = 0.3000$$

8.16

I	VALUE OF FACTOR	VALUE OF EQ. 8.14
18%	0.28591	+$423
20%	0.30071	− 21

By interpolation

$$i\% = \frac{423}{444}\,(2\%) + 18\% = 19.905\%$$

Thus the expenditure of $30,000 for a resultant savings of $9,800 is justified, for it exceeds the minimum acceptable rate of return by 1.9%. The return on spending the $60,000 for Alternative D compared with the do-nothing case can be calculated:

$$\mathrm{AW}_{i\%}(\mathrm{D} - \mathrm{A}) = -\$60{,}000(A/P\,i\%,6) + \$22{,}000$$

$$(A/P\,i\%,6) = \frac{\$22{,}000}{\$60{,}000} = 0.36667$$

8.17

I	VALUE OF FACTOR	VALUE OF EQ. 8.15
20%	0.30071	$3957.40
30%	0.37839	− 703.40

$$i = \frac{\$3957.40}{3957.40 + 703.40}\,(10\%) + 20\% = 28.5\%$$

Internal Rate of Return

The rate of return calculated on the data of Table 8.10 has been referred to by most authors as the *internal rate of return*. The adjective *internal* implies that there might be an *external rate of return*. The IRR (internal rate of return) is a determination of the interest that is earned on the investment. At each period a part of that investment is returned, so that at the end of the time studied, *n*, the investment has been returned. If the portions of the investment returned at intervals were not reinvested, that is, if they reposed in a box somewhere, then the rate calculated would not be valid, because the entire amount of the original investment was not earning that interest for the full economic life. The addition of the rate of return on the returned investment would constitute what is called the *external rate of return*. If funds recovered were invested at the same rate of return as the original investment, then the internal rate of return would be the same as the external rate of return. If the funds recovered were invested at a lower rate of return, then the internal rate of return would be higher.

It being impossible to forecast with any accuracy what the minimum acceptable rate of return will be in economic horizons of 10, 20, or 30 years, it is also impossible to estimate opportunities for future investment. Thus, it is highly unlikely that the external rate of return will be used by practicing economic analysts to guide executive decision-makers in the future.

Merit of the Rate-of-Return Method

In our previous examples by either the present-worth method or the annual-worth methods, a minimum acceptable rate of return was specified. Only those projects or alternatives were considered approved that yielded a balance equal to or greater than zero. And when it was greater, all that could be said was that the value of the present worth or annual worth exceeded the interest i by a certain number of dollars. In the rate-of-return method the actual rate of return of each alternative or their difference can be calculated.

The actual rate of return obtained in comparing alternatives will permit classifying projects by return, as was done earlier in the chapter.

It is important that rate of return be clearly understood. In Example 8.5 where $30,000 was invested to save $13,000 per year for 6 years, the return was later calculated as 36.63%. This does not mean that $30,000 was invested for 6 years and returned 36.63% every year. Instead, the $13,000 returned in the 1st year was used to cover the 36.63% interest on the $30,000 of $10,989, and the remainder was applied to reduce the investment to $27,989. And each subsequent year, as described in Table 8.12, a portion of the dollars returned was used for interest and another portion for reducing the unrecovered balance of the investment. At the end of time n, the entire investment is returned and the unrecovered balance every year earns the rate of return, in this case 36.63%.

FUTURE WORTH

The future-worth basis for comparing the merits of alternative proposals will give the same ratio as present worth or annual worth. This was shown in Chapter 5. That is, if Alternative B is better than Alternative A by a certain percentage in a present-worth analysis, then the annual-worth and

Table 8.12 The Meaning of Rate of Return.

EOY-t	CASH FLOW AT END OF YEAR t $	UNRECOVERED BALANCE AT BEGINNING OF YEAR t $	INTEREST ON UNRECOVERED BALANCE IN YEAR t $	UNRECOVERED BALANCE BEGINNING OF YEAR $t + 1$ $
0	−30,000	−	−	−30,000
1	+13,000	−30,000	10,989	27,989
2	+13,000	−27,989	10,252	25,241
3	+13,000	−25,241	9,246	21,487
4	+13,000	−21,487	7,871	16,358
5	+13,000	−16,358	5,992	9,350
6	+13,000	− 9,350	3,650	0

future-worth analyses will show the same percentage advantage. In Example 5.12 in Chapter 5 we found that their ratio is constant

$$\frac{PW_B}{PW_A} = \frac{AW_B}{AW_A} = \frac{FW_B}{FW_A} = \text{constant} \qquad 8.18$$

and was equal to 2.23 in that example. This will be true as long as i and n are fixed.

PAYOUT PERIOD

Example 8.2 presented the investment necessary to buy and install a robot. Table 8.6 detailed the net revenue on an annual basis from the installation of the robot. These figures are repeated in Table 8.13.

Many executives are concerned about cash flow and desire to know the time required to recover the first cost of an investment. They are interested in the net cash flow at interest equal to zero. The figures in Table 8.13 indicate in this problem that the answer is almost 4½ years.

This determination used net profit and did not allow for cash flow resulting from depreciation. It is calculated this way in many industries today. Although the economic analyst would frown on not recognizing the time value of money, the analyst must recognize that financial officers must concern themselves with forecasts of cash requirements and availability for several years into the future.

Payout Period with Interest

There are also executives who are interested in the payout period, but recognize the time value of money. For those executives the tabulation shown in

Table 8.13   Payout Calculations.

EOY	CASH FLOW $	BALANCE OF INVESTMENT UNRECOVERED $
0	−67,060	−67,060
1	+13,008	−54,052
2	+15,011	−39,041
3	+16,491	−22,550
4	+15,891	− 6,659
5	+15,419	+ 8,760
6	+15,449	
7	+16,126	
8	+16,943	
9	+17,983	
10	+19,242	

Table 8.14 would be required, where each year is discounted back to the present worth at time zero at 20% interest. This gives the same answer as Table 8.6, as we should expect. Table 8.6 shows that the investment failed to yield a 20% return by $974. Table 8.14 provides the same answer because the same discounting was used.

Payout Period with Depreciation Included

If the depreciation were included in the cash flow, a shorter payout period would result. This is illustrated by Table 8.15, which calculates payout period

Table 8.14.   Payout Calculations with Interest.

EOY	CASH FLOW $	CASH FLOW DISCOUNTED @ 20% $	BALANCE OF INVESTMENT UNRECOVERED $
0	−67,060	−67,060	−67,060
1	+13,008	+10,840	+56,220
2	+15,011	+10,424	−45,796
3	+16,491	+ 9,544	−36,252
4	+15,891	+ 7,663	−28,589
5	+15,419	+ 6,197	−22,392
6	+15,449	+ 5,174	−17,218
7	+16,126	+ 4,500	−12,718
8	+16,943	+ 3,940	− 8,778
9	+17,983	+ 3,485	− 5,293
10	+19,242	+ 3,108	− 2,185
Salvage	7,500	+ 1,211	− 974

Table 8.15 Payout Period with Depreciation Included and Without Interest.

EOY	CASH FLOW WITH DEPRECIATION[a] $	BALANCE OF INVESTMENT UNRECOVERED $
0	−67,060	−67,060
1	+26,240	−40,820
2	+36,470	− 4,350
3	+32,585	+28,235
4	+26,621	

[a] From column entitled BTCF of Table 8.7.

without discounting. The payout period is reduced by allowing for the depreciation as part of cash flow, from the 4½ years of Table 8.13 to the 2.13 years shown in Table 8.15. If the cash flow resulting from net profit and depreciation is discounted at 20%, as shown in Table 8.16, payout time is slightly over 3 years, compared with Table 8.14, which discounted the cash flow without depreciation and did not return the original investment.

If the effect of taxes is included, the payout of Table 8.16 of a little over 3 years is extended to a little over 4 years, as shown in Table 8.17. The after-tax cash flow of Table 8.17 is less than the before-tax cash flow of Table 8.16, which increases the payout.

Five tables have been presented thus far showing different methods employed to calculate payout period. The most popular one in industry is depicted in Table 8.15, which is a payout period that employs a cash flow in the usual usage, consisting of net profit and depreciation.

There is an increasing tendency in industry to employ a payout period based on cash flow, including depreciation, but also allowing for tax effects, but without discounting. This calculation is summarized in Table 8.18, which yields an answer of about 2½ years.

Table 8.16 Payout Period with Depreciation and with Interest.

EOY	CASH FLOW WITH DEPRECIATION[a] $	CASH FLOW DISCOUNTED @ 20% $	BALANCE OF INVESTMENT UNRECOVERED $
0	−67,060	−67,060	−67,060
1	+26,420	22,017	−45,043
2	+36,470	25,326	−19,717
3	+32,585	18,857	− 860
4	+26,621	12,838	+11,978

[a] From column entitled BTCF of Table 8.7.

Table 8.17 Payout Period with Depreciation Included, Calculated After Tax.

EOY	AFTER-TAX CASH FLOW[a] $	ATCF DISCOUNTED @ 20% $	BALANCE OF INVESTMENT UNRECOVERED $
0	−67,060	−67,060	−67,060
1	+26,651	+22,209	−44,851
2	+28,998	+20,138	−24,713
3	+24,376	+14,106	−10,607
4	+18,710	+ 9,023	− 1,584
5	+13,108	+ 5,267	+ 3,683

[a] From Table 8.7.

Table 8.18 Payout Period with Depreciation Calculated after Tax without Discounting.

EOY	ATCF $	BALANCE OF INVESTMENT UNRECOVERED $
0	−60,354	−60,354
1	+19,945	−40,409
2	+28,998	−11,411
3	+24,376	12,965

SUMMARY

In this chapter the reader was introduced to various quantitative measures for determining the profitability of a venture. They included payout period, internal rate of return, present worth, future worth, and incremental analysis. With the advent of computers, the time value of money has been included in these analyses; therefore the older methods of calculating profitability without interest have been replaced by the newer methods.

Incremental analysis is used frequently, especially when new equipment is added to already existing facilities to increase production or improve product quality. One should be alert to comparisons which are not on the same basis. Erroneous results with exceptionally high rates of return can be obtained, often giving ludicrous answers.

The methods in this chapter will be applied in Chapter 10, "Feasibility Analysis."

Suggested Further Reading

DeGarmo, E. Paul, Sullivan, William G., and Canada, John R. *Engineering Economy*. New York: Macmillan Publishing Co.

Grant, Eugene L., Ireson, W. Grant, and Leavenworth, Richard S. *Principles of Engineering Economy*, 7th ed. New York: John Wiley & Sons.

White, John A., Agee, Marvin H., and Case, Kenneth E. *Principles of Engineering Economic Analysis*, 2nd ed. New York: John Wiley & Sons.

PROBLEMS

8.1 You are employed in the Economic Analysis and Planning Section of a company and are asked to evaluate the following project:

Fixed Capital Investment	$3,600,000
Plant Capacity	5,000,000 lb/yr
Construction Period	one year beginning January 1987
Land	$100,000
Working Capital	$300,000
Project Life	10 years
Depreciation Life	5 years straight line
Potential Sales	4,000,000 lb/yr in 1987 increasing at 10% per year for each year of project life.
Selling Price	$0.80/lb
Cash Operating Expenses	$0.25/lb in 1987 and increasing 5% per year thereafter.
Income Tax	46%

a. Prepare a cumulative cash position chart.
b. Calculate the payout period without interest.
c. What is the internal rate of return?
d. In today's economy is this a project which is likely to be funded? Support your answer with numerical justifications.

8.2 Farout Venture, Inc. is considering a proposal for a fixed capital investment of $2,200,000 which will be purchased and installed uniformly over a period of one year prior to startup. Land on which the project is to be installed cost $200,000. The working capital for this venture is to be calculated as 15% of the total capital investment. Only these three items constitute the total capital investment. The total sales and total cash operating expenses are:

YEAR	TOTAL SALES	TOTAL CASH OPERATING EXPENSES
1987	$3,000,000	$2,800,000
1988	4,000,000	3,200,000
1989	4,500,000	3,400,000
1990	5,000,000	3,700,000
1991	5,500,000	3,800,000
1992	5,000,000	3,800,000
1993	5,000,000	4,000,000
1994	4,500,000	3,800,000
1995	4,200,000	3,600,000
1996	4,000,000	3,500,000

It may be assumed that the 5-year ACRS depreciation system is used and a 46% federal income tax applies. Calculate

a. Payout period with interest.
b. Net present worth of the project.
c. Future worth of the project.
d. What are your recommendations to management about this project?

Note: In this problem money is worth 15%.

8.3 Rework Problem 8.1 but include a 10% investment tax credit and the 5-year ACRS depreciation rates. How do these answers compare with those in Problem 8.1?

8.4 Excelsior Products, Inc., manufactures a line of food additives and supplements. An Executive Committee meeting is scheduled for the first part of next week to consider proposed new ventures for next year's budget. You have been asked by your supervisor to prepare the necessary information which is listed below. In order to fund projects, the company would have to cash some long-term securities which are currently yielding 11% compounded daily before taxes. The company has a policy of not going outside to borrow funds. The Executive Committee requires an internal rate of return of at least 20% after taxes and a maximum after-tax payout period of 3 years at this stage of project development. A 46% federal income tax rate applies and the company uses the ACRS depreciation guidelines of 15, 22, 21, 21, 21%. The expected project life is 10 years. In both cases, you may assume that all the product made in a year is sold.

KEEN SALT SUBSTITUTE

The following information was obtained from the marketing and manufacturing liason personnel:

YEAR	SALES, M LB/YR	SALES PRICE, $/LB	CASH OPERATING EXPENSES, $/LB
1	15,000	$0.33	$0.18
2	17,000	0.35	0.17
3	19,000	0.36	0.16
4	20,000	0.35	0.16
5	22,000	0.35	0.16
6	20,000	0.30	0.18
7	18,000	0.30	0.18
8	17,000	0.32	0.19
9	15,000	0.31	0.19
10	12,000	0.29	0.20

Fixed Capital Investment = $6,000,000
Land   =   100,000
Working Capital   = 1,000,000

The equipment is to be purchased and installed over a period of 1½ years prior to startup.

MSG Substitute

For this project the data are:

YEAR	SALES, M LB/YR	SALES PRICE, $/LB	CASH OPERATING EXPENSES, $/LB
1	6,000	$0.86	$0.32
2	6,500	0.87	0.31
3	7,000	0.87	0.30
4	8,000	0.89	0.32
5	10,000	0.90	0.33
6	11,000	0.88	0.35
7	10,000	0.87	0.35
8	9,000	0.86	0.36
9	7,000	0.86	0.36
10	5,500	0.85	0.35

Fixed Capital Investment = $10,000,000
Land   =   100,000
Working Capital   =   2,000,000

The equipment is to be purchased and installed over a 2-year period prior to startup.

Management uses continuous compounding in project feasibility studies. What course of action would you recommend to management? Be sure to substantiate your recommendations.

8.5 The plant in which you are working is considering the installation of a small scrubbing system to recover a salable dust which is currently being lost through venting to the atmosphere. Also, the local pollution control commission has received a complaint from the company's neighbors. The following data have been collected on four commercial scrubbing systems:

	SYSTEM			
	1	2	3	4
Fixed Capital Investment	$10,000	$16,000	$20,000	$26,000
Cash Operating Expenses $/yr	100	200	250	300
Value of Product Recovered, $/yr	4,000	5,800	6,200	7,800

Depreciation may be taken as 20% of the Fixed Capital Investment per year. You may neglect the following for this analysis:

time value of money
income tax effects
working capital

If your company requires a 20% return before taxes, which system would you recommend?

9 SENSITIVITY AND UNCERTAINTY ANALYSIS

INTRODUCTION

In Chapter 8, we assumed that all values of applicable costs, revenues, economic lives, and minimum acceptable rates of return were known with certainty. This was done so that attention could be focused on the methodology of economic analysis and, therefrom, decision-making. The high degree of confidence in such values, supplied and used without reservation, is usually referred to as *analysis under assumed certainty*. And decisions made on the basis of an analysis with these values are usually referred to as *decisions under certainty*. These expressions are misleading, because it is rare indeed when estimates of future costs and revenues (or the quantities behind them) can be assumed to be exact or even reasonably so.

Of course, in simple contracts, such as an agreement to pay the jeweler $10 per month for 12 months for the $100 watch, the time, period cost, and present worth are fixed with certainty. But any capital investment designed to save money or reduce costs will be analyzed based on capital costs that may be in turn based on estimates of labor costs and productivity, as well as on estimates of the cost of capital building materials. Operating or manufacturing costs may also be based on estimates of labor costs and productivity, as well as material cost estimates. Revenues also may be based on estimates, which may be influenced by share of the market, market supply-and-demand flexibility, cost of selling and servicing, and any number of other factors, some of which may be hidden.

Thus in almost every situation there is some level of doubt as to the ultimate result of an investment. This chapter will present and discuss several methods used by practicing economists in analyzing investments where the exact value of an element is in doubt.

BREAK-EVEN ANALYSIS

In Chapter 8 the concept of equivalence was used by solving for the value of a given parameter, such that two cash profiles be equivalent. Another way of stating the problem would have been: "Find a value of *x*, such that a break-even situation will exist between the two alternatives." Break-even analysis is a familiar concept and can be of value when a level of uncertainty exists. Information obtained from a break-even analysis can be of assistance in decision-making when examining an investment alternative involving uncertainty in the value of one of the parameters, when determining the effect of lowering the price to achieve greater volume, or when examining the effect of a change in any of the parameters. Example 9.1 is an example of a solution for a break-even point, given certain conditions.

Classical Break-Even Chart

EXAMPLE 9.1

Suppose the ABC Co. is evaluating manufacturing a new product and the following data have been estimated:

Selling price per unit	$30.00
Capital investment required	$1,750,000
Fixed cost per year	$400,000
Operating and maintenance cost per hour	$200
Hours required to produce 1,000 units	25
Planning horizon	10 years
Minimum acceptable rate of return (MARR)	18%
Salvage at end of 10 years	$250,000

Letting *x* denote the annual sales or production of the product, and setting the equation equal to zero, we can determine a point where revenue is equal to cost, or the break-even point:

$$AW(18\%) = 0 = -[\$1,750,000(A/P\ 18,10) - \$150,000(A/F\ 18,10.)]$$
$$-\$400,000 - \frac{\$200(25)x}{1000} + \$30x$$

Solving for *x* gives a break-even value of 31,151 new products per year. This is the point at which the company will receive its 18% return on investment but no more. At volumes above 31,151 it will have increasing profit.

The break-even chart for Example 9.1 is shown in Fig. 9.1. The shaded area to the right of the break-even point represents profit (above the 18% return on invested capital), and the shaded area to the left of the break-

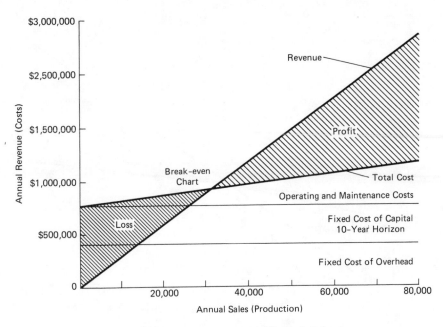

Figure 9.1. Breakeven chart for Example 9.1.

even point represents loss. The relationship among cost, volume, and revenue determines whether a venture will be profitable.

Profit is determined by interaction of selling price, volume, fixed costs, and variable costs. In Example 9.1 a major cost is the high fixed cost due to the high investment or capital cost. If capital cost were reduced by $500,000 and salvage value were correspondingly reduced to $150,000, but operating and maintenance costs increased by $80 per hour, would potential profit increase? Figure 9.2 shows the result. The break-even point is lowered from 31,818 to 29,207 units, but the potential profit at 70,000 units for example is reduced by about $150,000, or about 12% of the investment. The management would probably not decide to reduce capital cost with this exchange for increased operating cost and a resulting reduction in profit at higher sales and production rate.

By a similar analysis it could be determined whether a drop in price to achieve a larger share of the market were justified. If the price were dropped from $30 to $29 per unit, the total revenue curve would change as shown in Fig. 9.3. If the sales volume were to increase from 60,000 units to 80,000, because of an increase in the size of the total market, then the profit would probably increase from about $700,000 to about $1,000,000. If the total market volume did not increase—rather the increased volume was based on a larger

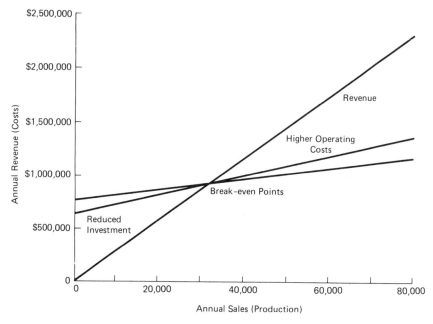

Figure 9.2. A reduction in fixed cost and an increase in variable cost.

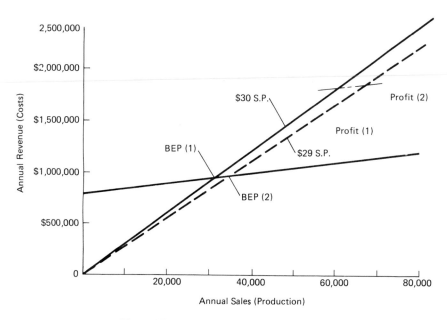

Figure 9.3. Effect of reduction in selling price.

share of the market—then the competition might also reduce prices to meet our drop, and we could drop without a change in volume to about $140,000 in total revenue. Based on a sales rate of 60,000 units per year, if the price is dropped from $30 to $29, an increase in sales of approximately 6,500 units must be achieved to maintain the same profit that was attained before the price was reduced.

Less Idealistic Break-Even Chart

The break-even chart is a simple pictorial representation that permits the decision-maker a graphic picture of the effects of changing parameters. The example used for the foregoing figures assumed a rather idealistic situation in which the sales were constant, yielding a straight revenue line. This seldom happens, because the revenue line represents net sales, allowing for selling, advertising, shipping, and warehousing costs, any of which might increase, causing a flattening of the revenue curve at higher volumes.

Also the total cost curve has been shown as a straight line, reflecting a constant variable cost. This is seldom the situation. Usually operating costs are high with very limited production, go through a minimum at some optimum productivity level, then increase as production is pushed beyond "normal" capacity.

As a result, a break-even chart could look like the one shown in Fig. 9.4, where the revenue line curves downward as it moves to the right, indicating that price reductions are necessary to get higher sales volume. A line from the origin (zero revenue and zero production) tangent to the total cost curve touches the cost curve at point x, which is the point of lowest average unit cost.

The slopes at any given point of the total cost and total revenue curves measure the margin cost (MC) and marginal revenue (MR), respectively. A line drawn from the origin to any point on the revenue curve will have a slope equal to the average unit selling price (total $/units sold). A line drawn from the origin to any point on the cost curve will have a slope equal to the average unit cost (total $/units produced). Where a vertical line will intersect both curves at points where the slopes of the two curves are equal, MR is equal to MC, and profits are at a maximum.

Cash Break-Even Analysis

In Chapter 6 we showed that depreciation is subtracted from income before obtaining profit. Thus a company could be breaking even, that is, not making a profit or experiencing a loss, and still have a positive cash flow, because depreciation is subtracted as though it were an expense, but it is paid to

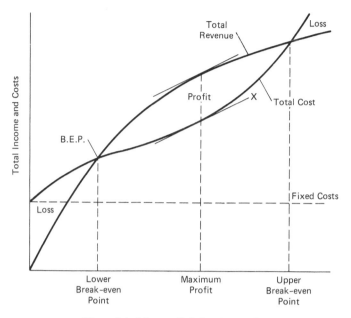

Figure 9.4. More realistic breakeven plot.

no one. This is described in Fig. 9.5. It will be noted that the break-even point is 31,818, and the cash flow break-even point is about 19,800 units. For illustrative purposes a straight-line depreciation over 5 years was used. In a cyclical business it would be possible for our hypothetical company to make large profits during years of high sales volume, be below the break-even point during years of low sales volume, and still be above the cash break-even point. Thus, risks of insolvency or inability to meet cash obligations would be small.

Operating Leverage

In the business world there are two types of leverage: (1) financial leverage, and (2) operating leverage. In both types, a high degree of leverage implies that a relatively small change in sales results in a large change in profits. Financial leverage was discussed in Chapter 1. Operating leverage is described in Fig. 9.6. Three companies, X, Y, and Z, are described with differing amounts of leverage. Each firm sells the same product at the same price. Firm X has the highest fixed costs and the lowest variable costs, while Firm Z has the lowest fixed costs and the highest variable costs. The characteristics of each firm are described in Table 9.1.

Note in Fig. 9.6 that Firm X has a high fixed cost, probably as a result

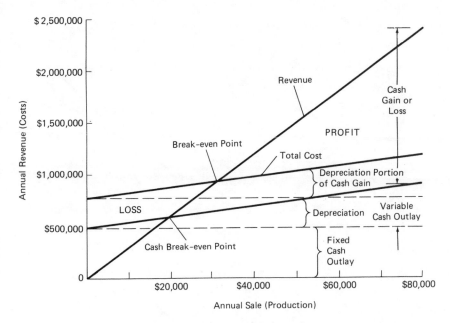

Figure 9.5. Cash flow breakeven point.

of a highly automated plant, resulting in a low variable cost relative to Firms Y and Z, because of a smaller labor force. Firm Z has little or no automated equipment and thus has low fixed costs and high labor or variable cost. Firm Y is in between. Firm Z has the highest slope variable cost line and the lowest break-even point, but the lowest profit above the 40,000-unit sales rate. At a 20,000-unit production level, Z breaks even, but Y loses $6,000 and X loses $18,000. But they may both have a positive cash flow. When X reaches its break-even point, its profits increase much faster than those of its competitors, exceeding them above 50,000 units.

Operating leverage is the change in profit resulting from a change in units sold, or, algebraically,

$$\text{Operating leverage} = \frac{\Delta \text{ Profits}}{\Delta \text{ Sales}}$$

$$OL(X) = \frac{\$15,000}{10,000 \text{ units}} = 1.5$$

$$OL(Y) = \frac{\$12,000}{10,000 \text{ units}} = 1.2$$

$$OL(Z) = \frac{\$7,500}{10,000 \text{ units}} = 0.75$$

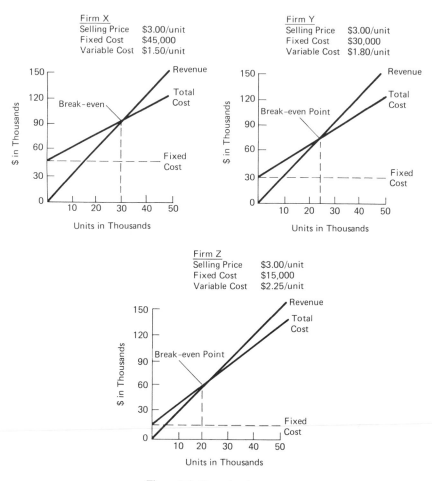

Figure 9.6. Operating leverage.

Table 9.1 Data for Fig. 9.6.

UNITS SOLD	SALES REVENUE	COSTS, $			PROFITS, $		
		X	Y	Z	X	Y	Z
10,000	30,000	60,000	48,000	37,500	−30,000	−18,000	−7,500
20,000	60,000	75,000	66,000	60,000	−15,000	−6,000	0
30,000	90,000	90,000	84,000	82,500	0	6,000	7,500
40,000	120,000	105,000	102,000	105,000	15,000	18,000	15,000
50,000	150,000	120,000	120,000	127,500	30,000	30,000	22,500
60,000	180,000	135,000	138,000	150,000	45,000	42,000	30,000

This will give a consistent value for operating leverage at any operating level with a linear break-even model. Operating leverage is also defined as the percentage change in profit resulting from a percentage change in units sold, or, algebraically,

$$\text{Operating leverage} = \frac{\dfrac{\Delta \text{ profit}}{\text{profit}}}{\dfrac{\Delta \text{ sales}}{\text{sales}}}$$

If this definition is used, the base sales level must be specified, for the same break-even graph for the same firm will give different values of operating leverage at different sales levels.

The calculated operating leverage figures show that Firm X, which has the highest operating leverage, is the most sensitive to sales volume, the same pattern that Fig. 9.6 shows graphically.

SENSITIVITY ANALYSIS

Almost all data used in an economic study are obtained as estimates of anticipated results, and therefore a degree of uncertainty exists. Questions reasonably occur, such as, "What if the capital investment is greater than the estimate?" or "What if the revenue turns out to be 10% less than estimated?" These questions, referred to as the "what-if" questions, can be resolved by determining the effect of percentage changes in pertinent variables. Plotting the results will many times give a good graphical picture of the effect of errors in estimates and may indeed indicate which variable ought to be studied more carefully. This is best illustrated by an example.

EXAMPLE 9.2

An investor is considering entering the fast-food business through one of the franchised chains. Investment, cost, and revenue have been estimated as follows:

Property	$200,000	
Building, landscaping, and parking	96,000	
Equipment	31,000	
Cost of franchise	50,000	
Total investment		$377,000
Time horizon	10 years	
Salvage value at 10 years		220,000
Revenue		735,000

Labor

Counter	$4/hr × 8 hr/day × 6 × 365 =	105,200
Cooks	$5/hr × 8 hr/day × 4 × 365 =	58,400
Managers	1. $6/hr × 2000 hr/yr	12,000
	2. $8/hr × 2000 hr/yr	16,000
	3. $10/hr × 2000 hr/yr	20,000
Fringe benefits	18%	38,300

Total payroll	$249,900
Food costs, 50% of revenue	367,500
Utilities	17,000
Local real estate taxes	2,300
Total operating costs	$636,700

Annual investment cost
$P(A/P, 15,10) - S(A/F, 15,10)$
377,000(.1993) − 220,000(.0493)
75,118 − 10,835   64,290

Annual profit
735,000 − 636,700 − 64,290   34.010

Thus if all the estimates were precise, the investor would receive a 15% return on his investment and in addition receive $34,010 per year profit above the 15%. But it is reasonable to expect that the estimates are not precise. In practice, depending on the time spent in obtaining data for the estimates, the estimates may be off by as much as 30%, as we have seen in Chapter 3.

So it is reasonable to examine the effects of errors in estimating the data. In Table 9.2 the effect of errors in the estimate of the cost of labor has been calculated. If the actual labor is increased by 10, 20, or 30%, the effects are shown on the right-hand side of the table; if the costs are less than the estimate, these costs are shown on the left-hand side. It will be noted that somewhere between a 10 and 20% increase above the estimate, the profit above a 15% return disappears.

Table 9.2 Effect of Errors in Estimates of Payroll Costs on Profit of the Fast-Food Restaurant.

	−30%	−20%	−10%	BASE CASE	+10%	+ 20%	+30%
Revenue	735,000	735,000	735,000	735,000	735,000	735,000	735,000
Labor Cost	164,930	199,920	224,910	249,900	274,890	299,880	324,870
Other Cost	386,800	386,800	386,800	386,800	386,800	386,800	386,000
Invest. Cost	64,290	64,290	64,290	64,290	64,290	64,290	64,290
Profit (loss)	118,980	83,990	59,000	34,010	9,020	(15,970)	(40,960)

Table 9.3   Effect of Errors in Estimates of Food Costs on Profit of the Fast-Food Restaurant (Dollars).

	−30%	−20%	−10%	BASE CASE	+10%	+20%	+30%
Revenue	735,000	735,000	735,000	735,000	735,000	735,000	735,000
Food Costs	257,250	294,000	330,750	367,500	404,250	441,000	477,750
Other Costs	269,200	269,200	269,200	269,200	269,200	269,200	269,200
Invest. Costs	64,290	64,290	64,290	64,290	64,290	64,290	64,290
Profit (Loss)	144,260	107,510	70,760	34,010	(2,740)	(39,490)	(76,240)

In Table 9.3 the effect of errors in the estimate of food costs is calculated. It will be noted that if the actual food costs turn out to be a little less than 10% greater than estimated, profitability is eliminated.

In Table 9.4 the effect of possible error in the estimate of revenue of the fast-food restaurant is calculated. If actual revenue drops below estimate by a little less than 10%, profitability is eliminated.

In Table 9.5 the effect of an error is the estimate of the capital expenditures in getting into the business is shown. It is apparent that the profitability is

Table 9.4   Effect of Errors in Estimates of Revenue on Profit of the Fast-Food Restaurant (Dollars).

	−30%	−20%	−10%	BASE CASE	+10%	+20%	+30%
Revenue	514,500	588,000	661,500	735,000	808,500	882,000	955,500
Food costs[a]	257,250	294,000	330,750	367,500	404,250	441,000	477,750
Other costs	269,200	269,200	269,200	269,200	269,200	269,200	269,200
Invest. Cost	64,290	64,290	64,290	64,290	64,290	64,290	64,290
Profit (Loss)	(76,249)	(39,390)	(2,740)	34,010	70,760	107,510	144,760

[a] It is assumed that as revenue drops, food costs will also be reduced, remaining 50% of revenue.

Table 9.5   Effects of Errors in Estimates of Investment Costs on Profit of Fast-Food Restaurant (Dollars).

	−30%	−20%	−10%	BASE CASE	+10%	+20%	+30%
Revenue	735,000	735,000	735,000	735,000	735,000	735,000	735,000
Oper. Costs	636,700	636,700	636,700	636,700	636,700	636,700	636,700
Capital Est.[a]	263,900	301,600	339,300	377,000	414,700	452,400	490,100
Invest. Cost	45,003	51,432	57,861	64,290	70,719	77,148	83,577
Profit (Loss)	53,297	46,868	40,439	34,010	27,581	21,152	14,723

[a] Assumes salvage value is 58.36% of investment cost.

Table 9.6 Effect of Change in Minimum Acceptable Rate of Return on Fast-Food Restaurant (Dollars).

	−30%	−20%	−10%	BASE CASE	+10%	+20%	+30%
Revenue	735,000	735,000	735,000	735,000	735,000	735,000	735,000
Oper. Costs	636,700	636,700	636,700	636,700	636,700	636,700	636,700
Invest. Costs	49,209	54,189	59,214	64,290	69,366	74,534	79,714
Profit (Loss)	49,091	44,111	39,086	34,010	28,934	23,766	18,586

relatively insensitive to errors in estimate of investment cost. If the cost is 10%, or $37,700, greater than estimated, profit will be reduced by $6,429 or 19%. This assumes that the ratio of salvage value remains a constant percentage of first cost. It should be noted that over 50% of the first cost is the cost of land. This is because fast-food restaurants must have high visibility and access. But because land seldom depreciates, it keeps the salvage value of the enterprise high.

If the minimum acceptable rate of return changes from the estimated 15%, caused by a change in the general level of interest rate or a change in attitude by the investor, the result is shown in Table 9.6. It may be noted that a 30% change in this variable results in less than a 50% increase or decrease in net annual return.

If the time horizon changes, Table 9.7 will indicate that within the 30% error range, there is relatively little effect on net annual worth. The net annual worth would not be reduced to zero until the time horizon was reduced to 3 years.

Sensitivity Chart

It is many times more clearly seen if the data as developed in the foregoing tables are presented in graphical form. This has been done in Fig. 9.7. It will be noted from the graphical presentation that the two most critical variables are food costs and revenues. A 10% reduction in revenue or a similar

Table 9.7 Effect of a Change in Time Horizon on Profit of Fast-Food Restaurant (Dollars).

	−30%	−20%	−10%	BASE CASE	+10%	+20%	+30%
Revenue	735,000	735,000	735,000	735,000	735,000	735,000	735,000
Oper. Costs	636,700	636,700	636,700	636,700	636,700	636,700	636,700
Invest. Costs	70,737	67,987	65,903	64,290	62,998	61,963	61,120
Profit (Loss)	27,563	30,313	32,397	34,010	35,302	36,337	37,180

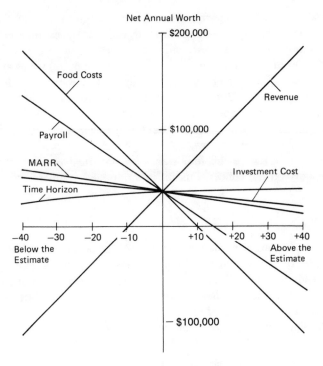

Figure 9.7. Sensitivity chart.

increase in food costs would reduce the net annual worth to zero. Thus estimates of revenue need to be examined closely. And food costs as a percentage of revenue need to be reviewed. It would be well to pursue the firm offering the franchise to make sure the figures are as good as possible.

Profitability is also very sensitive, in our example, to payroll costs. In the estimate given, payroll costs were kept constant as revenue increased or decreased. This is of course unrealistic. The number of personnel should be adjusted to the level of business to allow for cycles hourly, daily, or seasonally. Proper adjustment of personnel levels based on the level of business activity could have an appreciable effect on the slope of the payroll line.

The sensitivity chart indicates that food costs, revenue, and payroll are the three main variables in this example that need close attention in terms of the effect on the business venture.

ANALYSIS OF RISK

Up to this point we have treated all values of input into our calculations, such as investment, operating cost, salvage value, etc., as though they were unequivocally correct or deterministic. As such we have been concerned with decisions under certainty. Economic analysis requires the estimation of future events, or, more precisely, the estimation of values at some time in the future. And the farther in the future our crystal ball is required to give us an answer, the greater the chance of error. We usually pick a number with the best chance of being correct. But there is always a possibility or probability that the estimate is below or above the actual value.

To allow for the range of values around the average, or best value, statistical decision theory must be employed. Although we like to deal with certainty, it seldom exists. Despite the importance of statistical decision theory, we will touch only on the concepts useful in an applied manner.

Probability

Probability is the long-run relative frequency of the occurrence of an outcome. For example, there are two possible outcomes of flipping a coin. It will be either a head or a tail. Over an infinitely long period of time we would expect that half of the time heads would occur and half the time tails would occur. Thus the probability of flipping a head would be 0.50 and of flipping a tail 0.50. The sum of the probabilities is 1, that is,

Probability of a head	0.50
Probability of a tail	0.50
Sum of all possible outcomes	1.00

Probabilities are defined so that the sum of all probabilities for all possible outcomes is 1. A more complex set of possible outcomes is the result of rolling one-half of a pair of dice. Because the die has six sides, the probability of any side appearing is $1/6$, and thus the probabilities are as follows:

$$\text{Probability of rolling a 1, or } p(1) = 1/6$$
$$2, \text{ or } p(2) = 1/6$$
$$3, \text{ or } p(3) = 1/6$$
$$4, \text{ or } p(4) = 1/6$$
$$5, \text{ or } p(5) = 1/6$$
$$6, \text{ or } p(6) = 1/6$$
$$\text{Sum of all possible outcomes} \quad 6/6 \text{ or } 1.00$$

The probability of rolling a 3, 4, or 5, is $1/6 + 1/6 + 1/6 = 1/2$.

With a die and a coin our probabilities for any of the possible events were equal. But consider a pair of dice. Table 9.8 describes the possible sums that might be rolled with a pair of dice. It can be seen that there are

Table 9.8   Opportunities to Roll Certain Sums with Two Dice.

SPOTS ON EACH DIE	SUM ROLLED	2	3	4	5	6	7	8	9	10	11	12
1 1		1										
1 2			1									
1 3				1								
1 4					1							
1 5						1						
1 6							1					
2 2				1								
2 3					1							
2 4						1						
2 5							1					
2 6								1				
3 3						1						
3 4							1					
3 5								1				
3 6									1			
4 4								1				
4 5									1			
4 6										1		
5 5										1		
5 6											1	
6 6												1
Total Times Sum Rolled		1	1	2	2	3	3	3	2	2	1	1

21 different combinations of a pair of dice producing sums from 2 to 12. There are three different ways to roll a 7. It could be 6 and a 1, a 5 and 2, or a 4 and 3. Thus 3 of the 21 different rolls will yield a 7. Thus the probability of rolling something that is not a 7 is $(1 - \frac{1}{7})$ or $\frac{6}{7}$. The probability of any total from 2 to 12 is shown in Table 9.9.

If the probabilities are plotted as contiguous bars, the resulting figure is called a histogram. Figure 9.8a is the histogram of the probabilities of rolling various numbers with one die. The distribution is discrete, not continuous, because only integers appear on the face of the die. When outcomes such as this have an equal probability, in this case $\frac{1}{6}$, it is called a *uniform distribution*.

Simulation

If the probabilities of the sums from two dice are plotted as a histogram, Fig. 9.8b would be the result. Figures 9.8a and 9.8b are the plot of frequencies

Table 9.9   Probability of Rolling Various Sums on Two Dice.

PROBABILITY OF ROLLING A SUM OF:

2	$p(2) = 1/21$, or 4.76%
3	$p(3) = 1/21$, or 4.65%
4	$p(4) = 2/21$, or 9.52%
5	$p(5) = 2/21$, or 9.52%
6	$p(6) = 3/21$, or 14.29%
7	$p(7) = 3/21$, or 14.29%
8	$p(8) = 3/21$, or 14.29%
9	$p(9) = 2/21$, or 9.52%
10	$p(10) = 2/21$, or 9.52%
11	$p(11) = 1/21$, or 4.76%
12	$p(12) = 1/21$, or 4.76%
Sum of all possible outcomes:	21/21, or 1.00 or 100%

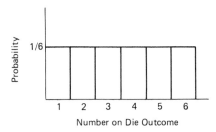

Figure 9.8a. Histogram of probabilities from the roll of one die.

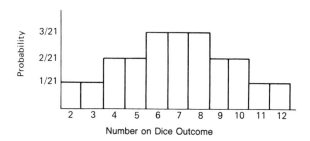

Figure 9.8b. Histogram of probabilities from the roll of 2 dice.

to be expected over an infinite number of trials. It is obvious that if we rolled two dice only 21 times, we would not get each of the 21 different outcomes shown in the left-hand column of Table 9.8. If we wanted to duplicate the uniform distribution of Figure 9.8b without rolling the dice, we could simulate the distribution by the use of random numbers. Table 9.10 contains an array of two-digit random numbers. It is possible to simulate the rolling of the dice by assigning numbers to the value of the die as follows:

Random Numbers	Value on Face of Die
01–04	1,1
05–08	1,2
09–12	1,3
13–16	1,4
17–20	1,5
21–24	1,6
25–28	2,2
29–32	2,3
33–36	2,4
37–40	2,5
41–44	2,6
45–48	3,3
49–52	3,4
53–56	3,5
57–60	3,6
61–64	4,4
65–68	4,5
69–72	4,6
73–76	5,5
77–80	5,6
81–84	6,6
85–00	Not Used

Table 9.10   240 Two-Digit Random Numbers.

02	41	52	40	85	19	17	22	47	55	15	03	99	55	23	72
89	61	37	04	97	06	53	31	61	24	03	27	92	57	15	71
22	40	38	18	71	15	24	55	21	34	61	71	66	80	69	41
06	68	35	15	40	46	19	87	43	10	21	87	02	40	75	17
87	71	39	32	82	23	39	67	65	71	94	20	47	29	49	18
60	81	94	90	14	50	69	75	03	55	00	77	96	14	45	52
22	90	08	38	72	16	77	50	34	16	05	66	20	78	45	84
24	30	76	05	80	58	08	96	74	17	88	87	10	14	74	00
19	88	17	47	08	48	20	94	29	66	34	30	65	79	56	21
33	42	44	34	83	70	19	99	09	27	76	44	31	61	87	41
21	16	81	40	95	38	47	32	74	93	64	19	53	08	18	44
49	32	54	02	83	23	94	79	14	42	21	64	48	66	00	69
73	39	90	82	88	55	80	31	69	63	57	02	74	18	90	11
55	73	37	15	90	40	97	13	86	31	65	28	89	97	32	15
62	31	44	45	56	94	11	49	75	15	30	76	41	64	69	51

Using the random numbers of Table 9.10 as a random number generator, we can select a row or column and proceed horizontally or vertically from there. If we chose column 1 and proceeded vertically until we had picked 15 numbers from that column and started again down column 2, the data of Table 9.11 and a distribution of Fig. 9.9 would be obtained. The distributions of Fig. 9.9 do not correspond to Fig. 9.8b, nor should they be expected to. If a computer were used and the selection of random numbers and their relation to the dots on the dice were run through several thousand times, the distribution pictured by the histogram of Fig. 9.8b would be approached.

Continuous Distributions

The distributions discussed thus far have been discrete distributions. Discrete distributions result from counting discrete objects or happenings, such as

Table 9.11   Randon Numbers and the Resultant Values of the Dice.[a]

RANDOM NUMBER	VALUE OF SUM OF DICE	RANDOM NUMBER	VALUE OF SUM OF DICE	RANDOM NUMBER	VALUE OF SUM OF DICE
02	2	16	5	15	5
89	–	32	5	32	5
22	7	39	7	90	7
06	3	73	10	38	7
87	–	31	5	5	3
60	9	52	7	47	6
22	7	37	7	34	6
24	7	38	7	40	7
19	6	35	6	02	2
33	6	39	7	82	12
21	7	94	–	15	5
49	7	08	3	45	6
73	10	76	10	85	–
55	8	18	6	97	–
62	8	44	8	71	10
41	8	81	12	40	7
61	8	54	8	82	12
40	7	90	–	14	5
68	9	37	7	72	10
71	10	44	8	80	12
81	12	40	7	08	3
90	–	04	2	83	12
30	5	18	6	95	–
88	–			83	12
42	8				

[a] Twenty-one assignable random numbers were used for each column.

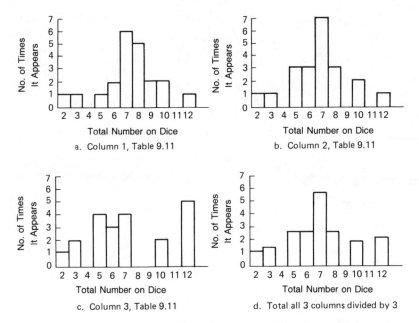

Figure 9.9. Histogram of the simulation of the dice rolls.

the dots on a pair of dice, where this count is an expression of (x), a random variable, and where the sum of the probabilities of each discrete happening or count are equal to unity.

If a smooth curve can be drawn through the plot of probability of occurrence versus the random variable (x), a continuous distribution is obtained. The fitted curve must have a reasonable shape, and the sum of the relative frequencies under the curve must be equal to 1.0.

Probability distributions of many shapes have been devised, analyzed, and described mathematically. The best known distribution and the most important one is the normal, or Gaussian, distribution. The normal distribution is the familiar, symmetrical, bell-shaped curve of Fig. 9.10a. A distribution may be skewed to one side or the other, as shown in Fig. 9.10b, which is skewed to the right. In Figure 9.10a the normal distribution curve is enlarged to show its significant features. The vertical axis of symmetry rising to the node at the top is the mean μ, or average, value of the distribution. A measure of the magnitude of variability around that mean is the standard deviation σ. Within the ± 1 σ limits, 68.26% of the values of the random variable x will be found. Within ± 2 σ limits around the mean μ, 95.45% of the values of the random variable x will be found. And within ± 3 σ limits, 99.73% of the values of x will be found.

Variance is the square of the standard deviation and is defined as the

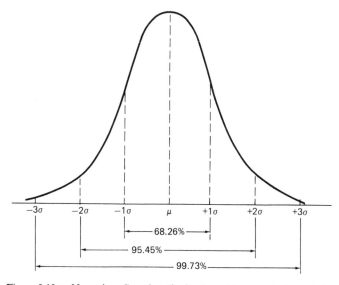

Figure 9.10.a. Normal or Gaussian distribution with percent of population.

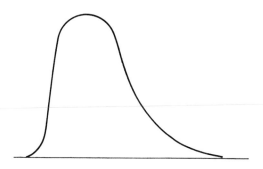

Figure 9.10.b. Skewed distribution.

mean of the squares of the variation from the mean of a frequency distribution, or, mathematically, for a population,

$$\text{Variance} = \frac{\Sigma(x - \bar{x})^2}{n}$$

When dealing with a sample of the total population, the denominator is reduced to $n - 1$ to reduce bias. This will be noted in Eq. 9.1.

Population Sampling

The mean symbol used above, μ, denotes the mean of the population, and σ denotes the standard deviation of the population that might be sampled. If the population being sampled were professional baseball players, but the sample consisted of 30 players, then the notation used for the mean of a sample is $\bar{x}$ and for standard deviation of the sample, s. The ages of the sample of the 30 professional baseball players were:

$$
\begin{array}{cccccccccc}
21 & 29 & 19 & 32 & 26 & 25 & 32 & 20 & 24 & 23 \\
27 & 24 & 22 & 23 & 28 & 18 & 22 & 26 & 23 & 30 \\
25 & 27 & 23 & 29 & 26 & 25 & 21 & 26 & 27 & 24
\end{array}
$$

For this group of people, assume the ages are normally distributed. The sum of these ages is 747;

$$\text{Mean } \bar{x} = \frac{747}{30} = 24.9 \text{ years}$$

The standard deviation is the square root of the sum of the square of the deviations around the mean, divided by 1 less than the sample size:

$$\text{Standard deviation } s = \sqrt{\frac{\Sigma(x - \bar{x})}{n - 1}} \qquad 9.1$$

Grouping the 30 ball players:

AGE GROUP	NO. IN AGE GROUP	$x - \bar{x}$	$(x - \bar{x})^2$	$n(x - \bar{x})^2$
18	1	−6.9	47.61	47.61
19	1	−5.9	34.81	34.81
20	1	−4.9	24.01	24.01
21	2	−3.9	15.21	30.42
22	2	−2.9	8.41	16.82
23	4	−1.9	3.61	14.44
24	3	−0.9	.81	2.43
25	3	0.1	.01	.03
26	4	1.1	1.21	4.84
27	3	2.1	4.41	13.23
28	1	3.1	9.61	9.61
29	2	4.1	16.81	33.62
30	1	5.1	26.01	26.01
31	0	6.1	37.21	0
32	2	7.1	50.41	100.82

$$\Sigma(x - \bar{x})^2 = 358.70$$

$$s = \sqrt{\frac{\Sigma(x - \bar{x})^2}{n - 1}} = \sqrt{\frac{358.70}{29}} = \sqrt{12.37} = 3.52 \text{ yr}$$

The standard deviation may also be solved by the equation:

$$s = \sqrt{\frac{\Sigma x^2}{n - 1} - \frac{(\Sigma x)^2}{n(n - 1)}} \qquad 9.2$$

And in this problem

$$\Sigma x^2 = 18^2 + 19^2 + 20^2 + (2)21^2 + (2)22^2 + (4)23^2$$
$$+ \ldots = 18,959$$
$$\Sigma x = 747$$
$$s = \sqrt{\frac{18,959}{29} - \frac{(747)^2}{30(29)}} = \sqrt{653.76 - 641.39}$$
$$= \sqrt{12.37} = 3.52 \text{ yr}$$

Thus, from the sample of 30 ball players, we have found the average age $\bar{x}$ of the 30 to be 24.9 years and the standard deviation s to be 3.52 years. The sample mean is our best estimate of μ, the average age of the population, and the sample standard deviation our best estimate of σ, the standard deviation of the age of the population.

Assuming the distribution is not skewed (inherent in the assumption of a normal distribution), it could be described by Fig. 9.11. If it were desired to determine the percentage of professional baseball players under 27 years of age, it would be difficult from Fig. 9.11 with a mean and standard deviation that are not integers. But the distribution can be standardized by using the formula

$$z = \frac{x - \mu}{\sigma} \qquad 9.3$$

where z is the standardized variable, or the number of standard deviations from the mean, x is the particular value of the random variable of interest, and μ and σ are the mean and standard deviation of the distribution, respectively. Thus if the particular value of the random variable is at one σ away from the mean, then $x - \mu = \sigma$ or $z = \sigma/\sigma = 1.0$.

Appendix D gives the values of the standard normal distribution function, which lists values of the distribution for values of z from 0.00 to 3.09. Going back to the problem of the percentage of players under 27 years of age, and using Eq. 9.3,

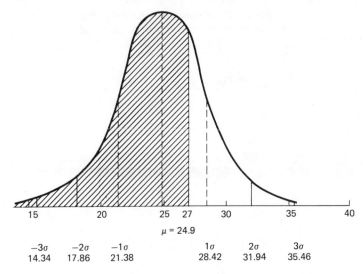

Figure 9.11. The normal distribution curve.

$$z = \frac{x - \mu}{\sigma} = \frac{27 - 24.9}{3.52} = .597$$

From the Appendix, by interpolation between z values of 0.59 and 0.60, a value of 0.2254 is obtained. This is the area under the curve between the mean μ and the value of x selected. The area to the left of 27 years of age is the area to the left of the mean (.50) plus 0.2254, or 0.7254, or 72.54%. Thus 72½% of the baseball players are younger than 27 years.

DISCRETE DISTRIBUTIONS

Individual random variables in economic analysis seldom can be described by equations that yield continuous distributions. Instead the random variable, such as investment cost, operating cost, maintenance cost, overhead cost, material costs, selling price, size of the market, share of the market, economic life, etc., are described as probabilities of the variable having certain discrete values. For example, the investment cost of a new product manufacturing facility might have a probability distribution of values as shown in Table 9.12. This distribution could be described by the histogram of Fig. 9.12.

Expected Values

Many of the random variables involved in the engineering economist's investment decision can be described by probability estimates, such as subjective

Table 9.12 Probability of Certain Values of the Investment Cost of a New Facility.

COST OF FACILITY	PROBABILITY OF THIS COST OCCURRING
$110,000	.10
130,000	.20
150,000	.35
170,000	.25
190,000	.10

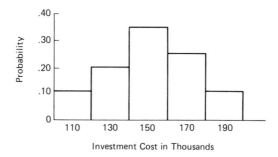

Figure 9.12. Histogram of the data of Table 9.12.

probability estimates. In working with such estimates, the expected values E_j may be calculated by the following equation:

$$\bar{E}_j = \sum_{s=1}^{n} E_{js}\, P_s \qquad 9.4$$

where E_{js} = Estimated Cost
P_s = Probability
and the standard deviations σ_j from

$$\sigma_j = \left[\sum_{s=1}^{n} (E_{js} - \bar{E}_j)^2\, P_s \right]^{1/2} \qquad 9.5$$

Thus the expected value of the distribution of Table 9.12 would be calculated as shown in Table 9.13.

Table 9.13 Calculation of the Mean $\bar{E}_j$ and Standard Deviation from the Distribution of Table 9.12.

STATE	PROBABILITY P_s	VALUE $E_{js} \times 10^{-3}$	$E_{js}P_s \times 10^{-3}$	$(E_{js} - \bar{E}_j)^2 \times 10^{-6}$	$(E_{js} - \bar{E}_j)^2 P_s \times 10^{-6}$
1	.10	110	11.0	1681	168.10
2	.20	130	26.0	441	88.20
3	.35	150	52.5	2	.35
4	.25	170	42.5	361	90.25
5	.10	190	19.0	1521	152.10

$$\bar{E}_j = 151.0$$

$$\sum_{s=1}^{5} (E_{js} - \bar{E}_j)^2 \cdot P_s = 499.00$$

$$\sigma_j = \left[\sum_{s=1}^{5} E_{js} - \bar{E}_j)^2 \cdot P_s \right]^{1/2}$$

$$= [499 \times 10^6]^{1/2} = 22,340$$

Highest, Lowest, and Most Likely Values

There are times when it is not possible to obtain even the limited subjective detail described in Table 9.12. In these cases it is usually possible to obtain estimates corresponding to three different values as follows:

L = the optimistic number that would be the lowest reasonable cost that might be expected or the highest reasonable revenue, profit, etc., that might be expected.

H = the pessimistic number that would be the highest reasonable cost that might be expected or the lowest reasonable revenue, profit, etc., that might be expected.

M = the most likely cost, revenue, profit, etc., that might be expected.

The range thus defined by the optimistic and pessimistic values supposedly includes every possible estimate of the variable being considered. The most likely estimate need not coincide with the midpoint, $(L + H)/2$, but may be to the left or to the right of the midpoint. The distribution as estimated may follow a beta distribution, with its modal point at M with end points L and H. Figure 9.13 illustrates three possible beta distributions.

The midpoint of the optimistic and pessimistic values, $(L + H)/2$, is assumed to have half the weight of the most likely point, M. Thus the mean, $\bar{E}$, is the arithmetic average of $(L + H)/2$ and $2M$:

$$\bar{E} = \frac{(L + H)/2 + 2M}{3} = \frac{L + 4M + H}{6} \qquad 9.6$$

By interpretation, the range (L, H) covers six standard deviations, because about 90% or more of *any* probability distribution lies within three standard deviations of its mean. Thus the variance, V, is obtained by

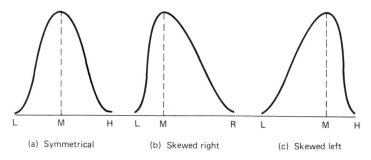

(a) Symmetrical   (b) Skewed right   (c) Skewed left

Figure 9.13. Three possible beta distributions.

$$V = \left(\frac{H - L}{6}\right)^2 \qquad 9.7$$

If several variables or elements of an economic study are estimated this way and can be assumed to be independent of each other and are added together, the distribution of the total cost will approximately follow a normal distribution. This follows from the *central limit theorem,* which states that the mean is the sum of the means, and the variance the sum of the variances. If the individual variables or elements are independent, it is assumed that the tendency to skew left or right or be symmetrical is random, so that the distribution of the sum of the costs will be normal despite the individual shapes of the distribution of each variable. There must be at least four elements to satisfy the conditions of the central limit law.

$$\bar{E}_t = \bar{E}_1 + \bar{E}_2 + \bar{E}_3 + \ldots + \bar{E}_n \ (n \geq 4) \qquad 9.8$$

and the variance V

$$V_T = V_1 + V_2 + V_3 + \ldots + V_n \qquad 9.9$$

where $\bar{E}_T$ = expected total cost, and V_T = variance of the total cost.

The central limit theory requires the random variables or elements to be mutually independent. They seldom are. The more variables that are considered in the total figures, the more assurance the central limit theory will produce a normal distribution. Table 9.14 illustrates an example of this approach using a total of five variables. It should be noted that a mean and a variance obtained by the *expected value* calculation could be added to the mean, such as the mean and variance from Table 9.13, and variance obtained from the most likely, highest, and lowest calculations.

Once a mean and a variance have been obtained, various statements regard-

Table 9.14 Calculation of Total Cost and Variance.

ELEMENT	OPTIMISTIC L	MOST LIKELY M	PESSIMISTIC H	$\bar{E}_j$	V_j
1. Direct labor cost	38.5	42.3	45.8	42.25	1.48
2. Indirect labor cost	68.5	75.8	85.6	7.22	8.12
3. Indirect costs	20.1	25.1	28.3	24.80	1.87
4. Overhead costs	41.2	47.3	52.0	47.07	3.24
5. Fixed costs	34.7	38.1	44.7	40.30	2.78
				$\bar{E}_T = 231.57$	$V_T = 17.49$

ing the interval for the future can be made. For example, what is the probability that the total cost will not exceed $239? Using Eq. 9.3

$$z = \frac{x - \mu}{\sigma} = \frac{239 - 231.57}{(17.49)^{1/2}} = \frac{7.43}{4.182}$$
$$= 1.78$$

From Appendix D, the area under the right side of the curve is 0.4625. Adding 0.50 for the area of probabilities less than the mean, we can state that the probability that the cost will not exceed $239 is 96.25%.

Simulation

Table 9.12 and Fig. 9.12 describe a subjective estimate of the investment cost of a new facility. Several subjective estimates of factors involved in an economic analysis might be made. This list of factors could include: direct manufacturing labor, direct materials, indirect labor, indirect materials, energy or utility costs, maintenance costs, office employee or overhead costs, volume of product sold, average price of produce sold, etc. When all these subjective tabulations are made, they may look like Table 9.15. There need not be five estimates with probabilities of each. There may be fewer or more than five. After each table is complete, then random numbers should be assigned with ranges that correspond to the probability of that particular value. Table 9.15 is an example of elements that might be used in an economic analysis of a capital investment.

If the minimum acceptable rate of return were 15% and the economic life 10 years, the present worth of the cash flows would be described by the following equation:

$$PW_{(15\%)} = -P - [DC + IC + 0 + SC - R](P/A\ 15\%,10)$$
$$+ P(F_P)(P/F\ 15,10) \qquad 9.10$$

Earlier in this chapter, we described simulation as an alternative to rolling dice. It may also be used to determine the value of an economic equation when various probability distributions are involved. To evaluate the equation, a source of random numbers is used to select a value of each random variable. Using Table 9.10 as a source of random numbers and using rows, starting with row 1 and applying the first seven numbers to the seven random variables of Table 9.15, we can develop the values of Table 9.16. The final value in each trial is the present worth as derived by substituting the values in Eq. 9.10. Only nine simulation trials are shown, with an average value for the present worth of $19,161, with values as low as ($166,936) and as high as

Table 9.15 Various Analysis Elements.

VALUE	PROBABILITY	RANDOM NUMBER RANGES
a. Initial Investment, $(P)		
110,000	.10	01 to 10
130,000	.20	11 to 30
150,000	.35	31 to 65
170,000	.25	66 to 90
190,000	.10	91 to 00
b. Annual Direct Manufacturing Costs, $(DC)		
24,000	.05	01 to 05
28,000	.15	06 to 20
32,000	.25	21 to 45
36,000	.30	46 to 75
40,000	.15	76 to 90
44,000	.10	91 to 00
c. Annual Indirect Manufacturing Costs, $(IC)		
13,000	.25	01 to 25
16,000	.55	26 to 80
19,000	.20	81 to 00
d. Annual Factory Overhead, $(O)		
15,000	.05	01 to 05
17,000	.25	06 to 30
19,000	.40	31 to 70
21,000	.25	71 to 95
23,000	.05	96 to 00
e. Salvage Value as a Percentage of Investment, $(F_P)		
8	.10	01 to 10
9	.30	11 to 40
10	.40	41 to 80
12	.20	81 to 00
f. Annual Selling Cost, $(SC)		
20,000	.10	01 to 10
23,000	.20	11 to 30
25,000	.40	31 to 70
27,000	.20	71 to 90
30,000	.10	91 to 00
g. Annual Revenue, $(R)		
80,000	.10	01 to 10
110,000	.25	11 to 35
140,000	.40	36 to 75
170,000	.20	76 to 95
185,000	.05	96 to 00

Table 9.16   Simulation Values for Variables from Table 9.14.

	TRIAL 1		TRIAL 2		TRIAL 3	
VARIABLE	RANDOM NUMBER	VALUE	RANDOM NUMBER	VALUE	RANDOM NUMBER	VALUE
P	02	110,000	89	170,000	22	130,000
DC	41	32,000	61	36,000	40	32,000
IC	52	16,000	37	16,000	38	16,000
O	40	19,000	04	15,000	18	17,000
F_P	85	12%	97	12%	71	10%
SC	19	23,000	06	20,000	15	23,000
R	17	110,000	53	140,000	24	110,000
PW		($6,361)		$101,038		($10,373)

	TRIAL 4		TRIAL 5		TRIAL 6	
VARIABLE	RANDOM NUMBER	VALUE	RANDOM NUMBER	VALUE	RANDOM NUMBER	VALUE
P	06	110,000	87	170,000	60	150,000
DC	68	36,000	71	36,000	81	40,000
IC	35	16,000	39	16,000	94	19,000
O	15	17,000	32	19,000	90	21,000
F_P	40	9%	82	12%	14	9%
SC	46	25,000	23	23,000	50	25,000
R	19	110,000	39	140,000	69	140,000
		($27,252)		(65,905)		$28,995

	TRIAL 7		TRIAL 8		TRIAL 9	
VARIABLE	RANDOM NUMBER	VALUE	RANDOM NUMBER	VALUE	RANDOM NUMBER	VALUE
P	22	130,000	24	130,000	19	130,000
DC	90	40,000	30	32,000	88	40,000
IC	08	13,000	76	16,000	17	13,000
O	38	19,000	05	15,000	47	19,000
F_P	72	10%	80	10%	08	8%
SC	16	23,000	58	25,000	48	25,000
R	77	170,000	08	80,000	20	110,000
PW		$249,620		($166,936)		($62,185)

$249,620. Usually simulations are run on computers with several hundred trials being made. When these are completed, the means and standard deviations are calculated. From these statistical data, a probability (based on Appendix D) can be developed of exceeding the 15% MARR.

Summary of Probability Analyses

Simulation using subjective data (of which Table 9.15 is a good example) is the most accurate method of obtaining the final probability information for whatever measure of merit may be desired. In Table 9.16 present worth was used as the measure of merit. It could as easily have been annual worth or rate of return. But several hundred iterations should be performed to establish reasonably representative values of the mean and standard deviation.

The same data of Table 9.15 could have been processed using only the most optimistic, most likely, and most pessimistic values using Eqs. 9.6, 9.7, 9.8, and 9.9. According to this method, the values from Table 9.15a used would be

Most optimistic	$110,000
Most likely	150,000
Most pessimistic	190,000

ignoring the values of $130,000 and $170,000.

Though less time-consuming than simulation, the method is less accurate. And certainly some data are discarded.

Even less accurate than the H, M, L method is the *expected value method,* which utilized Eqs. 9.4 and 9.5. Utilizing this method and obtaining the expected value for each variable, the present worth would be $54,952, compared with the mean value obtained in nine simulation iterations of $19,161 (a value that is expected not to be representative after only nine trials).

To the analyst who is not statistically minded and who wants only one value for each variable, the *most probable* value of each variable should be the only one used. Thus, one would use $150,000 for the investment, $36,000 for the direct manufacturing costs, and $16,000 for the indirect manufacturing costs. On this basis, the analyst would obtain a present worth of $74,534, assuming with certainty that each variable would have only one possible value. The analyst would have no idea of the probability that the investment could have less than a 15% rate of return.

The process of developing probability distributions of the variables to be used in an economic analysis is admittedly quite subjective. But what is sought is a probability distribution that best describes the analysts' beliefs about the random variable. Those beliefs will be based on numerous interviews; analyses of data, historical and current; and investigations, but in the end it is the analyst who must believe that the probabilities used best describe the probability of the values of each random variable, because it is the analyst's recommendation whether a capital expenditure should be made or not made.

There are many who criticize the degree of subjectivity involved in the development of probability distributions. But it remains the most accurate method available requiring a minimum amount of statistical theory for the practitioner.

Probability Distributions of Future Years

Our ability to forecast, or estimate, costs becomes less precise as the length of time moves farther into the future. And as we would expect, the variance increases as our forecast moves farther into the future. For this reason it becomes even more desirable to apply statistical probabilities to economic analysis. The expected cash flow for any year t may be derived from

$$\bar{E}_t = \sum_{s=1}^{n} (E_{js} P_s) \qquad\qquad 9.11$$

and the standard deviation σ_t for the year t from

$$\sigma_t = \left[\sum_{s=1}^{n} (E_{ts} - \bar{E}_t)^2 P_{ts} \right]^{1/2} \qquad\qquad 9.12$$

If we assume the probability distribution P_{ts} to be normally distributed and the cash flow from year t to be independent from the cash flow of year $(t-1)$, then the present worth of an uncertain stream of returns may be determined from

$$PW = \sum_{t=1}^{n} \left[\frac{\bar{E}_t}{(1+i)^t} \right] \qquad\qquad 9.13$$

The standard deviation of this PW may be calculated by the following equation:

$$\sigma_{PW} = \left[\sum_{t=0}^{n} \frac{\sigma_t^2}{(1+i)^{2t}} \right]^{1/2} \qquad\qquad 9.14$$

An example will best illustrate the use of these equations. Assume $150 is invested for 3 years with cash flows of different probabilities for each year, as shown in Table 9.17. The investor hopes to receive 10% on the investment. It will be noted that the present worth of $23.78 indicates that he can expect a 10% return on the investment and in addition can expect to exceed the 10% by $23.78. What is the probability that the investor will exceed a 10% return on the $150 investment? From Eq. 9.3,

Table 9.17   Calculation of Expected Return for the Investment of $150.

A. Calculation of Expected Cash Flows

	PERIOD 1			PERIOD 2			PERIOD 3		
STATE$_s$	E_{1s}	P_{1s}	$E_{1s}P_{1s}$	E_{2S}	P_{2s}	$E_{2s}P_{2s}$	E_{3s}	P_{3s}	$E_{3s}P_{3s}$
1	60	.10	6	40	.10	4.0	10	.10	1.0
2	70	.20	14	55	.24	13.2	35	.30	10.5
3	80	.40	32	70	.32	22.4	60	.30	18.0
4	90	.20	18	85	.24	20.4	85	.20	17.0
5	100	.10	10	100	.10	10.0	110	.10	11.0
			$\bar{E}_1 = \sum_{s=1}^{5}(E_{1s}\,P_{1s}) = 80$			$\bar{E}_2 = 70$			$\bar{E}_3 = 57.5$

B. Calculation of Standard Deviation

	PERIOD 1			PERIOD 2			PERIOD 3		
STATE$_s$	$(E_{1s} - \bar{E}_1)^2$	P_{1s}	$(E_{1s} - \bar{E})^2 P_{1s}$	$(E_{2s} - \bar{E}_2)^2$	P_{2s}	$(E_{2s} - \bar{E})^2 P_{2s}$	$(E_{2s} - \bar{E}_2)^2$	P_{2s}	$(E_{2s} - \bar{E})^2 P_{2s}$
1	400	.10	40	900	.10	90	2,256	.10	225.6
2	100	.20	20	225	.24	54	506	.30	151.8
3	0	.40	0	0	.32	0	6	.30	1.8
4	100	.20	20	225	.24	54	756	.20	151.2
5	400	.10	40	900	.10	90	2,756	.10	275.6
			$\sigma_1^2 = \sum_{s=1}^{5}(E_{1s} - \bar{E})^2 P_{1s} = 120$			$\sigma_2^2 = 288$			$\sigma_3^2 = 806$
			$\sigma_1 = \sqrt{120} = 10.95$			$\sigma_2 = \sqrt{288} = 16.97$			$\sigma_3 = 28.39$

C. Present Worth of the Expected Cash Flows

$$PW = -150 + \frac{80}{1.10} + \frac{70}{(1.10)^2} + \frac{57.5}{(1.10)^3} = \$23.78$$

D. Standard Deviation of the Present Worth

$$\sigma = \left[\frac{120}{(1.10)^2} + \frac{288}{(1.10)^4} + \frac{806}{(1.10)^6}\right]^{1/2} = \$27.40$$

$$z = \frac{x - \mu}{\sigma} = \frac{0 - 23.78}{\$27.40} = 0.868$$

At z equal to 0.868 (by Appendix D), 30.7% of the area under one side of the normal curve will lie between the mean and a value of zero dollars (the point at which the investor can expect a 10% return on the investment). This is shown in Fig. 9.14. Adding 50% to the 30.7% gives the probability of 80.73% of exceeding a 10% return. This conclusion assumes that the summary data would fit the normal distribution, which they do not do exactly. Industrial practice generally ignores small deviations from normal distributions and treats the sum of several probability functions as approximating a normal distribution closely enough to use the table of areas under the normal curve in Appendix D as we have done.

Figure 9.15 illustrates the increasing standard deviation as forecast years are increased farther into the future.

SUMMARY

In this chapter the reader was acquainted with the procedures for preparing sensitivity and uncertainty analyses. In the corporate world today, most companies will prepare some sort of sensitivity analysis. The results of such studies may be in tabular or graphical format. The authors prefer the graphical

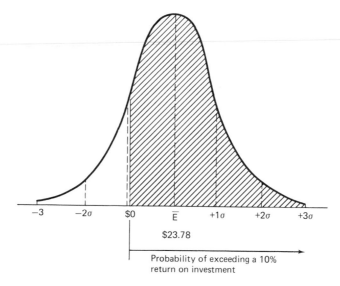

Figure 9.14. A normal distribution applied to the problem of Table 9.17.

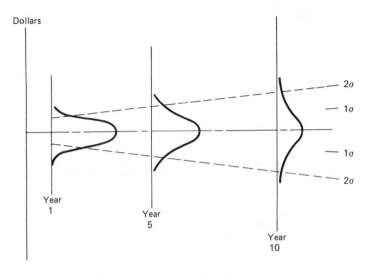

Figure 9.15. Forecasting is less precise with time.

presentation because at a glance the busy executive can quickly see what project variables create the greatest variation in the profitability measure used in a project analysis. Again, a word of caution: sensitivity analysis allows the user to inspect only one variable at a time and it does not take into account any synergistic effects occurring between two or more variables.

Uncertainty analysis will allow the user to account for variable interaction but probability distributions must be assigned for each variable being considered. Often the user does not know what distribution model best fits a variable. Further, a Monte Carlo type uncertainty analysis requires a computer with a large capacity, and a considerable amount of main-frame computer time is easily consumed unless careful planning of the programming is exercised. The results from a Monte Carlo analysis are only as good as the data fed to the simulation model. More research and improvements in matching probability models to variables are needed to improve the results from a Monte Carlo uncertainty analysis. Further, managers need to be educated about uncertainty analysis and how to interpret the results of such studies. For the foregoing reasons, companies will often not perform uncertainty analyses.

The application of sensitivity and uncertainty analysis will be demonstrated in Chapter 10, "Feasibility Analysis."

Suggested Further Reading

DeGarmo, Paul E., Sullivan, William G., and Canada, John R. *Engineering Economy,* 7th ed. New York: Macmillan Publishing Co.

Stevens, G. T., Jr. *Economic and Financial Analyses of Capital Investments.* New York: John Wiley & Sons.

White, John A., Agee, Marvin H., and Case, Kenneth E. *Principles of Engineering Economic Analysis.* New York: John Wiley & Sons.

PROBLEMS

9.1 Rustic Furniture is a small company that produces a line of antique model chairs. The following data were obtained from the plant accountants:

Fixed Costs	$90,000/yr
Variable Costs	$5.00/chair
Capacity	25,000 chairs/yr
Selling Price	$18.95/yr

    a. Determine the break-even point for this operation.
    b. In order to meet the target profit of $40,000/yr, how many chairs must be sold?
    c. At 75% capacity, what is the fixed cost per chair?
    d. At 75% capacity, what is the variable cost per year?

9.2 An electronics manufacturer is considering the installation of one of two types of machines to make an electronic component. A long-term sales forecast indicates that the sales will not fall below 8,200 units per year for the next 5 years, the expected life of the machine. Machine 1 will increase the fixed costs by $20,000 per year but will reduce the variable costs by $6.00 per unit produced. Machine 2 will increase the fixed costs by $4,000 per year but will reduce the variable costs by $4.00 per unit. Variable costs now amount to $20.00 per unit. At what point will it make no difference which machine is purchased? Which machine should be bought?

9.3 The Aeolian Record Shop is selling as many records as the storage and physical facilities will allow. Current fixed costs are $250,000 for up to 800,000 records. The manager has found that in order to sell more than this, overtime is necessary. The result is that for each additional 100,000 records sold (or fraction thereof), $10,000 in additional fixed costs is required. An addition to the building has been proposed to enable the store to operate at a higher volume. The addition to the facilities would cost $100,000, depreciated at the rate of $5,000 per year for the next 20 years. The addition is expected to increase the sales income by 10%, while additional operating costs are expected to be about $25,000 per year. The distribution of sales among the lines and proportion of records sold during overtime are expected to remain constant. On the basis of the data given for the present sales levels, would the proposed addition be a profitable one?

RECORD GROUP	SELLING PRICE	V. C. PER UNIT	UNITS SOLD
A	$7	$5	100,000
B	5	4	100,000
C	3	2	300,000
D	2	1	450,000

9.4 In 1977, Ajax Petrochemical, Inc. considered the manufacture of a plasticizer for potential customers in the plastics fabrication business. At the time, a market survey was made, but the results did not appear to be promising. The project was shelved.

In 1980, Ajax was acquired by Fusible Plastics Corporation, a large plastics manufacturer that wanted to integrate backwards. Since the acquisition, the surviving company has been reviewing the profitability of all Ajax's former projects. The Marketing Department of Fusible has prepared the following 10-year market survey for the chlorinated hydrocarbon plasticizer:

YEAR	POTENTIAL SALES	ESTIMATED SALES PRICE
1	20.0 MM lb/yr	$0.52/lb
2	20.5 MM lb/yr	0.52
3	21.0 MM lb/yr	0.51
4	22.0 MM lb/yr	0.50
5	23.0 MM lb/yr	0.50
6–10	25.0 MM lb/yr	0.48

In 1977, the total fixed capital investment for the hydrocarbon was estimated to be $5,000,000 for a 20 MM lb/yr plant. It is the company's standard procedure to update costs using the Chemical Engineering Index. Working capital may be taken at 15% of the total capital investment. For the purpose of this evaluation, land value may be ignored.

The chlorine to manufacture the chlorinated hydrocarbon is obtained from an existing chlorine plant at Ajax's facility. The capacity of the chlorine plant is 200 T/day of which the chlorinated hydrocarbon is expected to use 10 T/day. The total capital investment in the chlorine plant is $10 MM.

The operating costs for the proposed chlorinated chemical are:

Raw Materials	$0.12/lb product
Labor and Supervision	$0.05/lb product up through 17.0 MM lb/yr and $0.04/lb product above this rate
Maintenance	6%/yr of the fixed capital investment
Other Direct Costs	$0.01/lb product
Depreciation	10$yr (straight line)
Other Indirect Costs	$0.01/lb product
General O'head Expenses	$0.02/lb product
Utilities	$0.03/lb product up through 17.0 MM lb/yr and $0.02/lb product above this rate

In the screening stage, unless a proposed project shows a rate of return of 20% calculated by the DCF method, the venture will not be considered. A Federal and State Income Tax rate of 48% may be assumed. You may consider that the fixed capital is purchased uniformly over a 2-year period prior to start-up which is expected to be in the first quarter 1988.

In order to conform to the standard evaluation procedure of Fusible Plastics, prepare the following.

a. An estimate of the total capital requirements for a 25 MM lb/yr plant in 1988 using the CE Index and an inflation rate of 3% in 1986, 4% in 1987.

b. An annual operating cost sheet using only the data above the 100% of capacity case for January 1, 1988.

c. An estimate of the profitability by the DCF method using SL depreciation.

d. A cash position chart.

e. Prepare a sensitivity analysis to determine the effect of the following variables on the DCF return:

(1) ±5, ±10, ±15% variation in sales price.

(2) ±10, ±20, ±30% variation in market (sales volume).

(3) ±5, ±15, ±25% variation in raw material costs.

(4) ±10, ±15, ±25% variation in fixed capital investment.

f. Based upon your calculations, what recommendations would you make to management concerning this venture?

9.5 Using the data in Problem 9.4, prepare an uncertainty analysis. Probabilities will have to be assigned to sales price, sales volume, raw material costs and fixed capital investment. Propose statistical models for the variables. What is the probability of achieving an after-tax internal rate of return of 20%?

9.6 For a proposed project involving the manufacture of a product, the following data are available:

	MEAN VALUE, $\bar{Y}$	VARIANCE, $S^2(Y)$
Production, p	15,000 kg/mo	250,000 kg/mo
Net Sales Price, S-135	165	1.563
Fixed Capital Investment, FCI	4.1×10^6	1.04×10^{11}

Previous calculations have resulted in the following present worth equation:

$$\text{Net Present Worth} = 2.10p\,(\text{S} - 135) - 0.9(\text{FCI}) - 1.25 \times 10^{-6}$$

The input variables p, S-135, and FCI are assumed to follow the normal distribution curve. What is the probability that the net present worth will be less than zero?

10 FEASIBILITY ANALYSIS

INTRODUCTION

Economic evaluations are prepared to determine whether or not a proposed investment meets certain minimum economic requirements established by management. A feasibility analysis is prepared of sufficient detail and quality to provide management with the facts necessary to make a practical investment decision. In this chapter, a detailed solution for a proposed investment will be presented to demonstrate the steps necessary in the preparation of a feasibility analysis. Those people responsible for preparing this analysis should have an appreciation of the factors that affect the reliability of an analysis and also a sense of the expected accuracy.

INFORMATION REQUIRED

The amount of information required to prepare a feasibility study will depend upon the use of the study and management's desire. If the analysis is prepared to determine whether further research and/or pilot plant work is necessary, then preliminary capital cost estimates may be satisfactory with their inherent accuracy. Then again, if the decision involves a request for the appropriation of funds, firmer information will be required to prepare a detailed or definitive estimate.

The minimum information required to prepare a feasibility analysis would involve estimates of the following:

fixed capital investment
total capital investment
total operating expenses
cash flow analysis
measure of profitability
marketing data

To this list, management may also add break-even analysis, sensitivity study and, uncertainty analysis.

Fixed Capital Investment. To prepare an estimate of the fixed capital, it is recommended that a form be developed and used with all the necessary items included. A list including the purchased or delivered equipment costs is the first step. From this basic information, it is a simple matter to calculate the fixed capital investment using the Lang, Hand, or Wroth factors described in Chapter 3. If the Chilton method is to be used, another form similar to Table 3.16 is recommended. A detailed estimate would require establishing a code of accounts, a listing similar to Table 3.28. The use of the Chilton form will be demonstrated in Example 10.1.

Total Capital Investment. The major items constituting the total capital investment are presented in tabular format in Table 10.1. Blank spaces have been left to allow the user the option of adding other capital items. In the parentheses next to the dollar sign, the date of the cost data should be entered. If working capital is estimated using the inventory method, Table 10.2 might be useful, otherwise the working capital calculated by the percentage methods may be inserted directly into Table 10.1.

Total Operating Expenses. The total operating expenses may be calculated using two forms. The first is the total product cost discussed in Chapter 4; it includes the raw materials expenses, by-product credit, direct expenses, and indirect expenses, as well as packaging and shipping costs. The bottom line of this form, Table 10.3, is then the expenses involved in manufacturing, packaging and loading a product for delivery to a customer. Table 10.4, the general overhead expense form, is frequently used for detailed estimation purposes. As an alternative, the overhead expenses may be calculated as a

Table 10.1 Total Capital Investment.

	$( )
Land	
Fixed Capital	
Offsite Capital	
Allocated Capital	
Working Capital	
Startup Expenses	
Catalysts and Chemicals	
Licenses, Patents, Royalties	
Interest on Borrowed Funds	
- - - - - - - - - - - - - - - - - - -	
- - - - - - - - - - - - - - - - - - -	
Total Capital Investment	_____

Table 10.2 Working Capital Inventory Method.

	$( )
Raw Materials Inventory	
Goods-in-Progress Inventory	
Finished Goods Inventory	
Stores and Supplies Inventory	
Cash	
Accounts Receivable	
Accounts Payable	
- -	
- -	
Total Working Capital	

Table 10.3 Total Product Expense.

Total Operating Expenses:
 Product
 Total Annual Sales
 Rated Capacity
 Location
 Fixed Capital Investment
 Operating Hours per Year
 Date
 By

- -

Raw Materials: Material:	UNIT	ANNUAL AMOUNT	$/UNIT	$/YEAR

Gross Material Expense

- -

By-Products:	UNIT	ANNUAL AMOUNT	$/UNIT	$/YEAR

By-Product Credit

- -

Net Material Expense

Table 10.3 (Continued)

Direct Expenses:	UNIT	ANNUAL AMOUNT	$/UNIT	$/YEAR
Utilities				
Steam, Low-Press.				
Steam, Med-Press.				
Steam, High-Press.				
Gross Steam Expense				
Steam Credit				
Net-Steam Expense				
Electricity				
Cooling Water				
Fuel Gas				
City Water				
Total Utilities:				
Labor:				
Men/Shift				
Annual Labor Rate/Man				
Labor Expense				
Supervision:				
% of Labor Expense				
Payroll Charges, Fringe Benefits:				
% of Labor and Supervision				
Maintenance:				
% of Fixed Capital Expense				
Maintenance Expense				
Supplies:				
% of Labor				
Supplies Expense				
Laboratory Charges:				
Hours/Year				
Cost/Hour				
Laboratory Expense				
Royalties:				
Waste Disposal:				
Tons/Year				
Waste Charge/Ton				
Clothing and Laundry:				
% of Labor				
Waste Disposal:				
Tons/Year				
Waste Charge/Ton				
Clothing and Laundry:				
% of Labor				
Clothing Expense				
Other:				

- -

Total Direct Expense

Table 10.3   (Continued)

Total Direct + Net Material Expenses

- -

Indirect Expenses
Depreciation:
  % Fixed Capital Investment
  Depreciation Expense
Plant Indirect Expense:
  % Fixed Capital Investment
  Plant Indirect Expense

- -

Total Indirect Expenses

- -

Total Manufacturing Expense
Packaging and Shipping:
  Annual Production
  Cost/Ton
  Packaging and Shipping Expense

- -

Total Product Expense

Table 10.4   General Overhead Expense.

	$( )
Administration	
Sales	
Research and Engineering	
Finance	
- -	
- -	
Total General Overhead Expense	

percentage of annual sales, and Table 10.4 need not be used. The sum of the bottom lines of Table 10.3 and Table 10.4 is the total operating expense.

Cash Flow Analysis. A cash flow analysis sheet similar to Table 10.5 is very useful in presenting in concise, clear format those items involved in cash flow. The table can be constructed with enough flexibility to allow a choice of time zero and to allow management to add or delete certain items.

Table 10.5   Cash Flow Analysis.

	CASH FLOW SUMMARY		
YEAR	(19—)	(19—)	(19—)
Investment			
Land			
Fixed Capital Investment			
Offsite Capital			
Allocated Capital			
Working Capital			
Startup Expenses			
Interest			
Catalysts and Chemicals			
Licenses, Patents, etc.			
Total Capital Investment			
Profit-Loss Statement			
Income			
Expenses			
Cash Operating Expenses			
Depreciation			
Total Operating Expenses			
Operating Income			
Net Income Before Taxes			
Federal Income Taxes			
Net Income After Taxes			
Cash Flow			
Capital Recovery			
Cumulative Cash Flow			

Measures of Profitability. The profitability of a project may be included as part of the cash flow analysis or the results may be presented in a form like Table 10.6. In this table, the major measures of profitability are listed. A company may compute only certain values, so the table can be modified

Table 10.6   Profitability Analysis.

Return on Original Investment
Return on Average Investment
Payout Period
Payout Period with Interest
Present Worth (%)
Present Worth Index
Internal Rate of Return

for a specific use. In Table 10.6, the interest rate used in the calculation of present worth is to be placed in the parentheses.

Marketing Data. A major part of all feasibility studies is the marketing or income data. It is essential to have the best estimate of the market position for management's consideration. A tabulation of the projected sales volume, share of the market, and sales prices are minimal information. Table 10.7 is a sample of a marketing data table.

Break-Even Analysis. Often management requests a break-even chart as part of the feasibility analysis. Such charts are predicated on numerous assumptions, but will give some indication of the sensitivity of production rates to profitability. This kind of plot may be constructed like Fig. 10.1 to indicate not only the break-even point, but also the shutdown point. Break-even analysis is helpful in marketing and production planning.

Sensitivity Analysis. The effect of errors upon profitability measures is determined by means of a sensitivity analysis. The results may be presented in tabular or graphical form. We prefer a graphical format similar to Fig. 10.2 developed by Strauss (1968). At a glance, busy executives can quickly note those variables that affect profitability the most. Searching through tabulations of data can be time-consuming and tedious.

Uncertainty Analysis. The use of uncertainty analysis in feasibility studies has been adopted by some companies. The objective is to determine the probability of receiving a greater (or lesser) return on the investment. Probabilities must be assigned to each variable in the analysis. Some executives feel that to do this is an exercise in futility, for little is known about the probability distribution for a given variable. When uncertainty analyses are included, the results are plotted as shown in Fig. 10.3.

Procedure

For uniformity, it is essential that management establish a procedure for preparing a feasibility analysis. As a suggestion, the following steps might be followed:

1. Assemble all the necessary forms required for the feasibility analysis following company policy.
2. Decide on an appropriate quality for the fixed capital investment estimate, considering the time frame and money available.
3. Develop the data necessary for substitution in the various forms.

Table 10.7 Marketing Data.

PROFIT CENTER: _____ PROJECT TITLE: _____ APPROPRIATION NO.: _____

BASIS: SALES AND MARKET PROJECTIONS ARE NOT INFLATED (19__ DOLLARS)

| | 19__ | | 19__ | | 19__ | | 19__ | | 19__ | |
	AMOUNT	% TOTAL MARKET	AMOUNT	% TOTAL MARKET	AMOUNT	% TOTAL MARKET	AMOUNT	% TOTAL MARKET	AMOUNT	% TOTAL MARKET
Total Market:										
Units										
Average Realistic Price, $/Unit										
Value, $M										
Estimated Product Sales: (with AR)*			(Table Extends to the Right for the Number of Project Years)							
Units										
Average Realistic Price, $/Unit										
Value, $M										
Current Product Sales: (without AR)										
Unit										
Average Realistic Price, $/Unit										
Value, $M										
Incremental Product Sales: (with AR)										
Units										
Average Realistic Price, $/Unit										
Value, $M										
Current Product Sales Displaced By Improved Product Sales:										
Units										
Value, $M										
Total Improved Product Sales:										
Units										
Value, $M										

* AR is Appropriation Request.

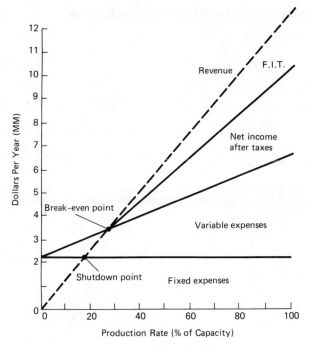

Figure 10.1. Typical break-even plot

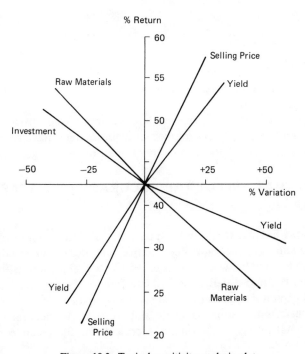

Figure 10.2. Typical sensitivity analysis plot.

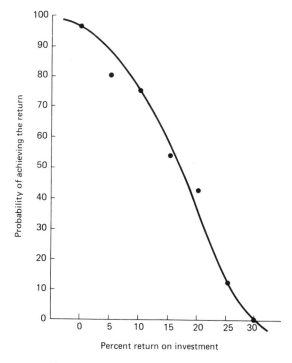

Figure 10.3. Typical uncertainty analysis plot.

4. Determine the economic feasibility of the project, including sensitivity and uncertainty analyses, if appropriate.

The use of standardized forms cannot be emphasized strongly enough. They serve as a checklist to ensure that all requisite items have been included and that the stepwise results are presented in an orderly, organized manner.

FACTORS THAT AFFECT THE ACCURACY OF A FEASIBILITY ANALYSIS

Capital Cost Estimates. In Chapter 3, the various types of capital cost estimates had limits of accuracy. For example, an order-of magnitude estimate accuracy might vary between −30% to +50%, a preliminary estimate from −15% to +30%, and a definitive estimate from −5% to +15%. The basis of any fixed capital investment estimate is the equipment costs. It is desirable to use the best information available and to know its accuracy. Further, the fixed capital investment estimate is critical, for the result computed is used to estimate working capital, startup expenses, and certain items of the total operating expenses. As early as possible the scope of the project must be defined. A poorly defined scope contributes to serious errors and considerable uncertainty regarding a project's feasibility.

Operating Expense Estimates. In the preparation of these estimates, it is wise to seek the counsel of manufacturing personnel. Their expertise will help temper the estimates and prevent the use of wild guesses. In particular, they are valuable sources with regard to labor requirements for a manufacturing operation. Raw material usage can be obtained with reasonable reliability from material balances, research reports, or pilot plant studies. Utilities may be estimated from material and energy balances. It is a good idea to check with the plant utilities supervisor for up-to-date or projected costs.

Marketing Data. One of the largest sources of error in feasibility analyses is the quality of marketing data. The market volume is difficult to predict, because the users often change their minds, substitute other products, or purchase a competitor's product. Any one of these alternatives can deal a devastating blow to projections of sales volume. Sales price is a volatile variable affected by the sales volume and competition in the marketplace from similar or substitute products. In many sensitivity analyses, market volume and market price affect the return of investment to the greatest extent. Therefore, a substantial amount of time and effort should be expended to obtain the best possible marketing data.

Inflation. In the recent past with rapidly increasing inflation, feasibility analyses often erred considerably. Various models might be included in an analysis, but at best the inflation rates used were educated guesses.

There are two excellent references on how to treat inflation in economic analyses. Appendix G of a book by Smith (1979) is devoted to that topic, and Jones (1982) published a text that deals more broadly with the subject. In general, there are two schools of thought on the matter.

Some authorities suggest that a specific time should be selected and all economic data regarding a project be corrected and reported on a constant-dollar basis as of that date.

The other alternative is to make an effort to project the percentage inflation rate based upon past experience and near-recent trends. Forecasting models have been used in this approach. One major oil company projects an inflation rate 6 months at a time and then corrects the rate as current data are obtained. They employ a corrected moving-average forecasting technique.

Whatever approach is used, and company policy will dictate this, those people who prepare feasibility analyses should not gloss over inflation, but should seriously consider its effect upon capital cost estimation and operating expenses.

Griest (1979) summarized the affect of inflation upon evaluations as follows:

1. Inflation does affect the profitability of a project. Longer depreciation lives reflect unfavorably upon the present worth.
2. Inflation can change the order of preference of projects in a capital budgeting decision.
3. Inflation may be built into the discount rate used in calculation of present worth.
4. If inflation is a variable in an analysis, then it can be handled statistically in an uncertainty analysis.
5. High rates of inflation tend to improve the attractiveness of a lease alternative relative to a capital investment.
6. High rates of inflation tend to favor lower capital projects.

Depreciation Method. Through the years depreciation methods have been modified by the Congress and Internal Revenue Service. These revisions often occurred when the economy was depressed. The reported intent of the revisions was to stimulate the economy by encouraging capital spending. The write-off periods were shortened, which increased the cash flow during the early years of a project. Therefore, because depreciation methods result in different cash flow patterns, a feasibility analysis can be drastically altered. In some cases, unattractive or "borderline" projects were reconsidered. When preparing a feasibility analysis, if alternative depreciation methods are allowable, it would be advisable to determine their affect on project attractiveness.

Production Rate. The amount of material to be produced is highly dependent upon marketing data. From these data, production schedules are prepared. Should the market volume decline, the company could quickly build inventories that would be economically unhealthy or the company might have to reduce the production rate below an economically feasible level. Operation at or near 100% capacity is not always possible. Many processes do not enjoy the flexibility of having a very low break-even point. Some processes require 50–60% of rated plant capacity to just break even. Even small variations in the production rate may affect the attractiveness of the project. To have this information available for management's consideration, a break-even chart is often included as part of the feasibility analysis. At a glance, the affect of changing production rates upon profitability of a project can be observed.

Tax Credits. The purpose of a tax credit is to reduce the income tax a company pays as a result of making an investment under specified conditions.

This concept began in the 1960s, but has been halted, revised, and commenced again. Although tax credits based upon investments in manufacturing equipment did alter a project's cash flow pattern, in most cases the credit did not have the strong influence that revisions to depreciation had. Tax credits are more volatile than depreciation, but should be included in any feasibility analysis.

EXAMPLE 10.1

PROBLEM STATEMENT

Ajax Petrochemical, Inc. in 1980 considered the manufacture of a plasticizer for potential customers in the plastics industry. At that time, a market survey was made, but the results did not appear to be promising. The project was shelved.

In 1984, Ajax was acquired by Fusible Plastics Corp., a large plastics manufacturer that wanted to integrate backward to raw materials. Since the merger, the surviving company has been reviewing the profitability of all Ajax projects. The marketing department of Fusible Plastics has prepared the following 10-year market survey for the hydrocarbon plasticizer:

YEAR	POTENTIAL SALES, LB/YR	ESTIMATED SALES PRICE, $/LB
1988	20.0 MM	0.52
1989	20.5 MM	0.52
1990	21.0 MM	0.51
1991	22.0 MM	0.50
1992	23.0 MM	0.50
1993–97	25.0 MM	0.48

The process to manufacture the plasticizer involves fluids only. The delivered equipment cost of the process equipment as of 1987 is as follows:

Tanks	$ 230,000
Pumps	75,000
Heat Exchangers	525,000
Filters	120,000
Reactors	1,200,000
Miscellaneous Equipment	350,000
TOTAL DELIVERED EQUIPMENT COST	$2,500,000

The company uses 1988 figures as a constant dollar basis, therefore, all figures are assumed to be in 1988 dollars, except the equipment costs. Land for this analysis may be considered as negligible, but working capital may be taken as 15% of the total capital investment. Apex Contractors has prepared a detailed estimate for the fixed capital investment of $12 million. The fixed capital investment is purchased and installed over a 2-year period prior to startup, which is expected to be January 1, 1988.

Chlorine is used to manufacture the hydrocarbon plasticizer. The chlorine is supplied by Fusibles' 200-ton per day plant located adjacent to the area where the proposed plasticizer unit is to be located. Ten tons per day of chlorine are required for the manufacture of the plasticizer. The total capital investment of the chlorine plant is $10 million.

Operating expenses for the proposed new unit are:

Raw Materials	$0.12/lb product
Labor and Supervision	$0.05/lb product up through 17.0 MM lb/yr and $0.04/lb product above this rate
Maintenance	6% per year of the fixed capital investment
Utilities	$0.03/lb product up through 17.0 MM lb/yr and $0.02/lb product above this rate
Other Direct Expenses	$0.01/lb product
Depreciation	10-year straight-line
Other Indirect Expenses	$0.01/lb product
General Overhead Expenses	$0.02/lb product

In the screening stage, unless a proposed project reflects an internal rate of return of 20% after taxes, the venture will not be considered. A federal income plus state tax rate of 48% may be assumed.

To conform to the standard evaluation procedure of Fusible Plastics, please prepare the following components of a feasibility study:

a. an estimate of the total capital investment for a 25-MM lb/yr batter-limits plant as of January 1, 1988 (use a 5% inflation factor to update 1987 to 1988 figures.)
b. annual operating expense sheets for all production rates
c. an estimate of the profitability by the IRR method, using straight-line depreciation and continuous interest
d. a cash position plot
e. a sensitivity analysis to determine the affect of the following variables upon the IRR:
   1. sales price ± 15% variation
   2. sales volume ± 15% variation
   3. raw material costs ± 15% variation
   4. fixed capital investment ± 15% variation

Based upon your analysis, what recommendations would you make to management concerning this proposed venture? Substantiate your answer with numerical results.

PROBLEM SOLUTION:

Estimate of total capital investment as of January 1, 1988

Apex Contractors has performed a detailed estimate of the fixed capital investment. The detailed estimate was $12,000,000, but could have an error of −5 to +15%. As a matter of policy, it might be wise to also estimate the fixed capital investment by the Lang, Hand, and Chilton methods to compare the results with Apex's figures. Often these shortcut methods mentioned can be used to obtain a preliminary fixed capital investment estimate before the outside contractor finishes his estimate.

LANG METHOD

Because the date of the delivered equipment price was given as 1987, let's assume it is January 1, 1987. Therefore, an inflation factor must be included in the calculations. The Lang factor for a fluid-processing unit given in Chapter 3 is 4.74 times the delivered equipment cost. Therefore, the fixed capital investment as of January 1, 1988 is:

$$(\$2.5\ MM)(4.74)(1.05) = \$12.5\ MM$$

HAND METHOD

This method involves the use of different factors for different types of equipment. The factors may be obtained in Chapter 3.

Item	Delivered Price	Factor	Component Cost
Tanks	$ 230,000	4.0	$ 920,000
Pumps	75,000	4.0	300,000
Heat Exchangers	525,000	3.5	1,838,000
Filters	120,000	4.0	480,000
Reactors	1,200,000	4.0	4,800,000
Miscellaneous	350,000	4.0	1,400,000
TOTAL	$2,500,000		$9,738,000

The total component cost must then be multiplied by the inflation factor to bring the costs to January 1, 1988:

$$(\$9,738,000)(1.05) = \$10,225,000$$

The fixed capital investment by the Hand method rounded off is $10,200,000.

CHILTON METHOD

As the estimate is for a battery-limits unit, only minimal services, utilities, and extensions will be assumed.

Item No.	Item	% of Item	Factor	Component Cost
1.	Delivered Equipment Cost	1	1.0	$ 2,500,000
2.	Installed Equipment Cost	1	1.43	3,575,000
3.	Process Piping (Fluid)	2	0.60	2,145,000
4.	Instrumentation (Extensive)	2	0.20	715,000
5.	Buildings and Site Development (Outdoor)	2	0.20	715,000
6.	Auxiliaries (Minor)	2	0.03	107,000
7.	Outside Lines (Minor)	2	0.03	107,000
8.	TOTAL PHYSICAL PLANT COSTS			$ 7,364,000
9.	Engineering (Simple)	8	0.25	1,841,000
10.	Contingencies (Firm)	8	0.15	1,105,000
11.	Size > $2 MM	8	0.03	221,000
12.	TOTAL FIXED CAPITAL INVESTMENT			$10,531,000

The fixed capital investment by the Chilton method may be rounded to $10,500,000.

The estimates of the fixed capital investment by all methods are:

Lang	$12,500,000
Hand	10,200,000
Chilton	10,500,000
Apex Contractor	12,000,000

If the errors in each method are considered, the estimates of the fixed capital investment are close. Because Apex's is a detailed estimate, its figures will be used in the rest of the feasibility study.

a. Total Capital Investment

ITEM	INVESTMENT
Land	$ 0
Fixed Capital Investment	$12,000,000
Allocated Capital $\left(\dfrac{10}{200}\right)(\$10,000,000)$	500,000
Working Capital	2,200,000
All Other Items	0
TOTAL CAPITAL INVESTMENT	$14,700,000

b. Operating Expenses

The most efficient way to present the results of these calculations is in tabular format. If the problem statement is followed, then a table similar to Table 10.8 will result. Care should be exercised, because certain unit costs change above the 17 million pounds per year production rate.

c. Cash Flow Analysis

The next step in a feasibility study is to develop a cash flow analysis. Again, like the operating expenses, it is advisable to present this analysis in tabular form. At this point, it should be apparent that both the operating expenses and cash flow analyses could have been prepared using an electronic spreadsheet. The cash flow analysis for this study is presented in Table 10.9.

PROFITABILITY ANALYSIS

The internal rate of return method is used by Fusible as the measure of a venture's profitability. Because the cash flow is uniform over the last 5 years of the project, Section D of the continuous interest tables in the appendix may be used. The cash flow each year is multiplied by 5 to obtain the total cash flow for that 5-year period, and then the weighted interest factor for the 6th to the 10th year is multiplied by that result to give the total cash flow discounted over that period. Detailed calculations for the study are presented in tabular format, Table 10.10.

Table 10.8   Operating Expenses.[a]

YEAR	1988	1989	1990	1991	1992	1993–97
Production, MM lb/yr	20.0	20.5	21.0	22.0	23.0	25.0
Raw Materials	2,400	2,460	2,520	2,640	2,760	3,000
Labor/Supv.	800	800	840	880	920	1,000
Maint.	720	720	720	720	720	720
Utilities	400	410	420	440	460	500
Other Dir.	200	205	210	220	230	250
Total Directs	4,520	4,615	4,710	4,900	5,090	5,470
Deprec.	1,200	1,200	1,200	1,200	1,200	1,200
Other Indirect	200	205	210	220	230	250
Total Indirect	1,400	1,405	1,410	1,420	1,430	1,450
Total Mfg Cost	5,920	6,020	5,120	5,320	6,520	6,920
General O'Head	400	410	420	440	460	500
Total Op. Exp.	6,320	6,430	6,540	6,760	6,980	7,420
Deprec.	1,200	1,200	1,200	1,200	1,200	1,200
Cash Op. Exp.	5,120	5,230	5,340	5,560	5,780	6,220

[a] All figures are expressed in $MM/yr.

Table 10.9   Cash Flow Analysis.[a]

YEAR	1988	1989	1990	1991	1992	1993–97
Prod., MM lb/yr	20.0	20.5	21.0	22.0	23.0	25.0
Sales, $	10,400	10,660	10,710	11,000	11,500	12,000
Cash Op. Expenses	5,120	5,230	5,340	5,560	5,780	6,220
Op. Income	5,280	5,430	5,370	5,440	5,720	5,780
Deprec.	1,200	1,200	1,200	1,200	1,200	1,200
NPBT	4,080	4,230	4,170	4,240	4,520	4,580
FIT (48%)	1,960	2,030	2,000	2,035	2,170	2,200
NPAT	2,120	2,200	2,170	2,205	2,350	2,380
DEP.	1,200	1,200	1,200	1,200	1,200	1,200
Cash Flow	3,320	3,400	3,370	3,405	3,550	3,580

[a] All figures are expressed in $MM.

d. Cash Position Plot

A cumulative cash position plot for this project was developed from the cash flow analysis Table 10.9. The plot is presented in Fig. 10.4.

e. Sensitivity Analysis

With the aid of a computer the sensitivity analysis can be prepared in a matter of minutes. By hand, the calculations will take hours.

Some companies prefer the results of the sensitivity analysis in tabular format, though others prefer a plot. Both will be presented here as Table 10.11 and Fig. 10.5.

This proposed venture does not meet Fusible's required minimum acceptable return of 20% after taxes. The base case gave a 15% return. Inasmuch as a number of items in this study are subject to error, the sensitivity analysis results show that at best only one variable, sales price, if in error, could possibly cause the return to exceed the barrier rate. Therefore, at this time, Fusible should not consider integrating backward in this product line. (NOTE: If statistical models had been proposed for the variables in this study, an uncertainty analysis could have been performed. We considered this possibility, but decided not to include an uncertainty analysis because of the considerable controversy over the methods and results).

SUMMARY

A feasibility analysis combines all the topics presented in Chapter 3 through Chapter 9. These include the preparation of a capital cost estimate, an estimate

Table 10.10   Profitability Analysis.[a]

TIME	INVESTMENT	CASH FLOW	15% FACTORS	PRESENT WORTH @ 15%	10% FACTORS	PRESENT WORTH @ 10%
2 Yr Before during	12,000	−12,000	1.350	−16,200	1.221	−14,652
Time 0	2,700	−2,700	1	−2,700	1	−2,700
1		3,320	0.929	3,084	0.952	3,161
2		3,400	0.799	2,717	0.861	2,927
3		3,370	0.688	2,319	0.799	2,693
4		3,405	0.592	2,016	0.705	2,401
5		3,550	0.510	1,811	0.638	2,265
6		3,580	0.439	1,572	0.577	2,066
7		3,580	0.378	1,353	0.522	1,869
8		3,580	0.325	1,164	0.473	1,693
9		3,580	0.280	1,002	0.428	1,532
10		3,580	0.241	863	0.387	1,385
End Tenth Year	2,700		0.223	602	0.368	994
			Net Present Worth	− 397	Net Present Worth	+ 5,634

$$IRR = 10 + \frac{5(5634)}{5634 - (-397)} = 14.7, \text{ say, } 15\%$$

[a] All figures are in $M/Yr.

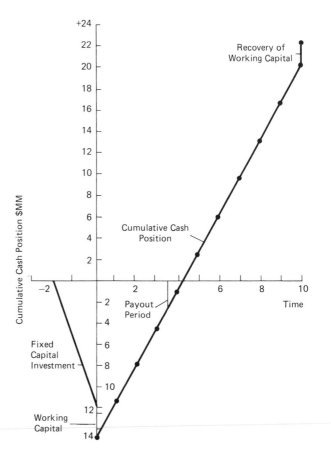

Figure 10.4. Example 10.1 Cumulative cash position plot.

Table 10.11 Results of Sensitivity Analysis.

ITEM	VARIATION FROM BASE CASE VALUES	RESULTING IRR
Sales Price	+15%	21
	−15%	12
Sales Volume	+15%	18
	−15%	11
Raw Materials	+15%	14
	−15%	16
Fixed Capital Investment	+15%	13
	−15%	18
	Base Case IRR 15%	

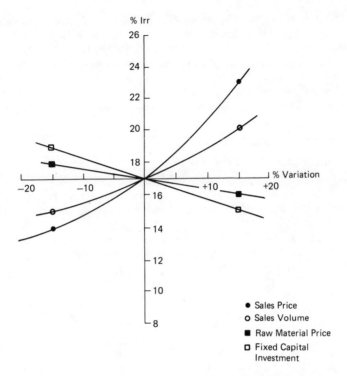

Figure 10.5. Example 10.1. Results of sensitivity analysis.

of the operating expenses, the calculation of a project's cash flow and its profitability. All these calculations are based upon estimates which are subject to error, it is then essential to determine what effect potential errors have upon the quantitative results of the study. This information is obtained by performing a sensitivity and, perhaps, an uncertainty analysis for the project.

The results of a feasibility analysis as has been seen are quantitative. Just as important as the quantitative data are the qualitative factors in the decision-making process. The next chapter addresses this topic.

PROBLEMS

10.1 The Spurline Co., Inc., is a small but stable young company manufacturing high-quality organic intermediates. The management of this company is also young and aggressive in its investment policy.

When Spurline enters a new venture, it evaluates profitability by measuring the cash flow and internal rate of return.

The staff engineering department has prepared a preliminary fixed capital cost estimate by the Chilton method. The estimated fixed capital investment is $5,000,000. Land alloted to the project is worth $200,000. Working capital is taken at $900,000, and startup expenses are $400,000.

The long-range planning group, of which you are a member, prepares economic evaluations that are then acted upon by the executive committee and ultimately by the board of directors. The planning group has the following operational guidelines for feasibility studies at this stage of development:

1. The project must yield a 20% IRR.
2. A payout period of less than 3 years.
3. ACRS depreciation guidelines.
4. A federal income tax rate of 46%.

It is expected that the construction will take 1½ years and that startup will be January 1988. Therefore, if approval is given, construction could not begin before July 1986.

After you consulted representatives of the manufacturing, marketing, and engineering departments, you estimated the net profit before taxes (NPBT) over a 10-year project life:

YEAR	NPBT, $M
0	0
1	$2,100
2	2,500
3	3,000
4	4,000
5	4,200
6	4,200
7	4,200
8	3,800
9	3,600
10	3,000

You may assume all the dollar figures have been corrected for inflation to January 1, 1988.

For the executive committee to review this project, please prepare the following information:

a. Estimate of the total capital investment
b. The payout period
c. The IRR
d. A sensitivity analysis of the effect on IRR for the following variables:
    1. Fixed capital investment ±20% variation
    2. Net profit before taxes ±20% variation
e. Your recommendations to management. Be sure to substantiate your recommendations.

10.2 The manufacture of a new specialty product is being considered by Tumbleweed, Inc. Although the market for this material is in the East, the plant is located in the southwestern United States because of the proximity of raw materials and the availability of a reliable source of labor. The market department has just completed a preliminary survey, which revealed the following sales potential and sales prices:

SALES VOLUME	SALES PRICE, $/LB
1,000,000 lb/yr	$0.32
2,000,000 lb/yr	0.30
3,000,000 lb/yr or more	0.26

For intermediate sales volumes, a straight-line interpolation of price may be assumed.

On November 1, the development department issued a preliminary report based upon a promising process developed by the research department. As a result of this study, the following costs were estimated for a plant producing 1,000,000 pounds per year of product, based upon 300 days of operation:

OPERATING COSTS PER DAY	
Raw Materials	$200
Labor	170
Sales Overhead	40
Depreciation	75
Maintenance	50
Utilities and other Fixed Costs	40
TOTAL	$575

The total fixed capital costs exclusive of land total $225,000. The plant is assumed to have a 10-year technical life.

The total fixed capital costs exclusive of land for capacities between 1 and 3 million pounds per year will vary directly as the 0.6 power of the capacity. Assume that an adequate land parcel is available at $4,000 for all plant sizes. Working capital is estimated to be 15% of the total capital investment.

The raw materials costs will be directly proportional to the amount of material produced. The labor cost will be constant between 1 and 2 million pounds per year. For more than 2 million pounds per year, the labor cost may be taken as 1.4 times that of the 1-million-pound rate.

Sales and overhead costs per year will be 1 cent/pound plus $40/day. Maintenance will be 6.7%/year of the total fixed capital investment, exclusive of land. Depreciation may be assumed to be 10%/year calculated by the straight-line method. Utilities and fixed operating expenses will be 5.34% of the total fixed capital costs. Income tax will be 46%.

The following information for a feasibility analysis is required to present to the planning board:

1. summaries of capital requirements, operating expenses, and profit-loss statements for 1.0, 1.5, 2.0, and 3.0 MM lb/yr

2. the optimum size plant, calculated by the IRR method
3. the break-even point
4. a sensitivity analysis showing the effect on the IRR optimum case of the following variables:
   a. sales price ±10 and ±25% variation
   b. fixed and working capital investment ±10 and ±25% variation

(NOTE: There are several possibilities that might be explored as variations on these two problems. For example, different depreciation methods might be used to develop different cash flow patterns. Cumulative cash position charts and break-even plots might be required. These problems could also be modified to include uncertainty analysis. Last, the calculations and summaries may be prepared by hand or by computers.)

REFERENCES

Strauss, R. *Chem. Eng.*, 112–116 (March 25, 1968).
Jones, B. W. *Inflation in Engineering Economic Analysis.* John Wiley & Sons, Inc., New York, 1982.
Smith, G. W., *Engineering Economy,* 3rd ed. Iowa State University Press, Ames, Iowa, 1979.
Griest, W. H. *Chem. Eng. Progr.,* 13–18 (June 1979).

11 CRITERIA FOR INVESTMENT

INTRODUCTION

A company continuously confronts investment decisions. Management has the responsibility of investing the earnings in financially attractive ventures. The decisions made by management affect the company's profitability and future success. The decision-making process is complex, requiring the skillful consideration of company objectives, such quantitative factors as internal rate of return, and such qualitative considerations as environmental and safety issues. The literature is replete with articles, essays, and books devoted to the subject of making investment decisions. This chapter is concerned with many of the factors that managers must consider for the investment of corporate funds.

ORIGIN OF INVESTMENT OPPORTUNITIES

The idea for a new product, process, service, or other venture may originate in a variety of ways. The manufacture of a product new to the company may have occurred as a result of a chance discovery in a research laboratory or by orderly, planned research through which existing company products are developed. Contact with customers or potential customers by a company's marketing staff often leads to improved or new products. New ventures may arise to protect or improve a company's competitive position.

To overcome process obsolescence or reduce operating expenses, projects are often initiated for new or improved processes. In the chemical process industries, batch processing equipment is frequently replaced by a continuous process that has a substantial amount of automatic process control equipment. In such instances, capital investment is justified by raw materials savings, better process yields, more efficient use of utilities, and savings in labor costs.

In the service industries, a project for capital expenditure, for example, personal computers, might be justified on the basis of better data base management and faster service to customers. In recent years, the presence of computers in insurance companies, retail marketing, accounting firms, engineering offices, etc., is evident.

Joint ventures are undertaken to take advantage of raw materials supplies or marketing and manufacturing expertise. These ventures lead to capital investment decisions by all parties involved. For example, a recent, domestic, three-company joint venture was undertaken. Company A had an excellent raw materials supply, Company B, the manufacturing expertise, and Company C, the marketing experience. All three companies were required to make investment contributions to the venture. Another recent example involves a foreign and a domestic company in the manufacture and sales of a petroleum-derived product. The domestic company has the technical competence for the design and construction of the manufacturing facilities, as well as the training of personnel. The foreign company has the raw materials supply, adequate at a low price for many years. A part of the capital investment is to be appropriated by both firms, and both will share in the profits. Therefore joint ventures of this type, which seem to be on the increase, are a source of new investment opportunities. A word of caution, however, is appropriate. Like people, companies have a "personality" or perhaps a style of management that might strain relationships between the parties.

Today mergers and acquisitions are daily news. These ventures require huge capital expenditures or transfers and are extremely critical decisions for all parties involved. What may appear to be an ideal merger or acquisition later may go sour. A company may try to acquire a favored raw materials position by obtaining another company, only to find later that funds were not available to meet the obligations of interest and principal on borrowed funds. A part of the acquired company might have to be sold to satisfy the obligations.

Although some examples of investment opportunities have been cited in this section, there are many sources of ideas that could ultimately lead to investment opportunities.

OBJECTIVES OF A COMPANY

One might ask: "What are the objectives of a company?" Before attempting to answer this question, we must recognize that companies exist for some economic gain or advantage, unlike government or nonprofit organizations. Corporate objectives change as the economy changes. Managers, be they from the business or technical areas of a company, are being educated in the newer management tools through various educational programs and experiences. A company that retains static objectives in this rapidly changing world is surely approaching economic stagnation.

If a group of executives were asked to state the financial objectives of their respective firms, a wide variety of answers would be received. Some of the answers might be: developing growth, maximizing return on net assets, a larger share of the market, increasing the net present value, etc. Petty, Scott, and Bird (1975) reported the results of a study of a select group of the Fortune 500 companies and found their financial objectives ranked as shown in Table 11.1.

From this study it is apparent that maximizing the percentage of return on assets, maximizing the aggregate earnings, and targeting the earnings per share growth rate are the most often stated objectives. Although a company may claim to state many objectives, most top management focuses on one or two. Weaver (1975) pointed out that ICI Americas had two objectives:

1. to maximize cash flow from all existing investments, and
2. to find outlets for a maximum of additional investment at returns that were greater than the minimum acceptable rate of return

He believed that other objectives interfered with the accomplishment of these two or limited their potential scope. With these comments as a preface, the rest of this chapter will deal with the criteria for investment that do influence the achievement of corporate objectives.

INVESTMENT CLASSIFICATION

Most firms have a priority or classification system for considering projects as they are brought before the executive committee or board of directors. A priority system categorizes projects according to project type and/or risk. Management will apply different investment criteria for each category. For

Table 11.1 Financial Objectives: Analysis by Rank.

RANKINGS	MAXIMIZE PERCENTAGE RETURN ON ASSET	MAXIMIZE AGGREGATE EARNINGS	TARGET EARNINGS PER SHARE GROWTH RATE	TARGET SHARE OF THE MARKET	MAXIMIZE COMMON STOCK PRICE	TOTAL
Percentage of times ranked first	37	15	36	2	11	100
Percentage of times ranked second	25	28	32	5	9	100
Percentage of times ranked third	23	18	19	22	18	100
Percentage of times ranked fourth	11	25	10	36	18	100
Percentage of times ranked fifth	6	13	0	42	40	100

example, a project involving a new product would have more stringent criteria than one involving quality improvement of an existing product that is being successfully marketed.

The number of categories in the priority system will depend upon the firm's product lines, company size, type of manufacturing, and management style. For example, a specialty chemical company in the mid-South categorizes projects as follows: cost reduction, expansion, new or improved products, replacement, safety problems, environmental control, research and development, and employee welfare. Some companies may find a two- or three-item priority system satisfactory.

For the purpose of discussion, let's consider the following classification:

Group 1: cost improvement projects
Group 2: product improvement projects
Group 3: expansion projects
Group 4: new ventures
Group 5: necessity projects

Cost improvement projects are usually associated with an operating process. Proposals in this category might include the installation of a waste-heat boiler to generate steam from a waste-heat stream or installation of process control equipment to reduce labor. Product improvement projects are justified on the basis of product quality. The installation of a filter system to remove suspended particles or a charcoal filter to remove color from a liquid stream are examples. The justification for such product improvements would be based upon preservation of an existing market that might be jeopardized or the possibility of an increased sales price for a higher quality product.

Expansion projects occur as the result of a need for increased production to meet a sales demand. Often a small amount of capital added to an existing process will yield excellent returns based on the incremental capital.

Ventures in Group 4 are by their very nature more risky. In this category, proposals might include a product or technology entirely new to the company and its operations or joint ventures with domestic or foreign partners. The investment decision for this group requires considerable study of all the possible ramifications.

Necessity projects are those that are essential to the company's operation or well-being. These proposals might include correction of an environmental or safety problem; elimination of a nuisance, such as noise; complying with laws; and improving public relations and company image. Necessity projects by their very nature do not have barrier rates of return to be met. Often it is a matter of proceeding with the project or ceasing operation. At best, the economics calculations made might show a decline in cash flow as a result of the project installation.

The approval of investment proposals in Group 1 incurs less risk than proposals in Group 3, expansion projects. The latter projects are based upon projections of increased production to meet sales demands that could easily diminish by the time the equipment is installed. In like manner, new ventures might involve an entirely new market and marketing strategy unfamiliar to the company. The element of risk in Group 4 is greater than in the previous groups. So in the hypothetical classification system presented, different investment criteria would be used for each group. A uniform single criteria system for all projects might be too conservative for some projects and too liberal for others. Although a classification system as described does not guarantee results, it is an attempt to group projects with similar risks into the same groups when considering capital budgeting. Management will make capital expenditure decisions that are of greatest benefit to the company and at the same time attempt to minimize risk.

QUANTITATIVE INVESTMENT FACTORS

The quantitative financial criteria have become more sophisticated in the last 25 years. In the years following World War II up to the late 1950s, investment decisions were based quantitatively upon return on investment or payout period calculations without regard for the time value of money.

More sophisticated techniques were developed and were taught by the graduate schools of business throughout the country. Middle management and young managers on the rise were often sent by their companies to management programs geared to industrial needs. As these people returned to their respective companies, there followed a gradual infusion of the new knowledge in the quantitative decision-making process. Hayes and Garvin (1982) cited a survey conducted by Klammer (1972): of 184 large manufacturing companies, 57% were evaluating investment proposals using discount techniques, in contrast to only 19% in 1959. A later survey by Bringham (1975) indicated that 94% of the companies were using these techniques.

Minimum Acceptable Rate of Return (MARR)

In any industrial investment there is an element of risk, because profits and cash flow cannot be predicted with accuracy. From our previous discussion of investment classification, it is obvious that certain projects are riskier than others.

Management will establish the MARR for investment categories based upon a number of factors. The cost of borrowing money is a major consideration. For the purpose of discussion here, it is assumed that projects would have to be funded from external sources and not from retained earnings. A determination of the cost of capital, as illustrated in Chapter 8, is essential. Management will also review proposed projects with respect to their current return on assets or investments. The availability of capital is dependent upon its cost. The more available, the less the cost.

Competing investments will affect the minimum acceptable rate of return. Management may adjust this figure for each investment category to weed out the less attractive proposals from consideration. In any healthy company, there are more project requests than there is money available for investment purposes. The differences in risks and the time required to recover the fixed capital investment are of primary consideration. The shorter the period of time, the less the element of risk. Of course, the general economic climate of the country, the world, and the company play an important role in management's decision to invest.

Many industrial concerns will require a 20–30% return after taxes for those projects of low risk at a preliminary stage of evaluation. As a secondary guide a payout period of 1 to 3 years is reasonable. As subsequent, more detailed estimates with additional research and engineering are prepared, the return has a tendency to decline.

Earlier in this chapter, we presented a proposed investment grouping of projects. For each group, a "hurdle," "barrier," or "minimum acceptable rate of return" is established by management for a venture to be funded. Proposals with similar risk levels are classified in each group. Management, therefore, may increase the "hurdle" rate required for a risky project. Each group has a "barrier" rate that must be met for a project to be considered for funding.

In addition to these quantitative measures, the capital expenditure goals will be considered in the decision-making process. A sample of the goals might be:

to achieve a given share of the market
to maximize the aggregate earnings
to maximize the common stock price to the stockholder

Management then has the responsibility of establishing minimum acceptable levels of returns, sometimes called *hurdle* or *barrier* rates, based upon the considerations above, or investing alternative ventures. Often a policy of doing nothing, that is, leaving the funds where they are, is better than doing something that may be regretted later.

Some authorities intimate that a single criterion is used. Nothing could be further from the truth. One major U.S. corporation we know well used six quantitative measures, as well as seven qualitative indicators for each capital budgeting decision. Each quantitative measure has some disadvantages, and as a result a single quantitative decision criterion may ignore the influence of uncertainty, market strategy, opportunity cost, etc. Because of the interdependence of many criteria, the reporting of a single value is limiting and inappropriate.

Profitability Measures

Chapter 8 presented the various methods for calculating profitability. Each of these methods has certain inherent advantages and disadvantages.

Return on original investment (ROOI) is a simple method that has been in use for many years. It is a quick method often used for screening purposes. It can be used to calculate returns for various fractions of capacity for individual years. This method does not take into account the time value of money, and it does not account for the timing of cash flows. Because averaging of profits is used in the calculation, the method allows for laxity in market and production cost forecasting.

There are numerous methods for calculating returns based on average investments. The investment value is reported on the average over the investment life. Rachlin (1974) reviews the averaging techniques and gives examples of each. This method is a comparison of the average annual net profits over the earning life to the average book investment including working capital multiplied by 100. The result is expressed as a percentage.

Payout period (POP), although it does not include the time value of money, is a very popular measure of profitability. It is simple to use, and it considers taxes properly. From its definition, cash flow is an integral part of the method. Payout period is concerned only with the amount of time it takes to recover the fixed depreciable investment from cash flow. As such it ignores land, working capital, and any investments made beyond the payout period. It ignores the later years of the project with respect to income, cash flow, and recovery of capital.

The three methods mentioned then do not take into account the time value of money. The effect of interest is important in today's economy, and the next three methods do take it into account.

Payout period with interest (POP + I) has all the advantages and disadvantages of POP, but it does consider the effect of interest on the investment and on cash flow. The net present worth method (NPW) relates all cash flows to an arbitrarily selected time zero. Discount or compound factors are applied to each cash flow item. The method considers all investment items properly, as well as income amount, income timing, and capital recovery. It does have the shortcoming that the result obtained—does not indicate the size of the project. To overcome this disadvantage, a present worth index (PWI) is often calculated relating the net present worth to some investment item, either fixed capital or total capital investment.

The Internal Rate of Return Method, IRR, provides a multiplicity of answers for unusual cash flow patterns. This method does consider the time value of money but projects with different lives cannot be compared correctly. Also, like the Present Worth Method, the result does not indicate the magnitude of the project.

Use of Quantitative Measures

As was mentioned earlier, some companies use several quantitative factors when making an investment decision. In Petty, Scott, and Bird (1975), mentioned earlier in this chapter, top-level executives felt that IRR and PW methods were of prime importance and were thought to be "theoretically" correct. Payout period, although third in the ranking, was often used as a supplementary tool. It was interesting to note that the same general relationships among these three quantitative profitability measures existed whether the managers were considering existing product or new product lines.

Inherent in the Present Worth Method is the assumption that an opportunity exists to reinvest in another venture at at least the cost of capital. The assumption behind the IRR Method is that there is an opportunity to invest in another project at the calculated IRR rate and this may not be the case. Bingham (1975) points out that investment decisions based upon Present Worth and IRR calculations can produce conflicts. For mutually exclusive projects, conditions may exist which cause direct conflicts in the conclusions drawn from the results. One condition occurs when the sizes of two projects are vastly different. The other condition occurs when the timings of cash flows are vastly different. For example, one project may have most of the cash flow in the early years, and in the other project the cash flows would occur later. Brigham mentions that in such cases it is possible to make an incorrect decision. He recommends that the NPW method be used as a criterion for investment, rather than IRR, assuming reinvestment at the cost of capital is implicit in the NPW method and is the better assumption. Reinvestment at the IRR rate may not be realistic.

QUALITATIVE FACTORS AFFECTING INVESTMENT DECISIONS

Authors of texts on technical economics would have the reader believe that quantitative financial criteria are the basis for investment decisions. This has also been the focus of many engineering economy courses. However, the authors' experience indicates that other criteria and objectives frequently enter into or control the decision-making process. There are instances in which major decisions based upon intangible factors oppose the results of a quantitative study.

In this section intangible factors will be presented and discussed with respect to their potential influence upon an investment decision.

What Are Intangibles?

Minimal information has been published concerning intangibles. Therefore, most of the information in this section comes from our experiences or from the meager literature.

Perry, Scott, and Bird (1975) presented the results of a study of intangible investment criteria. Their results are presented in Table 11.2, based upon responses from selected companies in the Fortune 500 list. They found that intangibles play a much more important role in the boardroom than many authors would lead you to believe. This is especially true as the time and money for an investment increase. The consideration of intangibles is often left until the end of an analysis, though they should have been considered at first.

Let's consider these intangibles and their potential effects upon an investment decision.

Employee Morale. This factor is directly related to the efficiency of an operation. If the employees do not consider their jobs or working conditions to be good, then surely this factor will affect not only the amount of material produced, but also the quality of the product. Quality circles have done much to improve a workers' interests in their immediate job and in their

Table 11.2 Qualitative Factors Affecting Investment Decisions

FACTOR	ORDER OF IMPORTANCE*
Company Image	1
Legal	2
Employee Morale	3
Employee Safety	4
Environmental	5
Management Goals	6

* Descending order of importance.

company by giving employees the opportunity to suggest, criticize, and inject new ideas about the working environment into management's decision-making process. Management, in turn, has an obligation to listen, digest, and, if possible, put into action employees' suggestions. Employees who feel they "belong" to an organization will take more interest in it, be more content, and display high morale.

Employee Safety. A safe work place not only reduces the cost of operation through reduced injury and lost production but contributes markedly to employee morale. Safety should be regarded as a joint venture, not an adversary position between labor and management. Labor has done much to improve the safety in such work places as refineries, textile mills, steel mills, paper mills, and mining operations, to name a few. Unsafe conditions cause accidents to personnel and equipment, which in turn increases the costs of insurance of capital equipment, causes losses of raw materials, utilities, and production. A plant designed and constructed with safety considered early in the planning stages will result in overall operating cost savings and contribute also to employee morale.

Environmental Constraints. Increasingly tighter restrictions on water, air, land, and noise pollution have forced management to reconsider existing operations as well as future investments. There are daily examples of plant closings due to the inability of companies to meet environmental standards. Like the two preceding intangibles, it is impossible to determine dollar effects, that is cost and benefit. It is a simple matter to determine the capital requirements to meet environmental standards, but the benefits manifest themselves as continued operation and community recognition of a company's good citizenship. Management has the option of meeting the environmental standards or shutting down, but the latter action can seriously affect the community. From a quantitative standpoint, the capital costs, operating expenses, and change in cash flow can be calculated to meet environmental standards. A return is meaningless—as the options are very clear.

Legal Constraints. Local and federal laws are intangibles that must be considered whenever an investment decision is made. A proposed venture that violates or infringes upon a statute is doomed. Fines or high capital expenditures to avoid legal action can quantitatively affect a firm's operation. It is essential, before locating a new plant, to review the existing laws and seek advice on their influence upon a site location. Zoning ordinances, potential antitrust actions, and potential licensing or patent infringements are examples. Most firms want to avoid litigation, as such proceedings can be long and costly and damage a firm's image in the community.

Product Liability. In recent years this intangible has received public attention. Consumer advocates and the public demand that a product, be it a pharmaceutical or a child's toy, must be safe to use. Management should consider this intangible early in the project development stages. A company must be able to answer a strong "yes" to the question: "Is the product safe?" It would be a wiser decision to forego the installation of a plant until there is a high probability that the product will meet safety requirements. In the news media, examples of product liability cases seem to increase daily. Management, therefore, must take a responsible posture with regard to this intangible.

Corporate Image. How a company is perceived by the public is indeed an important factor in capital investment decisions. A poorly maintained plant is an eyesore in the community and indicates an indifference about concern for the locale. It also indicates to potential purchasers of the company's products a sloppiness in management that could carry over in the purchaser's mind as laxity in maintaining product quality. General housekeeping within the plant and its immediate environs is indicative of the type of management.

The corporate image also is expressed in how much positive interest a company takes in community affairs. Social responsibility, such as corporate giving or sponsoring scholarships and programs that benefit society and the community, contributes to a company's image. As a consequence, corporate public relations officials are especially cognizant of these intangible factors and must convey their ideas to top management. The company image is considered in any investment decision because capital expenditures often are required to maintain a good corporate image. Again, like other intangibles, it is difficult to calculate a return, because a dollar figure can not be assigned to the benefit obtained from an expenditure.

Management Goals. This is a complex intangible, because it involves not only the corporate goals, but also the personal goals of individual managers.

Although the question of corporate objectives were mentioned earlier in this chapter, it might be advisable to point out that company growth and cash flow are two of the goals by which management effectiveness is measured. These are important goals for the survival of any company and any manager.

On a personal basis, managers may make an investment decision on the basis of personal interests and not necessarily for the well-being of the organization, irrespective of company policy and/or ethics. For example, a manager may make a decision based upon the influence on his job security within the company. Certainly, he would not approve of an action that would diminish or eliminate his position. Some managers may promote an investment decision that would expand their "empire," giving them greater company visibility, perhaps a better title, as well as an increase in compensation. The number of people supervised affects a person's salary in some organizations. All these points promote personal gain. Although within most organizations there are checks and balances, it is doubtful that the personal aspect can be eliminated entirely.

Attempts to Quantify Intangible Factors

Numerous methods have been proposed in an attempt to present multiple intangible criteria in an explicit format. Multiple criteria, of course, could include factors that might be quantified, such as price, payout period, etc., but also might include safety, environmental criteria, or image. Five methods for formulating these criteria are:

simple ordinal scale (1965)
symbolic scorecard (1977)
product profile chart (1961)
Churchman-Ackoff method (1965)
ranking and rating with additives model (1965)

The details of these approaches can be found in the references cited.

The first three listed form a group that uses one form or another of ordinal (numerical) ranking. The last two methods involve a weighted ranking. The symbolic scorecard and product profile chart are elaborations of the simple ordinal scale. These methods illustrate differences among factors, but also have the problem of equality of factors. To emphasize the inequality of factors, the Churchman-Ackoff and ranking and rating with additive model methods attempt to apply weighting factors, but these two methods are not as explicit as the three previous methods. Furthermore, the complexity of the methods tends to obscure the evaluation of intangible factors.

Another point of view is: Why do any of this? Why, because the five methods go into considerable detail to tell a manager what he already knows, namely, his own personal preferences. Angelelli (1983) pointed out that the "management decision maker may not always know what his own preferences are within the context of the firm's objectives." Nevertheless, the methods outlined above, when used properly, can present the manager with an explicit and consistent interpretation of intangible values. This exercise forces the manager to assign weighting factors and will have the effect of clarifying his own preferences.

Shepard (1962) discussed psychological factors that affect the manager's decision making process, and Cochran and Zeleny (1978) considered morality as a value criterion.

Concluding Remarks

Both authors of this text have been in company positions where they observed the strong influence of intangible factors upon the decision making process. Certainly, there are no formulas or cookbook methods for placing these factors in a value judgment array. Perhaps sometime in the future a methodology will be devised. In the meantime, the mental exercise of attempting to prioritize the intangible factors is worthy of consideration.

A VIEW FROM THE TOP

Executive Committee

After a proposal has passed through the various stages of approval, if it still appears to be attractive, it will ultimately be brought to the corporation's executive committee. In some companies, a proposal may be received by a person or a small review committee prior to executive committee action. The purpose of this review is to ensure that all the requisite information is available and in the proper format. If not, the proposal may be sent back to the originator or, if the corrections or additions are minor, the review committee may make the changes.

Executive committee meetings may be held weekly, biweekly, or monthly, depending upon company policy and the amount of material on the agenda. It is essential that the proposals brought before the executive committee be in a specified format, so that the committee members can quickly read and digest the request.

Often proposals coming from an operating division may be voluminous, containing substantial data. The members of the executive committee may not wish to read all the material, so frequently the proposal is simplified to a one- or two-page summary sheet attached to the proposal. The proposal sheet may have been developed by the originator of the proposal or the review committee. Nevertheless, the detailed data used to develop the proposal are on hand should they be needed in the executive committee meeting. The members of this committee are busy, and there are usually many items on the meeting agenda; therefore, there is a need for the information to be in a succinct yet factual format.

The person who developed the proposal for investment and his immediate superior or division manager may make the formal oral presentation to the executive committee. The time allotted for such a presentation is of the order of minutes, perhaps 15 to 20. It is essential that the person or persons making the formal presentation be well informed about the proposal. Therefore, it is wise to rehearse the presentation, so that all pertinent information is presented clearly and concisely. Often this is an opportunity for young people to have their talents recognized.

In executive committee meetings not only are the quantitative factors discussed, but the qualitative factors in the decision making process, as mentioned earlier in the chapter, are becoming increasingly important. One of the authors of this text was assigned the task of attending executive committee and board meetings to note the intangible factors used in each capital investment decision. Management was intensely interested in the affect these intangibles had upon the approval or disapproval of a proposed investment.

Board of Directors

A board of directors consists of the key corporate officers plus prominent people in business, government, military, or educational affairs. Board meetings occur about once a month. In an effort to make the most efficient use of time, the actions of the executive committee are summarized. Investment proposals that may have been voluminous originally are usually condensed to one page or even one paragraph. This condensation must contain the absolutely essential information upon which the board can act. Of course, the information supporting the proposed investment is available at the board meeting should the directors want to pursue some detail. The same personnel who presented the project to the executive committee may be required to be available in an anteroom, should their assistance be needed. Usually they are not in attendance at the board meeting.

Boards of directors comprise busy people who have many interests, and some members may not be entirely knowledgeable about the corporation's business ventures. All presentations therefore should be cloaked in simple terminology easily understood by the members. They are interested in the cost of a proposed venture and the ultimate benefits to the company, its future growth, as well as to the stockholders.

SUMMARY

Investment decisions are not simple because many factors must be considered. Although some authors would have the reader believe that one or perhaps two quantitative factors are needed to invest in a venture, usually several quantitative factors are computed. Qualitative factors are playing a more significant role in today's decision-making process than they have in the past. In part this is due to the social consciousness of industry and in part to great consumer advocacy. Qualitative factors cannot be expressed effectively in numerical terms. In any decision the quantitative and qualitative factors considered for a specific venture must be consistent with the objectives of the firm. The decision process is multifaceted and complex, without simple or easy answers.

It is essential that the factors discussed in this chapter be clearly and effectively stated in any proposal for investment. Thuesen, Fabrycky, and Thuesen (1977) published a critical fact: "Responsibility for the acceptance or rejection of an engineering proposal is exercised more often than not by persons who have not been concerned with the technical phases of the proposal. Also, the persons who control acceptance are likely not to understand technical matters."

Management, in the final analysis, may be required to consider economic tradeoffs in a given operating environment, becoming more sensitive to the impact of intangible factors in the decision making process.

The next step in funding a venture is to prepare the necessary documentation for the Executive Committee or the Board of Directors. This documentation, including not only the quantitative but also the qualitative data, is called a Request for Capital Appropriation. Once the appropriation is approved, the project is then scheduled for capital budgeting. The process of developing the capital appropriation and the capital budget are discussed in the next chapter.

REFERENCES

Harris, J. S. *Chem. Eng. News,* 110–118 (April 17, 1961).

Shepard, R. N. "On Subjectively Optimum Selection Among Multi-Attribute Alternatives." Paper presented at annual meeting of American Association for the Advancement of Science, Philadelphia, December 26, 1962.

Dean, B. V., and Nishry, M. J. ORSA, 13 (4) (1965).

Klammer, T. P. *J. Bus.,* 393 (July 1972).

Rachlin, R. *How To Use Return-on-Investment Concepts and Techniques for Profit Improvement.* New York: Pilot Books, 1974.

Weaver, J. B. *Eng. Econ.,* 20 (1), 1–35 (1975).

Petty, J. W., Scott, D. F., and Bird, M. M. *Eng. Econ.,* 20 (3), 159–172 (1975).

Bringham, E. E. *Financial Management,* 18, Autumn 1975.

Narasimham, S. L. "A Survey of Business Applications of Multiple Criteria Decision Making Techniques." Paper presented at TIMS/ORSA National Meeting, San Francisco, May 1977.

Thuesen, H. G., Fabrycky, W. J., and Thuesen, G. J. *Engineering Economy,* 5th ed. Englewood Cliffs, New Jersey: Prentice-Hall, Inc., 1977.

Cochrane, J. L., and Zeleny, M. ed. *Multiple Criteria Decision Making.* University of South Carolina Press, Columbia, 1978.

Brigham, E. E. *Financial Management: Theory and Practice,* 3rd ed. Chicago: Dryden Press, 1981.

Hayes, R. A., and Garvin, T. J., *Harvard Bus. Rev.* 60 (3), 71–79 (May-June 1982).

Angelelli, T. A. Private communication (1983).

12 CAPITAL APPROPRIATION—CAPITAL BUDGETING

INTRODUCTION

The two most important areas of management responsibilities or functions are capital budgeting and tactical and strategic planning. These functions determine the conceptualization, continuing life, and growth of a successful, vigorous enterprise. Both capital budgeting and planning involve selecting and implementing sound productive investments. Top management relinquishes control of a business organization if it delegates any part of these responsibilities.

Committees or groups may be formed to analyze capital budgets and planning documents. But their observations or conclusions should be merely recommendations to top management. Preparing or reviewing budget proposals is usually the concern, in manufacturing organizations, of the engineering economic analyst, who performs a vital and responsible role that requires objective scientific analysis of alternative proposals. There is no room for biased judgment, intuitive hunches, or influenced decision making.

The capital budgeting function can be divided into three categories depending on the time involved.

1. Strategic planning—setting goals, objectives, and broad business plans, including financial planning for 5 to 10 years into the future.
2. Tactical planning—determining the detail planning for following the strategic plan for the next 2 to 5 years, including financial planning.
3. Capital budgeting—this usually involves the request, analysis, and approval of expenditures to be initiated during the following fiscal year.

Our discussion of the competition for capital dollars will treat the periods in that order.

STRATEGIC PLANNING

The long-term goals of the organization are set by the strategic plan, which charts the course of the company or corporation for the next 5 years at a minimum. This plan may call for vertical integration, that is, expanding back into the production of raw materials used in the current production facilities or expanding forward by using current product to make another product, bringing the company a step closer to the consumer. For example, a chemical company may make vinyl acetate from acetic acid and ethylene and sell its product, the vinyl acetate, for the manufacture of many other products including adhesives and paint. Investing in a plant to produce acetic acid or ethylene would be integrating backward, but investing in a plant to produce adhesives or paint would be a vertical integration forward toward the ultimate consumer of the product.

Or a company may decide to expand into related products sold in essentially the same markets. For example, a chemical company that sells ethyl alcohol may elect to sell methyl alcohol or methyl ethyl ketone also. Or a company that has equipment for producing one type of product may use the same equipment, if it has idle capacity, to produce products in another market. For example, a producer of vending machines may elect to produce steel lockers for educational and industrial organizations.

The addition of a new major product line will many times require years of planning, market analysis, and assignment and acquisition of human and capital resources and equipment. For example, a company that has produced and marketed typewriters and office equipment will be making a major commitment of financial assets to hire experienced technical personnel and train many of its supervisors and employees, if it decides to enter into microprocessors and produce word processors.

Any company that decides to automate a large manufacturing facility should do so on the basis of a well-thought-out plan for the manufacturing system and then work toward that master plan. This should be done for several reasons.

1. An overall plan for automating the entire manufacturing system will permit an estimate of the capital requirements in completion of the total objective.
2. The overall plan will also permit determining in detail the final personnel requirements, from the standpoint of both numbers and qualifications required, so that training can be initiated at the appropriate time. And do not neglect the cost of reassignment of personnel and their training as part of the economic analysis.
3. Once the overall plan is complete, the key portions of this master plan may be selected for early detail design, acquisition, and installation. Thus, tactical plans may be developed from the strategic plan.
4. Being aware of the master process flow in the system will help avoid costly mistakes. Such mistakes include buying the wrong automated devices, buying an automated device that has more features than required

and thus was more expensive than needed, and location of new equipment in the wrong place.

Scientists and engineers must recognize that decisions made at the manufacturing level may set the nature of the entire organization's thrust in the marketplace. There are important tradeoff decisions. In the plant equipment area, should it be general purpose or special purpose? Should the tooling be temporary, minimal tooling or production tooling? In production, does the plant design for minimum downtime or labor cost or time in process or maximum output or minimum raw material and product inventory?

Setting the strategic plan is the responsibility of top management with assistance, as deemed necessary, by scientists and engineers in the organization. This is the roadmap for the future for the organization.

TACTICAL PLANNING

It is the tactical plan of the corporation, company, or plant in which more engineers and scientists will become involved than in the strategic plan. Each location in a multiplant corporation should lay out its tactical plans for meeting the strategic goals of the corporation. With a few exceptions for emergency expenditures, the yearly capital budget should have few surprises and should follow a defined, moving, 5-year tactical plan. The plan should have contingencies to allow for product demand that exceeds the forecasted growth and for product demand that falls short of the product growth.

A well-managed plant will have records indicating when key pieces of equipment need to be replaced and the cost of replacement. Plant engineers will know where the plant bottlenecks are and what level of production will require a capital expenditure to eliminate the bottlenecks. Automation, if justified in the manufacturing facilities, of individual operations in the plant should be part of an integrated evaluation plan that includes manpower planning, facilities planning, and product planning.

But typical of the industrial environment, the capability of an organization to convert its incoming purchased materials to the best product in the market at the lowest price is restrained by the resource base of the company and the existing levels of technology. So the challenge is to satisfy the consumer demand, limited always by human, material, and capital resources in exploiting the existing levels of technology. Thus it is incumbent on the technical personnel to plan carefully and spend wisely to avoid wasting any of the precious resources. And of necessity, they must be aware of the latest technology, to avoid being put out of business by competition.

It can be expected that demand will exceed the supply of funds. If demand does not exceed supply, it is apparent that management and technical people are failing to be imaginative and creative. It is their function and obligation to suggest better methods, better equipment, improved processes, and replacement of old and obsolete equipment. It is management's duty to come up with ideas for expenditures, not to avoid expenditures.

Some products have a life that is practically infinite. For such commodity products as nuts, bolts, and others, inventiveness and improvements can be applied only in materials handling, scheduling, and equipment, with little change in the product itself. Other products appear to have an infinite life cycle, but are constantly improved or changed to improve customer appeal. Such items include appliances, lawn mowers, etc. Other products are improved to the point of essentially making earlier models obsolete. This category includes such items as radios and television sets. Sometimes the major change is in materials of construction. In the past we have talked about the pounds of plastic in a steel automobile. In the very near future we will be talking about the pounds of steel or metal in a plastic automobile.

Other products have a finite life cycle and almost require the conception of a new product as soon as the first product is introduced into the marketplace. And so while manufacturing equipment is busy with the first product, studies are underway to determine how to modify the equipment to produce the new product.

We are currently in the midst of at least three technical revolutions.

1. The silicon revolution. The silicon chip with its tremendous capacity for storing data and instructions is rapidly changing the manufacturing environment. It has been the force that has converted this nation to an information society.
2. The robotics and automation revolution. Whereas the silicon revolution has been under way for 30 or more years, the robotics and automation revolution is just beginning. It will have more impact on the way we live, on the industrial environment, and the type of employment available than the silicon revolution, though indeed it, too, is part of the silicon revolution, because automated devices rely on the silicon chip. The social changes caused by automation will be as great as the great Industrial Revolution of history.
3. The biotechnical revolution. Younger than the robotics and automation revolution, the biotechnical revolution is just getting under way, but its occurrence is as sure as the changing of the seasons. The biotechnical revolution will have three separate thrusts.
   a. Fermentation technology. Continuous fermentation with "yeasts" will be capable of producing drugs and chemicals from new and cheaper raw materials.
   b. Enzymes technology. These "living catalysts" will permit more efficient production of chemical substances.

c. Bioengineering or gene splicing. From the simplest elements of life to medicines and agricultural products, the potential of this technology for serving mankind is awesome.

But why mention these revolutions in a chapter about budgeting? Because the technical personnel of the organization must be aware of where technology is heading and how this exploding technology will affect their company's operations. Though most scientists and engineers are specialists, becoming experts, in a selected field, they must also be generalists to the extent that they have an idea of what is going on, technically, in the industrial world around them. This can be accomplished by reading, by being involved in technical associations and professional groups, and by keeping in touch with salespeople who will tout the latest technical innovations in their equipment.

THE ANNUAL CAPITAL BUDGET

Decisions to make capital expenditures can be based on any of a number of principles. Some of the more common ones are listed below.

Probably the most frequently used nonanalytical approach to decision making is the *intuitive decision.* This decision is based on the hunch that it is the right decision. Unfortunately, there are those managers who made a decision in the past based on a hunch, and it fortunately (or unfortunately) turned out to be the right decision. As a result, the manager decided that he or she possessed supernatural powers that permitted him or her to guide the company with decisions with no basis of fact or of analysis. The overall result was predictable.

Another too often employed basis of decision is the *squeaky wheel approach.* Based on the concept that the squeaking wheel is the one that gets greased, managers resort to verbal barrages in memoranda and oral pleas for money until approval is given to stop the noise. It would have been better to put the vehicle with the squeaky wheel (the manager) in the barn for a rest and an opportunity to come up with an analytical justification for the rest.

There is also the *outside expert* basis of making a decision. It culminates in an executive reply that may be phrased: "I spoke to a man at the club yesterday who knew a man who said, 'Don't get into the (   ) business. I know a man who lost his shirt in that business.' " Or, "I heard a stock analyst the other day say that the (   ) business is due to grow." The comments, of course, are irresponsible and lack backup detail.

There's also the *necessity method,* which is the result of waiting until a piece of equipment must be replaced almost immediately or the plant will shut down. This method is foolproof, because no one can deny that the replacement is not necessary. Of course, the plant that uses this method is protecting extravagantly high operating costs to guarantee minimum profits.

Taking a step closer to an analytical approach, but leaving much to be desired, is the *payback period,* which is generally used in its simplest form, that is, without allowance for the time value of money. The misled management that feels this to be a valid measure of merit will be making decisions unrelated to the investment concept. Usually the management that employs this measure of merit has no understanding of the time value of money or the concept of engineering economic analysis.

No proposal will be accepted unless it has an extremely short payback (or payout) period. Usually these are set at 1 or 2 years. Such managers fail to realize that they may be blocking out some projects that would have had excellent returns. In decisions involving cost savings of automation or in simple replacement economy, this type of stipulation tends to extend the use of obsolete and uneconomical equipment.

In any of the above methods, personal bias often plays a major role in the decision making. Whether used consciously or not, many psychological and personal interest factors are likely to weigh for or against a particular choice.

SCIENTIFIC ANALYSIS IN PRACTICE

Most well-managed companies achieving good returns on invested dollars are doing so by careful analysis of investment proposals. In most companies 3 or 4 months before the end of a fiscal year capital budget requests are prepared. This activity is going on at the same time that the operating forecast is being prepared. If the corporation's fiscal year coincides with the calendar year, then shortly after the summer is over, plant engineers document their most promising capital expenditures. And concurrently financial people are preparing an estimate of the year-end financial condition and the expected cash flow during the coming year. The source of funds for capital investment was discussed in Chapter 2, and the setting of the minimum acceptable rate of return or barrier return was discussed in Chapter 8.

Standard Form Use

Most industrial organizations provide a detailed multipage form known by various names, such as a *Request for Approval of Capital Expenditure* (RACE) or *Request for Expenditure* (RFE) or *Authority for Expenditure* (AFE), etc.

This is usually a loosely structured cover page that has more the appearance of a memorandum than a form. It should describe the essential features of the investment proposal, such as:

1. Is it a cost savings or profit improvement investment? (In this regard, cost savings is a reduction in cost, and a profit improvement involves an increase in revenue by means of a new product or an increase in volume or price of an old product as a result of product or packaging changes.)
2. A discussion of the market involved if a new product. What is the total market, what area, what is the projected increase in share of the market, and what will be the reaction of the competition?
3. Pertinent positive and negative considerations other than economic ones, for example, safety, environment, personnel, union or employee relations, community relations, etc.
4. The location of the investment.
5. The effect on human resources, for example, how many personnel will be required and of what nature? Will we promote from within or go outside for special qualifications?

Some of these questions may be answered. Some may be noted as being studied.

The cover page is followed by several pages that present the economic analysis of the investment proposal. Table 12.1 presents an example of a form that could be used. Page A covers the manufacturing cost summary of the product, allowing for cost reduction investments as well as profit improvement investments. Note that one sheet is required to develop the net income from operations for each year of the time horizon being studied.

The results of these sheets are placed on page B, Discounted Cash Flow of Income from Operations. Figures are entered on the appropriate lines under the column titled Pretax/pgs A. From this, the tax can be calculated and the after-tax income posted, which, along with depreciation from line 22, pg A, will give the cash flow year by year. The factors under 10%, 15%, etc., can then be multiplied by the yearly cash flows to discount their value to a present worth. When they are totaled, the discounted cash flow of income from operations is available, discounted at that specific percentage.

Page C is the summary of expenditures, including capitalized items that are depreciable. It will be noted that the invested cost and estimated accuracy of investment are requested. The latter figure is a beneficial feature of the form. The sheet provides for expense items and working capital to give total expenditures.

The results of page C are transmitted to page D, which permits totaling

Table 12.1   Request for Approval of Capital Expenditure.

Project No. _____

SUMMARY: PRETAX INCOME FROM OPERATIONS

Page A_____ Year _____

Project Name _____   Economic Life _____

Analyst _____ Date _____   Period No. _____

		INCREASE	DECREASE
REVENUE CHANGE RESULT OF PROJECT			
Production Capacity (Gain or loss resulting from change in capacity)	1.	_____	_____
Product Quality or Reliability (Gain or loss in revenue resulting from change in quality)	2.	_____	_____
Other Changes (Gain or loss resulting from other changes) Note here:	3.	_____	_____
Selling Costs			
TOTAL REVENUE CHANGE	4.	_____ A	_____ B
DIRECT COST CHANGE			
Direct Labor (including fringes)	5.	_____	_____
Direct Materials	6.	_____	_____
Subcontract Work	7.	_____	_____
Overtime	8.	_____	_____
Other	9.	_____	_____
TOTAL DIRECT COST CHANGE	10.	_____ A	_____ B
INDIRECT COST CHANGE			
Indirect Labor (including fringes)	11.	_____	_____
Indirect Materials	12.	_____	_____
Rework	13.	_____	_____
Scrap	14.	_____	_____
Quality Control	15.	_____	_____
Maintenance	16.	_____	_____
Tooling	17.	_____	_____
Downtime	18.	_____	_____
Utilities	19.	_____	_____
Inventory	20.	_____	_____
Overtime	21.	_____	_____
Depreciation	22.	_____	_____
TOTAL INDIRECT COST CHANGE	23.	_____ A	_____ B
RESULTING CHANGE			
Net Increase in Revenue, 4A - 4B	24.	_____	(Note: one sheet required for each year.)
Net Decrease in Direct Cost, 10B - 10A	25.	_____	
Net Decrease in Indirect Cost, 23B - 23A	26.	_____	
NET INCOME FROM OPERATIONS, 24 + 25 + 26	27.		

Table 12.1 (Continued)

REQUEST FOR APPROVAL OF CAPITAL EXPENDITURE

Project No. _____

DISCOUNTED CASH FLOW OF INCOME FROM OPERATIONS
Page B_____

Economic Life _____   Date of Startup (Zero Point) _____

Depreciation Schedule Used _____   Tax Rate Used _____

End of Year	Income from Operation			Cash Flow (0%)	D.C.F. at Various %							
	Pretax Pgs. A	After Tax	Depr.		10%		15%		20%		25%*	
					Factor	P.W.	Factor	P.W.	Factor	P.W.	Factor	P.W.
1					0.909		0.870		0.833		0.800	
2					0.826		0.756		0.694		0.640	
3					0.751		0.658		0.579		0.512	
4					0.683		0.572		0.482		0.410	
5					0.621		0.497		0.402		0.328	
6					0.565		0.423		0.335		0.262	
7					0.513		0.356		0.279		0.210	
8					0.467		0.327		0.233		0.168	
9					0.424		0.284		0.194		0.134	
10					0.386		0.247		0.162		0.107	
11					0.351		0.215		0.135		0.086	
12					0.319		0.187		0.112		0.069	
13					0.290		0.163		0.094		0.055	
14					0.263		0.141		0.078		0.044	
15					0.239		0.123		0.065		0.035	
16					0.218		0.107		0.054		0.028	
17					0.198		0.093		0.045		0.023	
18					0.180		0.081		0.038		0.018	
19					0.164		0.070		0.031		0.014	
20					0.149		0.061		0.026		0.012	
Sal-vage**					0.149		0.061		0.026		0.012	
Tot.												

*If higher percentages are needed, attach additional page B.
**Salvage value of fixed assets.
NOTE: Operating income is after changes for depreciation but excludes tax credits and credit for displaced or idled equipment.

Analyst _____   Date _____

Table 12.1 (Continued)

REQUEST FOR APPROVAL OF CAPITAL EXPENDITURE

Project No. _____

SUMMARY OF EXPENDITURES

Page C_____

CASH OUTFLOW

CAPITALIZED ITEMS	Cost	Date of Payment	Expected Accuracy of Estimate
Major Pieces of Equipment			
Delivered Cost	_____		
Installation Costs	_____		
Piping	_____		
Building Additions	_____		
Electrical	_____		
Heating, Ventilating, Air Conditioning	_____		
Engineering	_____		
Purchasing	_____		
Contractor's Fee	_____		
Other	_____		
Prestartup Training	_____		
Licensing	_____		
Contingency	_____		
TOTAL	_____		

TOTAL OF CAPITAL ITEMS

Payment by Years

    -3 to -2   _____

    -2 to -1   _____

    -1 to 0   _____

ITEMS EXPENSED   _____

TOTAL   _____

     _____

Working Capital Required   _____

TOTAL EXPENDITURES   _____

Analyst _____   Date _____

Table 12.1   (Continued)

REQUEST FOR APPROVAL OF CAPITAL EXPENDITURE

Project No. _____

INTERNAL RATE OF RETURN

CASH OUTFLOW O -- From Page C

Page D_____

	0%	10%		15%		20%		25%	
		Factor	P.W.	Factor	P.W.	Factor	P.W.	Factor	P.W.
Capitalized Items									
Year -3 to -2	____	1.210	____	1.343	____	1.440	____	1.563	____
Year -2 to -1	____	1.100	____	1.150	____	1.200	____	1.250	____
Year -1 to 0	____	1.000	____	1.000	____	1.000	____	1.000	____
Total Capital Items	____		____		____		____		____
Expensed Items	____								
Working Capital									
Total Capital, O	____		____		____		____		____
CASH INFLOW I									
Operating Cash Flow, Page B	____		____		____		____		____
Investment Credit	____	1.000	____	1.000	____	1.000	____	1.000	____
Expense Tax Credit	____	1.000	____	1.000	____	1.000	____	1.000	____
Disposal of Idled Asset	____	1.000	____	1.000	____	1.000	____	1.000	____
Total Inflow, I	____		____		____		____		____

Ratio O/I

The internal rate of return is the interest rate at which the sum of the total of the present worth of the receipts I is equal to the present worth of the expenditures O.

Interpolation Chart

I.R.R.

Ratio O/I

Internal Rate of Return _____

Analyst _____   Date _____

the capital requirements as cash outflow [O] and the operating cash inflow from page B to be added to the investment tax credit, expense tax credit, and idled asset disposal to give total inflow [I]. This is done at each progressive interest rate listed, until that rate of discount is used that discounts the cash inflow [I] until it is equal to or less than the value of the cash outflow [O]. The values of the ratio of O to I at the applied interest rates are plotted on the interpolation chart, and the intersection of the line drawn through these points with an O/I ratio of 1.0 will give that value of the interest that represents the internal rate of return for that project.

This analysis procedure may be adapted or changed to the unique cost elements or conditions of a particular plant or company's cost elements. In some companies financial leverage is used by borrowing money against the asset. Most companies allow for the reduced net cost of the investment through further considerations at corporate headquarters, where the effect of borrowed money can be determined at the plant or divisional offices. Interest must be considered as a cost and may be subtracted from taxable income. Payments to the lending agency of both capital and interest are deducted from the cash flow.

REVIEW OF CAPITAL APPROPRIATIONS

Every capital expenditure should be reviewed at three time intervals. Most organizations make these reviews mandatory, to develop improved techniques for this very important decision-making process. The three reviews should cover three distinct areas:

1. review of capital expenditure estimate
2. review of operating expense estimate
3. review of the overall project, including revenue

Each of these reviews, or audits, is discussed further.

The Capital Estimate Review

Shortly after completion of the capital investment and after startup, when all the costs have been accumulated, the detailed estimate of capital investment should be compared with the detail of actual expenditures. Where appreciable differences between the estimated cost and actual cost are found, they should be reviewed by the estimator to determine the reason for the difference, whether the actual was greater than or less than the estimate. This accomplishes two purposes:

1. It keeps the estimators on their toes when they know an audit will be made, and
2. It assists the estimators in refining their estimating factors.

Capital cost estimating is a highly developed skill, and the practitioners are professionals who constantly strive to improve their ability to make more accurate estimates. Chapter 3 discusses the preparation of capital investments.

Review of Operating Cost Estimate

As soon as operation of the new capital investment has lined out, or become routine, or at least at the end of a year of operation, the operating cost estimates should be compared to actual operating cost in detail. And, again, any discrepancies between estimated and actual operating costs should be studied to determine where errors in estimating might have occurred to avoid these errors in future estimations.

Operating cost estimation is discussed in detail in Chapter 4.

Overall Review of the Capital Investment

After 1 or 2 years of operation of a new facility, a final review of the capital investment should be made. The final review at this time will permit an analysis of the overall project with particular emphasis on revenue. Has market penetration been as forecast? Is net selling price close to estimate? Are the total market and market share equivalent to forecast? Analysis of inventory levels should be compared to forecast, including raw material, in-process, and product inventory. Selling costs and distribution costs should also be compared to forecast.

PRESENTATION OF REQUESTS FOR CAPITAL EXPENDITURES

There are two significant steps in obtaining approval for capital expenditures: presentation to operating executives and presentation to corporate staff or board of directors.

Presentation to Operating Executives

The scientist or engineer who recommends a capital expenditure most usually will have his project reviewed by his immediate manager and probably the plant manager, the production superintendent, and other technical people, including possibly a corporate vice president and/or other corporate technical people. For this presentation, the proponent should cover the following points.

1. A review of alternative solutions to the problem. This should include the technical feasibility of each of the alternatives considered with the advantages of each.
2. The alternative selected based on an economic evaluation using the measure of merit usually used by the company. For example, present worth using the minimum acceptable or required rate of return, equivalent uniform annual worth on the same basis or expected internal rate of return. The payout period should be evaluated to answer that question if posed.
3. A review of the assumptions made regarding economic life, salvage value, market price and share of market (if applicable to a new product), labor and other savings (if a cost savings project). Be ready to demonstrate the thoroughness of your analysis.
4. Other justifications, including consideration of safety, occupational health, employee attitudes, possible union reactions, environmental impact, community relations, etc.
5. Use projected transparencies, keeping them simple and to the point. Exude confidence and assurance.
6. Wherever possible, depending on the importance and level of expenditure, discuss the project with key people who will be significant members of the review group. You will be less apprehensive if you have several people agree with your conclusion beforehand.
7. If your proposal is rejected, don't be too disheartened. Endeavor to find out why, either in the meeting or afterward. Nobody has a 100% sales record.

Presentation to Corporate Executives

If your project has passed the technical review, you will be asked to make your presentation to a higher review group. Depending on the amount of investment involved, this could be a plant group including the financial people or, with major expenditures, the corporate board of directors. At this level, there will be more concern with financial matters than technical ones. In this presentation:

1. It will be assumed that you are competent technically, so do not get involved in technical details. Let your audience know what your project does, briefly how it does it, and where it does it. But be prepared to answer questions in this regard. Do not bore these busy executives with details to prove how competent you are. They will find this out after the project is completed.
2. Describe the economic justification by whatever measure of merit the

corporation uses, but be prepared to answer with other measures of merit, because there may be a maverick present.

3. Inquire around and try to find someone, including your managers, who has made a presentation, to determine what the interests of the group are and what types of questions the group will present.

4. Respect, but do not be awed by, the titles or levels of responsibility of those in the group. They are asking your help in guiding the organization to make the proper decisions to carrying out the short-range and long-term objectives of the company. Know what they are.

5. When you are through and there are no more questions, pick up your notes and be prepared to leave. Chances are the decision will be made after you have left the meeting, unless you are invited to stay.

Whether your project is approved or rejected at either level, you will have had a growing experience.

SUMMARY

In this chapter the reader was introduced to the capital appropriation—capital budgeting process. This is one of the most important areas of management responsibility. The decisions made by management affect the growth, direction and the ultimate life of a company. Engineers and scientists as they move up the management ladder become more intimately involved in the planning process. From the business plans requests for capital appropriations are generated. After approval of a project, then plans for budgeting projects must be prepared.

Data obtained from estimate of capital investment, operating expenses, cash flow, and profitability as well as results of sensitivity analyses are part of the information needed in the capital appropriation—capital budgeting process. The development of the necessary information has been the subject of previous chapters in this book. The engineer or scientist is charged with the responsibility of preparing the data and submitting it in the proper format for management's review and action.

Suggested Further Reading

Petty, J. W., D. F. Scott and M. M. Bird, "The Capital Expenditure Decision-Making Process of Large Corporation," *The Engineering Economist,* 20 (8), 159–172 (1975).

Day, J. E., "A Screening Model for Investment Proposals," Management Accounting (48–52) January, 1975.

Vandell, R. F. and P. J. Stonich, "Capital Budgeting: Theory or Results?," *Financial Executive,* 46–52 (August, 1973).

Mao, J. C. T., "Survey of Capital Budgeting: Theory and Practice," *J. of Finance*, 349–360 (May, 1970).

Klammer, T., "Empirical Evidence of the Adoption of Sophisticated Capital Budgeting Techniques," *Journal of Business*, 387–397 (July, 1972).

Fregman, J. M., "Capital Budgeting Practices: A Survey," *Management Accounting*, 19–25 (May, 1973).

Brigham, E. F., "Financial Management: Theory and Practice," 3rd ed. Chapter 11, Dryden Press, Chicago, IL (1979).

13 CONCLUDING COMMENTS

The authors of this text stated in the preface that the intent of this book was to present a fundamental, practical approach to financial and economic analysis as currently used in industry. The text was primarily directed to those scientists and engineers in industry who suddenly find themselves at the first level of management. In this new situation, these people often confront financial terminology that is foreign to them. They may not have had any courses in college or on-the-job training in practical economics. To understand the basic definitions and terminology is not difficult. The actual practice of what is contained in this text takes experience, which ultimately comes with time.

A person who enters the first level of management is often confronted with an unfamiliar world of financial terminology. In addition, companies frequently have developed their own set of jargon for use in their industry or locale. These new terms and the associated concepts are confusing to the person who has been engrossed in scientific or engineering terminology. The topic headings of each chapter illustrate the new management world that the first-level manager might encounter. He or she learns soon that capital cost estimates, operating expenses, and profitability are estimated, often based upon preliminary information. Depending upon management policy, perhaps a feasibility estimate is prepared, or perhaps the cost estimates are returned to the originator for refinement. A return of this information may not be considered as rejection, for often the manager is not sure of what is desired.

The first-level manager learns how important marketing data are. These data may drastically alter an investment decision, and, in fact, these data may embody more errors than capital cost or operating expense estimates. It is important to remember that all estimates are subject to error and that none of the values reported are chiseled in stone.

The new manager is frequently involved in developing projected cash flow analyses and, if not making calculations of profitibility measures, should thoroughly understand their limitations. Depending upon company policy, sensitivity and/or uncertainty analyses may be prepared. Although the new manager may not prepare these elements of a feasibility analysis, he or she should fully understand what information is required and the methodologies used.

Frequently, the new manager will be given the opportunity of presenting a project to divisional officers, the executive committee, or the board of directors. Often to the persons far removed from this upper level management, little is understood of what must be considered to evaluate a potentially attractive project.

Capital appropriation requests are prepared, and the new manager is deeply involved in this process. It should be borne in mind that any healthy corporation has more demand on its funds than it has funds available. Therefore, top-level management must prioritize capital projects, depending upon quantitative and qualitative criteria for investment. A capital budget is prepared for all projects being considered. The time when a given project is to commence is of utmost significance. If the product enters the marketplace too late, it will not come to full economic bloom. The budgeting process must then include not only the capital requirements, but also the requisite marketing information, cash flow analysis, and project timing.

Of importance, but often not in the new manager's domain is how a venture is to be funded. Upper level management is concerned with this step. The strategies employed in seeking funds should not put the corporation in a financial bind. A person ultimately seeking an upper level position must have a fundamental knowledge of financing.

In this text the various chapters have been concerned with each of these economic and financial concepts. If a person seeking upward mobility does not have a clear understanding of how projects begin and their paths through the administrative framework, then he or she will be at a serious disadvantage. Often those at the lower end of the management ladder cannot understand why their pet projects were not funded. This text has presented the basic steps that are considered in project funding. To be successful in technical management today, a manager must be knowledgeable and conversant with economic and financial calculations, terminology, and procedures.

Appendix A
DISCRETE COMPOUND INTEREST FACTORS

TABLE A.1   1/2% DISCRETE COMPOUND INTEREST FACTORS

	Single Payment		Uniform Series				Uniform Gradient
n	Compound Amount Factor F/P	Present Worth Factor P/F	Compound Amount Factor F/A	Sinking Fund Factor A/F	Present Worth Factor P/A	Capital Recovery Factor A/P	Gradient Conversion Factor A/G
1	1.0050	0.9950	1.0000	1.0000	0.9950	1.0050	0.0000
2	1.0100	0.9901	2.0050	0.4988	1.9851	0.5038	0.4988
3	1.0151	0.9852	3.0150	0.3317	2.9703	0.3367	0.9967
4	1.0202	0.9803	4.0301	0.2481	3.9505	0.2531	1.4938
5	1.0253	0.9754	5.0503	0.1980	4.9259	0.2030	1.9900
6	1.0304	0.9705	6.0755	0.1646	5.8964	0.1696	2.4855
7	1.0355	0.9657	7.1059	0.1407	6.8621	0.1457	2.9801
8	1.0407	0.9609	8.1414	0.1228	7.8230	0.1278	3.4738
9	1.0459	0.9561	9.1821	0.0189	8.7791	0.1139	3.9668
10	1.0511	0.9514	10.228	0.0978	9.7304	0.1028	4.4589
11	1.0564	0.9466	11.279	0.0877	10.677	0.0937	4.9501
12	1.0617	0.9419	12.336	0.0811	11.619	0.0861	5.4406
13	1.0670	0.9372	13.397	0.0747	12.556	0.0797	5.9302
14	1.0723	0.9326	14.464	0.0691	13.489	0.0741	6.4190
15	1.0777	0.9279	15.537	0.0644	14.417	0.0694	6.9069
16	1.0831	0.9233	16.614	0.0602	15.340	0.0652	7.3940
17	1.0885	0.9187	17.697	0.0565	16.259	0.0615	7.8803
18	1.0939	0.9141	18.786	0.0532	17.173	0.0582	8.3658
19	1.0994	0.9096	19.880	0.0503	18.083	0.0553	8.8504
20	1.1049	0.9051	20.979	0.0477	18.987	0.0527	9.3342
21	1.1104	0.9006	22.084	0.0453	19.888	0.0503	9.8172
22	1.1160	0.8961	23.194	0.0431	20.784	0.0481	10.299
23	1.1216	0.8916	24.310	0.0411	21.676	0.0461	10.781
24	1.1272	0.8872	25.432	0.0393	22.563	0.0433	11.261
26	1.1328	0.8828	26.559	0.0377	23.446	0.0427	11.741
30	1.1614	0.8610	32.280	0.0310	27.794	0.0360	14.127
35	1.1907	0.8398	38.145	0.0262	32.035	0.0312	16.492
40	1.2208	0.8191	44.159	0.0227	36.172	0.0277	18.836
50	1.2832	0.7793	56.645	0.0177	44.143	0.0227	23.462
60	1.3489	0.7414	69.770	0.0143	51.726	0.0193	28.006
∞	∞	0	∞	0	200	0.005	200

TABLE A.2 2/3% DISCRETE COMPOUND INTEREST FACTORS

	Single Payment		Uniform Series				Uniform Gradient
n	Compound Amount Factor F/P	Present Worth Factor P/F	Compound Amount Factor F/A	Sinking Fund Factor A/F	Present Worth Factor P/A	Capital Recovery Factor A/P	Gradient Conversion Factor A/G
1	1.0067	0.9934	1.0000	1.0000	0.9934	1.0067	0.0000
2	1.0134	0.9868	2.0067	0.4983	1.9802	0.5050	0.4983
3	1.0201	0.9803	3.0200	0.3311	2.9604	0.3378	0.9956
4	1.0269	0.9738	4.0402	0.2475	3.9342	0.2542	1.4917
5	1.0338	0.9673	5.0671	0.1974	4.9015	0.2040	1.9867
6	1.0407	0.9609	6.1009	0.1639	5.8625	0.1706	2.4806
7	1.0476	0.9546	7.1416	0.1400	6.8170	0.1467	2.9734
8	1.0546	0.9482	8.1892	0.1221	7.7652	0.1288	3.4651
9	1.0616	0.9420	9.2438	0.1082	8.7072	0.1148	3.9557
10	1.0687	0.9357	10.305	0.0970	9.6429	0.1037	4.4452
11	1.0758	0.9295	11.374	0.0879	10.572	0.0946	4.9336
12	1.0830	0.9234	12.450	0.0803	11.496	0.0870	5.4208
13	1.0902	0.9172	13.533	0.0739	12.413	0.0806	5.9070
14	1.0975	0.9112	14.623	0.0684	13.324	0.0751	6.3920
15	1.1048	0.9051	15.721	0.0636	14.229	0.0703	6.8760
16	1.1122	0.3991	16.825	0.0594	15.239	0.0661	7.3588
17	1.1196	0.8932	17.938	0.0557	16.022	0.0624	7.8406
18	1.1270	0.8873	19.057	0.0525	17.909	0.0591	8.3212
19	1.1346	0.8814	20.184	0.0495	17.790	0.0562	8.8007
20	1.1421	0.8755	21.319	0.0469	18.666	0.0536	9.2791
21	1.1497	0.8698	22.461	0.0445	19.536	0.0512	9.7564
22	1.1574	0.8640	23.611	0.0424	20.400	0.0490	10.233
23	1.1651	0.8583	24.768	0.0404	21.258	0.4070	10.708
24	1.1729	0.8526	25.933	0.0386	22.111	0.0452	11.182
25	1.1807	0.8470	27.106	0.0369	22.958	0.0436	11.655
30	1.2206	0.8193	33.089	0.0302	27.109	0.0369	14.003
35	1.2618	0.7925	39.274	0.0255	31.125	0.0321	16.323
40	1.3045	0.7666	45.668	0.0219	35.009	0.0286	18.616
50	1.3941	0.7173	59.110	0.0169	42.402	0.0236	23.119
60	1.4898	0.6712	73.4769	0.0136	49.318	0.0203	27.513
∞	∞	0	∞	0	150	0.0067	150

TABLE A.3   3/4% DISCRETE COMPOUND INTEREST FACTORS

	Single Payment		Uniform Series				Uniform Gradient
n	Compound Amount Factor F/P	Present Worth Factor P/F	Compound Amount Factor F/A	Sinking Fund Factor A/F	Present Worth Factor P/A	Capital Recovery Factor A/P	Gradient Conversion Factor A/G
1	1.0075	0.9926	1.0000	1.0000	0.9926	1.0075	0.0000
2	1.0151	0.9852	2.0075	0.4981	1.9777	0.5056	0.4981
3	1.0227	0.9778	3.0276	0.3309	2.9556	0.3384	0.9950
4	1.0303	0.9706	4.4052	0.2472	3.9261	0.2547	1.4907
5	1.0381	0.9633	5.0752	0.1970	4.8894	0.2045	1.9851
6	1.0459	0.9562	6.1136	0.1636	5.8456	0.1711	2.4782
7	1.0537	0.9491	7.1595	0.1397	6.7946	0.1472	2.9701
8	1.0616	0.9420	8.2132	0.1218	7.7366	0.1293	3.4608
9	1.0696	0.9350	9.2748	0.1078	8.6716	0.1153	3.9502
10	1.0776	0.9280	10.344	0.0967	9.5996	0.1042	4.4384
11	1.0857	0.9211	11.422	0.0876	10.521	0.0951	4.9253
12	1.0938	0.9152	12.508	0.0800	11.435	0.0875	5.4110
13	1.1020	0.9074	13.601	0.0735	12.342	0.0810	5.8954
14	1.1103	0.9007	14.703	0.0680	13.243	0.0755	6.3786
15	1.1186	0.8940	15.814	0.0632	14.137	0.0707	6.8606
16	1.1270	0.8873	16.932	0.0591	15.024	0.0666	7.3413
17	1.1354	0.8807	18.059	0.0554	15.905	0.0629	7.8207
18	1.1440	0.8742	19.195	0.0521	16.779	0.0596	8.2989
19	1.1525	0.8677	20.339	0.0492	17.647	0.0567	8.7759
20	1.1612	0.8612	21.491	0.0465	18.508	0.0540	9.2517
21	1.1699	0.8548	22.652	0.0442	19.363	0.0517	9.7261
22	1.1787	0.8484	23.822	0.0420	20.211	0.0495	10.199
23	1.1875	0.8421	25.001	0.0400	21.053	0.0475	10.671
24	1.1964	0.8358	26.188	0.0382	21.889	0.0457	11.142
25	1.2054	0.8296	27.385	0.0365	22.719	0.0440	11.612
30	1.2513	0.7992	33.503	0.0299	26.775	0.0374	13.941
35	1.2989	0.7699	39.854	0.0251	30.683	0.0326	16.239
40	1.3483	0.7417	46.446	0.0215	34.447	0.0290	18.506
50	1.4530	0.6883	60.394	0.0166	41.567	0.0241	22.948
60	1.5657	0.6387	75.424	0.0311	48.173	0.0208	27.267
∞	∞	0	∞	0	133.33	0.0075	133.33

TABLE A.4 1% DISCRETE COMPOUND INTEREST FACTORS

	Single Payment		Uniform Series				Uniform Gradient
n	Compound Amount Factor F/P	Present Worth Factor P/F	Compound Amount Factor F/A	Sinking Fund Factor A/F	Present Worth Factor P/A	Capital Recovery Factor A/P	Gradient Conversion Factor A/G
1	1.0100	0.9901	1.0000	1.0000	0.9901	1.0100	0.0000
2	1.0201	0.9803	2.0100	0.4975	1.9704	0.5075	0.4975
3	1.0303	0.9706	3.0301	0.3300	2.9410	0.3400	0.9934
4	1.0406	0.9610	4.0604	0.2463	3.9020	0.2563	1.4876
5	1.0510	0.9515	5.1010	0.1960	4.8534	0.2060	1.9801
6	1.0615	0.9421	6.1520	0.1626	5.7955	0.1726	2.4710
7	1.0721	0.9327	7.2135	0.1386	6.7282	0.1486	2.9602
8	1.0829	0.9235	8.2857	0.1207	7.6517	0.1307	3.4478
9	1.0937	0.9143	9.3685	1.1068	8.5660	0.1168	3.9337
10	1.1046	0.9053	10.462	0.0956	9.4713	0.1056	4.4179
11	1.1157	0.8963	11.567	0.0865	10.368	0.0965	4.9005
12	1.1268	0.8875	12.683	0.0789	11.255	0.0889	5.3815
13	1.1381	0.8787	13.809	0.0724	12.134	0.0824	5.8607
14	1.1495	0.8700	14.947	0.0669	13.004	0.0769	6.3384
15	1.1610	0.8614	16.097	0.0621	13.865	0.0721	6.8143
16	1.1736	0.8528	17.258	0.0580	14.718	0.0680	7.2887
17	1.1843	0.8444	18.430	0.0543	15.562	0.0643	7.7613
18	1.1961	0.8360	19.615	0.0510	16.398	0.0610	8.2323
19	1.2081	0.8277	20.811	0.0481	17.225	0.0581	8.7017
20	1.2202	0.8196	22.019	0.0454	18.046	0.0554	9.1694
21	1.2324	0.8114	23.239	0.0430	18.857	0.0530	9.6354
22	1.2447	0.8034	24.472	0.0409	19.660	0.0509	10.100
23	1.2572	0.7955	25.716	0.0389	20.456	0.0489	10.563
24	1.2797	0.7876	26.973	0.0371	21.243	0.0471	11.024
25	1.2824	0.7798	28.243	0.0354	22.023	0.0454	11.483
30	1.3478	0.7419	34.785	0.0288	25.808	0.0388	13.756
35	1.4166	0.7059	41.660	0.0240	29.409	0.0340	15.987
40	1.4889	0.6717	48.886	0.0205	32.835	0.0305	18.178
50	1.6446	0.6080	64.463	0.0155	39.196	0.0255	22.436
60	1.8167	0.5505	81.670	0.0123	44.955	0.0223	26.533
∞	∞	0	∞	0	100.0	0.0100	100.0

TABLE A.5   1-1/2% DISCRETE COMPOUND INTEREST FACTORS

	Single Payment		Uniform Series				Uniform Gradient
n	Compound Amount Factor F/P	Present Worth Factor P/F	Compound Amount Factor F/A	Sinking Fund Factor A/F	Present Worth Factor P/A	Capital Recovery Factor A/P	Gradient Conversion Factor A/G
1	1.0150	0.9852	1.000	1.0000	0.9852	1.0150	0.0000
2	1.0302	0.9707	2.015	0.4963	1.9559	0.5113	0.4963
3	1.0457	0.9563	3.045	0.3284	2.9122	0.3434	0.9901
4	1.0614	0.9422	4.091	0.2445	3.8544	0.2595	1.4814
5	1.0773	0.9283	5.152	0.1941	2.7827	0.2091	1.9702
6	1.0934	0.9146	6.230	1.1605	5.6972	0.1755	2.4566
7	1.1098	0.9010	7.323	0.1366	6.5982	0.1516	2.9405
8	1.1265	0.8877	8.433	0.1186	7.4859	0.1336	3.4219
9	1.1434	0.8746	9.559	0.1046	8.3605	0.1196	3.9008
10	1.1605	0.8617	10.703	0.0934	9.2222	0.1084	4.3772
11	1.1779	0.8489	11.863	0.0843	10.071	0.0993	4.8512
12	1.1956	0.8364	13.041	0.0767	10.908	0.0917	5.3227
13	1.2136	0.8240	14.237	0.0703	11.732	0.0853	5.7917
14	1.2318	0.8119	15.450	0.0647	12.543	0.0797	6.2582
15	1.2502	0.7999	16.682	0.0600	13.343	0.0750	6.7223
16	1.2690	0.7880	17.932	0.0558	14.131	0.0708	7.1839
17	1.2880	0.7764	19.201	0.0521	14.908	0.0671	7.6431
18	1.3073	0.7649	20.489	0.0488	15.673	0.0638	8.0997
19	1.3270	0.7536	21.797	0.0459	16.426	0.0609	8.5539
20	1.3469	0.7425	23.124	0.0433	17.169	0.0583	9.0057
21	1.3671	0.7315	24.471	0.0409	17.900	0.0559	9.4550
22	1.3876	0.7207	25.838	0.0387	18.621	0.0537	9.9018
23	1.4084	0.7100	27.225	0.0367	19.331	0.0517	10.346
24	1.4300	0.6996	28.634	0.0349	20.030	0.0499	10.788
25	1.4509	0.6892	30.063	0.0333	20.720	0.0483	11.228
30	1.5631	0.6398	37.539	0.0266	24.016	0.0416	13.388
35	1.6839	0.5939	45.592	0.0219	27.076	0.0369	15.488
40	1.8140	0.5513	54.268	0.0184	29.916	0.0334	17.528
50	2.105	0.4750	73.683	0.0136	35.000	0.0286	21.428
60	2.443	0.4093	96.215	0.0104	39.380	0.0254	25.093
∞	∞	0	∞	0	66.667	0.0150	66.667

TABLE A.6 2% DISCRETE COMPOUND INTEREST FACTORS

	Single Payment		Uniform Series				Uniform Gradient
n	Compound Amount Factor F/P	Present Worth Factor P/F	Compound Amount Factor F/A	Sinking Fund Factor A/F	Present Worth Factor P/A	Capital Recovery Factor A/P	Gradient Conversion Factor A/G
1	1.0200	0.9804	1.0000	1.0000	0.9804	1.0200	0.0000
2	1.0408	0.9612	2.0200	0.4951	1.9416	0.5151	0.4951
3	1.0612	0.9423	3.0604	0.3268	2.8839	0.3468	0.9868
4	1.0824	0.9239	4.1216	0.2426	3.8077	0.2626	1.4753
5	1.1041	0.9057	5.2040	0.1922	4.7135	0.2122	1.9604
6	1.1262	0.8880	6.3081	0.1585	5.6012	0.1785	2.4423
7	1.1487	0.8706	7.4343	0.1345	6.4720	0.1545	2.9208
8	1.1717	0.8535	8.5830	0.1165	7.3255	0.1365	3.3961
9	1.1951	0.8368	9.7546	0.1025	8.1622	0.1225	3.8681
10	1.2190	0.8204	10.950	0.0913	8.9826	0.1113	4.3367
11	1.2434	0.8043	12.169	0.0822	9.7869	0.1022	4.8021
12	1.2682	0.7885	13.412	0.0746	10.575	0.0946	5.2643
13	1.2936	0.7730	14.680	0.0681	11.348	0.0881	5.7231
14	1.3195	0.7579	15.974	0.0626	12.106	0.0826	6.1786
15	1.3459	0.7430	17.293	0.0578	12.849	0.0778	6.6309
16	1.3728	0.7285	18.639	0.0537	13.578	0.0737	7.0799
17	1.4002	0.7142	20.012	0.0500	14.292	0.0700	7.5256
18	1.4282	0.7002	21.412	0.0567	14.992	0.0667	7.9681
19	1.4568	0.6864	22.841	0.0438	15.675	0.0638	8.4073
20	1.4859	0.6730	24.297	0.0412	16.351	0.0612	8.8433
21	1.5157	0.6598	25.783	0.0388	17.011	0.0588	9.2760
22	1.5460	0.6468	27.299	0.0366	17.658	0.0566	9.7055
23	1.5769	0.6342	28.845	0.0347	18.292	0.0547	10.132
24	1.6084	0.6217	30.422	0.0329	18.914	0.0529	10.555
25	1.6406	0.6095	32.030	0.0312	19.524	0.0512	10.975
30	1.8114	0.5521	40.568	0.0247	22.397	0.0447	13.025
35	2.0000	0.5000	49.994	0.0200	24.999	0.0400	14.996
40	2.2080	0.4529	60.402	0.0166	27.355	0.0366	16.8885
50	2.6916	0.3715	84.579	0.0118	31.4236	0.0318	20.4420
60	3.2810	0.3048	114.05	0.0088	34.7609	0.0288	23.6961
∞	∞	0	∞	0	50.000	0.0200	50.000

TABLE A.7   3% DISCRETE COMPOUND INTEREST FACTORS

	Single Payment		Uniform Series				Uniform Gradient
n	Compound Amount Factor F/P	Present Worth Factor P/F	Compound Amount Factor F/A	Sinking Fund Factor A/F	Present Worth Factor P/A	Capital Recovery Factor A/P	Gradient Conversion Factor A/G
1	1.0300	0.9709	1.0000	1.0000	0.9709	1.0300	0.0000
2	1.0609	0.9426	2.0300	0.4926	1.9135	0.5226	0.4926
3	1.0927	0.9152	3.0909	0.3235	2.8286	0.3535	0.9803
4	1.1255	0.8885	4.1836	0.2390	3.7171	0.2690	1.4631
5	1.1593	0.8626	5.3091	0.1884	4.5797	0.2184	1.9409
6	1.1941	0.8375	6.4684	0.1546	5.4172	0.1846	2.4138
7	1.2299	0.8131	7.6625	0.1305	6.2303	0.1605	2.8819
8	1.2668	0.7894	8.8923	0.1125	7.0197	0.1425	3.3450
9	1.1348	0.7664	10.159	0.0984	7.7861	0.1284	3.8032
10	1.3439	0.7441	11.464	0.0872	8.5302	0.1172	4.2565
11	1.3842	0.7224	12.808	0.0781	9.2526	0.1081	4.7049
12	1.4258	0.7014	14.192	0.0705	9.9540	0.1005	5.1485
13	1.4685	0.6810	15.618	0.0640	10.635	0.0940	5.5872
14	1.1525	0.6611	17.086	0.0585	11.296	0.0885	6.0211
15	1.5580	0.6419	18.599	0.0538	11.938	0.0838	6.4501
16	1.6047	0.6232	20.157	0.0496	12.561	0.0796	6.8742
17	1.6528	0.6050	21.762	0.0460	13.166	0.0760	7.2936
18	1.7024	0.5874	23.414	0.0427	13.754	0.0727	7.7081
19	1.7535	0.5703	25.117	0.0398	14.326	0.0698	8.1179
20	1.8061	0.5537	26.870	0.0372	14.878	0.0672	8.5229
21	1.8603	0.5376	28.676	0.0349	15.415	0.0649	8.9231
22	1.9161	0.5219	30.537	0.0328	15.937	0.0628	9.3186
23	1.9736	0.5067	32.453	0.0308	16.444	0.0608	9,7094
24	2.0328	0.4919	34.426	0.0291	16.936	0.0591	10.095
25	2.0938	0.4776	36.459	0.0274	17.413	0.0573	10.477
30	2.4273	0.4120	47.575	0.0210	19.601	0.0510	12.314
35	2.8139	0.3554	60.462	0.0165	21.487	0.0465	14.038
40	3.2620	0.3066	75.401	0.0133	23.115	0.0433	15.650
50	4.3839	0.2281	112.80	0.0089	25.730	0.0389	18.558
60	5.8916	0.1697	163.05	0.0061	27.676	0.0361	21.067
∞	∞	0	∞	0	33.333	0.0300	33.333

TABLE A.8 4% DISCRETE COMPOUND INTEREST FACTORS

	Single Payment		Uniform Series				Uniform Gradient
n	Compound Amount Factor F/P	Present Worth Factor P/F	Compound Amount Factor F/A	Sinking Fund Factor A/F	Present Worth Factor P/A	Capital Recovery Factor A/P	Gradient Conversion Factor A/G
1	1.0400	0.9615	1.0000	1.0000	0.9615	1.0400	0.0000
2	1.0816	0.9246	2.0400	0.4902	1.8861	0.5302	0.4902
3	1.1249	0.8890	3.1216	0.3204	2.7751	0.3604	0.9739
4	1.1699	0.8548	4.2465	0.2355	3.6299	0.2755	1.4510
5	1.2167	0.8219	5.4163	0.1846	4.4518	0.2246	1.9216
6	1.2653	0.7903	6.6330	0.1508	5.2421	1.1908	2.3857
7	1.3159	0.7599	7.8983	0.1266	6.0021	0.1666	2.8433
8	1.3686	0.7307	9.2142	0.1085	6.7328	0.1485	3.2944
9	1.4233	0.7026	10.583	0.0945	7.4353	0.1345	3.7391
10	1.4802	0.6756	12.006	0.0833	8.1109	0.1233	4.1773
11	1.5395	0.6496	13.486	0.0742	8.7605	0.1142	4.6090
12	1.6010	0.6246	15.026	0.0666	9.3851	0.1066	5.0344
13	1.6651	0.6006	16.627	0.0602	9.9857	0.1002	5.4533
14	1.7317	0.5775	18.292	0.0547	10.563	0.0947	5.8659
15	1.8009	0.5553	20.024	0.0500	11.118	0.0900	6.2721
16	1.8730	0.5339	21.825	0.0458	11.652	0.0858	6.6720
17	1.9479	0.5134	23.698	0.0422	12.166	0.0822	7.0656
18	2.0258	0.4936	25.645	0.0390	12.659	0.0790	7.4530
19	2.1068	0.4747	27.671	0.0361	13.134	0.0761	7.8342
20	2.1911	0.4564	29.778	0.0336	13.590	0.0736	8.2091
21	2.2788	0.4388	31.969	0.0313	14.029	0.0713	8.5780
22	2.3699	0.4220	34.248	0.0292	14.451	0.0692	8.9407
23	2.4647	0.4057	36.618	0.0273	14.857	0.0673	9.2973
24	2.5633	0.3901	39.083	0.0256	15.247	0.0656	9.6479
25	2.6658	0.3751	41.646	0.0240	15.622	0.0640	9.9925
30	3.2434	0.3083	56.085	0.0178	17.292	0.0578	11.627
35	3.9461	0.2534	73.652	0.0136	18.665	0.0536	13.120
40	4.8010	0.2083	95.026	0.0106	19.799	0.0505	14.477
50	7.1067	0.1407	152.667	0.0066	21.482	0.0466	16.812
60	10.520	0.0951	237.991	0.0042	22.624	0.0442	18.697
∞	∞	0	∞	0	25.000	0.0400	25.000

TABLE A.9 5% DISCRETE COMPOUND INTEREST FACTORS

	Single Payment		Uniform Series				Uniform Gradient
n	Compound Amount Factor F/P	Present Worth Factor P/F	Compound Amount Factor F/A	Sinking Fund Factor A/F	Present Worth Factor P/A	Capital Recovery Factor A/P	Gradient Conversion Factor A/G
1	1.0500	0.9524	1.0000	1.0000	0.9524	1.0500	0.0000
2	1.1025	0.9070	2.0500	0.4878	1.8594	0.5378	0.4878
3	1.1576	0.8638	3.1525	0.3172	2.7233	0.3672	0.9675
4	1.2155	0.8227	4.3101	0.2320	3.5460	0.2820	1.4391
5	1.2763	0.7835	5.5256	0.1810	4.3295	0.2310	1.9025
6	1.3401	0.7462	6.8019	0.1470	5.0757	0.1970	2.3579
7	1.4071	0.7107	8.1420	0.1228	5.7864	0.1728	2.8052
8	1.4775	0.6768	9.5491	0.1047	6.4632	0.1547	3.2445
9	1.5513	0.6446	11.027	0.0907	7.1078	0.1407	3.6758
10	1.5289	0.6139	12.587	0.0795	7.7217	0.1295	4.0991
11	1.7103	0.5847	14.207	0.0704	8.3064	0.1204	4.5145
12	1.7959	0.5568	15.917	0.0628	8.8633	0.1128	4.9219
13	1.8856	0.5303	17.713	0.0565	9.3936	0.1065	5.3215
14	1.9799	0.5051	19.599	0.0510	9.8987	0.1010	5.7133
15	2.0789	0.4810	21.579	0.0464	10.380	0.0964	6.0973
16	2.1829	0.4581	23.658	0.0423	10.838	0.0923	6.4736
17	2.2920	0.4363	25.840	0.0387	11.274	0.0887	6.8423
18	2.4066	0.4155	28.132	0.0356	11.690	0.0856	7.2034
19	2.5270	0.4957	30.539	0.0328	12.085	0.0828	7.5569
20	2.6533	0.3769	33.066	0.0303	12.462	0.0803	7.9030
21	2.7860	0.3590	35.719	0.0280	12.821	0.0780	8.2416
22	2.9253	0.3419	38.505	0.0260	13.163	0.0760	8.5730
23	3.0715	0.3256	41.430	0.0241	13.489	0.0741	8.8971
24	3.2251	0.3101	44.502	0.0225	13.799	0.0725	9.2140
25	3.3864	0.2953	47.727	0.0210	14.094	0.0710	9.5238
30	4.3219	0.2314	66.439	0.0151	15.373	0.0651	10.969
35	5.5160	0.1813	90.320	0.0111	16.374	0.0611	12.250
40	7.0400	0.1241	120.80	0.0083	17.159	0.0583	13.378
50	11.467	0.0872	209.35	0.0048	18.256	0.0548	15.223
60	18.679	0.0535	353.58	0.0028	18.929	0.0528	16.606
∞	∞	0	∞	0	20.000	0.0500	20.000

TABLE A.10 6% DISCRETE COMPOUND INTEREST FACTORS

	Single Payment		Uniform Series				Uniform Gradient
n	Compound Amount Factor F/P	Present Worth Factor P/F	Compound Amount Factor F/A	Sinking Fund Factor A/F	Present Worth Factor P/A	Capital Recovery Factor A/P	Gradient Conversion Factor A/G
1	1.0600	0.9434	1.0000	1.0000	0.9434	1.0600	0.0000
2	1.1236	0.8900	2.0600	0.4854	1.8334	0.5454	0.4854
3	1.1910	0.8396	3.1836	0.3141	2.6730	0.3741	0.9612
4	1.2625	0.7921	4.3746	0.2286	3.4651	0.2886	1.4272
5	1.3382	0.7473	5.6371	0.1774	4.2124	0.2374	1.8836
6	1.4185	0.7050	6.9753	0.1434	4.9173	0.2034	2.3304
7	1.5036	0.6651	8.3938	0.1191	5.5824	0.1791	2.7676
8	1.5938	0.6274	9.8975	0.1010	6.2098	0.1610	3.1952
9	1.6895	0.5919	11.491	0.0870	6.8017	0.1470	3.6133
10	1.7908	0.5584	13.181	0.0759	7.3601	0.1359	4.0220
11	1.8983	0.5268	14.972	0.0668	7.8869	0.1268	4.4213
12	2.0122	0.4970	16.870	0.0593	8.3839	0.1193	4.8113
13	2.1329	0.4688	18.882	0.0530	8.8527	0.1130	5.1920
14	2.2609	0.4423	21.015	0.0476	9.2950	0.1076	5.5635
15	2.3966	0.4173	23.276	0.0430	9.7123	0.1030	5.9260
16	2.5404	0.3937	25.673	0.0390	10.106	0.0990	6.2794
17	2.6928	0.3714	28.213	0.0355	10.477	0.0955	6.6240
18	2.8543	0.3504	30.906	0.0324	10.828	0.0924	6.9597
19	3.0256	0.3305	33.760	0.0296	11.158	0.0896	7.2867
20	3.2071	0.3118	36.786	0.0272	11.470	0.0872	7.6052
21	3.3996	0.2942	39.993	0.0250	11.764	0.0850	7.9151
22	3.3035	0.2775	43.392	0.0231	12.042	0.0831	8.2166
23	3.8197	0.2618	46.996	0.0213	12.303	0.0813	8.5099
24	4.0489	0.2470	50.816	0.0197	12.550	0.0797	8.7951
25	4.2919	0.2330	54.865	0.0182	12.783	0.0782	9.0722
30	5.7435	0.1741	79.058	0.0127	13.765	0.0727	10.342
35	7.6861	0.1301	111.4	0.0090	14.498	0.0690	11.432
40	10.2857	0.0972	154.76	0.0065	15.046	0.0665	12.359
50	18.4202	0.0543	290.34	0.0035	15.762	0.0635	13.796
60	32.9877	0.0303	533.13	0.0019	16.161	0.0619	14.791
∞	∞	0	∞	0	16.667	0.0600	16.667

TABLE A.11   7% DISCRETE COMPOUND INTEREST FACTORS

	Single Payment		Uniform Series				Uniform Gradient
n	Compound Amount Factor F/P	Present Worth Factor P/F	Compound Amount Factor F/A	Sinking Fund Factor A/F	Present Worth Factor P/A	Capital Recovery Factor A/P	Gradient Conversion Factor A/G
1	1.0700	0.9346	1.0000	1.0000	0.9346	1.0700	0.0000
2	1.1449	0.8734	2.0700	0.4831	1.8080	0.5531	0.4831
3	1.2250	0.8163	3.2149	0.3111	2.6243	0.3811	0.9549
4	1.3108	0.7629	4.4399	0.2252	3.3872	0.2952	1.4155
5	1.4026	0.7130	5.7507	0.1739	4.1002	0.2439	1.8650
6	1.5007	0.6664	7.1533	0.1398	4.7665	0.2098	2.3032
7	1.6058	0.6228	8.6540	0.1156	5.3893	0.1856	2.7304
8	1.7182	0.5820	10.260	0.0975	5.9713	0.1675	3.1466
9	1.8385	0.5439	11.978	0.0835	6.5152	0.1535	3.5517
10	1.9672	0.5084	13.816	0.0724	9.0236	0.1424	3.9461
11	2.1049	0.4751	15.784	0.0634	7.4987	0.1334	4.3296
12	2.2522	0.4440	17.888	0.0559	7.9427	0.1259	4.7025
13	2.4093	0.4150	20.141	0.0497	8.3577	0.1197	5.0649
14	2.5785	0.3878	22.550	0.0444	8.7455	0.1144	5.4167
15	2.7590	0.3625	25.129	0.0398	9.1079	0.1098	5.7583
16	2.9522	0.3387	27.888	0.0359	9.4467	0.1059	6.0897
17	3.1588	0.3166	30.840	0.0324	9.7632	0.1024	6.4110
18	3.3799	0.2959	33.999	0.0294	10.059	0.0994	6.7225
19	3.6165	0.2765	37.379	0.0268	10.336	0.0968	7.0242
20	3.8697	0.2584	40.996	0.0244	10.594	0.0944	7.3163
21	4.1405	0.2415	44.865	0.0223	10.836	0.0923	7.5990
22	4.4304	0.2257	49.006	0.0204	11.061	0.0904	7.8725
23	4.7405	0.2110	53.436	0.0187	11.272	0.0887	8.1369
24	5.0724	0.1972	58.177	0.0172	11.469	0.0872	8.3923
25	5.4274	0.1843	63.249	0.0158	11.654	0.0858	8.6391
30	7.6123	0.1314	94.461	0.0106	12.409	0.0806	9.7487
35	10.6766	0.0937	138.24	0.0072	12.948	0.0772	10.669
40	14.9745	0.0668	199.64	0.0050	13.332	0.0750	11.423
50	29.4570	0.0340	406.53	0.0025	13.801	0.0725	12.529
60	57.9464	0.0173	813.52	0.0012	14.039	0.0712	13.232
∞	∞	0	∞	0	14.286	0.0700	14.286

TABLE A.12 8% DISCRETE COMPOUND INTEREST FACTORS

	Single Payment		Uniform Series				Uniform Gradient
n	Compound Amount Factor F/P	Present Worth Factor P/F	Compound Amount Factor F/A	Sinking Fund Factor A/F	Present Worth Factor P/A	Capital Recovery Factor A/P	Gradient Conversion Factor A/G
1	1.0800	0.9259	1.0000	1.0000	0.9259	1.0800	0.0000
2	1.1664	0.8573	2.0800	0.4808	1.7833	0.5608	0.4808
3	1.2597	0.7938	3.2464	0.3080	2.5771	0.3880	0.9488
4	1.3605	0.7350	4.5061	0.2219	3.3121	0.3019	1.4040
5	1.4693	0.6806	5.8666	0.1705	3.9927	0.2505	1.8465
6	1.5869	0.6302	7.3359	0.1363	4.6229	0.2163	2.2764
7	1.7138	0.5835	8.9228	0.1121	5.2064	0.1921	2.6937
8	1.8509	0.5403	10.637	0.0940	5.7466	0.1740	2.0985
9	1.9990	0.5003	12.488	0.0801	6.2469	0.1601	3.4910
10	2.1489	0.4632	14.487	0.0690	6.7101	0.1490	3.8713
11	2.3316	0.4289	16.645	0.0601	7.1390	0.1401	4.2395
12	2.5182	0.3971	18.977	0.0527	7.5361	0.1327	4.5958
13	2.7196	0.3677	21.495	0.0465	7.9038	0.1265	4.9402
14	2.9372	0.3405	24.215	0.0413	8.2442	0.1213	5.2731
15	3.1722	0.3153	27.152	0.0368	8.5595	0.1168	5.5945
16	3.4259	0.2919	30.324	0.0330	8.8514	0.1130	5.9046
17	3.7000	0.2703	33.750	0.0296	9.1216	0.1096	6.2038
18	3.9960	0.2503	37.450	0.0267	9.3719	0.1067	6.4920
19	4.3157	0.2317	41.446	0.0241	9.6036	0.1041	6.7697
20	4.6610	0.2146	45.762	0.0219	9.8182	0.1019	7.0370
21	5.0338	0.1987	50.423	0.0198	10.017	0.0998	7.2940
22	5.4365	0.1840	55.457	0.0180	10.201	0.0980	7.5412
23	5.8715	0.1703	60.893	0.0164	10.371	0.0964	7.7786
24	6.3412	0.1577	66.765	0.0150	10.529	0.0950	8.0066
25	6.8485	0.1460	73.106	0.0137	10.675	0.0937	8.2254
30	10.063	0.0994	113.28	0.0088	11.258	0.0888	9.1897
35	14.785	0.0676	172.32	0.0058	11.655	0.0858	9.9611
40	21.725	0.0460	259.06	0.0039	11.925	0.0839	10.570
50	46.902	0.0213	573.77	0.0018	12.234	0.0818	11.411
60	101.257	0.0099	1253.21	0.0008	12.377	0.0808	11.902
∞	∞	0	∞	0	12.500	0.0800	12.500

TABLE A.13 9% DISCRETE COMPOUND INTEREST FACTORS

	Single Payment		Uniform Series				Uniform Gradient
n	Compound Amount Factor F/P	Present Worth Factor P/F	Compound Amount Factor F/A	Sinking Fund Factor A/F	Present Worth Factor P/A	Capital Recovery Factor A/P	Gradient Conversion Factor A/G
1	1.0900	0.9174	1.0000	1.0000	0.9174	1.0900	0.0000
2	1.1881	0.8417	2.0900	0.4785	1.7591	0.5685	0.4785
3	1.2950	0.7722	3.2781	0.3051	2.5313	0.3951	0.9426
4	1.4116	0.7084	4.5731	0.2187	3.2397	0.3087	1.3925
5	1.5386	0.6499	5.9847	0.1671	3.8897	0.2571	1.8282
6	1.6771	0.5963	7.5233	0.1329	4.4859	0.2229	2.2498
7	1.8280	0.5470	9.2004	0.1087	5.0330	0.1987	2.6574
8	1.9926	0.5019	11.028	0.0907	5.5348	0.1807	3.0512
9	2.1719	0.4604	13.021	0.0768	5.9953	0.1668	3.4312
10	2.3674	0.4224	15.193	0.0658	6.4177	0.1558	3.7978
11	2.5804	0.3875	17.560	0.0570	6.8052	0.1470	4.1510
12	2.8127	0.3555	20.141	0.0497	7.1607	0.1397	4.4910
13	3.0658	0.3262	22.953	0.0436	7.4869	0.1336	4.8182
14	3.3417	0.2993	26.019	0.0384	7.7862	0.1284	5.1326
15	3.6425	0.2745	29.361	0.0341	8.0607	0.1241	5.4346
16	3.9703	0.2519	33.003	0.0303	8.3126	0.1203	5.7245
17	4.3276	0.2311	36.974	0.0271	8.5436	0.1171	6.0024
18	4.7171	0.2120	41.301	0.0242	8.7556	0.1142	6.2687
19	5.1417	0.1945	46.018	0.0217	8.9501	0.1117	6.5236
20	5.6044	0.1784	51.160	0.0196	9.1286	0.1096	6.7675
21	6.1088	0.1637	56.765	0.0176	9.2923	0.1076	7.0006
22	6.6576	0.1502	62.873	0.0159	9.4424	0.1059	7.2232
23	7.2579	0.1378	69.532	0.0144	9.5802	0.1044	7.4358
24	7.9111	0.1264	76.790	0.0130	9.7066	0.1030	7.6384
25	8.6231	0.1160	84.701	0.0118	9.8226	0.1018	7.8316
30	13.268	0.0754	136.31	0.0073	10.274	0.0973	8.6657
35	20.414	0.0490	215.71	0.0046	10.567	0.0946	9.3083
40	31.409	0.0318	337.88	0.0030	10.757	0.0930	9.7957
50	74.358	0.0135	815.08	0.0012	10.962	0.0912	10.430
60	176.03	0.0057	1944.8	0.0005	11.048	0.0905	10.768
∞	∞	0	∞	0	11.111	0.0900	11.111

TABLE A.14 10% DISCRETE COMPOUND INTEREST FACTORS

	Single Payment		Uniform Series				Uniform Gradient
n	Compound Amount Factor F/P	Present Worth Factor P/F	Compound Amount Factor F/A	Sinking Fund Factor A/F	Present Worth Factor P/A	Capital Recovery Factor A/P	Gradient Conversion Factor A/G
1	1.1000	0.9091	1.0000	1.0000	0.9091	1.1000	0.0000
2	1.2100	0.8265	2.1000	0.4762	1.7355	0.5762	0.4762
3	1.3310	0.7513	3.3100	0.3021	2.4869	0.4021	0.9366
4	1.4641	0.6830	4.6410	0.2155	3.1699	0.3155	1.3812
5	1.6105	0.6209	6.1051	0.1638	3.7908	0.2638	1.8101
6	1.7716	0.5645	7.7156	0.1296	4.3553	0.2296	2.2236
7	1.9487	0.5132	9.4872	0.1054	4.8684	0.2054	2.6216
8	2.1436	0.4665	11.436	0.0875	5.3349	0.1875	3.0045
9	2.3579	0.4241	13.579	0.0737	5.7590	0.1737	3.3724
10	2.5937	0.3856	15.937	0.0628	6.1446	0.1628	3.7255
11	2.8531	0.3505	18.531	0.0540	6.4951	0.1540	4.0641
12	3.1384	0.3186	21.384	0.0468	6.8137	0.1468	4.3884
13	3.4523	0.2897	24.523	0.0408	7.1034	0.1408	4.6988
14	3.7975	0.2633	27.975	0.0358	7.3667	0.1358	4.9955
15	4.1772	0.2394	31.772	0.0315	7.6061	0.1315	5.2789
16	4.5950	0.2176	35.950	0.0278	7.8237	0.1278	5.5493
17	5.0545	0.1979	40.545	0.0247	8.0216	0.1247	5.8071
18	5.5599	0.1799	45.599	0.0219	8.2014	0.1219	6.0526
19	6.1159	0.1635	51.159	0.0196	8.3649	0.1196	6.2861
20	6.7275	0.1487	57.275	0.0175	8.5136	0.1175	6.5081
21	7.4002	0.1351	64.003	0.0156	8.6487	0.1156	6.7189
22	8.1403	0.1229	71.403	0.0140	8.7716	0.1140	6.9189
23	8.9543	0.1117	79.543	0.0126	8.8832	0.1126	7.1085
24	9.8497	0.1015	88.497	0.0113	8.9848	0.1113	7.2881
25	10.835	0.0923	98.347	0.0102	9.0771	0.1102	7.4580
30	17.449	0.0573	164.49	0.0061	9.4269	0.1061	8.1762
35	28.102	0.0356	271.02	0.0037	9.6442	0.1037	8.7086
40	45.259	0.0221	442.59	0.0023	9.7791	0.1023	9.0962
50	117.391	0.0085	1163.9	0.0009	9.9148	0.1009	9.5704
60	304.482	0.0033	3034.8	0.0003	9.9672	0.1003	9.8023
∞	∞	0	∞	0	10.000	0.1000	10.000

TABLE A.15   12% DISCRETE COMPOUND INTEREST FACTORS

	Single Payment		Uniform Series				Uniform Gradient
n	Compound Amount Factor F/P	Present Worth Factor P/F	Compound Amount Factor F/A	Sinking Fund Factor A/F	Present Worth Factor P/A	Capital Recovery Factor A/P	Gradient Conversion Factor A/G
1	1.1200	0.8929	1.000	1.0000	0.9029	1.1200	0.0000
2	1.2544	0.7972	2.120	0.4717	1.6901	0.5917	0.4717
3	1.4049	0.7118	3.374	0.2964	2.4018	0.4164	0.9246
4	1.5735	0.6355	4.779	0.2092	3.0374	0.3292	1.3589
5	1.7623	0.5674	6.353	0.1574	3.6048	0.2774	1.7746
6	1.9738	0.5066	8.115	0.1232	4.1114	0.2432	2.1721
7	2.2107	0.4524	10.089	0.0991	4.5638	0.2191	2.5515
8	2.4760	0.4039	12.300	0.0813	4.9676	0.2013	2.9132
9	2.7731	0.3606	14.776	0.0677	5.3283	0.1877	3.2574
10	3.1058	0.3220	17.549	0.0570	5.6502	0.1770	3.5847
11	3.4785	0.2875	20.655	0.0484	5.9377	0.1684	3.8953
12	3.8960	0.2567	24.133	0.0414	6.1944	0.1614	4.1897
13	4.3635	0.2292	28.029	0.0357	6.4236	0.1557	4.4683
14	4.8871	0.2046	32.393	0.0309	6.6282	0.1509	4.7317
15	5.4736	0.1827	37.280	0.0268	6.8109	0.1468	4.9803
16	6.1304	0.1631	42.753	0.0234	6.9740	0.1434	5.2147
17	6.8660	0.1457	48.884	0.0205	7.1196	0.1405	5.4353
18	7.6900	0.1300	55.750	0.0179	7.2497	0.1379	5.6427
19	8.6128	0.1161	63.440	0.0158	7.3658	0.1358	5.8375
20	9.6463	0.1037	72.052	0.0139	7.4695	0.1339	6.0202
21	10.804	0.0926	81.699	0.0123	7.5620	0.1323	6.1913
22	12.100	0.0827	92.503	0.0108	7.6447	0.1308	6.3514
23	13.552	0.0738	104.60	0.0096	7.7184	0.1296	6.5010
24	15.179	0.0659	118.16	0.0085	7.7843	0.1285	6.6407
25	17.000	0.0588	133.33	0.0075	7.8431	0.1275	6.7708
30	29.960	0.0334	241.33	0.0042	8.0552	0.1242	7.2974
35	52.800	0.0189	431.66	0.0023	8.1755	0.1223	7.6577
40	93.051	0.0108	767.09	0.0013	8.2438	0.1213	7.8988
50	289.00	0.0035	2400.0	0.0004	8.3045	0.1204	8.1597
60	897.60	0.0011	7471.6	0.0001	8.3240	0.1201	8.2664
∞	∞	0	∞	0	8.3333	0.1200	8.3333

TABLE A.16   15% DISCRETE COMPOUND INTEREST FACTORS

	Single Payment		Uniform Series				Uniform Gradient
n	Compound Amount Factor F/P	Present Worth Factor P/F	Compound Amount Factor F/A	Sinking Fund Factor A/F	Present Worth Factor P/A	Capital Recovery Factor A/P	Gradient Conversion Factor A/G
1	1.1500	0.8696	1.000	1.0000	0.8696	1.1500	0.0000
2	1.3225	0.7562	2.150	0.4651	1.6257	0.6151	0.4651
3	1.5209	0.6575	3.473	0.2880	2.2832	0.4380	0.9071
4	1.7490	0.5718	4.993	0.2003	2.8550	0.3503	1.3263
5	2.0114	0.4972	6.742	0.1483	3.3522	0.2983	1.7228
6	2.3131	0.4323	8.754	0.1142	3.7845	0.2642	2.0972
7	2.6600	0.3759	11.067	0.0904	4.1604	0.2404	2.4499
8	3.0590	0.3269	13.727	0.0729	4.4873	0.2229	2.7813
9	3.5179	0.2843	13.786	0.0596	4.7716	0.2096	3.0922
10	4.0456	0.2472	20.304	0.0493	5.0188	0.1993	3.3832
11	4.6524	0.2150	24.349	0.0411	5.2337	0.1911	3.6550
12	5.3502	0.1869	29.002	0.0345	5.4206	0.1845	3.9082
13	6.1528	0.1625	34.352	0.0291	5.5832	0.1791	4.1438
14	7.0757	0.1413	40.505	0.0247	5.7245	0.1747	4.3624
15	8.1371	0.1229	47.580	0.0210	5.8474	0.1710	4.5650
16	9.3576	0.1069	55.717	0.0180	5.9542	0.1680	4.7523
17	10.761	0.0929	65.075	0.0154	6.0472	0.1654	4.9251
18	12.375	0.0808	75.836	0.0132	6.1280	0.1632	5.0843
19	14.232	0.0703	88.202	0.0113	6.1982	0.1613	5.2307
20	16.637	0.0611	102.44	0.0098	6.2593	0.1598	5.3651
21	18.822	0.0531	118.81	0.0084	6.3125	0.1584	5.4883
22	21.645	0.0462	137.63	0.0073	6.3587	0.1573	5.6010
23	24.891	0.0402	159.28	0.0063	6.3988	0.1563	5.7040
24	28.625	0.0349	184.17	0.0054	6.4338	0.1554	5.7979
25	32.919	0.0304	212.79	0.0047	6.4642	0.1547	5.8834
30	66.212	0.0151	434.75	0.0023	6.5660	0.1523	6.2066
35	133.18	0.0075	881.17	0.0011	6.6166	0.1511	6.4019
40	267.86	0.0037	1779.1	0.0006	6.6418	0.1506	6.5168
50	1083.7	0.0009	7217.7	0.0002	6.6605	0.1501	6.6205
60	4384.0	0.0002	29220.	0.0001	6.6651	0.1500	6.6530
∞	∞	0	∞	0	6.6667	0.1500	6.6667

TABLE A.17 16% DISCRETE COMPOUND INTEREST FACTORS

	Single Payment		Uniform Series				Uniform Gradient
n	Compound Amount Factor F/P	Present Worth Factor P/F	Compound Amount Factor F/A	Sinking Fund Factor A/F	Present Worth Factor P/A	Capital Recovery Factor A/P	Gradient Conversion Factor A/G
1	1.1600	0.8621	1.0000	1.0000	0.862	1.1600	0.0000
2	1.3456	0.7432	2.160	0.4630	1.605	0.6230	0.4630
3	1.5609	0.6407	3.5056	0.2853	2.246	0.4453	0.9012
4	1.8106	0.5523	5.0664	0.1974	2.798	0.3574	1.3156
5	2.1003	0.4761	6.8771	0.1454	3.274	0.3054	1.7059
6	2.4364	0.4104	8.9775	0.1114	3.685	0.2714	2.0728
7	2.8262	0.3538	11.414	0.0876	4.039	0.2476	2.4169
8	3.2784	0.3050	14.240	0.0702	4.344	0.2302	2.7388
9	3.8030	0.2630	17.519	0.0571	4.607	0.2171	3.0391
10	4.4114	0.2267	21.321	0.0469	4.833	0.2069	3.3187
11	5.1173	0.1954	25.733	0.0389	5.234	0.1989	3.5783
12	5.9360	0.1685	30.850	0.0324	5.197	0.1924	3.8189
13	6.8858	0.1452	36.786	0.0272	5.342	0.1872	4.0413
14	7.9875	0.1252	43.672	0.0229	5.468	0.1829	4.2464
15	9.2655	0.1079	51.660	0.0194	5.575	0.1794	4.4352
16	10.748	0.0930	60.925	0.0164	5.668	0.1764	4.6086
17	12.468	0.0802	71.673	0.0140	5.749	0.1740	4.7676
18	14.463	0.0691	84.141	0.0119	5.818	0.1719	4.9129
19	16.777	0.0596	98.603	0.0101	5.877	0.1701	5.0457
20	19.461	0.0514	115.38	0.0087	5.929	0.1687	5.1667
21	22.575	0.0443	134.84	0.0074	5.973	0.1674	5.2766
22	26.186	0.0382	157.42	0.0064	6.011	0.1664	5.3765
23	30.376	0.0329	183.60	0.0055	6.044	0.1655	5.4670
24	35.236	0.0284	213.98	0.0047	6.073	0.1647	5.5490
25	40.874	0.0245	249.21	0.0040	6.097	0.0640	5.6230
30	85.850	0.0116	530.31	0.0019	6.177	0.1619	5.8964
35	180.31	0.0055	1120.7	0.0009	6.215	0.1609	6.0548
40	378.72	0.0026	2360.8	0.0004	6.233	0.1604	6.1441
50	1670.7	0.0006	10436	0.0001	6.246	0.0601	6.2200
∞	∞	0	∞	0	6.250	0.01600	6.250

TABLE A.18 18% DISCRETE COMPOUND INTEREST FACTORS

	Single Payment		Uniform Series				Uniform Gradient
n	Compound Amount Factor F/P	Present Worth Factor P/F	Compound Amount Factor F/A	Sinking Fund Factor A/F	Present Worth Factor P/A	Capital Recovery Factor A/P	Gradient Conversion Factor A/G
1	1.1800	0.8475	1.0000	1.0000	0.8475	1.1800	0.0000
2	1.3924	0.7182	2.1800	0.4587	1.5656	0.6387	0.4587
3	1.6430	0.6086	3.5724	0.2799	2.1743	0.4599	0.8902
4	1.9388	0.5158	5.2154	0.1917	2.6901	0.3717	1.2947
5	2.2878	0.4371	7.1542	0.1398	3.1272	0.3198	1.6728
6	2.6996	0.3704	9.4420	0.1059	3.4976	0.2859	2.0252
7	3.1855	0.3139	12.142	0.0824	3.8115	0.2624	2.3526
8	3.7589	0.2660	15.327	0.0652	4.0776	0.2452	2.6558
9	4.4355	0.2255	19.086	0.0524	4.3030	0.2324	2.9358
10	5.2338	0.1911	23.521	0.0425	4.4941	0.2225	3.1936
11	6.1759	0.1619	28.755	0.0348	4.6560	0.2148	3.4303
12	7.2876	0.1372	34.931	0.0286	4.7932	0.2086	3.6470
13	8.5994	0.1163	42.219	0.0237	4.9095	0.2037	3.8449
14	10.147	0.0985	50.818	0.0197	5.0081	0.1997	4.0250
15	11.974	0.0835	60.965	0.0164	5.0916	0.1964	4.1887
16	14.129	0.0708	72.939	0.0137	5.1624	0.1937	4.3369
17	16.672	0.0600	87.068	0.0115	5.2223	0.1915	4.4708
18	19.673	0.0508	103.74	0.0096	5.2732	0.1896	4.5916
19	23.214	0.0431	123.41	0.0081	5.3162	0.1881	4.7003
20	27.393	0.0365	146.63	0.0068	5.3528	0.1868	4.7978
21	31.324	0.0309	174.02	0.0057	5.3837	0.1857	4.8851
22	38.142	0.0262	206.34	0.0048	5.4099	0.1848	4.9632
23	45.008	0.0222	244.49	0.0041	5.4321	0.1841	5.0329
24	53.109	0.0188	289.49	0.0035	5.4510	0.1835	5.0950
25	62.669	0.0160	342.60	0.0029	5.4669	0.1829	5.1502
30	143.37	0.0070	790.95	0.0013	5.5168	0.1813	5.3448
35	328.00	0.0030	1816.7	0.0006	5.5386	0.1806	5.4485
40	750.38	0.0013	4163.2	0.0002	5.5482	0.1802	5.5022
50	3927.4	0.0003	21813.	0.0000	5.5541	0.1800	5.5428
∞	∞	0	∞	0	5.5556	0.1800	5.5556

TABLE A.19 20% DISCRETE COMPOUND INTEREST FACTORS

	Single Payment		Uniform Series				Uniform Gradient
n	Compound Amount Factor F/P	Present Worth Factor P/F	Compound Amount Factor F/A	Sinking Fund Factor A/F	Present Worth Factor P/A	Capital Recovery Factor A/P	Gradient Conversion Factor A/G
1	1.2000	0.8333	1.0000	1.0000	0.8333	1.2000	0.0000
2	1.4400	0.6945	2.2000	0.4546	1.5278	0.6546	0.4546
3	1.7280	0.5787	3.6400	0.2747	2.1065	0.4747	0.8791
4	2.0736	0.4823	5.3680	0.1863	2.5887	0.3863	1.2742
5	2.4883	0.4019	7.4416	0.1344	2.9906	0.3344	1.6405
6	2.9860	0.3349	9.9299	0.1007	3.3255	0.3007	1.9788
7	3.5832	0.2791	12.916	0.0774	3.6046	0.2774	2.2902
8	4.2998	0.2326	16.499	0.0606	3.8372	0.2606	2.5756
9	5.1598	0.1938	20.799	0.0481	4.0310	0.2481	2.8364
10	6.1917	0.1615	25.959	0.0385	4.1925	0.2385	3.0739
11	7.4301	0.1346	32.150	0.0311	4.3271	0.2311	3.2893
12	8.9161	0.1122	39.581	0.0253	4.4392	0.2253	3.4841
13	10.699	0.0935	48.497	0.0206	4.5327	0.2206	3.6597
14	12.839	0.0779	59.196	0.0169	4.6106	0.2169	3.8175
15	15.407	0.0639	72.035	0.0139	4.6755	0.2139	3.9589
16	18.488	0.0541	87.442	0.0114	4.7296	0.2114	4.0851
17	22.186	0.0451	105.93	0.0095	4.7746	0.2095	4.1976
18	26.623	0.0376	128.12	0.0078	4.8122	0.2078	4.2975
19	31.948	0.0313	154.74	0.0065	4.8435	0.2065	4.3861
20	38.338	0.0251	186.69	0.0054	4.8696	0.2054	4.4644
21	46.005	0.0217	225.03	0.0045	4.8913	0.2045	4.5334
22	55.206	0.0181	271.03	0.0037	4.9094	0.2037	4.5942
23	66.247	0.0151	326.24	0.0031	4.9245	0.2031	4.6475
24	79.497	0.0126	392.48	0.0026	4.9371	0.2026	4.6943
25	95.396	0.0105	471.98	0.0021	4.9476	0.2021	4.7352
30	237.38	0.0042	1181.9	0.0009	4.9789	0.2009	4.8731
35	590.67	0.0017	2948.3	0.0003	4.9915	0.2003	4.9407
40	1469.8	0.0007	7343.9	0.0002	4.9966	0.2001	4.9728
50	9100.4	0.0001	45497.	0.0000	4.9995	0.2000	4.9945
∞	∞	0	∞	0	5.0000	0.2000	5.0000

TABLE A.20 25% DISCRETE COMPOUND INTEREST FACTORS

	Single Payment		Uniform Series				Uniform Gradient
n	Compound Amount Factor F/P	Present Worth Factor P/F	Compound Amount Factor F/A	Sinking Fund Factor A/F	Present Worth Factor P/A	Capital Recovery Factor A/P	Gradient Conversion Factor A/G
1	1.2500	0.8000	1.0000	1.0000	0.8000	1.2500	0.0000
2	1.5625	0.6400	2.2500	0.4445	1.4400	0.6945	0.4445
3	1.9531	0.5120	3.8125	0.2623	1.9520	0.5123	0.8525
4	2.4414	0.4096	5.7656	0.1735	2.3616	0.4234	1.2249
5	3.0518	0.3277	8.2070	0.1219	2.6893	0.3719	1.5631
6	3.8147	0.2622	11.259	0.0888	2.9514	0.3388	1.8683
7	4.7684	0.2097	15.073	0.0664	3.1611	0.3164	2.1424
8	5.9605	0.1678	19.842	0.0504	3.3289	0.3004	2.3873
9	7.4506	0.1342	25.802	0.0388	3.4631	0.2888	2.6048
10	9.3132	0.1074	33.253	0.0301	3.5705	0.2801	2.7971
11	11.642	0.0859	42.566	0.0235	3.6564	0.2735	2.9663
12	14.552	0.0687	54.208	0.0185	3.7251	0.2685	3.1145
13	18.190	0.0550	68.760	0.0146	3.7801	0.2646	3.2438
14	22.737	0.0440	86.949	0.0115	3.8241	0.2615	3.3560
15	28.422	0.0352	109.69	0.0091	3.8593	0.2591	3.4530
16	35.527	0.0282	138.11	0.0073	3.8874	0.2573	3.5366
17	44.409	0.0225	173.64	0.0058	3.9099	0.2558	3.6084
18	55.511	0.0180	218.05	0.0046	3.9280	0.2546	3.6698
19	69.389	0.0144	273.56	0.0037	3.9424	0.2537	3.7222
20	86.736	0.0115	342.95	0.0029	3.9539	0.2529	3.7667
21	108.42	0.0092	429.68	0.0023	3.9631	0.2523	3.8045
22	135.53	0.0074	538.10	0.0019	3.9705	0.2519	3.8365
23	169.41	0.0059	673.63	0.0015	3.9764	0.2515	3.8634
24	211.76	0.0047	843.03	0.0012	3.9811	0.2512	3.8861
25	264.70	0.0038	1054.8	0.0010	3.9849	0.2510	3.9052
30	807.79	0.0012	3227.2	0.0003	3.9951	0.2503	3.9628
35	2465.2	0.0004	9856.8	0.0001	3.9984	0.2501	3.9858
40	7523.2	0.0001	30089.	0.0001	3.9995	0.2500	3.9947
∞	∞	0	∞	0	4.0000	0.2500	4.0000

TABLE A.21   30% DISCRETE COMPOUND INTEREST FACTORS

	Single Payment		Uniform Series				Uniform Gradient
n	Compound Amount Factor F/P	Present Worth Factor P/F	Compound Amount Factor F/A	Sinking Fund Factor A/F	Present Worth Factor P/A	Capital Recovery Factor A/P	Gradient Conversion Factor A/G
1	1.3000	0.7692	1.0000	1.0000	0.7692	1.3000	0.0000
2	1.690	0.5917	2.3000	0.4348	1.3610	0.7348	0.4348
3	2.1970	0.4552	3.9900	0.2506	1.8161	0.5506	0.8271
4	2.8561	0.3501	6.1870	0.1616	2.1663	0.4616	1.1783
5	3.7129	0.2693	9.0431	0.1106	2.4356	0.6104	1.4903
6	4.8268	0.2072	12.756	0.0784	2.6428	0.3784	1.7655
7	6.2749	0.1594	17.583	0.0569	2.8021	0.3569	2.0063
8	8.1573	0.1226	23.858	0.0419	2.9247	0.3419	2.2156
9	10.605	0.0943	32.015	0.0312	3.0190	0.3312	2.3963
10	13.786	0.0725	42.620	0.0235	3.0915	0.3235	2.5512
11	17.922	0.0558	56.405	0.0177	3.1473	0.3177	2.6833
12	23.298	0.0429	74.327	0.0135	3.1903	0.3135	2.7952
13	30.288	0.0330	97.625	0.0103	3.2233	0.3103	2.8895
14	39.374	0.0254	127.91	0.0078	3.2487	0.3078	2.9685
15	51.186	0.0195	167.29	0.0060	3.2682	0.3060	3.0345
16	66.542	0.0150	218.47	0.0046	3.2832	0.3046	3.0892
17	86.504	0.0116	285.01	0.0035	3.2948	0.3035	3.1345
18	112.46	0.0089	371.52	0.0027	3.3037	0.3027	3.1718
19	146.19	0.0069	483.97	0.0021	3.3105	0.3021	3.2025
20	109.05	0.0053	630.17	0.0016	3.3158	0.3016	3.2276
21	247.07	0.0041	820.22	0.0012	3.3199	0.3012	3.2480
22	321.18	0.0031	1067.3	0.0009	3.3230	0.3009	3.2646
23	417.54	0.0024	1388.5	0.0007	3.3254	0.3007	3.2781
24	542.80	0.0019	1806.0	0.0006	3.3272	0.3006	3.2890
25	705.64	0.0014	2348.8	0.0004	3.3286	0.3004	3.2979
30	2620.0	0.0004	8730.0	0.0001	3.3321	0.3001	3.3219
35	9727.8	0.0001	32423.	0.0000	3.3330	0.3000	3.3297
∞	∞	0	∞	0	3.3333	0.3000	3.3333

TABLE A.22 40% DISCRETE COMPOUND INTEREST FACTORS

	Single Payment		Uniform Series				Uniform Gradient
n	Compound Amount Factor F/P	Present Worth Factor P/F	Compound Amount Factor F/A	Sinking Fund Factor A/F	Present Worth Factor P/A	Capital Recovery Factor A/P	Gradient Conversion Factor A/G
1	1.4000	0.7143	1.000	1.0001	0.7143	1.4001	0.0000
2	1.9600	0.5103	2.400	0.4167	1.2245	0.8167	0.4167
3	2.7440	0.3645	4.360	0.2294	1.5890	0.6294	0.7799
4	3.8316	0.2604	7.104	0.1408	1.8493	0.5408	1.0924
5	5.3782	0.1860	10.946	0.0914	2.0352	0.4914	1.3580
6	7.5295	0.1329	16.324	0.0613	2.1680	0.4613	1.5811
7	10.541	0.0949	23.853	0.0420	2.2629	0.4420	1.7664
8	14.758	0.0678	34.395	0.0291	2.3306	0.4291	1.9186
9	20.661	0.0485	49.153	0.0204	2.3790	0.4204	2.0423
10	28.925	0.0346	69.814	0.0144	2.4136	0.4144	2.1420
11	40.496	0.0247	98.739	0.0102	2.4393	0.4102	2.2214
12	56.694	0.0177	139.234	0.0072	2.4560	0.4072	2.2846
13	79.371	0.0126	195.928	0.0052	2.4686	0.4052	2.3342
14	111.12	0.0090	275.299	0.0037	2.4775	0.4037	2.3729
15	155.57	0.0065	386.419	0.0026	2.4840	0.4026	2.4030
16	217.79	0.0046	541.986	0.0019	2.4886	0.4019	2.4262
17	304.91	0.0033	759.780	0.0014	2.4918	0.4014	2.4441
18	426.88	0.0024	1064.691	0.0010	2.4942	0.4010	2.4578
19	597.63	0.0017	1491.567	0.0007	2.4959	0.4007	2.4682
20	836.68	0.0012	2089.195	0.0005	2.4971	0.4005	2.4761
21	1171.3	0.0009	2925.871	0.0004	2.4979	0.4004	2.4821
22	1639.9	0.0007	4097.218	0.0003	2.4985	0.4003	2.4866
23	2295.8	0.0005	5737.105	0.0002	2.4990	0.4002	2.4900
24	3214.2	0.0004	8032.945	0.0002	2.4993	0.4002	2.4926
25	4499.8	0.0003	11247.110	0.0001	2.4995	0.4001	2.4945
30	24201.	0.0001	50400.580	0.0001	2.4999	0.4001	2.4988
∞	∞	0	∞	0	2.5000	0.4000	2.5000

TABLE A.23 50% DISCRETE COMPOUND INTEREST FACTORS

	Single Payment		Uniform Series				Uniform Gradient
n	Compound Amount Factor F/P	Present Worth Factor P/F	Compound Amount Factor F/A	Sinking Fund Factor A/F	Present Worth Factor P/A	Capital Recovery Factor A/P	Gradient Conversion Factor A/G
1	1.5000	0.6667	1.0000	1.0000	0.6667	1.5000	0.0001
2	2.2500	0.4445	2.5000	0.4000	1.1112	0.9001	0.4001
3	3.3750	0.2963	4.7500	0.2106	1.4075	0.7106	0.7369
4	5.0625	0.1976	8.1250	0.1231	1.6050	0.6231	1.0154
5	7.5938	0.1317	13.188	0.0759	1.7367	0.5759	1.2418
6	11.391	0.0878	20.781	0.0482	1.8245	0.5482	1.4226
7	17.086	0.0586	32.172	0.0311	1.8830	0.5311	1.5649
8	25.629	0.0391	49.258	0.0204	1.9220	0.5204	1.6752
9	38.443	0.0261	74.887	0.0134	1.9480	0.5134	1.7597
10	57.665	0.0174	113.33	0.0089	1.9654	0.5089	1.8236
11	86.498	0.0116	171.00	0.0059	1.9769	0.5059	1.8714
12	129.75	0.0078	257.49	0.0039	1.9846	0.5039	1.9068
13	194.62	0.0052	387.24	0.0026	1.9898	0.5026	1.9329
14	291.93	0.0035	281.86	0.0018	1.9932	0.5018	1.9519
15	437.89	0.0023	873.79	0.0012	1.9955	0.5012	1.9657
16	656.84	0.0016	1311.7	0.0008	1.9970	1.5008	1.9757
17	985.26	0.0011	1968.5	0.0006	1.9980	1.5006	1.9828
18	1477.9	0.0007	2953.8	0.0004	1.9987	0.5004	1.9879
19	2216.8	0.0005	4431.7	0.0003	1.9991	0.5003	1.9915
20	3325.3	0.0004	6648.5	0.0002	1.9994	0.5002	1.9940
21	4987.9	0.0003	9973.8	0.0002	1.9996	0.5002	1.9958
22	7481.8	0.0002	14962.	0.0001	1.9998	0.5001	1.9971
23	11223.	0.0001	22443.	0.0001	1.9999	0.5001	1.9980
24	16834.	0.0001	33666.	0.0001	1.9999	0.5001	1.9986
25	25251.	0.0001	50500.	0.0001	2.0000	0.5001	1.9991
∞	∞	0	∞	0	2.0000	0.5000	2.0000

Appendix B
CONTINUOUS COMPOUND INTEREST FACTORS

TABLE B.1 1/2% CONTINUOUS COMPOUND INTEREST FACTORS

	Single Payment		Uniform Series				Uniform Gradient
n	Compound Amount Factor F/P	Present Worth Factor P/F	Compound Amount Factor F/A	Sinking Fund Factor A/F	Present Worth Factor P/A	Capital Recovery Factor A/P	Gradient Conversion Factor A/G
1	1.0050	0.9950	1.0000	1.0000	0.9950	1.0050	0.0000
2	1.0100	0.9901	2.0049	0.4988	1.9850	0.5038	0.4988
3	1.0151	0.9851	3.0150	0.3317	2.9702	0.3367	0.9967
4	1.0202	0.9802	4.0301	0.2481	3.9503	0.2531	1.4938
5	1.0253	0.9753	5.0502	0.1980	4.9255	0.2030	1.9900
6	1.0305	0.9704	6.0755	0.1646	5.8960	0.1696	2.4854
7	1.0356	0.9656	7.1060	0.1407	6.8615	0.1457	2.9800
8	1.0408	0.9608	8.1417	0.1228	7.8225	0.1278	3.4738
9	1.0460	0.9560	9.1825	0.1089	8.7784	0.1139	3.9667
10	1.0513	0.9512	10.229	0.0978	9.7297	0.1028	4.4588
11	1.0565	0.9465	11.280	0.0887	10.6762	0.0937	4.9500
12	1.0618	0.9418	12.336	0.0811	11.6180	0.0861	5.4404
13	1.0672	0.9371	13.398	0.0736	12.5550	0.0796	5.9300
14	1.0725	0.9324	14.465	0.0691	13.4874	0.0741	6.4188
15	1.0799	0.9277	15.538	0.0644	14.4152	0.0694	6.9067
16	1.0833	9.9231	16.616	0.0602	15.3382	0.0652	7.3938
17	1.0887	0.9185	17.669	0.0565	12.2568	0.0615	7.8800
18	1.0942	0.9139	18.788	0.0532	17.1707	0.0582	8.3654
19	1.0997	0.9094	19.882	0.0503	18.0800	0.0553	8.8500
20	1.1052	0.9048	20.982	0.0477	18.9849	0.0527	9.3338
21	1.1107	0.9003	22.087	0.0453	19.8853	0.0503	9.8167
22	1.1163	0.8958	23.198	0.0431	20.7811	0.0481	10.299
23	1.1219	0.8914	24.314	0.0411	21.6725	0.0461	10.780
24	1.1275	0.8869	25.436	0.0393	22.5594	0.0443	11.261
25	1.1311	0.8825	26.563	0.0376	23.4419	0.0427	11.740
30	1.1618	0.8607	32.286	0.0310	27.7888	0.0360	14.126
35	1.1912	0.8395	38.154	0.0262	32.0284	0.0312	16.490
40	1.2214	0.8137	44.170	0.0226	36.1633	0.0277	18.834
50	1.2840	0.7783	56.663	0.0176	44.1294	0.0227	23.460
60	1.3499	0.7408	69.797	0.0143	41.7069	0.0193	28.003

TABLE B.2 1% CONTINUOUS COMPOUND INTEREST FACTORS

	Single Payment		Uniform Series				Uniform Gradient
n	Compound Amount Factor F/P	Present Worth Factor P/F	Compound Amount Factor F/A	Sinking Fund Factor A/F	Present Worth Factor P/A	Capital Recovery Factor A/P	Gradient Conversion Factor A/G
1	1.0100	0.9901	1.0000	1.0000	0.9901	1.0101	0.0000
2	1.0202	0.9802	2.0101	0.4975	1.9703	0.5076	0.4975
3	1.0305	0.9705	3.0303	0.3300	2.9407	0.3401	0.9933
4	1.0408	0.9608	2.0608	0.2463	3.9015	0.2563	1.4875
5	1.0513	0.9512	5.1016	0.1960	4.8527	0.2061	1.9800
6	1.0618	0.9418	6.1530	0.1625	4.7945	0.1726	2.4708
7	1.0725	0.9324	7.2148	0.1386	6.7269	0.1487	2.9600
8	1.0833	0.9231	8.2873	0.1207	7.6500	0.1307	3.4475
9	1.0942	0.9139	9.3707	0.1067	8.5639	0.1168	3.9334
10	1.1052	0.9048	10.465	0.0956	9.4688	0.1056	4.4175
11	1.1163	0.8958	11.570	0.0864	10.365	0.0965	4.9000
12	1.1275	0.8869	12.686	0.0788	11.252	0.0889	5.3809
13	1.1388	0.8781	13.814	0.0724	12.130	0.0825	5.8600
14	1.1503	0.8694	14.952	0.0669	12.999	0.0769	6.3376
15	1.1618	0.8607	16.103	0.0621	13.860	0.0722	6.8134
16	1.1735	0.8522	17.264	0.0579	14.712	0.0680	7.2876
17	1.1853	0.8437	18.438	0.0542	15.556	0.0643	7.7601
18	1.1972	0.8353	19.623	0.0510	16.391	0.0610	8.2310
19	1.2092	0.8270	20.821	0.0480	17.218	0.0581	8.7002
20	1.2218	0.8187	22.030	0.0454	18.037	0.0555	9.1677
21	1.2337	0.8106	23.251	0.0430	18.847	0.0531	9.6336
22	1.2461	0.8025	24.485	0.0409	19.650	0.0509	10.098
23	1.2586	0.7945	25.731	0.0389	20.444	0.0489	10.560
24	1.2712	0.7866	26.990	0.0371	21.231	0.0471	11.021
25	1.2840	0.7788	28.261	0.0354	22.010	0.0454	11.481
30	1.3499	0.7408	34.881	0.0287	25.789	0.0388	13.752
35	1.4191	0.7047	41.698	0.0240	29.384	0.0340	15.982
40	1.4918	0.6703	48.937	0.0204	32.803	0.0305	18.171
50	1.6487	0.6065	64.548	0.0155	39.151	0.0256	22.426
60	1.822	0.5488	81.802	0.0122	44.894	0.0223	26.519

TABLE B.3 1-1/2% CONTINUOUS COMPOUND INTEREST FACTORS

	Single Payment		Uniform Series				Uniform Gradient
n	Compound Amount Factor F/P	Present Worth Factor P/F	Compound Amount Factor F/A	Sinking Fund Factor A/F	Present Worth Factor P/A	Capital Recovery Factor A/P	Gradient Conversion Factor A/G
1	1.0151	0.9851	1.0000	1.0000	0.9851	1.0151	0.0000
2	1.0305	0.9704	2.0151	0.4963	1.9555	0.5114	0.4963
3	1.0460	0.9560	3.0456	0.3283	2.9116	0.3435	0.9900
4	1.0618	0.9418	4.0916	0.2444	3.8534	0.2595	1.4813
5	1.0779	0.9277	5.1535	0.1940	4.7811	0.2092	1.9700
6	1.0942	0.9139	6.2313	0.1605	5.6950	0.1756	2.4563
7	1.1107	0.9003	7.3256	0.1365	6.5954	0.1516	2.9400
8	1.1275	0.8869	8.4363	0.1185	7.4823	0.1336	3.4213
9	1.1445	0.8737	8.5638	0.1046	8.3560	0.1197	3.9000
10	1.1618	0.8607	10.708	0.0934	9.2168	0.1085	4.3763
11	1.1794	0.8479	11.870	0.0842	10.065	0.0994	4.8501
12	1.1972	0.8353	13.050	0.0766	10.900	0.0917	5.3213
13	1.2153	0.8228	14.247	0.0702	11.723	0.0853	5.7901
14	1.2337	0.8106	15.462	0.0647	12.533	0.0798	6.2564
15	1.2523	0.7985	16.696	0.0599	13.332	0.0750	6.7202
16	1.2712	0.7866	17.948	0.0557	14.119	0.0708	7.1816
17	1.2905	0.7749	19.220	0.0520	14.894	0.0671	7.6404
18	1.3100	0.7634	20.510	0.0488	15.657	0.0639	8.0967
19	1.3298	0.7520	21.820	0.0458	16.409	0.0609	8.5506
20	1.3499	0.7408	23.150	0.0432	17.150	1.0583	9.0020
21	1.3703	0.7298	24.500	0.0408	17.880	0.0559	9.4509
22	1.3910	0.7189	25.870	0.0387	18.598	0.0538	9.8973
23	1.4120	0.7082	27.261	0.0367	19.307	0.0518	10.341
24	1.4333	0.6977	28.673	0.0349	20.004	0.0500	10.783
25	1.4550	0.6873	30.106	0.0332	20.692	0.9483	11.222
30	1.5683	0.6376	37.605	0.0266	23.978	0.0417	13.3800
35	1.6905	0.5916	45.687	0.0219	27.026	0.0370	15.4770
40	1.8221	0.5488	54.399	0.0184	29.855	0.0335	17.5131
50	2.1170	1.4724	73.910	0.0135	34.913	0.0286	21.4052
60	2.4596	0.4066	96.580	0.0104	39.267	0.0255	25.0609

TABLE B.4 2% CONTINUOUS COMPOUND INTEREST FACTORS

	Single Payment		Uniform Series				Uniform Gradient
n	Compound Amount Factor F/P	Present Worth Factor P/F	Compound Amount Factor F/A	Sinking Fund Factor A/F	Present Worth Factor P/A	Capital Recovery Factor A/P	Gradient Conversion Factor A/G
1	1.0202	0.9802	1.0000	1.0000	0.9802	1.0202	0.0000
2	1.0408	0.9608	2.0203	0.4950	1.9410	0.5152	0.4950
3	1.0618	0.9418	3.0611	0.3267	2.8828	0.3469	0.9867
4	1.0833	0.9231	4.1229	0.2425	3.8060	0.2627	1.4750
5	1.1052	0.9048	5.2063	0.1921	4.7108	0.2123	1.9600
6	1.1275	0.8869	6.3115	0.1584	5.5978	0.1786	2.4417
7	1.1503	0.8694	7.4390	0.1344	6.4672	0.1546	2.9200
8	1.1735	0.8521	8.5893	0.1164	7.3193	0.1366	3.3950
9	1.1972	0.8353	9.7629	0.1024	8.1546	0.1226	3.8667
10	1.2214	0.8187	10.960	0.0912	8.9734	0.1114	4.3351
11	1.2461	0.8025	12.182	0.0821	9.7759	0.1023	4.8002
12	1.2712	0.7866	13.428	0.0745	10.563	0.0947	5.2619
13	1.2969	0.7711	14.699	0.0680	11.334	0.0882	5.7203
14	1.3231	0.7558	15.996	0.0625	12.090	0.0827	6.1754
15	1.3499	0.7408	17.319	0.0577	12.830	0.0779	6.6272
16	1.3771	0.7251	18.669	0.0536	13.557	0.0738	7.0757
17	1.4049	0.7118	20.046	0.0699	14.268	0.0701	7.5209
18	1.4333	0.6977	21.451	0.0466	14.966	0.0668	7.9628
19	1.4623	0.6839	22.885	0.0437	15.650	0.0639	8.4014
20	1.4918	0.6703	24.347	0.0411	16.320	0.0613	8.8368
21	1.5220	0.6570	25.834	0.0387	16.977	0.0589	9.2688
22	1.5527	0.6440	27.361	0.0365	17.621	0.0567	9.6976
23	1.5841	0.6313	28.914	0.0346	18.253	0.0548	10.123
24	1.6161	0.6188	30.498	0.0328	18.871	0.0530	10.545
25	1.6487	0.6065	32.114	0.0311	19.478	0.0513	10.964
30	1.8221	0.5488	40.697	0.0246	22.335	0.0448	13.011
35	2.0138	0.4966	50.184	0.0199	24.921	0.0401	14.977
40	2.2255	0.4493	60.668	0.0165	27.260	0.0367	16.863
50	2.7183	0.3679	85.060	0.0118	31.292	0.0320	20.403
60	3.3201	0.3012	114.853	0.0087	34.593	0.0289	23.641

TABLE B.5 3% CONTINUOUS COMPOUND INTEREST FACTORS

	Single Payment		Uniform Series				Uniform Gradient
n	Compound Amount Factor F/P	Present Worth Factor P/F	Compound Amount Factor F/A	Sinking Fund Factor A/F	Present Worth Factor P/A	Capital Recovery Factor A/P	Gradient Conversion Factor A/G
1	1.0305	0.9705	1.0000	1.0000	0.9705	1.0305	0.0000
2	1.0618	0.9418	2.0305	0.4925	1.9122	0.5230	0.4925
3	1.0942	0.9139	3.0923	0.3234	2.8262	0.3538	0.9800
4	1.1275	0.8869	4.1866	0.2389	3.7131	0.2693	1.4625
5	1.1618	0.8607	5.3141	0.1882	4.5738	0.2186	1.9400
6	1.1972	0.8353	6.4760	0.1544	5.4090	0.1849	2.4126
7	1.2337	0.8106	7.6732	0.1303	6.2196	0.1608	2.8801
8	1.2712	0.7866	8.9069	0.1123	7.0063	0.1427	3.3427
9	1.3100	0.7634	10.178	0.0983	7.7696	0.1287	3.8003
10	1.3499	0.7408	11.488	0.0871	8.5105	0.1175	4.2529
11	1.3910	0.7189	12.838	0.0779	9.2294	0.1084	4.7006
12	1.4333	0.6977	14.229	0.0703	9.9271	0.1007	5.1433
13	1.4770	0.6771	15.662	0.0639	10.6041	0.0943	5.5811
14	1.5220	0.6571	17.139	0.0584	11.2612	0.0888	6.0139
15	1.5683	0.6376	18.661	0.0536	11.8988	0.0841	6.4419
16	1.6161	0.6188	20.229	0.0494	12.5176	0.0799	6.8650
17	1.6653	0.6005	21.845	0.0458	13.1181	0.0762	7.2831
18	1.7160	0.5828	23.511	0.0425	13.7008	0.0730	7.6964
19	1.7683	0.5655	25.227	0.0397	14.2663	0.0703	8.1049
20	1.8221	0.5488	26.995	0.0371	14.8152	0.0675	8.5085
21	1.8776	0.5326	28.817	0.0347	15.3477	0.0652	8.9072
22	1.9348	0.5169	30.695	0.0326	15.8646	0.0630	9.3012
23	1.9937	0.5016	32.629	0.0307	16.3662	0.0611	9.6904
24	2.0544	0.4868	34.623	0.0289	16.8529	0.0593	10.075
25	2.1170	0.4724	36.678	0.0273	17.3253	0.0577	10.455
30	2.4595	0.4066	47.927	0.0209	19.4858	0.0513	12.282
35	2.8577	0.3499	60.998	0.0164	21.3453	0.0469	13.995
40	3.3201	0.3012	76.183	0.0131	22.9459	0.0436	15.595
50	4.4817	0.2231	114.32	0.0088	25.5092	0.0392	18.475
60	6.0496	0.1653	165.81	0.0060	27.4081	0.0365	20.954

TABLE B.6   4% CONTINUOUS COMPOUND INTEREST FACTORS

	Single Payment		Uniform Series				Uniform Gradient
n	Compound Amount Factor F/P	Present Worth Factor P/F	Compound Amount Factor F/A	Sinking Fund Factor A/F	Present Worth Factor P/A	Capital Recovery Factor A/P	Gradient Conversion Factor A/G
1	1.0408	0.9608	1.0000	1.0000	0.9608	1.0408	0.0000
2	1.0833	0.9231	2.0408	0.4900	1.8839	0.5308	0.4900
3	1.1275	0.8869	3.1241	0.3201	2.7708	0.3609	0.9734
4	1.1735	0.8522	4.2515	0.2352	3.6230	0.2760	1.4500
5	1.2214	0.8187	5.4251	0.1843	4.4417	0.2251	1.9201
6	1.2712	0.7866	6.6465	0.1505	5.2283	0.1913	2.3835
7	1.3231	0.7558	7.9178	0.1263	5.9841	0.1671	2.8402
8	1.3771	0.7262	9.2409	0.1082	6.7103	0.1490	3.2904
9	1.4333	0.6977	10.618	0.0942	7.4079	0.1350	3.7339
10	1.4918	0.6703	12.051	0.0830	8.0783	0.1238	4.1709
11	1.5527	0.6440	13.543	0.0738	8.7223	0.1147	4.6013
12	1.6161	0.6188	15.096	0.0663	9.3411	0.1071	5.0252
13	1.6820	0.5945	16.712	0.0598	9.9356	0.1007	5.4425
14	1.7507	0.5712	18.394	0.0544	10.5068	0.0592	5.8534
15	1.8221	0.5488	20.145	0.0497	11.0556	0.0509	6.2578
16	1.8965	0.5273	21.967	0.0455	11.5829	0.0863	6.6558
17	1.9739	0.5066	23.863	0.0419	12.0895	0.0827	7.0474
18	2.0548	0.4868	25.837	0.0387	12.5763	0.0795	7.4326
19	2.1383	0.4677	27.892	0.0359	13.0440	0.0767	7.8114
20	2.2255	0.4493	30.030	0.0333	13.4933	0.0741	8.1840
21	2.3164	0.4317	32.255	0.0310	13.9250	0.0718	8.5503
22	2.4109	0.4148	34.572	0.0289	14.3398	0.0697	8.9105
23	2.5093	0.3985	36.983	0.0270	14.7383	0.0479	9.2644
24	2.6117	0.3829	39.492	0.0253	15.1212	0.0661	9.6122
25	2.7183	0.3679	42.104	0.0238	15.4981	0.0646	9.9539
30	3.2301	0.3012	56.851	0.0176	17.1231	0.0584	11.573
35	4.0552	0.2466	74.863	0.0134	18.4609	0.0542	13.048
40	4.9530	0.2019	96.862	0.0103	19.5562	0.0511	14.385
50	7.3891	0.1353	156.55	0.0064	21.1872	0.0472	16.678
60	11.023	0.0907	245.60	0.0041	22.2805	0.0449	18.517

TABLE B.7   5% CONTINUOUS COMPOUND INTEREST FACTORS

	Single Payment		Uniform Series				Uniform Gradient
n	Compound Amount Factor F/P	Present Worth Factor P/F	Compound Amount Factor F/A	Sinking Fund Factor A/F	Present Worth Factor P/A	Capital Recovery Factor A/P	Gradient Conversion Factor A/G
1	1.0513	0.9512	1.0000	1.0000	0.9512	1.0513	0.0000
2	1.1052	0.9048	2.0513	0.4875	1.8561	0.5388	0.4875
3	1.1618	0.8607	3.1565	0.3168	2.7168	0.3681	0.9667
4	1.2114	0.8187	4.3185	0.2316	3.5355	0.2829	1.4376
5	1.2840	0.7788	5.5397	0.1805	4.3143	0.2318	1.9001
6	1.3499	0.7408	6.8238	0.1466	5.0551	0.1978	2.3544
7	1.4191	0.7047	8.1737	0.1224	5.7598	0.1736	2.8004
8	1.4918	0.6703	9.5927	0.1043	6.4301	0.1555	3.2382
9	1.5683	0.6376	11.085	0.0902	7.0778	0.1415	3.6678
10	1.6487	0.6065	12.653	0.0790	7.6743	0.1303	4.0892
11	1.7333	0.5770	14.301	0.0699	8.2513	0.1212	4.5025
12	1.8221	0.5488	16.035	0.0624	8.8001	0.1136	4.9077
13	1.9155	0.5221	17.857	0.0560	9.3221	0.1073	5.3049
14	2.0138	0.4966	19.772	0.0506	9.8187	0.1019	5.6941
15	2.1170	0.4724	21.786	0.0459	10.291	0.0972	6.0753
16	2.2255	0.4493	23.903	0.0418	10.740	0.0931	6.4487
17	2.3396	0.4274	26.129	0.0383	11.168	0.0896	6.8143
18	2.4596	0.4066	28.468	0.0351	11.574	0.0864	7.1721
19	2.5857	0.3868	30.928	0.0323	11.961	0.0836	7.5222
20	2.7183	0.3679	33.514	0.0298	12.329	0.0811	7.8646
21	2.8577	0.3499	36.232	0.0276	12.679	0.0789	8.1996
22	3.0042	0.3329	39.090	0.0256	13.012	0.0769	8.5270
23	3.1582	0.3166	42.094	0.0238	13.328	0.0750	8.8471
24	3.3201	0.3012	45.252	0.0221	13.630	0.0734	9.1599
25	3.4903	0.2865	48.572	0.0206	13.916	0.0719	9.4654
30	4.4817	0.2231	67.907	0.0147	15.152	0.0660	10.888
35	5.7546	0.1738	92.735	0.0108	16.115	0.0621	12.143
40	7.3891	0.1353	124.61	0.0080	16.865	0.0593	13.244
50	12.1825	0.0821	218.11	0.0046	17.903	0.0559	16.033
60	20.0855	0.0498	372.25	0.0027	18.533	0.0540	16.360

TABLE B.8 6% CONTINUOUS COMPOUND INTEREST FACTORS

	Single Payment		Uniform Series				Uniform Gradient
n	Compound Amount Factor F/P	Present Worth Factor P/F	Compound Amount Factor F/A	Sinking Fund Factor A/F	Present Worth Factor P/A	Capital Recovery Factor A/P	Gradient Conversion Factor A/G
1	1.0618	0.9418	1.0000	1.0000	0.9418	1.0618	0.0000
2	1.1275	0.8869	2.0618	0.4850	1.8287	0.5469	0.4850
3	1.1972	0.8353	3.1893	0.3136	2.6640	0.3754	0.9600
4	1.2712	0.7866	4.3866	0.2280	3.4506	0.2898	1.4251
5	1.3499	0.7408	5.6578	0.1768	4.1914	0.2386	1.8802
6	1.4333	0.6977	7.0077	0.1427	4.8891	0.2045	2.3254
7	1.5220	0.6571	8.4410	0.1185	5.5461	0.1803	2.7607
8	1.6161	0.6188	9.9630	0.1004	6.1649	0.1622	3.1862
9	1.7160	0.5828	11.579	0.0864	6.7477	0.1482	3.6020
10	1.8221	0.5488	13.295	0.0752	7.2965	0.1371	4.0080
11	1.9348	0.5169	15.117	0.0662	7.8133	0.1280	4.4044
12	2.0544	0.4868	17.052	0.0587	8.3001	0.1205	4.7912
13	2.1815	0.4584	19.106	0.0523	8.7585	0.1142	5.1685
14	2.3164	0.4317	21.288	0.0470	9.1902	0.1088	5.5363
15	2.4506	0.4066	23.604	0.0424	9.5968	0.1042	5.8949
16	2.6117	0.3829	26.064	0.0384	9.9797	0.1002	6.2442
17	2.7732	0.3606	28.676	0.0349	10.340	0.0967	6.5845
18	2.9447	0.3396	31.449	0.0318	10.680	0.0936	6.9157
19	3.1268	0.3198	34.393	0.0291	11.000	0.0909	7.2379
20	3.3201	0.3012	37.520	0.0267	11.301	0.0885	7.5514
21	3.5254	0.2837	40.840	0.0245	11.585	0.0863	7.8562
22	3.7434	0.2671	44.366	0.0225	11.852	0.0844	8.1525
23	3.9749	0.2516	48.109	0.0208	12.103	0.0826	8.4403
24	4.2207	0.2369	52.084	0.0192	12.340	0.0810	8.7199
25	4.4817	0.2231	56.305	0.0178	12.563	0.0796	8.9913
30	6.0495	0.1653	81.661	0.0123	13.499	0.0741	10.231
35	8.1662	0.1225	115.89	0.0086	14.191	0.0705	11.288
40	11.0232	0.0907	162.09	0.0062	14.705	0.0680	12.181
50	20.0855	0.0498	308.65	0.0032	15.367	0.0651	13.552
60	36.5982	0.0273	575.68	0.0017	15.730	0.0636	14.490

TABLE B.9 7% CONTINUOUS COMPOUND INTEREST FACTORS

	Single Payment		Uniform Series				Uniform Gradient
n	Compound Amount Factor F/P	Present Worth Factor P/F	Compound Amount Factor F/A	Sinking Fund Factor A/F	Present Worth Factor P/A	Capital Recovery Factor A/P	Gradient Conversion Factor A/G
1	1.0725	0.9324	1.0000	1.0000	0.9324	1.0725	0.0000
2	1.1503	0.8694	2.0725	0.4825	1.8018	0.5550	0.4825
3	1.2337	0.8106	3.2228	0.3103	2.6123	0.3828	0.9534
4	1.3231	0.7558	4.4565	0.2244	3.3681	0.2969	1.4126
5	1.4191	0.7047	5.7796	0.1730	4.0728	0.2455	1.8603
6	1.5220	0.6571	7.1987	0.1389	4.7299	0.2114	2.2965
7	1.6323	0.6126	8.7207	0.1147	5.3425	0.1872	2.7211
8	1.7507	0.5712	10.353	0.0966	5.9137	0.1691	3.1344
9	1.8776	0.5326	12.104	0.0826	6.4463	0.1551	3.5364
10	2.0138	0.4966	13.981	0.0715	6.9429	0.1440	3.9272
11	2.1598	0.4630	15.995	0.0625	7.4059	0.1350	4.3069
12	2.3164	0.4317	18.155	0.0551	7.8376	0.1276	4.6756
13	2.4843	0.4025	20.471	0.0489	8.2401	0.1214	5.0334
14	2.6645	0.3753	22.955	0.0436	8.6154	0.1161	5.3804
15	2.8576	0.3499	25.620	0.0390	8.9654	0.1161	5.7168
16	3.0649	0.3263	28.478	0.0351	9.2917	0.1076	6.0428
17	3.2871	0.3042	31.542	0.0317	9.5959	0.1042	6.3585
18	3.5254	0.2837	34.829	0.0287	9.8795	0.1012	6.6640
19	3.7810	0.2645	38.355	0.0261	10.144	0.0986	6.9596
20	4.0552	0.2466	42.136	0.0237	10.391	0.0963	7.2453
21	4.3492	0.2299	46.191	0.0217	10.621	0.0942	7.5215
22	4.6646	0.2144	50.540	0.0198	10.835	0.0923	7.7882
23	5.0028	0.1999	55.205	0.0191	11.035	0.0906	8.0456
24	5.3656	0.1864	60.208	0.0166	11.221	0.0891	8.2940
25	5.7546	0.1738	65.573	0.0153	13.395	0.0878	8.5335
30	8.1662	0.1225	98.833	0.0101	12.103	0.0826	9.6052
35	11.588	0.0863	146.03	0.0069	12.601	0.0794	10.486
40	16.445	0.0608	213.01	0.0047	12.953	0.0772	11.202
50	33.115	0.0302	442.92	0.0023	13.375	0.0748	12.235
60	66.686	0.0150	905.92	0.0011	13.585	0.0736	12.878

TABLE B.10   8% CONTINUOUS COMPOUND INTEREST FACTORS

	Single Payment		Uniform Series				Uniform Gradient
n	Compound Amount Factor F/P	Present Worth Factor P/F	Compound Amount Factor F/A	Sinking Fund Factor A/F	Present Worth Factor P/A	Capital Recovery Factor A/P	Gradient Conversion Factor A/G
1	1.0833	0.9231	1.0000	1.0000	0.9231	1.0833	0.0000
2	1.1735	0.8522	2.0833	0.4800	1.7753	0.5633	0.4800
3	1.2712	0.7866	3.2568	0.3071	2.5619	0.3903	0.9467
4	1.3771	0.7262	4.5281	0.2209	3.2880	0.3041	1.4002
5	1.4918	0.6703	5.9052	0.1694	3.9584	0.2526	1.8405
6	1.6161	0.6188	7.3971	0.1352	4.5772	0.2185	2.2676
7	1.7507	0.5712	9.0131	0.1110	5.1484	0.1942	2.6817
8	1.8965	0.5273	10.764	0.0929	5.6757	0.1762	3.0829
9	2.0545	0.4868	12.660	0.0790	6.1624	0.1623	3.4713
10	2.2255	0.4493	14.715	0.0680	6.6117	0.1513	3.8470
11	2.4109	0.4148	16.940	0.0590	7.0265	0.1423	4.2102
12	2.6117	0.3829	19.351	0.0517	7.4094	0.1350	4.5611
13	2.8292	0.3535	21.963	0.0455	7.7629	0.1288	4.8998
14	3.0649	0.3263	24.792	0.0403	8.0891	0.1236	5.2265
15	3.3201	0.3012	27.857	0.0359	8.3903	0.1192	5.5415
16	3.5966	0.2780	31.177	0.0321	8.6684	0.1154	5.8449
17	3.8962	0.2567	34.774	0.0288	8.9250	0.1121	6.1369
18	4.2207	0.2369	38.670	0.0259	9.1620	0.1092	6.4178
19	4.5722	0.2187	42.891	0.0233	9.3807	0.1066	6.6879
20	4.9530	0.2019	47.463	0.0211	9.5826	0.1044	6.9473
21	5.3656	0.1864	52.416	0.0191	9.7689	0.1024	7.1963
22	5.8124	0.1721	57.781	0.0173	9.9410	0.1006	7.4352
23	6.2965	0.1588	63.594	0.0157	10.0998	0.0990	7.6642
24	6.8210	0.1466	59.890	0.0143	10.2464	0.0976	7.8836
25	7.3891	0.1353	76.711	0.0130	10.3818	0.0963	8.0937
30	11.023	0.0907	120.35	0.0083	10.9175	0.0916	9.0136
35	16.445	0.0608	185.44	0.0054	11.2765	0.0887	9.7405
40	24.533	0.0408	282.55	0.0035	11.5173	0.0868	10.307
50	54.598	0.0183	643.54	0.0016	11.7868	0.0849	11.074
60	121.51	0.0082	1446.93	0.0007	11.9079	0.0840	11.509

TABLE B.11   9% CONTINUOUS COMPOUND INTEREST FACTORS

	Single Payment		Uniform Series				Uniform Gradient
n	Compound Amount Factor F/P	Present Worth Factor P/F	Compound Amount Factor F/A	Sinking Fund Factor A/F	Present Worth Factor P/A	Capital Recovery Factor A/P	Gradient Conversion Factor A/G
1	1.0942	0.9139	1.0000	1.0000	0.9139	0.0942	0.0000
2	1.1972	0.8353	2.0942	0.4775	1.7492	0.5717	0.4775
3	1.3100	0.7634	3.2914	0.3038	2.5126	0.3980	0.9401
4	1.4333	0.6977	4.6014	0.2173	3.2103	0.3115	1.3878
5	1.5683	0.6376	6.0347	0.1657	3.8479	0.2599	1.8206
6	1.7160	0.5828	7.6031	0.1315	4.4306	0.2257	2.2388
7	1.8776	0.5326	9.3191	0.1073	4.9632	0.2015	2.6424
8	2.0544	0.4868	11.197	0.0893	5.4500	0.1835	3.0316
9	2.2479	0.4449	13.251	0.0755	5.8948	0.1697	3.4065
10	2.4596	0.4066	15.499	0.0645	6.3014	0.1587	3.7674
11	2.6912	0.3716	17.959	0.0557	6.6730	0.1499	4.1145
12	2.9447	0.3396	20.650	0.0484	7.0126	0.1426	4.4479
13	3.2220	0.3104	23.594	0.0424	7.3230	0.1366	4.7680
14	3.5254	0.2837	26.816	0.0373	7.6066	0.1315	5.0750
15	3.8574	0.2593	30.342	0.0330	7.8658	0.1271	5.3691
16	4.2207	0.2369	34.199	0.0293	0.1028	0.1234	5.6507
17	4.6182	0.2165	38.420	0.0260	8.3193	0.1202	5.9201
18	5.0531	0.1979	43.038	0.0232	8.5172	0.1174	6.1776
19	5.5290	0.1809	48.091	0.0208	8.6981	0.1150	6.4234
20	6.0496	0.1653	53.620	0.0187	8.8634	0.1128	6.6579
21	6.6184	0.1511	59.670	0.0168	9.0133	0.1109	6.8815
22	7.2427	0.1381	66.289	0.0151	9.1525	0.1093	7.0945
23	7.9248	0.1262	73.532	0.0136	9.2787	0.1078	7.2972
24	8.6711	0.1153	81.457	0.0123	9.3940	0.1065	7.4900
25	9.4877	0.1054	90.128	0.0111	9.4994	0.1053	7.6732
30	14.880	0.0672	147.38	0.0068	9.9050	0.1010	8.4572
35	23.336	0.0429	237.18	0.0042	10.1636	0.0984	9.0516
40	36.598	0.0273	378.00	0.0027	10.3285	0.0968	9.4950
50	90.017	0.0111	945.24	0.0011	10.5007	0.0952	10.057
60	221.406	0.0045	2340.41	0.0004	10.5707	0.0946	10.346

TABLE B.12 10% CONTINUOUS COMPOUND INTEREST FACTORS

	Single Payment		Uniform Series				Uniform Gradient
n	Compound Amount Factor F/P	Present Worth Factor P/F	Compound Amount Factor F/A	Sinking Fund Factor A/F	Present Worth Factor P/A	Capital Recovery Factor A/P	Gradient Conversion Factor A/G
1	1.1052	0.9048	1.0000	1.0000	0.9048	1.1052	0.0000
2	1.2214	0.8187	2.1052	0.4750	1.7236	0.5802	0.4750
3	1.3499	0.7408	3.3266	0.3006	2.4644	0.4058	0.9335
4	1.4918	0.6703	4.6765	0.2138	3.1347	0.3190	1.3754
5	1.6487	0.6065	6.1683	0.1621	3.7412	0.2673	1.8009
6	1.8221	0.5488	7.8170	0.1279	4.2901	0.2331	2.2101
7	2.0138	0.4966	9.6392	0.1038	4.7866	0.2089	2.6033
8	2.2255	0.4493	11.653	0.0858	5.2360	0.1910	2.9806
9	2.4396	0.4066	13.878	0.0721	5.6425	0.1772	3.3423
10	2.7183	0.3679	16.338	0.0612	6.0104	0.1664	3.6886
11	3.0042	0.3329	19.056	0.0525	6.3433	0.1577	4.0198
12	3.3201	0.3012	22.060	0.0453	6.6445	0.1505	4.3362
13	3.6693	0.2725	25.381	0.0394	6.9170	0.1446	4.6381
14	4.0552	0.2466	29.050	0.0344	7.1636	0.1396	4.9260
15	2.4817	0.2231	33.105	0.0302	7.3867	0.1354	5.2001
16	3.9530	0.2019	37.587	0.0266	7.5886	0.1318	5.4608
17	5.4739	0.1827	42.540	0.0235	7.7713	0.1287	5.7086
18	6.0496	0.1653	48.014	0.0208	7.9366	0.1260	5.9437
19	6.6859	0.1496	54.063	0.0185	8.0862	0.1237	6.1667
20	7.3890	0.1353	60.749	0.0165	8.2215	0.1216	6.3780
21	8.1662	0.1225	68.138	0.0147	8.3440	0.1199	6.5779
22	9.0250	0.1108	76.305	0.0131	8.4548	0.1183	6.7669
23	9.9742	0.1003	85.330	0.0117	8.5550	0.1169	6.9454
24	11.023	0.0907	95.304	0.0105	8.6458	0.1157	7.1139
25	12.183	0.0821	106.33	0.0094	8.7279	0.1146	7.2727
30	20.086	0.0498	181.47	0.0055	9.0349	0.1107	7.9365
35	33.115	0.0302	305.36	0.0033	0.2212	0.1085	8.4185
40	54.598	0.0183	509.63	0.0020	9.3342	0.1071	8.7620
50	148.41	0.0067	1401.7	0.0007	9.4443	0.1059	9.1692
60	403.43	0.0025	3826.4	0.0003	9.4848	0.1054	9.3592

TABLE B.13 12% CONTINUOUS COMPOUND INTEREST FACTORS

	Single Payment		Uniform Series				Uniform Gradient
n	Compound Amount Factor F/P	Present Worth Factor P/F	Compound Amount Factor F/A	Sinking Fund Factor A/F	Present Worth Factor P/A	Capital Recovery Factor A/P	Gradient Conversion Factor A/G
1	1.1275	0.8869	1.0000	1.0000	0.8869	1.1275	0.0000
2	1.2712	0.7866	2.1275	0.4700	1.6736	0.5975	0.4700
3	1.4333	0.6977	3.3987	0.2942	2.3712	0.4217	0.9202
4	1.6161	0.6188	4.8321	0.2070	2.9900	0.3345	1.3506
5	1.8221	0.5488	6.4481	0.1551	3.5388	0.2826	1.7615
6	2.0544	0.4868	8.2703	0.1209	4.0256	0.2484	2.1531
7	2.3164	0.4317	10.325	0.0969	4.4573	0.2244	2.5257
8	2.6117	0.3829	12.641	0.0791	4.8402	0.2066	2.8796
9	2.9447	0.3396	15.253	0.0656	5.1798	0.1931	3.2153
10	3.3201	0.3012	18.197	0.0550	5.4810	0.1825	3.5332
11	3.7434	0.2671	21.518	0.0465	5.7481	0.1740	3.8337
12	4.2207	0.2369	25.261	0.0396	5.9850	0.1670	4.1174
13	4.7588	0.2101	29.482	0.0339	6.1952	0.1614	4.3848
14	5.3656	0.1864	34.241	0.0292	6.3815	0.1567	4.6364
15	6.0496	0.1653	39.606	0.0253	6.5468	0.1528	4.8728
16	6.8210	0.1466	45.656	0.0219	6.6935	0.1494	5.0947
17	7.6906	0.1300	52.477	0.0191	6.8235	0.1466	5.3025
18	8.6711	0.1153	60.156	0.0166	6.9388	0.1441	5.4969
19	9.7767	0.1023	68.838	0.0145	7.0411	0.1420	5.6785
20	11.023	0.0907	78.615	0.0127	7.1318	0.1402	5.8480
21	12.429	0.0805	89.638	0.0112	7.2123	0.1387	6.0058
22	14.013	0.0714	102.06	0.0098	7.2836	0.1373	6.1528
23	15.800	0.0633	116.08	0.0086	6.3469	0.1361	6.2893
24	17.814	0.1561	131.88	0.0076	7.4031	0.1351	6.4160
25	20.086	0.0498	149.69	0.0067	7.4528	0.1342	6.5334
30	36.598	0.0273	279.21	0.0036	7.6290	0.1311	7.0006
35	66.686	0.0150	525.20	0.0020	7.7257	0.1294	7.3105
40	121.51	0.0082	945.20	0.0011	7.7788	0.1286	7.5114
50	403.43	0.0025	3156.4	0.0003	7.8239	0.1278	7.7191

TABLE B.14   15% CONTINUOUS COMPOUND INTEREST FACTORS

	Single Payment		Uniform Series				Uniform Gradient
n	Compound Amount Factor F/P	Present Worth Factor P/F	Compound Amount Factor F/A	Sinking Fund Factor A/F	Present Worth Factor P/A	Capital Recovery Factor A/P	Gradient Conversion Factor A/G
1	1.1618	0.8607	1.0000	1.0000	0.8607	1.1618	0.0000
2	1.3499	0.7408	2.1618	0.4626	1.6015	0.6244	0.4626
3	1.5683	0.6376	3.5117	0.2848	2.2392	0.4466	0.9004
4	1.8221	0.5488	5.0800	0.1969	2.7880	0.3587	1.3137
5	2.1170	0.4724	6.9021	0.1449	3.2603	0.3067	1.7029
6	2.4596	0.4066	9.0191	0.1109	3.6669	0.2727	2.0685
7	2.8576	0.3499	11.479	0.0871	4.0168	0.2490	2.4110
8	3.3201	0.3012	14.336	0.0698	4.3180	0.2316	2.7311
9	3.8574	0.2593	17.657	0.0566	4.5773	0.2185	3.0295
10	4.4817	0.2231	21.514	0.0465	4.8004	0.2083	3.3070
11	5.2070	0.1921	25.996	0.0385	4.9925	0.2003	3.5645
12	6.0496	0.1653	31.203	0.0321	5.1578	0.1939	3.8028
13	7.0287	0.1423	37.252	0.0269	5.3000	0.1887	4.0228
14	8.1662	0.1225	44.281	0.0226	5.4225	0.1844	4.2255
15	9.4877	0.1054	52.447	0.0191	5.5279	0.1809	4.4119
16	11.023	0.0907	61.935	0.0162	5.6186	0.1780	4.5829
17	12.807	0.0781	72.958	0.0137	5.6967	0.1756	4.7394
18	14.880	0.0672	85.765	0.0117	5.7639	0.1735	4.8823
19	17.288	0.0579	100.65	0.0099	5.8217	0.1718	5.0127
20	20.086	0.0498	117.93	0.0085	5.8715	0.1703	5.1313
21	23.336	0.0429	138.02	0.0073	5.9144	0.1691	5.2390
22	27.113	0.0369	161.35	0.0062	5.9513	0.1680	5.3367
23	31.500	0.0318	188.47	0.0053	5.9830	0.1672	5.4251
24	36.598	0.0273	219.97	0.0046	6.0103	0.1664	5.5050
25	42.521	0.0235	256.57	0.0039	5.0339	0.1657	5.5771
30	90.017	0.0111	550.05	0.0018	6.1105	0.1637	5.8422
35	190.57	0.0053	1171.4	0.0009	6.1467	0.1627	5.9945
40	403.43	0.0025	2486.7	0.0004	6.1639	0.1622	6.0798
50	1808.0	0.0006	11166.	0.0001	6.1758	0.1619	6.1515

TABLE B.15   18% CONTINUOUS COMPOUND INTEREST FACTORS

	Single Payment		Uniform Series				Uniform Gradient
n	Compound Amount Factor F/P	Present Worth Factor P/F	Compound Amount Factor F/A	Sinking Fund Factor A/F	Present Worth Factor P/A	Capital Recovery Factor A/P	Gradient Conversion Factor A/G
1	1.1972	0.8353	1.0000	1.0000	0.8353	1.1972	0.0000
2	1.4333	0.6977	2.1972	0.4551	1.5330	0.6523	0.4551
3	1.7160	0.5827	3.6305	0.2754	2.1157	0.4727	0.8806
4	2.0544	0.4868	5.3466	0.1870	2.6025	0.3843	1.2770
5	2.4596	0.4066	7.4010	0.1351	3.0090	0.3323	1.6450
6	2.9447	0.3396	9.8606	0.1014	3.3486	0.2986	1.9852
7	3.5254	0.2837	12.805	0.0781	3.6323	0.2753	2.2987
8	4.2207	0.2369	16.331	0.0612	3.8692	0.2585	2.5866
9	5.0531	0.1979	20.551	0.0487	4.0671	0.2459	2.8500
10	6.0497	0.1653	25.605	0.0391	4.2324	0.2363	3.0902
11	9.2427	0.1381	31.654	0.0316	4.3705	0.2288	3.3085
12	8.6711	0.1153	38.897	0.0257	4.4858	0.2229	3.5062
13	10.381	0.0963	47.568	0.0210	4.5821	0.2182	3.6848
14	12.429	0.0805	57.949	0.0173	4.6626	0.2145	3.8456
15	14.880	0.0672	70.378	0.1421	4.7298	0.2114	3.9898
16	17.814	0.0561	85.258	0.1173	4.7859	0.2089	4.1190
17	21.328	0.0469	103.07	0.0970	4.8328	0.2069	4.2342
18	25.534	0.0392	124.40	0.0804	4.8720	0.2053	4.3369
19	30.570	0.0327	149.93	0.0667	4.9047	0.2039	4.4280
20	36.598	0.0273	180.50	0.0554	4.9320	0.2028	4.5087
21	43.816	0.0228	217.10	0.0461	4.9548	0.2018	4.5801
22	52.457	0.0191	260.97	0.0383	4.9739	0.2011	4.6430
23	62.803	0.0159	313.37	0.0319	4.9898	0.2004	4.6984
24	75.189	0.0133	376.18	0.0266	5.0031	0.1999	4.7471
25	90.017	0.0111	451.37	0.0222	5.0142	0.1994	4.7897
30	221.41	0.0045	1117.6	0.0089	5.0476	0.1981	4.9344
35	544.57	0.0018	2756.2	0.0036	5.0612	0.1976	5.0062
40	1339.4	0.0007	6786.6	0.0015	5.0668	0.1974	5.0407
50	8103.1	0.0001	41082.	0.0002	5.0699	0.1972	5.0644

TABLE B.16   20% CONTINUOUS COMPOUND INTEREST FACTORS

	Single Payment		Uniform Series				Uniform Gradient
n	Compound Amount Factor F/P	Present Worth Factor P/F	Compound Amount Factor F/A	Sinking Fund Factor A/F	Present Worth Factor P/A	Capital Recovery Factor A/P	Gradient Conversion Factor A/G
1	1.2214	0.8187	1.000	1.0000	0.8187	1.2214	0.0000
2	1.41918	0.6703	2.221	0.4502	1.4891	0.6716	0.4502
3	1.8221	0.5488	3.713	0.2693	2.0379	0.4907	0.8676
4	2.2255	0.4493	5.535	0.1807	2.4872	0.4021	1.2528
5	2.7183	0.3679	7.761	0.1289	2.8551	0.3503	1.6068
6	3.3201	0.3012	10.479	0.0954	3.1563	0.3168	1.9306
7	4.0552	0.2466	13.799	0.0725	3.4029	0.2939	2.2255
8	4.9530	0.2019	17.854	0.0560	3.6048	0.2774	2.4929
9	4.0496	0.1653	22.808	0.0439	3.6601	0.2653	2.7344
10	7.3891	0.1353	28.857	0.0347	3.9054	0.2561	2.9515
11	9.0250	0.1108	36.246	0.0276	4.0162	0.2490	3.1460
12	11.023	0.0907	45.271	0.0221	4.1069	0.2435	3.3194
13	13.464	0.0743	56.294	0.0178	4.1812	0.2392	3.4736
14	16.445	0.0608	69.758	0.0143	4.2420	0.2357	3.6102
15	20.086	0.0498	86.203	0.0116	4.2918	0.2330	3.7307
16	24.553	0.0408	105.29	0.0094	4.3326	0.2308	3.8368
17	29.964	0.0334	130.82	0.0077	4.3659	0.2291	3.9297
18	36.598	0.0273	160.79	0.0062	4.3933	0.2276	4.0110
19	44.701	0.0224	197.38	0.0051	4.4156	0.2265	4.0819
20	54.598	0.0183	242.08	0.0041	4.4339	0.2255	4.1435
21	66.686	0.0150	296.68	0.0034	4.4489	0.2248	4.1970
22	81.451	0.0123	363.37	0.0028	4.4612	0.2242	4.2432
23	99.484	0.0101	444.82	0.0023	4.4713	0.2237	4.2831
24	121.51	0.0082	544.30	0.0018	4.4795	0.2232	4.3175
25	148.41	0.0067	665.81	0.0015	4.4862	0.2229	4.3471
30	403.43	0.0025	1817.6	0.0006	4.5055	0.2220	4.4421
35	1096.6	0.0009	4948.6	0.0002	4.5125	0.2216	4.4847
40	2981.0	0.0004	13459.	0.0001	4.5152	0.2215	4.5032
50	22026.	0.0001	99481.	0.0000	4.5165	0.2214	4.5144

TABLE B.17 25% CONTINUOUS COMPOUND INTEREST FACTORS

	Single Payment		Uniform Series				Uniform Gradient
n	Compound Amount Factor F/P	Present Worth Factor P/F	Compound Amount Factor F/A	Sinking Fund Factor A/F	Present Worth Factor P/A	Capital Recovery Factor A/P	Gradient Conversion Factor A/G
1	1.2840	0.7788	1.0000	1.0000	0.7788	1.2840	0.0000
2	1.6487	0.6065	2.2840	0.4378	1.3853	0.7219	0.4378
3	2.1170	0.4724	3.9327	0.2543	1.8577	0.5383	0.8351
4	2.7183	0.3679	6.0498	0.1653	2.2256	0.4493	1.1929
5	3.4903	0.2865	8.7680	0.1141	2.5121	0.3981	1.5131
6	4.4817	0.2231	12.258	0.0816	2.7352	0.3656	1.7975
7	5.7546	0.1738	16.740	0.0597	2.9090	0.3438	2.0486
8	7.3891	0.1353	22.495	0.0445	30.443	0.3285	2.2687
9	9.4877	0.1054	29.884	0.0335	3.1497	0.3175	0.4605
10	12.184	0.0821	39.371	0.0254	3.2318	0.3094	2.6266
11	15.643	0.0639	51.554	0.0194	3.2957	0.3034	2.7696
12	20.086	0.0498	67.197	0.0149	3.3455	0.2989	2.8921
13	25.790	0.0388	87.282	0.0115	3.3843	0.2955	2.9964
14	33.115	0.0302	113.07	0.0089	3.4145	0.2929	3.0849
15	42.521	0.0235	146.19	0.0069	3.4380	0.2909	3.1596
16	54.598	0.0183	188.71	0.0053	3.4563	0.2893	3.2223
17	70.105	0.0143	243.31	0.0041	3.4706	0.2881	3.2748
18	90.017	0.0111	313.41	0.0032	3.4817	0.2872	3.3186
19	115.58	0.0087	403.43	0.0025	3.4904	0.2865	3.3550
20	148.41	0.0067	519.01	0.0019	3.4971	0.2860	3.3851
21	190.57	0.0053	667.43	0.0015	3.5023	0.2855	3.4100
22	244.69	0.0041	857.99	0.0012	3.5064	0.2852	3.4305
23	314.19	0.0032	1102.7	0.0009	3.5096	0.2849	3.4474
24	403.43	0.0025	1416.8	0.0007	3.5121	0.2847	3.4612
25	518.01	0.0019	1820.3	0.0006	3.5140	0.2846	3.4725
30	1808.0	0.0006	6362.2	0.0002	3.5189	0.2842	3.5042
35	6310.7	0.0002	22215.	0.0001	3.5203	0.2841	3.5153

TABLE B.18   30% CONTINUOUS COMPOUND INTEREST FACTORS

	Single Payment		Uniform Series				Uniform Gradient
n	Compound Amount Factor F/P	Present Worth Factor P/F	Compound Amount Factor F/A	Sinking Fund Factor A/F	Present Worth Factor P/A	Capital Recovery Factor A/P	Gradient Conversion Factor A/G
1	1.3499	0.7408	1.0000	1.0000	0.7408	1.3499	0.0000
2	1.8221	0.5488	2.3499	0.4256	1.2896	0.7754	0.4256
3	2.4596	0.4066	4.1720	0.2397	1.6962	0.5896	0.8030
4	3.3201	0.3012	6.6317	0.1508	1.9974	0.5007	1.1343
5	4.4817	0.2231	9.9517	0.1005	2.2205	0.4504	1.4222
6	6.0496	0.1653	14.433	0.0693	2.3858	0.4192	1.6701
7	8.1662	0.1225	20.483	0.0488	2.5083	0.3987	1.8815
8	11.023	0.0907	28.649	0.0349	2.5990	0.3848	2.0602
9	14.880	0.0672	39.672	0.0252	2.6662	0.3751	2.2099
10	20.086	0.0498	54.552	0.0183	2.7160	0.3682	2.3343
11	27.113	0.0369	74.638	0.0134	2.7529	0.3633	2.4371
12	36.598	0.0273	101.75	0.0098	2.7802	0.3597	2.5212
13	49.402	0.0203	138.35	0.0072	2.8004	0.3571	2.5897
14	66.686	0.0150	187.75	0.0053	2.8154	0.3552	2.6452
15	90.017	0.0111	254.44	0.0039	2.8266	0.3538	0.6898
16	121.51	0.0082	344.45	0.0029	2.8348	0.3528	2.7255
17	164.02	0.0061	465.97	0.0022	2.8409	0.3520	2.7540
18	221.41	0.0045	629.99	0.0016	2.8454	0.3515	2.7766
19	298.87	0.0034	851.39	0.0012	2.8487	0.3510	2.7945
20	403.43	0.0025	1150.3	0.0009	2.8512	0.3507	2.8086
21	544.57	0.0018	1553.7	0.0007	2.8531	0.3505	2.8197
22	735.10	0.0014	2098.3	0.0005	2.8544	0.3503	2.8283
23	992.28	0.0010	2833.4	0.0004	2.8554	0.3502	2.8351
24	1339.4	0.0008	3825.6	0.0003	2.8562	0.3501	2.8404
25	1808.0	0.0006	5165.1	0.0002	2.8567	0.3501	2.8445
30	8103.1	0.0001	23158.	0.0001	2.8580	0.3499	2.8546
35	36316.	0.0000	10380.	0.0000	2.8582	0.3499	2.8573

TABLE B.19   40% CONTINUOUS COMPOUND INTEREST FACTORS

	Single Payment		Uniform Series				Uniform Gradient
n	Compound Amount Factor F/P	Present Worth Factor P/F	Compound Amount Factor F/A	Sinking Fund Factor A/F	Present Worth Factor P/A	Capital Recovery Factor A/P	Gradient Conversion Factor A/G
1	1.4918	0.6703	1.0000	1.0000	0.6703	1.4918	0.0000
2	2.2255	0.4493	2.4918	0.4013	1.1197	0.8931	0.4013
3	3.3201	0.3012	4.7174	0.2120	1.4208	0.7038	0.7402
4	4.9530	0.2019	8.0375	0.1244	1.6227	0.6162	1.0214
5	7.3891	0.1353	12.9905	0.0770	1.7581	0.5688	1.2507
6	11.023	0.0907	20.3796	0.0491	1.8488	0.5409	1.4346
7	16.445	0.0608	31.4027	0.0318	1.9096	0.5237	1.5800
8	24.533	0.0408	47.8474	0.0209	1.9504	0.5127	1.6933
9	36.598	0.0273	72.3799	0.0138	1.9777	0.5056	1.7804
10	54.598	0.0183	108.9782	0.0092	1.9960	0.5010	1.8467
11	81.451	0.0123	163.5763	0.0061	2.0083	0.4979	1.8965
12	121.51	0.0082	245.0272	0.0041	2.0165	0.4959	0.9337
13	181.27	0.0055	366.5376	0.0027	2.0220	0.4946	1.9611
14	270.43	0.0037	547.8100	0.0018	2.0257	0.4937	1.9813
15	403.43	0.0025	818.2362	0.0012	20.282	0.4930	1.9960
16	601.85	0.0017	1221.6650	0.0008	2.0299	0.4926	2.0066
17	897.85	0.0011	1823.5101	0.0005	2.0310	0.4924	2.0143
18	1339.4	0.0007	2721.3574	0.0004	2.0317	0.4922	2.0198
19	1998.2	0.0005	4060.7881	0.0002	2.0322	0.4921	0.0237
20	2981.0	0.0003	6058.9840	0.0002	2.0326	0.4920	2.0265
21	4447.1	0.0002	9039.9420	0.0001	2.0328	0.4919	0.0285
22	6634.2	0.0002	13487.009	0.0001	2.0329	0.4919	0.0299
23	9897.1	0.0001	20121.253	0.0000	2.0330	0.4919	2.0309
24	14765.	0.0001	30018.382	0.0000	2.0331	0.4919	2.0316
25	22026.	0.0000	44783.163	0.0000	2.0332	0.4918	2.0321

TABLE B.20   50% CONTINUOUS COMPOUND INTEREST FACTORS

	Single Payment		Uniform Series				Uniform Gradient
n	Compound Amount Factor F/P	Present Worth Factor P/F	Compound Amount Factor F/A	Sinking Fund Factor A/F	Present Worth Factor P/A	Capital Recovery Factor A/P	Gradient Conversion Factor A/G
1	1.6487	0.6065	1.0000	1.0000	0.6065	1.6487	0.0000
2	2.7183	0.3679	2.6487	0.3775	0.9744	1.0263	0.3775
3	4.4817	0.2231	5.3670	0.1863	1.1975	0.8350	0.6798
4	7.3891	0.1353	9.8487	0.1015	1.3329	0.7503	0.9154
5	12.183	0.0821	17.238	0.0580	1.4150	0.7067	1.0944
5	20.086	0.0498	39.420	0.0340	1.4648	0.6827	1.2271
6	33.116	0.0302	49.506	0.0202	1.4950	0.6689	1.3235
7	54.598	0.0183	82.621	0.0121	1.5133	0.6608	1.3922
8	90.017	0.0111	137.22	0.0073	1.5244	0.6560	1.4404
10	148.41	0.0067	227.24	0.0044	1.5311	0.6531	1.4737
11	244.69	0.0041	375.67	0.0027	1.5352	0.6514	1.4964
12	403.43	0.0025	620.34	0.0016	1.5377	0.6503	1.5117
13	665.14	0.0015	1023.78	0.0010	1.5392	0.5397	1.5219
14	1096.6	0.0009	1688.9	0.0006	1.5401	1.6493	1.5287
15	1808.0	0.0006	2785.5	0.0004	1.5406	0.6491	1.5332
16	2981.0	0.0003	4593.6	0.0002	1.5410	0.6489	1.5361
17	4914.8	0.0002	7573.5	0.0001	1.5412	0.6489	1.5380
18	8103.1	0.0001	12489.	0.0001	1.5413	0.6488	1.5383
19	13360.	0.0001	20592.	0.0000	1.5414	0.6488	1.5401
20	22026.	0.0000	33952.	0.0000	1.5414	0.6488	1.5406
21	36136.	0.0000	55979.	0.0000	1.5415	0.6487	1.5409
22	59874.	0.0000	92294.	0.0000	1.5415	0.6487	1.5411
23	98716.	0.0000	152170.	0.0000	1.5415	0.6487	1.5413
24	162750.	0.0000	250880.	0.0000	1.5415	0.6487	1.5414
25	268340.	0.0000	413640.	0.0000	1.5415	0.6487	1.5414

Appendix C
GRAPHS OF DISCRETE COMPOUND
INTEREST FACTORS

Graph C.1. PLOT OF DISCRETE COMPOUND INTEREST FACTORS

$$F/P\,(i,n) = (1 + i)^n$$

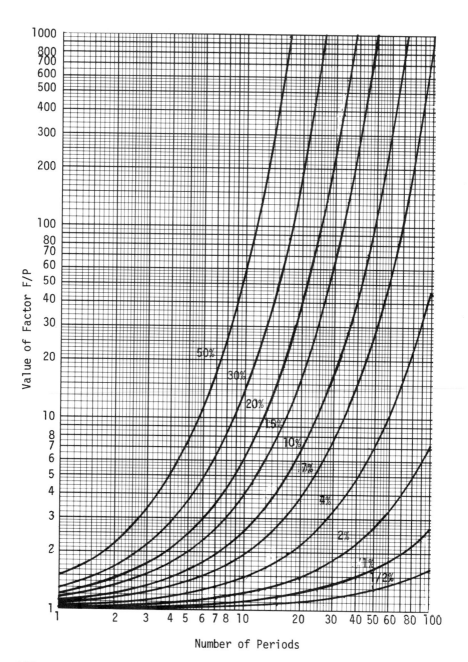

Number of Periods

Graph C.2. PLOT OF DISCRETE COMPOUND INTEREST FACTORS

$$P/F\ (i,n) = \frac{1}{(1 + i)^n}$$

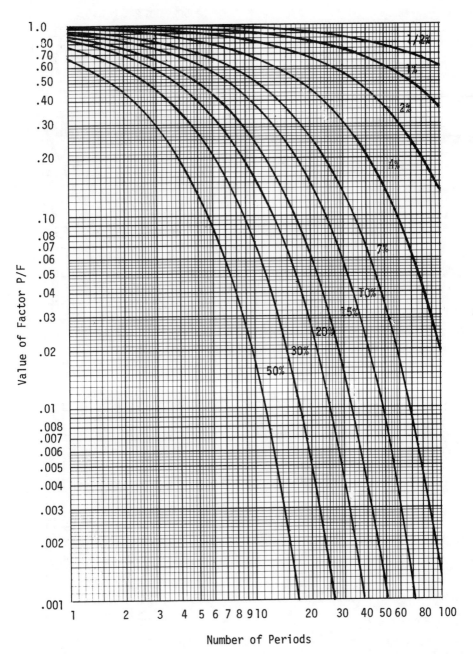

Value of Factor P/F

Number of Periods

Graph C.3. PLOT OF DISCRETE COMPOUND INTEREST FACTORS

$$F/A\,(\,i\,,n\,) = \frac{(1 + i)^n - 1}{i}$$

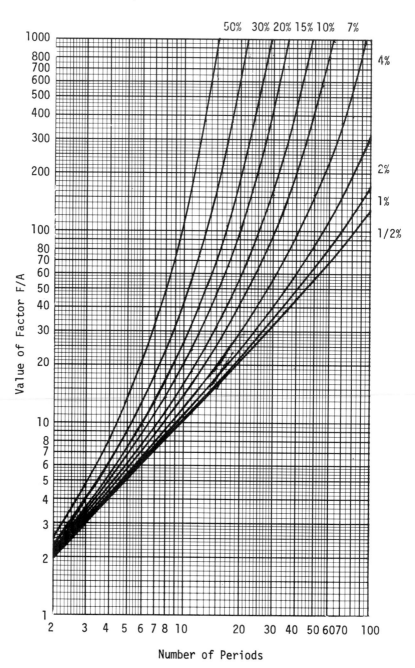

Number of Periods

Graph C.4.   PLOT OF DISCRETE COMPOUND INTEREST FACTORS

$$A/F\,(i,n) = \frac{i}{(1 + i)^n - 1}$$

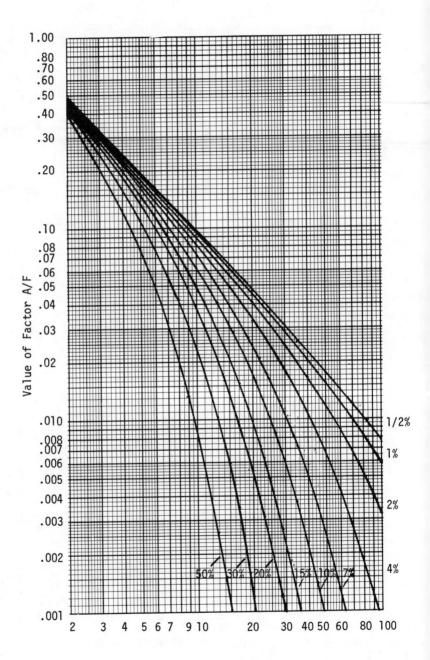

Number of Periods

Graph C.5. PLOT OF DISCRETE COMPOUND INTEREST FACTORS

$$P/A\,(i,n) = \frac{(1 + i)^n - 1}{i\,(1 + i)^n}$$

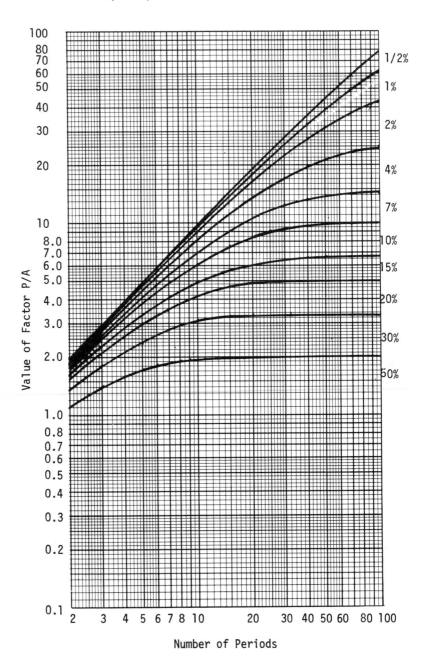

Number of Periods

Graph C.6. PLOT OF DISCRETE COMPOUND INTEREST FACTORS

$$A/P\,(\,i\,,n\,) = \frac{i(1 + i)^n}{(1 + i)^n - 1}$$

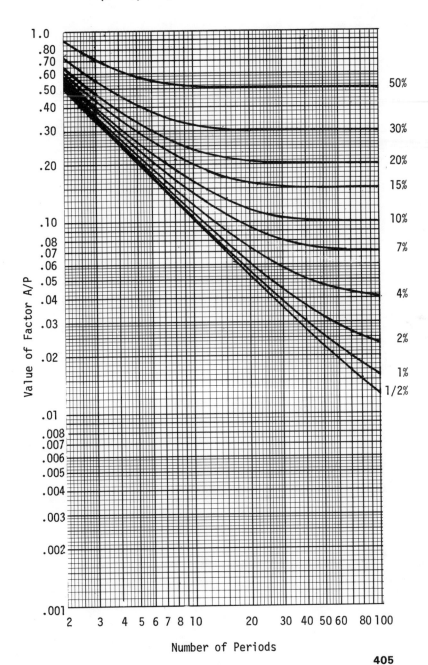

Number of Periods

Appendix D
AREAS UNDER THE NORMAL PROBABILITY DISTRIBUTION

Areas under the Normal Probability Distribution

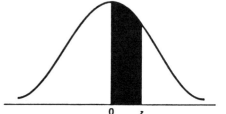

Values in the table represent the proportion of area under the normal curve between the mean ($\mu = 0$) and a positive value of z.

z	.00	.01	.02	.03	.04	.05	.06	.07	.08	.09
.0	.0000	.0040	.0080	.0120	.0160	.0199	.0239	.0279	.0319	.0359
.1	.0398	.0438	.0478	.0517	.0557	.0596	.0636	.0675	.0714	.0753
.2	.0793	.0832	.0871	.0910	.0948	.0987	.1026	.1064	.1103	.1141
.3	.1179	.1217	.1255	.1293	.1331	.1368	.1406	.1443	.1480	.1517
.4	.1554	.1591	.1628	.1664	.1700	.1736	.1772	.1808	.1844	.1879
.5	.1915	.1950	.1985	.2019	.2054	.2088	.2123	.2157	.2190	.2224
.6	.2257	.2291	.2324	.2357	.2389	.2422	.2454	.2486	.2517	.2549
.7	.2580	.2611	.2642	.2673	.2703	.2734	.2764	.2794	.2823	.2852
.8	.2881	.2910	.2939	.2967	.2995	.3023	.3051	.3078	.3106	.3133
.9	.3159	.3186	.3212	.3238	.3264	.3289	.3315	.3340	.3365	.3389
1.0	.3413	.3438	.3461	.3485	.3508	.3531	.3554	.3577	.3599	.3621
1.1	.3643	.3665	.3686	.3708	.3729	.3749	.3770	.3790	.3810	.3830
1.2	.3849	.3869	.3888	.3907	.3925	.3944	.3962	.3980	.3997	.4015
1.3	.4032	.4049	.4066	.4082	.4099	.4115	.4131	.4147	.4162	.4177
1.4	.4192	.4207	.4222	.4236	.4251	.4265	.4279	.4292	.4306	.4319
1.5	.4332	.4345	.4357	.4370	.4382	.4394	.4406	.4418	.4429	.4441
1.6	.4452	.4463	.4474	.4484	.4495	.4505	.4515	.4525	.4535	.4545
1.7	.4554	.4564	.4573	.4582	.4591	.4599	.4608	.4616	.4625	.4633
1.8	.4641	.4649	.4656	.4664	.4671	.4678	.4686	.4693	.4699	.4706
1.9	.4713	.4719	.4726	.4732	.4738	.4744	.4750	.4756	.4761	.4767
2.0	.4772	.4778	.4783	.4788	.4793	.4798	.4803	.4808	.4812	.4817
2.1	.4821	.4826	.4830	.4834	.4838	.4842	.4846	.4850	.4854	.4857
2.2	.4861	.4864	.4868	.4871	.4875	.4878	.4881	.4884	.4887	.4890
2.3	.4893	.4896	.4898	.4901	.4904	.4906	.4909	.4911	.4913	.4916
2.4	.4918	.4920	.4922	.4925	.4927	.4929	.4931	.4932	.4934	.4936
2.5	.4938	.4940	.4941	.4943	.4945	.4946	.4948	.4949	.4951	.4952
2.6	.4953	.4955	.4956	.4957	.4959	.4960	.4961	.4962	.4963	.4964
2.7	.4965	.4966	.4967	.4968	.4969	.4970	.4971	.4972	.4973	.4974
2.8	.4974	.4975	.4976	.4977	.4977	.4978	.4979	.4979	.4980	.4981
2.9	.4981	.4982	.4982	.4983	.4984	.4984	.4985	.4985	.4986	.4986
3.0	.4987	.4987	.4987	.4988	.4988	.4989	.4989	.4989	.4990	.4990

Source: From Paul G. Hoel, *Elementary Statistics*, 2d ed., John Wiley & Sons, Inc., New York, 1966. Reproduced by permission of the publisher.

Appendix E
GLOSSARY OF TERMS

Accounts Payable: The value of purchased services and materials which are being used.

Accounts Receivable: Credit extended to customers usually on a 30-day basis. Cash is set aside to take care of the probability that some of the customers won't pay their bills.

Administrative Cost: Includes administrative and office salaries, rent, auditing, legal, engineering, etc.

Amortization: Often used interchangeably with depreciation but there is a slight technical difference depending on whether or not the life of the item is known. If the period of time is definitely known the annual charge is called "amortization." If the life is estimated, it is called "Depreciation."

Annual Net Sales: lbs. of product sold times the net sales price.

Annual Report: The report of management to stockholders at the end of fiscal year showing the status of the company and its funds, profits, income, expenses, and other information.

Assets: The lists of money on hand, money due, investments, plants, properties, patents, inventory, etc. at cost, or market value, whichever is smaller.

Balance Sheet: A tabulation of numbers which shows the owners of an enterprise how their capital is distributed.

Bonds: When you purchase a bond you acquire an interest in debt, that is, you become a creditor of the corporation. A bond gives you the right to receive regular interest payments and the subsequent repayment of the principal. If the corporation defaults, the bondholders can start legal proceedings to foreclose the mortgage. The corporation's assets are then subject to sale to satisfy the bondholder's claims or, it may be desirable to reorganize the firm.

Book Value of Common Stock: Net worth divided by the number of shares of common stock issued at the time of the report.

Book Value: Original investment in an asset minus the accumulated depreciation.

Break-even Chart: Economic production chart

By-product: A production item made as a consequence of the production of a main item. The by-product may have value in itself or as a raw material for reuse.

Capital Ratio: Ratio of capital investment to sales dollars; it is the reciprocal of capital turnover.

Capital Turnover: The ratio of sales dollars to investment; it is the reciprocal of capital ratio.

Cash: Money which must be kept on hand for monthly operating expenses—e.g. wages, salaries and raw material purchases.

Cash Flow: Net income, depreciation, and depletion make up the cash flow into the company's treasury. Cash flow less dividends gives a measure of the money available to internal generation to expand the company business and is an important item in evaluating the common stock as an investment, or the desirability of seeking employment in that company.

Common Stock: Money paid into corporation for common stock becomes the permanent capital of the firm. It is not paid back as in the case of bonds. A common stockholder can sell his stock to individuals or firms and get his investment, showing profit or loss, depending on the price at which the stock is selling. The right to transfer ownership is one of the basic rights of the stockholder. Common stockholders have the right to vote.

Compound Interest: The interest charges under the condition that interest is charged on any previous interest earned in any time period, as well as on the principal.

Continuous Compounding: A mathematical procedure for evaluating compound interest factors based on a continuous interest function rather that discrete interest periods.

Conversion Cost: The cost of goods manufactured less the direct material costs, or the cost of converting the direct material into finished product.

Corporation: In 1819 Chief Justice Marshall defined a corporation as an artificial being invisible, intangible and existing only in contemplation of law." It exists by the grace of the state. The laws of a state govern the procedure for its formation. Generally, it involves the preparation of a certificate of incorporation setting forth the name of the corporation, purpose of its organization, number of shares and the amount of capital stock, the location of its main office, and, the names and addresses of the subscribers to stock including the amount each subscriber will take. If accepted by the state, a charter is given. Changes in the charter must be agreed upon by the stockholders and the state.

Cost of Capital: The cost of obtaining capital, expressed as an interest rate.

Cost of Sales: The sum of variable and fixed costs representing the cost of getting the product to the consumer.

Decision or Decision Making: A program of action undertaken as the result of (a) an established policy or (b) an analysis of the variables that can be altered to influence the final result.

Depreciation Cost: A noncash expense deductible from income for tax purposes to permit recovery of investment.

Direct Cost: The costs identifiable to a unit of output or portion of a business operation such as direct material or direct labor; also called prime cost.

Direct Labor Cost: The cost of labor involved in the actual production or service.

Direct Material Cost: The cost of materials which are consumed in or incorporated into a product or service.

Distribution Cost: Includes advertising, samples, travel and entertainment, rent, telephone, stationery, postage, freight out, warehousing, etc.

Dollar Volume: Dollar worth of product per unit time.

Earnings: The difference between income and costs. In general, earnings is synonymous with profit.

Effective Interest: The true value of interest rate computed by equations for compound interest rate for 1 year period.

Equity: The owners' actual capital held by the company for its operations.

External Funds: Capital obtained by selling stock, bonds or by borrowing.

Financial Cost: The charges for use of borrowed capital.

Fixed Assets: Real or material facilities that represent part of the capital in an economic venture.

Fixed Capital: Buildings and equipment.

Fixed Cost: A cost which is independent of the rate of output.

Fixed and Miscellaneous Costs: Includes such items as rent, insurance, depreciation, maintenance, utilities, small tools, ad valorem and inventory taxes.

Future Worth: An expected value of capital in the future according to some predetermined method of computation.

Goods-In-Process Inventory: Hold-up of product in a semifinished state either because the process is stopped or because its nature requires material in various stages of completion.

Goods Manufactured, Cost of: Also referred to as total plant costs, this is the total of prime or direct costs and plant overhead costs.

Goods Sold, Cost of: The total of all costs except income taxes which may be deducted from revenue to obtain profit.

Gross National Product: An economic indicator used to study the total business activity.

Gross Margin (Profit):   Total revenue less cost of goods manufactured.

Income Tax: Corporation profits are taxed by the Federal and /state government on a sliding scale. The rate varies from time to time.

Indirect Costs: Those costs which have a bearing upon product cost but are not directly related to the manufacture of a specific product. (Depreciation, local taxes, insurance, etc.)

Internal Funds: Capital available from depreciation and accumulated earnings.

Inventory: Quantity of material held in process or in storage.

Leverage: The influence of debt on the earning rate of a company.

Liabilities: An accounting term for capital owed by a company.

Manufacturing (Operating) Costs: Cost of raw materials, utilities, labor, repairs, depreciation, insurance, local taxes, etc. (Direct plus indirect costs).

Marginal Costs: The rate of change of costs with production or output.

Minimum Acceptable Rate of Return: The minimum interest rate management policy selects as acceptable for a financial investment.

Net Worth: The capital of a financial venture that is accountable to the owners. It is the sum of the stockholders' investment plus the surplus. Assets minus liabilities.

Nominal Interest: The number employed loosely to describe the annual interest rate.

Operating Cost: The general and administrative costs and selling costs.

Operating Margin: Gross margin less the general administrative and selling costs.

Payout Time: Fixed capital investment divided by Cash Flow.

Preferred Stock: So named because of certain prior claims that it commands over common stock. The preference usually related to dividends. Preferred stockholders must receive their dividends before any distribution is made to common stockholders. Preference may also be extended to proceeds from the sale of assets if the corporation is forced to dissolve. Preferred stockholders usually do NOT have voting rights.

Present Worth: The value at some datum time of expenditures, costs, profits, etc., according to some predetermined method of computation.

Production Rate: The amount produced in a given time period.

Profitability: A term applied in a broad sense to the economic feasibility of a proposed venture or a going operation.

Revenues: The net sales received for selling the product to the customer.

Sales Volume: Amount of sales, lbs., gal. cu. ft., etc. per unit time.

Selling Costs: Salaries and commissions of sales personnel.

Simple Interest: The interest charges under the condition that interest in any time period is only charged on the principal.

Sinking Fund: An accounting procedure computed according to a specified procedure to provide capital to replace an asset.

Surplus: The excess of earnings over expense which is not distributed to stockholders.

Tax Credit: The amount available to a firm as part of its annual return because of deductible costs for tax purposes.

Time Value of Money: The expected interest rate that capital should or will earn.

Variable Cost: Any expense that varies with output.

Working Capital: The excess of current assets over current liabilities. It consists of the total amount of money invested in raw material, inventory, goods-in-process, product inventory, mechanical stores inventory, accounts receivable and cash.

Appendix F
EQUIPMENT COST-CAPACITY CURVES

Equipment cost-capacity curves for the following equipment are included:

Centrifugal Pumps	Rotary
Fans	Bag Filters
Blower	Wet Scrubbers
Reciprocating Compressors	Cyclone Separators
Centrifugal Compressors	Electrostatic Precipitators
Storage Tanks	Cooling Towers
50–10,000 gal	Packaged Boilers
10,000–1,000,000 gal	Electical Substations
Heat Exchangers	Waste-heat Boilers
Plate	Inert Gas Generators
Shell-and-Tube	Packaged Industrial
Pressure Vessels	Wastewater Plants
Fractionation Towers	Tower Packings
Filters	Relative Costs of
Plate	Fabricated Equipment

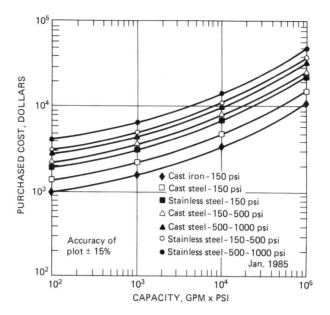

Fig. F.1. Centrifugal Pumps

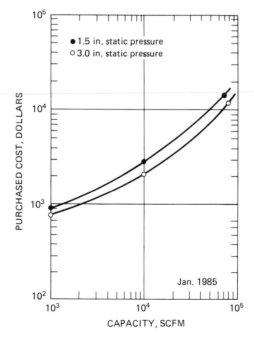

Fig. F.2. Centrifugal fans

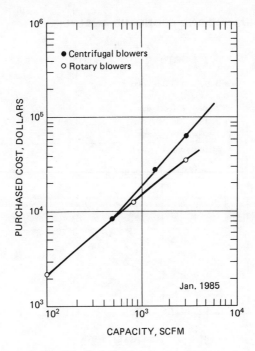

Fig. F.3. Centrifugal and rotary blowers

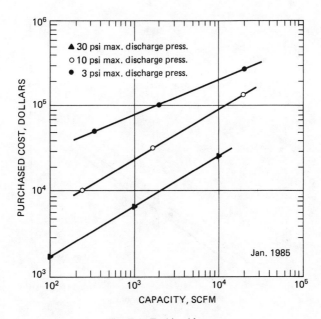

Fig. F.4. Turbine blowers

415

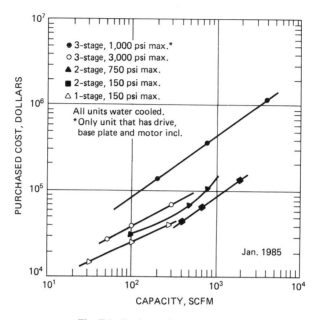

Fig. F.5. Reciprocating compressors

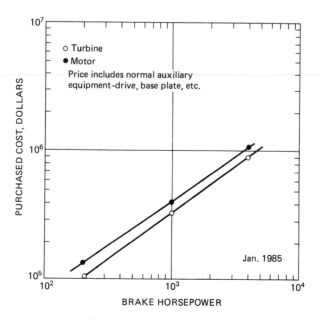

Fig. F.6. Centrifugal compressors

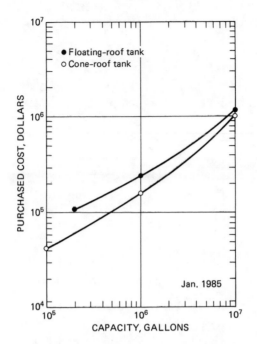

Fig. F.7. Receivers and small storage tanks

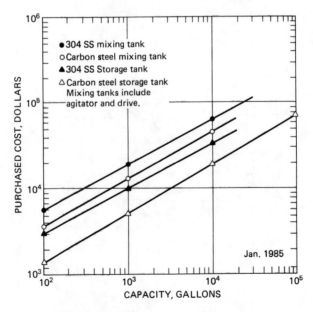

Fig. F.8. Large capacity storage tanks

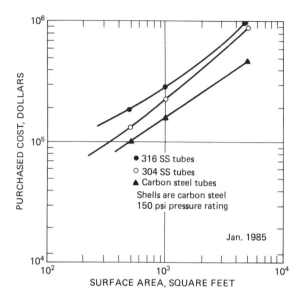

Fig. F.9. Heat exchangers, fixed head

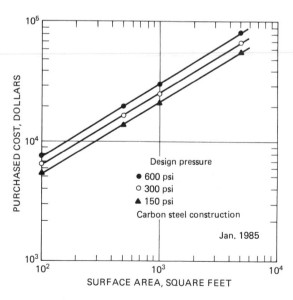

Fig. F.10. Heat exchangers, floating head

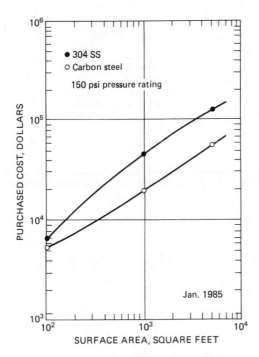

Fig. F.11. Heat exchangers, U-tube

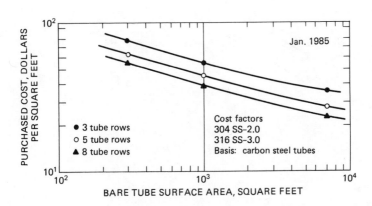

Fig. F.12. Heat exchangers, air-cooled

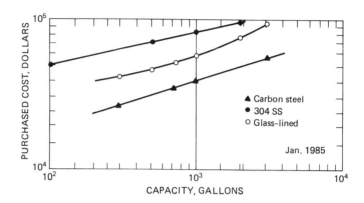

Fig. F.13. Reactors

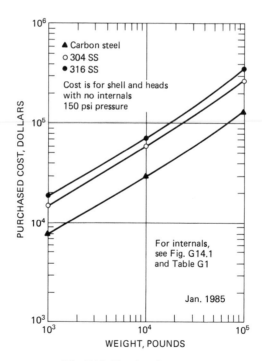

Fig. F.14. Fractionating towers

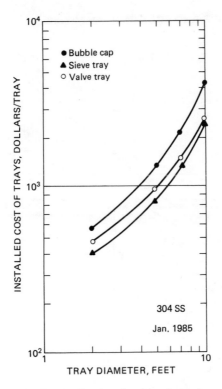

Fig. F.14.1. Fractionating tower internals

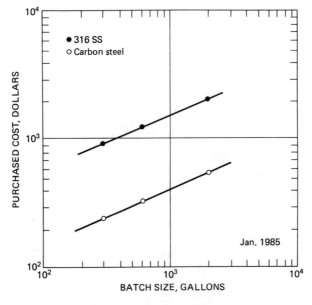

Fig. F.15. Filters, cartridge

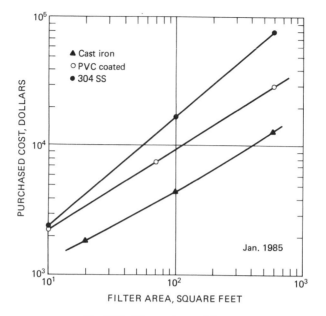

Fig. F.16. Filters, plate and frame

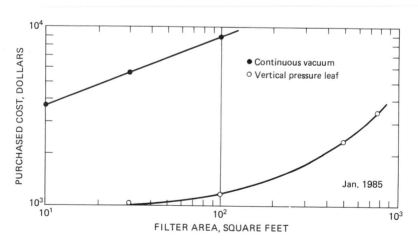

Fig. F.17. Filters, rotary vacuum and vertical leaf

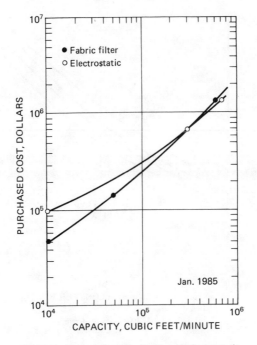

Fig. F.18. Dust collectors, fabric and electrostatic

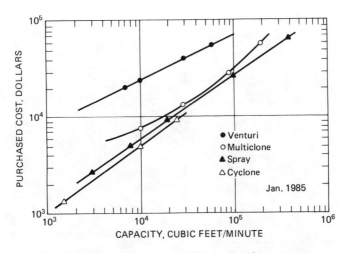

Fig. F.19. Dust collectors, wet scrubbers and cyclone separators

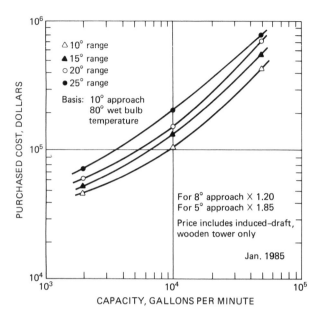

Fig. F.20. Cooling towers

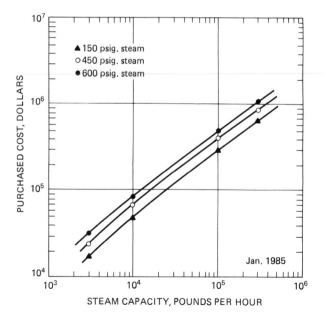

Fig. F.21. Packaged boilers

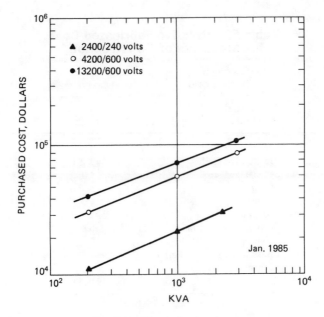

Fig. F.22. Electrical substations

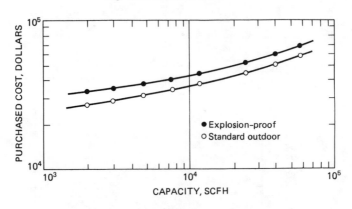

Fig. F.23. Inert gas generators

Table F1   Cost of Power Packings*

TYPE/SIZE	1 IN.	2 IN.	3 IN.
Berl Saddles	$32	$25	$10
Raschig Rings	15	10	8
Intalox Saddles	21	15	13

* 1985 prices for stoneware packings

Table F2   Relative Fabricated Cost for Materials of Construction.

MATERIAL OF CONSTRUCTION	RELATIVE COST
Carbon steel	1.0
400 stainless steel	2.0–2.5
Red brass	2.0–3.0
304 stainless steel	3.0
316 stainless steel	4.5–5.0
347 stainless steel	5.0
Monel	6.5–7.0
Inconel	8.0
Aluminum	2.0
Polyvinyl chloride plastic	0.8
Polypropylene	0.85
Epoxy-resin, glass reinforced	1.2
High silicon iron	2.0
Glass-lined	4.0–6.0

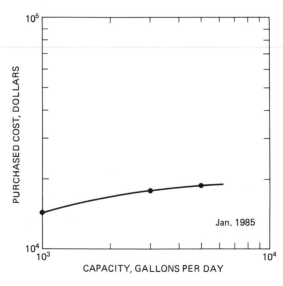

Fig. F.24. Packaged industrial wastewater plants

INDEX